Genes, Organisms, Populations

⨆ *Bradford Books*

Edward C. T. Walker, Editor. Explorations in THE BIOLOGY OF LANGUAGE. 1979.

Daniel C. Dennett. BRAINSTORMS. 1979.

Charles E. Marks. COMMISSUROTOMY, CONSCIOUSNESS, AND UNITY OF MIND. 1980.

John Haugeland, Editor. MIND DESIGN, 1981.

Fred I. Dretske. KNOWLEDGE AND THE FLOW OF INFORMATION. 1981.

Jerry A. Fodor. REPRESENTATIONS. 1981.

Ned Block, Editor. IMAGERY, 1981.

Roger N. Shepard and Lynn A. Cooper. MENTAL IMAGES AND THEIR TRANSFORMATIONS. 1982.

Hubert L. Dreyfus, Editor, in collaboration with Harrison Hall. HUSSERL, INTENTIONALITY, AND COGNITIVE SCIENCE. 1982.

John Macnamara. NAMES FOR THINGS. 1982.

Natalie Abrams and Michael D. Buckner, Editors. MEDICAL ETHICS. 1982.

Morris Hale and G. N. Clements. PROBLEM BOOK IN PHONOLOGY. 1983.

Jerry A. Fodor. MODULARITY OF MIND. 1983.

George D. Romanos. QUINE AND ANALYTIC PHILOSOPHY. 1983.

Robert Cummins. THE NATURE OF PSYCHOLOGICAL EXPLANATION. 1983.

Irwin Rock. THE LOGIC OF PERCEPTION. 1983.

Stephen Stich. FOLK PSYCHOLOGY AND COGNITIVE SCIENCE. 1983.

Jon Barwise and John Perry. SITUATIONS AND ATTITUTDES. 1983.

Izchak Miller. HUSSERL'S THEORY OF PERCEPTION. 1983.

Elliot Sober, Editor. CONCEPTUAL ISSUES IN EVOLUTIONARY BIOLOGY. 1984.

Norbert Hornstein. LOGIC AS GRAMMAR. 1984.

Paul M. Churchland. MATTER AND CONSCIOUSNESS. 1984.

Owen D. Flanagan. THE SCIENCE OF MIND. 1984.

Ruth Garrett Millikan. LANGUAGE, THOUGHT, AND OTHER BIOLOGICAL CONSIDERATIONS. 1984.

Myles Brand. INTENDING AND ACTING. 1984.

Herbert A. Simon and K. Anders Ericsson. PROTOCOL ANALYSIS. 1984.

Zenon W. Pylyshyn. COMPUTATION AND COGNITION. 1984.

Robert N. Brandon and Richard M. Burian, Editors. GENES, ORGANISMS, POPULATIONS. 1984.

Genes, Organisms, Populations:
Controversies over the Units of Selection

edited by Robert N. Brandon and Richard M. Burian

The MIT Press
Cambridge, Massachusetts
London, England

This book was set in IBM Press Roman by Horne Associates, Inc. and printed and bound by Halliday Lithograph in the United States of America.

Library of Congress Cataloging in Publication Data
Main entry under title:

Genes, organisms, populations.

   "A Bradford book."
   Bibliography: p.
   Includes index.
   1. Natural selection–Addresses, essays, lectures.
I. Brandon, Robert N.   II. Burian, Richard M.
QH375.G46   1984   575.01'62   83–24838
ISBN 0-262-02205-2

Contents

II

III

Natural selection is thought to be the major force of evolution. It favors the fitter over the less fit, and when the differences in the features underlying differential fitness are heritable, evolution occurs. But what are the objects that vary in fitness? At what level or levels does selection act? We have found the units-of-selection controversy exciting because these and other questions are of intrinsic biological and philosophical interest and have provoked mutually beneficial communication between the two fields. In recent years biologists and philosophers have published a large number of papers bearing on these questions. We hope that this anthology, which includes some of the most important of these papers, will stimulate further contact between the two communities. This hope has guided our selection of articles.

Our selection of articles was also guided by pedagogical considerations. Although the issues involved are difficult and sometimes highly technical, we have sought to include articles that are accessible to advanced undergraduates and graduate students in philosophy and biology.

This anthology was conceived during The Council for Philosophical Studies Summer Institute on Philosophy of Biology (1982), directed by Marjorie Grene. Like all collections of articles, this one is imperfect; however, it is far better than it would have been had we not received the suggestions of Robert Boyd, Ernst Mayr, Michael Ruse, and Michael Wade. We gratefully acknowledge their help.

The anthology is divided into three sections. The first focuses on the history of the topic. The second includes works explicating the conceptual issues at stake, and the third presents various models of selection, primarily models of kin and group selection. In addition to the general introduction we have written introductions to each section. Robert Boyd, James Collins, Robert Richardson, and Bruce Wallace have kindly read through all of this material and have made many helpful suggestions. We thank them. Of course, they should not be held responsible for our failure to heed all of their advice.

We also wish to thank John Maynard Smith, Ernst Mayr, and V.C. Wynne-Edwards for writing prefaces for their articles included in this volume.

Finally, for their forebearance during our long telephone conversations and harried attempts to meet deadlines, we want to thank our wives, Gloria and Linda, to whom we dedicate this volume.

Introduction

Ever since Darwin published the *Origin of Species* (Darwin, 1869), a nagging and persistent set of problems has plagued evolutionary theory. What is it that evolves, what is it that natural selection acts on, what are the fundamental units of reproduction? Increasingly recognized as being of fundamental importance, these problems affect both the proper articulation of the theory of evolution by means of natural selection and its substance. We will begin by sketching what we take to be Darwin's position and two competing contemporary alternatives within the Darwinian tradition. We will then step back to examine, briefly, the importance of the controversy. Finally, we will set out the scope and limits of this anthology.

The full title of the *Origin* already hints at the difficulties which concern us: *On the Origin of Species by Means of Natural Selection, or the Preservation of Favoured Races in the Struggle for Life.* In spite of Darwin's subtitle, the primary tendency of his thought is to treat (individual) organisms, not races, populations, or groups as the *target* of selection. That is, for Darwin selection acts primarily at the level of individual organisms. He usually construes the preservation of favored races as an effect (*sensu* G.C. Williams, 1966, i.e., a side effect) of the selective advantage of well-adapted organisms. When individuals of a population vary in a trait affecting adaptedness, those organisms which have a version of the trait advantageous with respect to the prevailing environment will tend, other things being equal, to be disproportionately represented in the next generation. Given a stable environment, favored races (i.e., conspecific organisms sharing an advantageous trait such as light coat color, high milk yield, or extreme heterostyly) will tend to be preserved because of the advantage that the resultant relatively greater adaptedness confers on *individuals* manifesting the trait. Thus, though Darwin would never have put it in these terms, *what evolves* is a population; *what selection acts on* are the (competing) organisms that make up the population in a given generation; and the reason that selection of this sort is effective is that *what reproduces differentially* are individuals with traits which are differentially adapted to the environment.

This description is, in certain respects, anachronistic. It presumes clearer distinctions among what evolves, what selection acts on, and what replicates than were available to Darwin. As the readings of Part I will indicate, the need to make such distinctions is itself the result of two lines of attack on the position just described. Both lines of attack belong within the Darwinian tradition, taken broadly. On the one hand there are those (beginning with Alfred Russel Wallace, whose views are discussed by Ruse, this volume) who hold that selection acts on groups, populations, and/or species as well as individuals, and who maintain that selection acting at these "higher" levels accounts for a variety of crucial traits, such as regulation of population size and density (Wynne-Edwards, 1962 and this volume), evolution of sterile castes (Darwin?, Wallace), and cooperation and altruism (Wallace, Wynne-Edwards, and many others, some reviewed in E. O. Wilson, 1975).

The other relevant departure from Darwin is based on a particular reading of twentieth-century genetics, which rests on the observation that organisms do not replicate nearly as faithfully as genes and proposes that (in spite of initial appearances and intuitions to the contrary) in the first instance it is genes, not organisms, which reproduce differentially. To be sure, the genes in question are always temporarily grouped with other genes, and their reproductive advantage depends on the detailed interactions between them and the genes with which they are grouped. But genes will have some net effect when averaged over all genetic backgrounds, and differences in these net effects are the ultimate means by which selection acts. This viewpoint, advocated by Williams (1966, excerpted in this volume) and Dawkins (1976 and in this volume) treats the gene as the fundamental unit of replication and sees differential replication of genes as the most fundamental consequence of selection. Accordingly, the position has come to be labeled *genic selectionism.*

Biologists have long recognized that nature is arranged in a hierarchy. Genes are located on chromosomes and chromosomes are located in cells. Cells form organs and whole organisms. Organisms form families, groups, demes, and finally species. Species or local populations form communities that, in turn, enter into ecosystems. The controversies in which the proponents of various forms of group selection, individual selection, and genic selection have become embroiled concern the location in this hierarchy of the target or targets of natural selection. Logically there are two options here: either there is some privileged level at which selection always acts, or selection may act at multiple levels. The first option is taken by genic selectionists as well as some neo-Darwinists who think selection occurs only at the level of individual organisms. The second is taken by all proponents of higher level (e.g., kin or group) selection. Thus no group selectionist maintains that groups are the sole units of selection.

The issues involved might seem to be straightforwardly empirical. They are not. One issue that is not concerns the role of reductionism in biology. Genic selectionsts seem to be motivated by a certain view of reductionism. For instance, G. C. Williams (this volume) and others have argued that the *principle of parsimony* requires that we explain biological adaptations at the lowest level possible. But why should lower levels have a privileged position relative to higher levels? If this invocation of the principle of parsimony is legitimate, what does that tell us about the biological world? If it is not legitimate, why not? And what does that tell us about the biological world and the relation of biology to other sciences? These questions are of biological and philosophical significance.

That the issues raised by the units of selection controversy are not straightforwardly empirical is evidenced by the large literature that the controversy has generated, within both theoretical biology and philosophy of biology. Philosophers have contributed mainly through terminological clarification and conceptual analysis. The units-of-selection controversy is not likely to be resolved until we figure out what such terms as "unit of selection" mean. As we will see in Part II, this term in particular has two distinct and equally important meanings. Disentangling them is, not surprisingly, a necessary step in resolving the controversy.

Not all of the questions are such that abstract qualitative analyses will answer them. Some are quantitative and require mathematical modeling for their solution. For instance, the standard argument against group selection is quantitative; given biologically realistic circumstances, it is argued, group selection can rarely overcome the force of individual selection.

Another, less obvious, case involves the relation between kin and group selection. One of the major catalysts of theoretical work on the units of selection has been the rise of sociobiology during the last decade. Biologists concerned with social species (e.g., social ants) have observed many traits (e.g., workers' sacrifice of life in defense of the colony) that seemingly are not beneficial to the individual, specifically not to the individual's genetic fitness. Important among such traits are *altruistic behaviors* which, by definition, decrease the fitness of the actor while increasing the fitness of the recipient. Thus altruism is an anomaly for the Darwinian paradigm of selection acting solely at the level of individual organisms. Most sociobiologists (e.g., Dawkins 1976, 1982) have sharply distinguished kin and group selection, rejecting group selection while using kin selection as the primary explanation of altruism in nature (but see Wilson, 1975, for a more eclectic view). Their arguments have been largely verbal and have been quite persuasive. But recent efforts to model the two processes have indicated that it is not possible to sharply distinguish them. This issue, which has considerable implications for sociobiological work, will be discussed in detail in Part III.

Of course there are, ultimately, empirical issues raised by the units of selection controversy. Once the necessary conceptual and theoretical work has been done, questions such as "Is group selection an important force in the evolution of this particular population?" should become empirically answerable. But, as it is not our purpose in this anthology to pursue such empirical questions, we will not, for instance, pursue the specific evidence concerning the relative biological importance of group versus individual or species selection. Rather, our purpose is to present the relevant work so that biologists can pose the empirical questions clearly and figure out the best ways to attack and solve them.

Although the co-editors of this volume are agnostic about the outcome of such empirical investigations, we do have opinions on the relevant conceptual and theoretical issues. These opinions have influenced our selection of articles and our substantive comments on them below. We do not say this apologetically. Any other approach would, we think, be of less value. At the same time, in order to maximize the usefulness of this anthology, we have sought to present the major positions even-handedly enough that their proponents can both teach from this book and find the issues that they must face raised in a challenging way.

References

Darwin, C. 1859. *On the Origin of Species.* London: John Murray.

Dawkins, R. 1976. *The Selfish Gene.* New York: Oxford University Press.

Dawkins, R. 1982. *The Extended Phenotype.* Oxford: W. H. Freeman and Company.

Williams, G. C. 1966. *Adaptation and Natural Selection.* Princeton: Princeton University Press.

Wilson, E. O. 1975. *Sociobiology: The New Synthesis.* Cambridge: Harvard University Press.

Wynne-Edwards, V. C. 1962. *Animal Dispersion in Relation to Social Behavior.* New York: Hafner.

I

Historical Readings

It may seem odd to some (as it did to one of the contributors to this volume) that nearly all of the materials in a section of "historical readings" were written within the last twenty-five years. Yet the readings presented in this book, though recent, set forth the classic positions that served as a backdrop for the controversies covered in parts II and III. And although, as Ruse shows, there have been significant disagreements over the levels at which natural selection acts from the earliest days of the theory of natural selection, the issues with which we are concerned did not receive a better formulation than that found in Darwin and Wallace until the 1960s. The works we have chosen to reprint are, we believe, particularly useful in setting up the conceptual issues that are the principal concern of this book.

There were, of course, significant steps along the way. Two are worthy of particular mention: Haldane's suggestion (1932) of the mechanism of kin selection and Sewall Wright's development of a theory of interdemic selection, one version of which is reprinted here. Another step of considerable importance was taken by Mayr in his many arguments from ca. 1949 against what he termed "beanbag genetics"—the treatment of genes as beads on a string that act independently of each other (or enough so that their interactions can be ignored) and accordingly are each separately subject to the scrutiny of natural selection. His article on the unity of the genotype presents a particularly clear articulation of his extremely influential view.

Surprisingly few evolutionists have recognized the deep conflict between Mayr's position and the stance taken by G. C. Williams in his pathbreaking *Adaptation and Natural Selection,* one chapter of which is excerpted. Written in reaction to Wynne-Edwards' articulation of selection acting on (and for the benefit of) *groups* of organisms (1962), Williams' book advocates a form of *genic* selectionism which cannot, in general, obtain if Mayr's claims about the unity of the genotype are correct. The disagreement between the two positions, often unrecognized, is but one facet of the controversies pursued in the later parts of this book.

We turn to a more specific consideration of the chapters in part I. Michael Ruse reviews the earliest modern (i.e., Darwinian) dispute over the workability and importance of group selection—namely, that between Darwin and the co-discoverer of natural selection, Alfred Russel Wallace. Their disagreement foreshadows a good part of the contemporary debate. As Ruse points out, even though Darwin did not have modern formulations of such concepts as kin selection and group selection at his disposal, he viewed selection as acting primarily on competing organisms. In those few cases in which Darwin thought that selection might act at a higher level (e.g., in producing the sterile castes of social insects), precisely because he did not have the modern distinctions available, his text is difficult to interpret in terms of these distinctions. For example, on p. 237 of (1859), Darwin suggests that since families with sterile workers have an advantage over those which do not, sterile castes can be explained "when it is remembered that selection may be applied to the family, as well as to the individual." On the very next page, however, Darwin redescribes the envisaged mechanism in the following way:

A slight modification of structure, or instinct, correlated with the sterile condition of certain members of the community, has been advantageous to the community: consequently the fertile males and females of the same community flourished, and transmitted to their fertile offspring a tendency to produce sterile members having the same modification.

Do these texts indicate that Darwin was committed to kin (i.e., family?) selection or to group (i.e., community?) selection? Since Darwin did not separate these positions in a way that dovetails with contemporary distinctions, we consider the full texts, in context, equivocal. Ruse, in contrast, interprets them as favoring kin selection. As Robert Richardson (who favors Ruse's reading of the *Origin*) has reminded us, Darwin's views shifted with time. In particular, he seems to have attached a greater importance to group selection, and appealed to it more frequently, in his later than in his earlier writings. Some of the later texts, as is illustrated by the following passage from the *Descent of Man* (Darwin, 1871, p. 155; in the 2nd edition moved to p. 70 and rephrased) seem unequivocal:

With strictly social animals, natural selection sometimes acts indirectly on the individual, through the preservation of variations which are beneficial only to the community. A community including a large number of well-endowed individuals increases in number and is victorious over other and less well-endowed communities; although each separate member may gain no advantage over the other members of the same community.

The matter is further complicated by the fact that contemporary theorists distinguish kin from group selection in quite different ways. Two of the principal positions, Maynard Smith (1964 and this volume) and D. S. Wilson (1975 and this volume), are discussed at greater length in part III. Ruse, following Maynard Smith, treats kin and group selection as exclusive alternatives—a stance that lends considerable importance to the claim that Darwin favored kin over group selection. D. S. Wilson (whose view we prefer) analyzes kin and group selection in such a way that they overlap along a continuum; if such an analysis is accepted, the precise localization of Darwin's stance comes to be of secondary importance. In the face of all these difficulties, it does not seem profitable to force Darwin into a contemporary mold with respect to an issue about which, for lack of the relevant distinctions, he did not have a clearly articulated position.

This is not to imply that Darwin is wishy-washy. As we shall see, it is quite clear, for example, that (if he were forced) he would prefer Wright's approach to group selection over Wynne-Edwards'. Both Wright and Wynne-Edwards argue that groups are structured so as to alter the course of selection in such a way that the path of evolution cannot be determined solely from the selectively relevant features of individual organisms plus knowledge of the environment. Nonetheless, the difference between them is immense. Wynne-Edwards is concerned with "group selection for group advantage" (Wright, this volume), deriving from this a selective force that is independent of (and typically acts contrary to) individual selection. Wright is concerned with a mechanism that he now views as "group selection for organismic advantage." It increases between-group variance in the population by exposing individuals in different demes to different selective regimes and by radically increasing the magnitude of the effects of genetic drift. Local extinctions plus repopulation from nearby demes accelerate the rate of evolution further. Wright holds that this mechanism does *not* interpose selection for group advantage as an additional force shaping the phenotype of individual organisms. Thus the primary effects of interdemic selection are to provide natural selection with more varied raw material on which to work and to allow local populations to depart further than they otherwise would from local fitness maxima. (Many biologists have interpreted Wright's position as being stronger than his present gloss suggests, perhaps with some justice. He clearly intended the mechanism of interdemic selection, when combined with the effects of random drift in small populations, to explain (1) nonadaptive and contra-adaptive features of organisms, and (2) features that would never have arisen in large panmictic populations shaped primarily by natural selection acting on individual organisms. Accordingly, Wright has frequently been seen as suggesting a mechanism of group selection which, at least occasionally, acts in opposition to organismic selection and to all forms of "selection acting for organismic advantage.")

Wynne-Edwards' views about group selection were shaped in good part by a tradition we have not yet mentioned, to wit the tradition in ecology built around the metaphor of the superorganism. (For examples, see Allee et al., 1949; Clements, 1916; Emerson, 1939; or Phillips, 1934–1935.) This metaphor treats social insects in particular, but also social animals generally and entire ecological communities as being analyzable in elaborate detail as organisms writ large. (A. E. Emerson, 1939, self-consciously cites Plato as founder of the view that societies have the attributes of organisms.) In an ant colony, for example, the queen represents the germ line, the distinct castes of workers correspond to distinct somatic cell lines, food sharing manifests combined aspects of circulation of blood and communication in the nervous system, and so on. At all levels where it was applied, this metaphor treated the preservation of the population (or community) as the function to be performed by its parts. Just as the heart, liver, and lungs of a vertebrate organism are homeostatically regulated so that each performs its function in the preservation of the individual, so the morphologies, numbers, and tasks of the various castes of ants (the various species of the community) are homeostatically regulated so that each performs its function in the preservation of the hive (the community).

This holistic vision was central to mid-century community and, to a degree, population ecology and apparently flourished side-by-side with a theoretical commitment to Darwinism. (See Collins, MS, for a discussion of the interrelations of superorganismic and evolutionary thinking in ecology.) Yet as soon as one asks for the population genetics used to support the holistic treatment of groups, populations, and species, an enormous gap becomes apparent. As Lawton (1982) argues, it is useful to see Wynne-Edwards as attempting to fill that gap. Wynne-Edwards' concern with population structure stems in part from the recognition of the need to provide a satisfactory explanation of the phenomena of population regulation, including the immensely complex social behaviors which that involves. And his treatment of groups and populations as wholes whose interests determine the behavior of their component individuals, shocking to many Darwinians, was entirely natural to practicing ecologists. His (1962) is an heroic effort to explain the social mechanisms that contribute to regulation of density in animal populations by reference to selection operating on whole populations rather than on individuals.

Heroic, but flawed. Wynne-Edwards' mechanism for population regulation requires animals to forego reproduction (or emigrate or reduce reproductive effort) when they have received appropriate conventional signals indicating, first, that the population is excessively dense and, second, that the individual's status is below the appropriate threshold. Groups in which the conventional signals are not honored will pay the penalty of overpopulation (with its associated risk of population crash). Groups in which they are honored will flourish.

Yet as he himself recognizes (Wynne-Edwards, 1977), in his earlier publications he does not develop plausible evolutionary mechanisms for (1) the origin of the required reproductive self-sacrifice, (2) its maintenance *within* the group, or (3) the subordination of individual to group reproductive interest. Nor does he fully consider alternative accounts according to which the devices by means of which density is regulated are in the reproductive interests of the *individuals* in the population. (It is to be hoped that he will address these matters in his projected volume on Animal Sociality and Group Selection, announced in the preface to his chapter in this book.) Given these difficulties, it is not surprising that his theory raised a storm of Darwinian criticism.

Perhaps the most important and influential of the Darwinian responses to Wynne-Edwards was G. C. Williams' (1966). Williams distinguishes sharply between an adapted population of organisms and a population of adapted organisms—between a fleet herd of deer and a herd of fleet deer. He argues, fundamentally, that whenever an adaptation of a population can be explained by means of the adaptation of its members (as the fleetness of a herd can be explained by the fleetness of its members plus the individual advantage of cooperative flight), there is no ground for supposing that any group-level process has molded the properties of the group. All that is needed is natural selection acting on individual organisms.

Williams carries this reductionistic analysis one step further by elevating his methodology into a principle, to wit, "adaptation should be attributed to no higher a level of organization than is demanded by the evidence" (p. vii). Organisms are built according to a design carried by the genes, and genes, unlike whole organisms, are "potentially immortal" (p. 24) in the sense that they can produce faithful copies of themselves, fully identical to their originals, in perpetuity. Accordingly, those genes (strictly, those alternative alleles) which reliably yield advantageous properties in organisms will be favored by selection, while those that do not reliably lead to such advantages will not. With appropriate caveats (for example, to take proper account of the fact that "selection of alternative alleles works only with an immediate better-vs.-worse among individuals in a population," p. vii), Williams concludes that "the question of population survival is irrelevant" in determining the effectiveness of selection (p. vii). For that matter, on an evolutionary time scale, *individual* survival is irrelevant too. "Natural selection is a statistical bias in the relative rates of survival of alternatives (genes, individuals, etc.)." Rate considerations show that phenotypes and genotypes do not survive long; in the end it is *genes* that are favored or disfavored by the statistical biases which operate on an evolutionary scale. In this sense, it is genes that are the ultimate unit of selection, genes that define the lowest level of organization back to which all explanations of adaptation should be traced.

Mayr's fundamental position, arrived at long before Williams wrote his book, is preadapted to provide a rationale for rejecting this second, reductionistic, step of tracing everything back to the genic level. (Others, too, reject this step—cf. our Introduction and Wimsatt's and Sober and Lewontin's articles in part II.) Even granting that genes have greater longevity via replication than gene complexes, Mayr insists on the inescapability and importance of gene interactions and the selective importance of balanced gene complexes. He argues that the "fitness of genes tied up in these complexes is determined more by the fitness of the complexes as a whole than by any functional qualities of individual genes." More important, the "targets" of selection—i.e., the units on which selection acts and which it modifies by its action—are, typically, neither genes nor gene complexes, but "such components of the phenotype as the eye, the legs, the flower, the thermoregulatory or photosynthetic apparatus, etc."

As we shall see in part II, some of the difficulties in resolving this disagreement between genic and organismic selectionism stem from ambiguities in the concept of a unit of selection. These ambiguities will be at least partially removed in our Introduction and in the articles by Brandon, Dawkins, and Hull. As a result, many of the issues between the contending parties can be set aside; the remainder, we believe, will be sharpened and clarified.

References

Allee, W. C., et al., 1949. *Principles of Animal Ecology*. Philadelphia: W. B. Saunders.

Clements, F. E., 1916. "Plant Succession: An Analysis of the Development of Vegetation." *Publications of the Carnegie Institution of Washington*, Publ. no. 242, pp. 1–512.

Collins, J. P., MS. "*Evolutionary Ecology* and the Changing Role of Natural Selection in Ecological Theory."

Darwin, C., 1859. *On the Origin of Species by Means of Natural Selection.* London: John Murray. Reprint edition, Cambridge, Mass.: Harvard University Press, 1964.

Darwin, C., 1871. *The Descent of Man, and Selection in Relation to Sex.* 2 vols. London: John Murray, 1871.

Emerson, A. E., 1939. "Social Coordination and the Superorganism." *American Midland Naturalist* 21:182–209.

Haldane, J. B. S., 1932. *The Causes of Evolution.* New York: Longmans, Green & Co. Reprinted, Ithaca, N.Y.: Cornell University Press, 1963.

Lawton, M. F., 1982. "Altruism and Sociobiology: A Critical Look at the Critical Issue." Dissertation, University of Chicago.

Maynard Smith, J., "Group Selection and Kin Selection." *Nature* 201:1145–47.

Phillips, J. F., 1934–1935. "Succession, Development, the Climax and the Complex Organism: An Analysis of Concepts." *Journal of Ecology* 22:554–571; 23:210–246, 488–508.

Williams, G. C., 1966. *Adaptation and Natural Selection.* Princeton: Princeton University Press.

Wilson, D. S., 1975. "A Theory of Group Selection." *Proceedings of the National Academy of Sciences* (USA) 72:143–146.

Wynne-Edwards, V. C., 1962. *Animal Dispersion in Relation to Social Behaviour.* Edinburgh and London: Oliver and Boyd.

Wynne-Edwards, V. C., 1977. "Society versus the Individual in Animal Evolution." In B. Stonehouse and L. Perrins, eds., *Evolutionary Ecology.* Baltimore: University Park Press, pp. 5–17.

1

Charles Darwin and Group Selection

Michael Ruse

1. Introduction

In recent years evolutionary biologists have shown much interest in the question of the levels at which natural selection can be said to operate.[1] Generally speaking, confining ourselves initially to the nonhuman world, it is probably true to say that although V. C. Wynne-Edwards in his *Natural Regulation of Animal Numbers* argued strongly for the widespread efficacy of some form of group selection,[2] most evolutionists would agree with G. C. Williams' reply, *Adaptation and Natural Selection,* in which it was argued that, essentially, selection must start with the individual.[3] Nevertheless, a number of studies have been aimed at showing how under certain circumstances selection could work at the group level.[4] Hence, it is probably true to say that matters are not yet definitively settled, either theoretically or empirically.

The debate about the levels of selection has been given added zest by the assumption that selection almost invariably centers on the individual, a crucial assumption to the theories and conclusions of the sociobiologists, those biologists interested in animal social behavior.[5] Indeed, what the sociobiologists claim, as a major distinguishing feature of their work from that of earlier students of the biology of animal behavior, is that they alone make the right choice of individual over group selection. This in itself would hardly be a matter of great controversy; but since most of the sociobiologists want to apply their theorizings from the animal world directly to the human world, inevitably there has been some rather heated discussion about whether one can properly use the notion of individual selection to explain the evolution and maintenance of all significant human behavior. The critics of sociobiology feel that such an attempt leads to a reactionary distortion of human sociality, and they argue that other causes of human behavior must be sought in explanation.[6]

Of course, one does not have to be a supporter of some form of group

From *Annals of Science* (1980), 37:615–630.

selection in the nonhuman world to be a critic of human sociobiology. Nevertheless, some eminent biologists do fall into both categories, and, moreover, I suspect they see important ideological links in their overall critique of the all-sufficiency of individual selection. For instance, both Levins[7] and Lewontin[8] have allowed the possibility of group selection in certain special situations; they are both against sociobiology; and by their own admission they see the totality of their work as part of an overall Marxist-oriented biology.[9]

Because both the sociobiologists and their critics resort to the familiar tactic of trying to legitimize the present by reference to the past—one finds protagonists on both sides claiming that they alone stand in the true evolutionary tradition[10]—there is some interest in seeing whether the debate about the levels of selection stretches back to the first announcement of the theory of evolution through natural selection, and where precisely the theory's chief formulator, Charles Darwin, stood on the matter. Such an historical inquiry is the aim of this paper. First, I shall consider Darwin's position on the levels of selection in his major work, *On the Origin of Species*.[11] Second, I shall see how his ideas developed over the next twelve years. Third, I shall look at his ideas in his major significant work on human beings, *The Descent of Man*.[12] For clarity in this paper, because there has been some confusion about terminology, by "individual selection"[13] I shall mean selection which in some sense affects an individual's reproductive interests. This could be directly through the individual, or indirectly in some way: for instance, by kin selection, where an individual's interests are furthered through close relatives; through parental manipulation, where a parent directs an offspring to its own interests; or through reciprocal altruism, where an individual is selected to do favors for others in the hope of returns.[14] By "group selection" I shall mean selection in some way causing characteristics which help others, including nonrelatives, in an individual's group, most probably by the species. There is not necessarily any hope of return for the individual.

2. On the Origin of Species

The early chapters of the *Origin,* those in which Darwin introduced his mechanisms for evolution, certainly give the impression of a Darwin who was going to be firmly committed to individual selection. As is well known, he did not just present natural selection without any theoretical backing, as an axiom, as it were. Rather, he argued first to a universal struggle for existence, from premises modeled on Malthus's ideas about available food and space. Then, from the struggle, assuming that there was heritable variation of the required amount and kind, Darwin went on to argue that the survivors and reproducers in the struggle will on average be different from the losers: natural selection.[15] Now as he introduced the struggle, Darwin gave strong evidence that he was going to be thinking at the level of the individual. To have some sort of group selection, one has got to minimize the tensions or rivalries within the group. When, for instance, the ethologist Konrad Lorenz invoked group selection, he did so because he was trying to show how it is that animals have mechanisms inhibiting all-out attacks on conspecifics.[16] Darwin, however, saw the struggle (which was going to lead to selection) as acting just as much between conspecifics as between any two organisms: ". . . as more individuals are produced than can possibly survive, there must in every case be a struggle for existence, either one individual with another of the same species, or with the individuals of distinct species, or with the physical conditions of life."[17] In fact, he then went on to say that the closer the relationship, the more severe the struggle: ". . . the struggle almost invariably will be most severe between the individuals of the same species."[18] It should be added, of course, that he was not necessarily thinking of struggle in the sense of hand-to-hand combat, but struggle for resources of various kinds and so forth. Nevertheless, the point remains that he was viewing the crucial biological tensions as much within the group as without.

Coming to selection itself, we find the same emphasis on the individual. For instance, to illustrate how natural selection might work Darwin gave the imaginary example of a group of wolves, hard-pressed for food.[19] He suggested that the swiftest and slimmest will be selected, because it will be they alone who will catch the prey: deer, and so forth. Hence, there will be evolution towards and maintenance of fast, lean wolves. Obviously, the crux of this explanation is that some wolves survive and reproduce, whereas others do not. There is no question here of selection working for a group: rather it is all a matter of individual against individual.

Although an example like this shows that Darwin thought natural selection itself to be individual oriented, his commitment to the individual is perhaps best illustrated by his variant form of selection, sexual selection.[20] This Darwin divided into two forms: sexual selection through male combat, where the males compete between themselves for the females, and sexual selection through female choice, where females choose between males displaying in various ways. It is true that Darwin was criticized for this mechanism, particularly on the grounds that female choice anthropomorphically supposes that animals have the same standards of beauty as humans.[21] But this is as it may be. What is important is how clearly sexual selection shows that Darwin was thinking of selection as something that could act between fellow species' members, preserving a characteristic that gives an organism an advantage over conspecifics. There is no place here for the preservation of characteristics of value to conspecifics at the expense of the individuals within a group.

Introducing selection and its foundations, therefore, Darwin gave the impression that he was going to be a fairly rigorous individual selectionist. But was he completely committed to individual selection? Did he feel that there could ever be a case where selection could and would act for the benefit of the group? In the *Origin,* as we turn from Darwin's introduction of his mechanisms to their applications, we find that with respect to the levels of selection dilemma there are two points at which Darwin had to make a decision: when he discussed social insects and when he discussed hybrid sterility. Let us take them in turn.

By "social insects" is meant insects with sterile castes, all living together in a community. The problem is how one explains the sterility of individuals in some of these castes, and how members of sterile castes could have evolved to be so very different from fertile fellow community members. Surely one must invoke some sort of group selection to explain how the sterile community members, so helpful to the group, so unhelpful to themselves, evolved? About the question of sterility, Darwin wrote as follows:

How the workers have been rendered sterile is a difficulty; but not much greater than that of any other striking modification of structure; for it can be shown that some insects and other articulate animals in a state of nature occasionally become sterile; and if such insects had been social, and it had been profitable to the community that a number should have been annually born capable of work, but incapable of procreation, I can see no very great difficulty in this being effected by natural selection. [22]

In a related fashion he tackled the problem of how the members of some sterile castes can be very different from their parents and can be different from the members of other castes. Drawing on a favorite analogy of the effects of artificial selection in the domestic world, Darwin pointed out how breeders can work indirectly, raising desired organisms (which are killed without reproducing), because the fertile parents can somehow latently carry the characteristics of these organisms. Similarly, in the wild, fertile parents could have sterile offspring who help the community, and also could pass on to their fertile offspring the potential to have such sterile offspring in turn. And if different kinds of sterile offspring could be used in a community, these too could be formed by selection. [23]

There is no group selection here, where "group selection" is understood in our above-defined sense as involving unreturned aid to nonrelatives. The key to Darwin's argument is that the sterile altruists are closely related to the fertile members of the community. The sterility occurs because it is of value to all the related members of the nest, and also, Darwin thought in part, because when one has two sterile castes, without sterility one would have interbreeding and less effective hybrid forms (that is, forms, less effective for the community). But selection is not preserving characteristics exclusively of value to nonrelatives.

One should nevertheless add that although Darwin was certainly an individual selectionist at this point, even an individual selectionist sufficiently sophisticated to see how individual selection can work through a closely related community, he did not really bring his argument to the level brought by today's sociobiologists. Some sociobiologists today argue that caste differentiation (in the Hymenoptera at least) is a function of kin selection: because of the haplodiploid method of sex determination in the Hymenoptera, sisters are more closely related to sisters than to daughters, and thus there is a genetic advantage in raising sisters.[24] Other of today's sociobiologists argue that the key is parental manipulation, where parents make some offspring sterile altruists towards siblings.[25] Both of these explanations see that there can be reproductive conflicts between community members, despite the close relationships. Darwin, however, saw the community members united in common interests. It would therefore be somewhat anachronistic to say that Darwin was a kin selectionist rather than a parental manipulator, or vice versa. Because of his ignorance about the proper principles of genetics, his analysis was just not that fine-grained. One might be tempted to say that Darwin was a shade closer to group selection than today's sociobiologists, because he saw no conflict between relatives, despite their lack of genetic identity. Perhaps so—but again I am inclined to think that anachronistically one is reading into Darwin's work something more subtle than is really there.

The other place in the *Origin* where Darwin might have been tempted towards a group-selection mechanism was over the question of sterility—either the sterility between members of different species, or, if hybrids were formed, the sterility of these hybrids.[26] A priori one might think that the very usual sterility between species or the sterility of hybrids between members of two different species (for instance, the sterile horse-donkey, the mule) would have been something fashioned by selection. If one has two forms, each adapted to its respective environment, a hybrid would be (literally!) neither fish nor fowl. Hence, it would be of advantage that such a hybrid either be barred altogether or, if possible, be sterile, because it could not then reproduce and give rise to further ill-adapted forms. The problem is, of course, to whom the absence or sterility of the hybrid would be of advantage. If the hybrid is not formed at all, then the parents lose any chance of offspring. If the hybrid is formed, then it would clearly not be of direct advantage to the hybrid itself to be sterile. Nor, differentiating this case from that of the social insects, would it be of advantage to the parents that the hybrid offspring be sterile—there is no question of the hybrid being freed through its sterility to aid its related community. At best the advantage from absence or sterility of hybrids would be to the parent species, who would thus gain better evolutionary prospects because no energies or resources would be going into ill-adapted hybrid offspring.

But to Darwin, apart from the fact that he could not see why in nature one gets so many degrees and forms of sterility (assuming selection does cause sterility), the unambiguous group selection required to cause sterility was apparently just not a live possibility. Although he did not provide a detailed theoretical attack on group selection, Darwin clearly hinted that he could not see how group selection, favoring the group over the individual, could work at all. Further, he went to some pains to show how individuals of different species frequently cannot interbreed at all because of incidentally formed differences, and similarly how hybrid sterility is an incidental fact, brought about by the lack of harmony between the different contributions by the parents to the hybrid's reproductive mechanisms:

On the theory of natural selection the case [of sterile hybrids] is especially important, inasmuch as the sterility of hybrids could not possibly be of any advantage to them, and therefore could not have been acquired by the continued preservation of successive profitable degrees of sterility. I hope, however, to be able to show that sterility is not a specially acquired or endowed quality, but is incidental on other acquired differences.[27]

3. Between the **Origin** and the **Descent**

There are two items of particular interest in the 1860s. First, there is the fact that Darwin himself wrestled at length with possible selective causes of sterility. Second, relatedly, Darwin and natural selection's co-discoverer, Alfred Russel Wallace, debated the individual-group selection problem. By the end of the decade, with respect to the animal and plant worlds, there was nothing implicit about Darwin's commitment to individual selection. He had looked long and hard at group selection and rejected it. Let us take in turn the matters which engaged Darwin in the levels-of-selection problem.

Almost immediately after the publication of the *Origin,* Darwin's interests turned to botany. Among other plants that he studied were members of the primula family, primroses and cowslips.[28] Members of this kind of species come in one of two different forms. Some have long styles, with the stamens tucked right away down the tube of the corolla; others have short styles, with the stigma right down the tube and the stamens at the mouth (see Figure 1). Hitherto, these different forms had been considered accidental varieties, but Darwin was able to show that the two forms play important roles in the cross-fertilization of the (hermaphroditic) plants. In particular, the crosses between plants of different types are far more fertile than crosses between plants of the same type (see Figure 2).

In the different degrees of fertility between the different kinds of crosses,

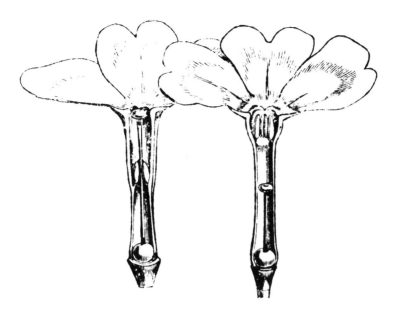

Figure 1. Long-styled (left) and short-styled (right).

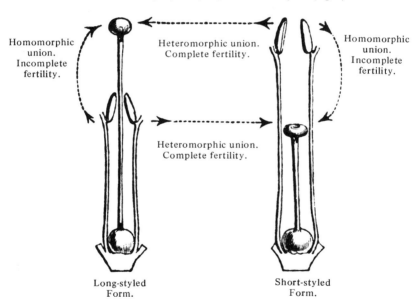

Homomorphic union. Incomplete fertility.

Heteromorphic union. Complete fertility.

Homomorphic union. Incomplete fertility.

Heteromorphic union. Complete fertility.

Long-styled Form.

Short-styled Form.

Figure 2. Heteromorphic and homomorphic unions.

Figures 1 and 2. From C. Darwin, "On the two forms, or dimorphic condition, in the species of *Primula,* and on their remarkable sexual relations," *Journal of the Proceedings of the Linnaean Society (Botany)* (1862), 6:77–96.

Darwin thought that he found a clue pointing to the possibility, in some special cases at least, that selection may have had a hand in sterility barriers. Why should a plant be barred from reproducing in a satisfactory way with half of its fellow species' members? Darwin hypothesized that this barrier may be a consequence of a selection acting to prevent something which is known to be positively deleterious, namely, self-fertilization (which produces inferior, inbred offspring). Plants, Darwin supposed, get selected for self-sterility, and then somehow accidentally (at least, not through selection) this gets transferred into a sterility with all forms like the plant itself. Furthermore, thought Darwin, if this hypothesis be true, we should find that the kind of plant which stands the greater chance of being self-fertilized has the greater barriers to prevent it. Since the primulae are fertilized by insects, it is obviously the short-styled form which runs this greater risk, and Darwin was happy to be able to confirm that short-short crosses were indeed even less fertile than long-long crosses. He therefore concluded:

Seeing that we thus have a groundwork of variability in sexual power, and seeing that sterility of a peculiar kind has been acquired by the species of *Primula* to favour intercrossing, those who believe in the slow modification of specific forms will naturally ask themselves whether sterility may not have been slowly acquired for a distinct object, namely, to prevent two forms, whilst being fitted for distinct lines of life, becoming blended by marriage, and thus less well adapted for their new habits of life.[29]

Judging from this passage alone, one might think that Darwin had now turned, not merely to a selection hypothesis for sterility, but to a group selection hypothesis, at least in partial explanation of sterility in those organisms which are hermaphroditic. (This latter clause about hermaphrodites was not necessarily that great a restriction, because his work on barnacles had convinced him that sexual organisms evolved from hermaphrodites.)[30] However, if we look at his explanation carefully, it is clear that Darwin had turned to nothing of the sort. Inasmuch as selection was supposed to cause sterility, it was for the good of the individual: so that it would not fertilize itself, thus causing only inferior inbred offspring. Insofar as sterility was being generalized from the individual to the group, it was accidental, in the sense of not being of selective value. There was no question of selection for the group, however much Darwin's rather sloppy use of language might hint otherwise.

At the end of the above-quoted passage, where Darwin had speculated that selection might cause sterility, wisely he added reservations: "But many great difficulties would remain, even if this view could be maintained."[31] It was perhaps just as well that he covered himself here, for it was not long afterwards that he discovered evidence which destroyed his hypothesis about the selective origin of sterility.[32] The plant *Lythrum salicaria* has three forms, and they are all involved in cross-fertilization of members of the species. In particular, given any one of the three forms, long-, mid-, and short-styled, one needs one of the other forms to effect the most efficient fertilization. If Darwin's hypothesis had been correct, then since the closer the stigma and the stamens, the greater the chance of self-fertilization; and the closer the stigma and the stamens on two plants being crossed, the greater should be the sterility barrier (excluding, of course, cases where stigmas and stamens were in exactly the same positions, because this could not happen on a single plant). In fact, however, it turned out that sterility was a direct function of the distance between stigmas and stamens—the very opposite to that predicted through the hypothesis. Hence, Darwin was led to reject his short-lived speculations and return to his original position: sterility was an accidental by-product of individual selection.

Perhaps as a warning to others, in the 4th edition of the *Origin* (published in 1866), Darwin inserted a somewhat stronger discussion than hitherto as to why selection could not cause sterility, although like most of us he found it difficult to reject a good idea—even if it was fairly clearly false (witness his reluctance to throw out his marine explanation of the parallel roads of Glen Roy).[33] Hence, in this edition of the *Origin* he did present his hypothesis about sterility in the primulae, but then he concluded that selection could not cause sterility![34]

In support of his strengthened claim that selection could not cause sterility, Darwin gave three reasons. First, he pointed out that selection could not be a necessary condition for sterility, because there are indisputable cases of species having developed in different geographical regions; yet, although selection could not possibly have made them intersterile, they prove to be so when they are brought together. Second, there are cases where only one of the possible crosses between members of species proves sterile and where the other cross is quite fertile (that is, male of species A crossed with female of species B is sterile, but male of species B crossed with female of species A is fertile). Darwin could not see how selection could cause this asymmetrical relationship. Third, and most important, he stated categorically that even if sterility is of value to the group, it is not of value to the individual, and it is at the level of the individual that selection operates. Sterility could not have been caused by natural selection, "for it could not have been of any direct advantage to an individual animal to breed poorly with another individual of a different variety, and thus to leave few offspring; consequently such individuals could not have been preserved or selected."[35] And in the 5th edition of the *Origin,* he added that if hybrids are born and they are less than fully fertile, then selection will act against them too. In short, he showed that he had thought consciously about and rejected group selection.

If, indeed, with his full discussion of the reasons why sterility could not be fashioned by selection, it was Darwin's aim to warn others against thinking that selection could fashion sterility or indeed anything of value to the group rather than the individual, his actions had exactly the opposite effect to that which he intended! In particular, his discussion (which he repeated practically verbatim two years later in his *Variation of Animals and Plants under Domestication*)[36] spurred Wallace to react by embracing whole-heartedly the cause and efficacy of the group selection:

It appears to me that, given a differentiation of a species into two forms, each of which was adapted to a special sphere of existence, every slight degree of sterility would be a positive advantage, not to the individuals who were sterile, but to each form. If you work it out, and suppose the two incipient species *a . . . b* to be divided into two groups, one of which contains those which are fertile when the two are crossed, the other being slightly sterile, you will find that the latter will certainly supplant the former in the struggle for existence . . .[37]

Although Darwin and Wallace each tried as politely as possible to see the viewpoint of the other, the beginning was basically the end of the matter also. Darwin reiterated that he could not see how sterility, so disadvantageous to the individual, could be preserved by selection; Wallace reiterated that he could not see how sterility, so advantageous to the group, could fail to be preserved by selection; and that was that.[38] It is true that Darwin and Wallace were not entirely apart: they both agreed that a disinclination to cross with members of another species could have been acquired by selection, even though Wallace, unlike Darwin, wanted to link this disinclination to sterility, should a cross ever so occur. But of course for Darwin this admission demanded no compromise on the matter of individual selection. Given a choice between hybrid offspring and offspring entirely of one's own species, it would certainly be in an organism's reproductive advantage not to waste effort on producing hybrids, well-adapted to neither parent's ecological niche. Hence, selection could help one avoid producing such hybrids in the first place. The point was, as Darwin saw it, if the coupling had in fact taken place, it would not then be in an individual's advantage to promote sterility. In other words, if an individual had mated with another, it would not then be in its interests to yield less than fully fertile offspring.

And so we find Darwin and Wallace divided. Rather sadly, Darwin concluded that "We shall, I greatly fear, never agree."[39] Wallace gallantly conceded that it was probably he himself who was wrong (although this did not stop him later in the century from repeating his own position in print!).[40] Wallace gallantly feared only that the problem of sterility would "become a formidable weapon in the hands of the enemies of Natural Selection."[41] Incidentally, it is interesting to note that in this disagreement there are faint echoes of the other matter which separated Darwin and Wallace at this time: sexual selection through female choice.[42] Darwin wanted to argue that the beauty of, say, the peacock as opposed to the peahen, is a function of the females choosing beautiful males. Wallace argued that the difference is essentially a function of the females being more drab than the males, this drabness coming through the female's need for camouflage from predators as they incubate their eggs and care for their young. In arguing this way, Wallace was certainly not invoking group selection. However, unlike Darwin, who was emphasizing the individual nature of selection by seeing the main competition (at this point) as coming from within the species, Wallace was deemphasizing competition within the group by seeing the threat coming from without.

Concluding this section dealing with the years immediately following the *Origin*, we see therefore that Darwin continued to think about the problem of the proper level of selection, and that he became even more convinced that in the nonhuman world selection acts at, and only at, the level of the individual. Let us see now what happened when Darwin turned his attention to human beings.

4. The Descent of Man

As is well known, what made Darwin's speculations in the *Origin* so unpalatable to so many were the obvious implications for man. As the geologist Charles Lyell sadly wrote to Darwin:

It is small comfort or consolation to me, who feels that Lamarck or Darwin have lessened the dignity of their ancestry, making them out to be with[t]. souls, to be told, 'Never mind, you will be succeeded in unbroken lineal descent by angels who, like the Superior Beings spoken of by Pope, "Will show a Newton as we show an ape."'[43]

In fact in the *Origin* itself, Darwin hardly mentioned man. Wisely deciding not to draw more controversy than he need, Darwin deliberately restricted himself to a single final comment: "Light will be thrown on the origin of man and his history."[44] And this, surely the most understated claim of the nineteenth century, Darwin added only so that he would not later be accused of dishonorably concealing his own true beliefs. But his reticence should not be confused with indecision. It is clear, from private notebooks that he kept, that right from the time when he first became an evolutionist in the late 1830s, he considered man as an animal on a par with other animals.[45] Indeed, the first hint that we have of his using natural selection as an evolutionary mechanism is a speculation about how selection might have improved human intelligence.[46]

Through the years, nothing at all changed, and so we find that when Darwin did write fully and publicly on man, in 1871 in his *Descent of Man,* he tried as carefully and thoroughly as he could to show that man evolved from other animals, by the same processes as hold throughout the organic world. For instance, "in the rudest state of society, the individuals who were the most sagacious, who invented and used the best weapons or traps, and were best able to defend themselves, would rear the greatest number of offspring." [47] The one thing perhaps noteworthy about Darwin's treatment of man, taken generally, is the very significant role he gave to the action of sexual selection. But even this, to a certain extent, was forced on him by external circumstances, namely, the apostasy of Wallace.

In his early years, Wallace had had even less religious belief than Darwin, and in fact after the *Origin,* when he first started to write on man, Wallace still treated him as a natural object. However, towards the end of the 1860s, chiefly because of a growing involvement with spiritualism, Wallace came to believe that there were aspects of human development which call for a creative power above any natural process of selection. [48] For instance, he argued that only through some kind of supernatural interference could one explain the relative hairlessness of members of the human species. To counter Wallace, although undoubtedly also as a natural development of ideas which he had had previously, Darwin included in the *Descent* a very large general discussion of sexual selection, and then he argued that many of the differences between humans, both between the sexes and between different races, are due to this kind of selection: men struggle for the women they want, women are attracted to the dominant men, and so forth. Thus something like human hairlessness can be explained as a function of early men finding hairy mates distasteful. [49]

The precise details of Darwin's general explanation of man's evolution are not our concern here. What is important to us is the obvious fact that normally he saw the individual man or woman as being the crucial unit in the selective process. There was no question that, when faced with his own species, he was going to swing round suddenly and start to argue as a general policy that for *Homo sapiens* alone the group, particularly the species, is the key element in the evolutionary mechanism. As we saw in the above quotation about the evolution of intelligence, it is when some individual man is brighter than his fellows that we get the important evolutionary consequences, for then it is that he (not everyone) will have an increased crop of children. Furthermore, whether he was indeed right in giving sexual selection so important a role in human development, the fact is that he did emphasize in even greater detail the extent to which he saw evolutionary competition occurring within the human species. As pointed out earlier, by its very definition sexual selection takes place within a species, pitting conspecific against conspecific.

Nevertheless, in dealing with man's evolution there was one point—a point incidentally noted by Wallace as inexplicable through selection—where Darwin for once did quaver in his commitment to individual selection. This was over the evolution of the human moral sense: man's awareness of and actions upon what is right and wrong. Darwin was certainly not about to follow Wallace in concluding that human morality implies that there must be a supernatural power guiding human morality; but for once he did lose sight of the individual and allow that possibly the unit of selection may have been the group, specifically the tribe. Rhetorically, Darwin asked: "...how within the limits of the same tribe did a large number of members first become endowed with [their] social and moral qualities, and how was the standard of excellence raised." [50] And then immediately he expressed his worries about the power of individual selection to bring about such morality:

It is extremely doubtful whether the offspring of the more sympathetic and benevolent parents, or of those which were the most faithful to their comrades, would be reared in greater number than the children of selfish and treacherous parents of the same tribe. He who was ready to sacrifice his life, as many a savage has been, rather than betray his comrades, would often leave no offspring to inherit his noble nature. The bravest men, who were always willing to come to the front in war, and who freely risked their lives for others, would on an average perish in larger number than other men. [51]

In short, it would seem that natural selection working at the level of the individual could not bring about or preserve a heritable moral sense.

Of course, asking rhetorical questions and setting forth the difficulties do not in themselves imply absolutely that Darwin believed that the only way in which one could explain the human moral sense was through some sort of group selection: that selection preserved a feeling for morality because the moral group was more fit than the immoral group, even though the moral individual may have been less fit than the immoral individual. However, shortly after the just-quoted passages, Darwin did give evidence that this was the way in which he inclined:

It must not be forgotten that although a high standard of morality gives but a slight or no advantage to each individual man and his children over the other men of the same tribe, yet that an advancement in the standard of morality and an increase in the number of well-endowed men will certainly give an immense advantage to one tribe over another. [52]

Moreover, apparently Darwin told one of his young followers that in the case of man's moral sense, he believed that selection had to be acting at the level of the type rather than the individual. [53]

It would seem, therefore, that although Darwin resolutely opposed group selection in the nonhuman world, when it came to our own species (although again for almost everything he was an individual selectionist) in one crucial respect of our culture—our morality—he weakened and allowed that selection must have acted at the level of the population. He could not see how helping our fellows simultaneously helps our own reproduction unless one makes the reference unit of selection the group rather than the individual. Apparently, at the final point of evolution, Darwin became a group selectionist.

Nevertheless, while one can hardly deny some truth to this conclusion, there are two modifying points which should be made. First, it must be noted that even if Darwin became something of a group selectionist, he was never a group selectionist thinking that the crucial unit of selection is the species. His concern was at most for the tribe, and he was quite explicit that morality as it developed was to benefit fellow tribesmen, to the detriment of other members of the human species: "There can be no doubt that a tribe including many members who, from possessing in a high degree the spirit of patriotism, fidelity, obedience, courage, and sympathy, were always ready to give aid to each other and to sacrifice themselves for the common good, would be victorious over most other tribes; and this would be natural selection."[54]

It is true indeed that Darwin allowed that as civilization rises, one's moral concerns extend through the human world and even to animals.[55] But it is probable that at this point he would have thought we would have left the strictly biological and have entered the realm of what we might anachronistically call "cultural evolution." In other words, here Darwin would possibly have thought that the biological individual – group selection debate was irrelevant. Certainly, he thought that modern culture transcends the biological; for instance, he rather lamented the fact that modern medicine allows the infirm to survive and reproduce, because, as he pointed out, biologically this leads to the race becoming less fit.[56]

It should also be noted that Darwin saw many of the tribe-members as being related,[57] and he was quite clear that, as in the case of social instincts, human virtues can be spread through relatives, even if an individual does not survive. I am not suggesting that Darwin went so far as to think that the only kind of group selection involved in promoting morality collapsed into an individualistic kin selection. It is fairly definite that his primitive morality was supposed to aid all fellow tribesmen, including nonrelatives. But it does seem fair to say that his group selection was of a rather mild variety.

The second modifying point about Darwin's acceptance of group selection is that, whatever its degree, it was hesitant at best. Indeed, along with his group-selection explanation of human morality, he offered an individual-selection explanation as well! He argued that morality could have come about through what today's sociobiologists call "reciprocal altruism," namely, a form of enlightened self-interest, where being nice to others pays from an evolutionary viewpoint because they in turn are nice to you.[58] Morality, Darwin suggested, may have begun because "as the reasoning powers and foresight of the members became improved, each man would soon learn from experience that if he aided his fellow-men, he would commonly receive aid in return."[59] In other words, it would seem that even as Darwin strayed from the pastures of individual selection to those of group selection, he checked himself. Hence, with respect to human morality he ended sitting firmly on the fence!

5. Conclusion

Let us conclude our discussion by linking things to the contemporary scene. This is worth doing, not to make Darwin seem more modern than he really is, a pseudo-member of the Harvard biology department—he is too great to need this revisionist treatment—but because, as we saw earlier, participants on both sides of today's debate about the levels of selection, particularly as they pertain to the evolution of humans, have invoked the past in defense of their own positions and criticism of their opponents'.

In the light of our discussion, one can only suspect that Darwin's sympathies today would lie with those who push individual selection a very long way. In the nonhuman world Darwin was a firm, even aggressive, individual selectionist. This did not, of course, stop him from arguing that peculiar phenomena like the social instincts would have evolved through such selection, although, as pointed out, his views on heredity were not sufficiently sophisticated to make worthwhile any attempt to decide which of the various modern hypotheses about the evolution of insect sociality he would have favored. We cannot, for instance, tell whether Darwin would have supported kin selection or parental manipulation as the true cause of hymenopteran sociality. But queries at this level do not negate the fact that for organisms other than man, he unequivocally invoked individual selection.

Given the facts covered in the last section, it is obvious that at least a slight gap starts to open up between the Darwin of the last century and the total believer in individual selection of this century. For almost all aspects of man, indeed, there would be agreement in principle about the power of individual selection, even though there might possibly be differences about the specific workings of such selection. However, it must be admitted that with respect to the evolution of morality Darwin seems to have been more sympathetic to group selection than would be a modern extremist like (for instance) R. L. Trivers. Nevertheless, given Darwin's general commitment to individual selection, his acceptance of group selection for morality seems to have been motivated more by the negative cause of being unable exactly to see how individual selection can cause morality than by the positive cause of thinking that group selection validates itself on its own merits. Thus, were

Darwin to have seen modern work like Trivers's explanation of morality through individualistic reciprocal altruism, he might well have responded positively: particularly since he himself gave the rudiments of a recripocal-altruism argument!

It might be added, moreover, that if one is determined to see Darwin in a modern light, even some of the most notorious human sociobiologists seem to allow that not everything is completely typical when we come to morality. Wilson, for instance, concedes that for human culture the genes have "given away most of their sovereignty,"[60] and he certainly thinks we can (and should) act morally in the interests of our group, rather than the individual. Otherwise he could not argue as he does about the need to eliminate the human population explosion.[61] Similarly, R. D. Alexander allows that we are now at the point where individual and group interest coincide, with respect to certain moral questions.[62] In other words, the individual-group selection tension vanishes, because the two modes of selection fuse together. We know that Darwin thought there comes a time when humans (in some respects) escape their biology. Hence, he would undoubtedly feel fairly sympathetic to the general kind of position that these biologists try to sketch out.

Finally, let us offer solace to the opponents of human sociobiology. If one is uncomfortable with a rather extreme individual selectionism, particularly as applied to man, and if one yet wants historical precedent to legitimize one's yearnings, then no less than the sociobiologists can one find the most respectable of intellectual ancestors. One may not be able to claim one of the fathers of evolutionism, but one can claim the other: Alfred Russel Wallace. He was a group selectionist and, moreover, he was not prepared to see man treated on a par with other organisms. I certainly do not want to pretend that today's biologists would find convincing the details of Wallace's doubts about the all-sufficiency of individual selection, or that those who criticize human sociobiology grind the same metaphysical axe as did Wallace (although it is interesting that, politically, Wallace was fairly left-wing, as are many of today's critics).[63] But given Wallace's conclusions, it does seem true that the critics of human sociobiology are not less part of the evolutionary tradition than those they criticize!

Notes

1 See R. C. Lewontin, "The units of selection," in *Annual Review of Ecology and Systematics*, ed. R. F. Johnston et al., California: Annual Reviews Inc. (1970), 1:1–23.

2 V. C. Wynne-Edwards, *Natural Regulation of Animal Numbers*, Edinburgh: Oliver and Boyd, 1962.

3 G. C. Williams, *Adaptation and Natural Selection,* Princeton: Princeton University Press, 1966.

4 See, e.g., R. Levins, "Extinction," in *Some Mathematical Questions in Biology,* ed. M. Gerstenhaber, Providence: American Mathematical Society (1970), 77–107; S. A. Boorman and P. R. Levitt, "Group selection on the boundary of a stable population," *Proceedings of the National Academy of Sciences,* 69 (1972), 2711–2713; their "Group selection of the boundary of a stable population," *Theoretical Population Biology,* 4 (1973), 85–128; and M. J. Wade, "A critical review of the models of group selection," *Quarterly Review of Biology,* 53 (1978), 101–114.

5 See E. O. Wilson, *Sociobiology: The New Synthesis,* Cambridge, Mass.: Harvard University Press, 1975; R. L. Trivers, "The evolution of reciprocal altruism," *Quarterly Review of Biology,* 46 (1971), 35–57; his "Parental investment and sexual selection," in B. Campbell, *Sexual Selection and the Descent of Man, 1871–1971,* Chicago: Aldine, 1972; his "Parent-offspring conflict," *American Zoologist,* 14 (1974), 249–264; D. P. Barash, *Sociobiology and Behavior,* New York: Elsevier, 1977; R. D. Alexander, "The search for an evolutionary philosophy," *Proceedings of the Royal Society of Victoria Australia,* 84 (1971), 99–120; his "The evolution of social behavior," *Annual Review of Ecology and Systematics,* 5 (1974), 325–384; his "The Search for a General Theory of Behavior," *Behavioral Science,* 20 (1975), 77–100; his "Evolution, human behavior, and determinism," *PSA 1976,* ed. F. Suppe and P. Asquith, Michigan: Philosophy of Science Association (1977), 2:3–21; "Natural selection and the analysis of human sociality," in *Changing Scenes in Natural Sciences,* ed. C. E. Goulden, Philadelphia: Philadelphia Academy of Natural Sciences, 1977; R. Dawkins, *The Selfish Gene,* Oxford: Oxford University Press, 1976; D. L. Hull, "Sociobiology: A scientific bandwagon or a traveling medicine show?" *Society,* 15 (1978), 50–59; M. Ruse, "Sociobiology: Sound science or muddled metaphysics?" in *PSA 1976,* ed. F. Suppe and P. Asquith (supra), 2:48–71; his "Sociobiology: A philosophical analysis," in *The Sociobiology Debate,* ed. A. Caplan, New York: Harper and Row, 1978; his "The genetics of altruism," (MS, forthcoming); and his *Sociobiology: Sense or Nonsense?* Dordrecht: Reidel, 1979.

6 E. Allen et al., "Letter to editor," *New York Review of Books* (Nov. 13, 1975), pp. 182, 184–186; their "Sociobiology: Another biological determinism," *BioScience,* 26 (1976), 182–186; their "Sociobiology: A new biological determinism," in *Biology as a Social Weapon,* ed. Sociobiology Study Group of Boston, Minneapolis: Burgess, 1977; and M. Sahlins, *The Use and Abuse of Biology,* Ann Arbor: University of Michigan, 1976.

7 Levins (note 4).

8 Lewontin (note 1).

9 R. C. Lewontin and R. Levins, "The problem of Lysenkoism," in *The Radicalisation of Science,* ed. H. and S. Rose, London: Macmillan, 1976.

10 See, e.g., Barash (note 5) and Sahlins (note 6).

11 C. Darwin, *On the Origin of Species,* 1st ed., London: John Murray, 1859.

12 Darwin, *The Descent of Man,* 1st ed., London: John Murray, 1871.

13 M. J. West Eberhard, "The evolution of social behavior by kin selection," *Quarterly Review of Biology*, 50 (1975), 1–33; and J. Maynard Smith, "Group selection," *Quarterly Review of Biology*, 51 (1976), 277–283.

14 See Ruse (note 5).

15 A. G. N. Flew, "The structure of Darwinism," *New Biology*, 28 (1959), 18–34; M. Ruse, "Natural selection in 'The origin of species,'" *Studies in the History and Philosophy of Science*, 1 (1971), 311–351; and his "Charles Darwin's theory of evolution: An analysis," *Journal of the History of Biology*, 8 (1975), 219–241.

16 K. Lorenz, *On Aggression,* New York: Harcourt Brace and World, 1966.

17 Darwin (note 11), 63.

18 Ibid., 75.

19 Ibid., 90.

20 Ibid., 87. See also M. Ghiselin, *The Triumph of the Darwinian Method,* Berkeley: University of California Press, 1969; and E. Mayr, "Sexual selection and natural selection," in B. Campbell (note 5), 87–106.

21 Such criticisms are still being made. See G. Himmelfarb, *Darwin and the Darwinian Revolution,* New York: Anchor, 1962.

22 Darwin (note 11), 236.

23 Ibid., 237–238.

24 W. D. Hamilton, "The genetical theory of social behaviour," *Journal of Theoretical Biology*, 7 (1964), 1–32; and R. Trivers and H. Hare, "Haplodiploidy and the evolution of social insects," *Science*, 191 (1976), 249–263.

25 Alexander (note 5).

26 M. J. Kottler, "Isolation and speciation, 1837–1900," Yale University Ph.D. thesis, 1976.

27 Darwin (note 11), 245.

28 C. Darwin, "On the two forms, or dimorphic condition, in the species of *Primula,* and on their remarkable sexual relations," *Journal of the Proceedings of the Linnaean Society (Botany),* 6 (1862), 77–96; reprinted in *The Collected Papers of Charles Darwin,* ed. P. H. Barrett, Chicago: University of Chicago Press (1977), 2:45–63. See also Ghiselin (note 20); and H. L. K. Whitehouse, "Cross-and self-fertilization in plants," in *Darwin's Biological Work,* ed. P. R. Bell, Cambridge: Cambridge University Press, 1959.

29 Darwin (note 28). *Papers,* 2:61.

30 C. Darwin, *A Monograph of the Sub-Class* Cirripedia, *with Figures of All the Species. The* Lepadidae; *or* Pedunculated Cirripedes, London: Ray Society, 1851; and his *A Monograph of the Sub-Class* Cirripedia, *with Figures of All the Species. The* Balamidae *(or* Sessile Cirripedes*); the* Verrucidae. *&c,* London: Ray Society, 1854. See also Ghiselin (note 20); and M. Ruse, *The Darwinian Revolution: Science Red in Tooth and Claw,* Chicago: University of Chicago Press, 1979.

31 Darwin (note 28). *Papers,* 2:62.

32 C. Darwin, "On the sexual relations of the three forms of *Lythrum salicaria*," *Journal of the Proceedings of the Linnaean Society (Botany)*, 8 (1865), 169-196, reprinted in Barrett (note 28), 2:106-131.

33 M. J. S. Rudwick, "Darwin and Glen Roy: A 'Great Failure' In Scientific Method?" *Studies in the History and Philosophy of Science*, 5 (1974), 97-185.

34 C. Darwin, *On the Origin of Species by Means of Natural Selection*, variorum text, ed. M. Pekham, Philadelphia: University of Pennsylvania Press (1959), 446.

35 Ibid., 444.

36 C. Darwin, *Variation of Animals and Plants under Domestication*, London: John Murray, 1868.

37 Letter from Wallace to Darwin, February, 1868, in *More Letters of Charles Darwin*, ed. F. Darwin and A. C. Seward, London: Murray (1903), 1:288.

38 Ibid., 288-297.

39 Ibid., 296.

40 A. R. Wallace, *Darwinism*, London: Macmillan, 1889.

41 Darwin and Seward (note 37), 1:297.

42 J. Marchant, *Alfred Russel Wallace: Life and Reminiscences*, New York: Harper (1916), 151-154.

43 L. Wilson, *Sir Charles Lyell's Scientific Journals on the Species Question*, New Haven: Yale University Press (1970), 382.

44 Darwin (note 11), 488.

45 G. de Beer, "Darwin's notebooks on transmutation of species," *Bulletin of the British Museum (Natural History)*, *Historical Series*, 2 (1960-67), 27-200 (pp. 129-176).

46 H. Gruber and P. Barrett, *Darwin on Man*, New York: Dutton (1974), Notebook M, p. 42.

47 Darwin (note 12), 1:196.

48 A. R. Wallace, "Sir Charles Lyell on geological climates and the origin of species," *Quarterly Review*, 126 (1869), 359-394; his "The limits of natural selection as applied to man," in *Contributions to the Theory of Natural Selection*, London: Macmillan, 1870; see also M. J. Kottler, "Alfred Russel Wallace, the origin of man, and spiritualism," *Isis*, 65 (1974), 145-192; and R. Smith, "Alfred Russel Wallace: Philosophy of nature and man," *British Journal for the History of Science*, 6 (1972), 177-199.

49 Darwin (note 12), 2:376-377.

50 Ibid., 1:163.

51 Ibid.

52 Ibid., 1:166.

53 E. R. Romanes, *Life and Letters of George John Romanes*, London: Longmans (1895), 173. It must be noted, however, that Romanes had his own special views on speciation, which might have made him a less-than-reliable reporter; see Kottler (note 26).

54 Darwin (note 12), 1:166.

55 Ibid., 103.

56 Ibid., 168.

57 Ibid., 161

58 Trivers (note 5).

59 Darwin (note 12), 1:163.

60 Wilson (note 5), 550.

61 E. O. Wilson, "Human decency is animal," *The New York Times Magazine* (12 October 1975), 38–50.

62 Alexander (note 5).

63 A. R. Wallace, *Studies: Scientific and Social,* London: MacMillan, 1900.

2

The Roles of Mutation, Inbreeding, Crossbreeding and Selection in Evolution

Sewall Wright

The enormous importance of biparental reproduction as a factor in evolution was brought out a good many years ago by East (1918). The observed properties of gene mutation—fortuitous in origin, infrequent in occurrence, and deleterious when not negligible in effect—seem about as unfavorable as possible for an evolutionary process. Under biparental reproduction, however, a limited number of mutations which are not too injurious to be carried by the species furnish an almost infinite field of possible variations through which the species may work its way under natural selection.

Estimates of the total number of genes in the cells of higher organisms range from 1000 up. Some 400 loci have been reported as having mutated in Drosophila during a laboratory experience which is certainly very limited compared with the history of the species in nature. Presumably, allelomorphs of all type genes are present at all times in any reasonably numerous species. Judging from the frequency of multiple allelomorphs in those organisms which have been studied most, it is reasonably certain that many different allelomorphs of each gene are in existence at all times. With 10 allelomorphs in each of 1000 loci, the number of possible combinations is 10^{1000}, which is a very large number. It has been estimated that the total number of electrons and protons in the whole visible universe is much less than 10^{100}.

However, not all of this field is easily available in an interbreeding population. Suppose that each type gene is manifested in 99 percent of the individuals, and that most of the remaining 1 percent have the most favorable of the other allelomorphs, which in general means one with only a slight differential effect. The average individual will show the effects of 1 percent of the 1000, or 10 deviations from the type, and since this average has a standard deviation of $\sqrt{10}$, only a small proportion will exhibit more than 20 deviations from type, where 1000 are possible. The population is thus confined to an infinitesimal

From *Proceedings of the Sixth International Congress of Genetics* (1932), 1:356–366.

portion of the field of possible gene combinations; yet this portion includes some 10^{40} homozygous combinations, on the above extremely conservative basis, enough so that there is no reasonable chance that any two individuals have exactly the same genetic constitution in a species of millions of millions of individuals persisting over millions of generations. There is no difficulty in accounting for the probable genetic uniqueness of each individual human being or other organism which is the product of biparental reproduction.

If the entire field of possible gene combinations be graded with respect to adaptive value under a particular set of conditions, what would be its nature? Figure 1 shows the combinations in the cases of 2 to 5 paired allelomorphs.

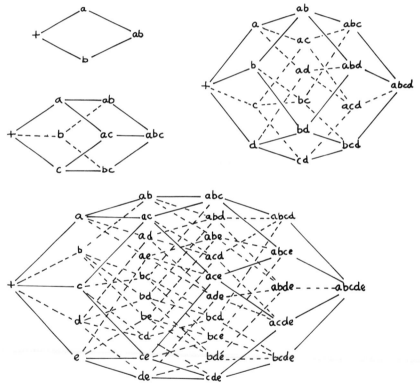

Figure 1. The combinations of from 2 to 5 paired allelomorphs.

In the last case, each of the 32 homozygous combinations is at one remove from 5 others, at two removes from 10, etc. It would require 5 dimensions to represent these relations symmetrically; a sixth dimension is needed to represent level of adaptive value. The 32 combinations here compare with 10^{1000} in a species with 1000 loci each represented by 10 allelomorphs, and the 5 dimensions required for adequate representation compare with 9000. The two dimensions of Figure 2 are a very inadequate representation of such a field. The contour lines are intended to represent the scale of adaptive value.

One possibility is that a particular combination gives maximum adaptation and that the adaptiveness of the other combinations falls off more or less regularly according to the number of removes. A species whose individuals are clustered about some combination other than the highest would move up the steepest gradient toward the peak, having reached which it would remain unchanged except for the rare occurrence of new favorable mutations.

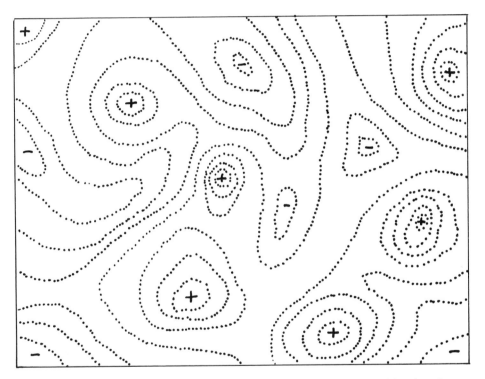

Figure 2. Diagrammatic representation of the field of gene combinations in two dimensions instead of many thousands. Dotted lines represent contours with respect to adaptiveness.

But even in the two-factor case (Figure 1) it is possible that there may be two peaks, and the chance that this may be the case greatly increases with each additional locus. With something like 10^{1000} possibilities (Figure 2) it may be taken as certain that there will be an enormous number of widely separated harmonious combinations. The chance that a random combination is as adaptive as those characteristic of the species may be as low as 10^{-100} and still leave room for 10^{800} separate peaks, each surrounded by 10^{100} more or less similar combinations. In a rugged field of this character, selection will easily carry the species to the nearest peak, but there may be innumerable other peaks which are higher but which are separated by "valleys." The problem of evolution as I see it is that of a mechanism by which the species may continually find its way from lower to higher peaks in such a field. In order that this may occur, there must be some trial and error mechanism on a grand scale by which the species may explore the region surrounding the small portion of the field which it occupies. To evolve, the species must not be under strict control of natural selection. Is there such a trial and error mechanism?

At this point let us consider briefly the situation with respect to a single locus. In each graph in Figure 3 the abscissas represent a scale of gene frequency, 0 percent of the type genes to the left, 100 percent to the right. The

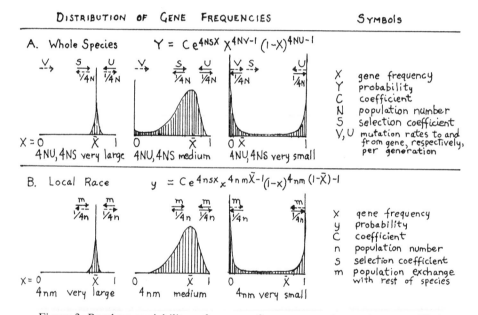

Figure 3. Random variability of a gene frequency under various specified conditions.

elementary evolutionary process is, of course, change of gene frequency, a practically continuous process. Owing to the symmetry of the Mendelian mechanism, any gene frequency tends to remain constant in the absence of disturbing factors. If the type gene mutates at a certain rate, its frequency tends to move to the left, but at a continually decreasing rate. The type gene would ultimately be lost from the population if there were no opposing factor. But the type gene is in general favored by selection. Under selection, its frequency tends to move to the right. The rate is greatest at some point near the middle of the range. At a certain gene frequency the opposing pressures are equal and opposite, and at this point there is consequently equilibrium. There are other mechanisms of equilibrium among evolutionary factors which need not be discussed here. Note that we have here a theory of the stability of species in spite of continuing mutation pressure, a continuing field of variability so extensive that no two individuals are ever genetically the same, and continuing selection.

If the population is not indefinitely large, another factor must be taken into account: the effects of accidents of sampling among those that survive and become parents in each generation and among the germ cells of these, in other words, the effects of inbreeding. Gene frequency in a given generation is in general a little different one way or the other from that in the preceding, merely by chance. In time, gene frequency may wander a long way from the position of equilibrium, although the farther it wanders, the greater the pressure toward return. The result is a frequency distribution within which gene frequency moves at random. There is considerable spread even with very slight inbreeding, and the form of distribution becomes U-shaped with close inbreeding. The rate of movement of gene frequency is very slow in the former case but is rapid in the latter (among unfixed genes). In this case, however, the tendency toward complete fixation of genes, practically irrespective of selection, leads in the end to extinction.

In a local race, subject to a small amount of crossbreeding with the rest of the species (Figure 3, lower half), the tendency toward random fixation is balanced by immigration pressure instead of by mutation and selection. In a small sufficiently isolated group all gene frequencies can drift irregularly back and forth about their mean values at a rapid rate, in terms of geologic time, without reaching fixation and giving the effects of close inbreeding. The resultant differentiation of races is, of course, increased by any local differences in the conditions of selection.

Let us return to the field of gene combinations (Figure 4). In an indefinitely large but freely interbreeding species living under constant conditions, each gene will reach ultimately a certain equilibrium. The species will occupy a certain field of variation about a peak in our diagram (heavy broken contour in upper left of each figure). The field occupied remains constant although no two individuals are ever identical. Under the above conditions further evolution can occur only by the appearance of wholly new (instead of recurrent) mutations, and ones which happen to be favorable from the first. Such mutations would change the character of the field itself, increasing the elevation of the peak occupied by the species. Evolutionary progress through this mechanism is excessively slow, since the chance of occurrence of such mutations is very small and, after occurrence, the time required for attainment of sufficient frequency to be subject to selection to an appreciable extent is enormous.

The general rate of mutation may conceivably increase for some reason. For example, certain authors have suggested an increased incidence of cosmic rays in this connection. The effect (Figure 4A) will be as a rule a spreading of the field occupied by the species until a new equilibrium is reached. There will be an average lowering of the adaptive level of the species. On the other hand, there will be a speeding up of the process discussed above, elevation of the peak itself through appearance of novel favorable mutations. Another possibility of evolutionary advance is that the spreading of the field occupied may go so far as to include another and higher peak, in which case the species will move over and occupy the region about this. These mechanisms do not appear adequate to explain evolution to an important extent.

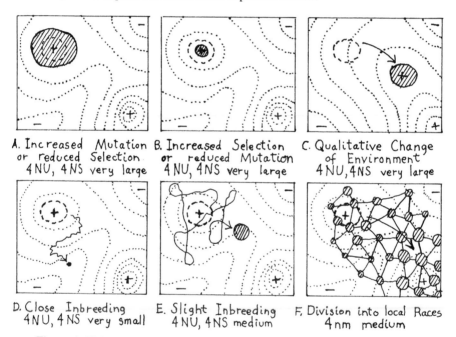

A. Increased Mutation or reduced Selection 4NU, 4NS very large   B. Increased Selection or reduced Mutation 4NU, 4NS very large   C. Qualitative Change of Environment 4NU, 4NS very large

D. Close Inbreeding 4NU, 4NS very small   E. Slight Inbreeding 4NU, 4NS medium   F. Division into local Races 4nm medium

Figure 4. Field of gene combinations occupied by a population within the general field of possible combinations. Type of history under specified conditions indicated by relation of initial field (heavy broken contour) and arrow.

The effects of reduced mutation rate (Figure 4B) are, of course, the opposite: a rise in average level but reduced variability, less chance of novel favorable mutation, and less chance of capture of a neighboring peak.

The effect of increased severity of selection (also 4B) is, of course, to increase the average level of adaptation until a new equilibrium is reached. But again this is at the expense of the field of variation of the species and reduces the chance of capture of another adaptive peak. The only basis for continuing advance is the appearance of novel favorable mutations which are relatively rapidly utilized in this case. But at best the rate is extremely slow even in terms of geologic time, judging from the observed rates of mutation.

Relaxation of selection has, of course, the opposite effects and thus effects somewhat like those of increased mutation rate (Figure 4A).

The environment, living and non-living, of any species is actually in continual change. In terms of our diagram this means that certain of the high places are gradually being depressed and certain of the low places are becoming higher (Figure 4C). A species occupying a small field under influence of severe selection is likely to be left in a pit and become extinct, the victim of extreme specialization to conditions which have ceased, but if under sufficiently moderate selection to occupy a wide field, it will merely be kept continually on the move. Here we undoubtedly have an important evolutionary process and one that has been generally recognized. It consists largely of change without advance in adaptation. The mechanism is, however, one that shuffles the species about in the general field. Since the species will be shuffled out of low peaks more easily than high ones, it should gradually find its way to the higher general regions of the field as a whole.

Figure 4D illustrates the effect of reduction in size of population below a certain relation to the rate of mutation and severity of selection. There is fixation of one or another allelomorph in nearly every locus, largely irrespective of the direction favored by selection. The species moves down from its peak in an erratic fashion and comes to occupy a much smaller field. In other words there is the deterioration and homogeneity of a closely inbred population. After equilibrium has been reached in variability, movement becomes excessively slow, and, such as there is, is nonadaptive. The end can only be extinction. Extreme inbreeding is not a factor that is likely to give evolutionary advance.

With an intermediate relation between size of population and mutation rate, gene frequencies drift at random without reaching the complete fixation of close inbreeding (Figure 4E). The species moves down from the extreme peak but continually wanders in the vicinity. There is some chance that it may encounter a gradient leading to another peak and shift its allegiance to this. Since it will escape relatively easily from low peaks as compared with high ones, there is here a trial and error mechanism by which in time the species may work its way to the highest peaks in the general field. The rate of progress, however, is extremely slow, since change of gene frequency is of the order of the reciprocal of the effective population size and this reciprocal must be of the order of the mutation rate in order to meet the conditions for this case.

Finally (Figure 4F), let us consider the case of a large species that is sub-divided into many small local races, each breeding largely within itself but occasionally crossbreeding. The field of gene combinations occupied by each of these local races shifts continually in a nonadaptive fashion (except insofar as there are local differences in the conditions of selection). The rate of move-ment may be enormously greater than in the preceding case, since the condi-tion for such movement is that the reciprocal of the population number be of the order of the proportion of crossbreeding instead of the mutation rate. With many local races, each spreading over a considerable field and moving relatively rapidly in the more general field about the controlling peak, the chances are good that one at least will come under the influence of another peak. If a higher peak, this race will expand in numbers and by crossbreeding with the others will pull the whole species toward the new position. The average adaptiveness of the species thus advances under intergroup selection, an enormously more effective process than intragroup selection. The conclu-sion is that subdivision of a species into local races provides the most effective mechanism for trial and error in the field of gene combinations.

It need scarcely be pointed out that with such a mechanism complete isola-tion of a portion of a species should result relatively rapidly in specific dif-ferentiation, and one that is not necessarily adaptive. The effective intergroup competition leading to adaptive advance may be between species rather than races. Such isolation is doubtless usually geographic in character at the outset but may be clinched by the development of hybrid sterility. The usual dif-ference of the chromosome complements of related species puts the impor-tance of chromosome aberration as an evolutionary process beyond question, but as I see it this importance is not in the character differences which they bring (slight in balanced types), but rather in leading to the sterility of hybrids and thus making permanent the isolation of two groups.

How far do the observations of actual species and their subdivisions con-form to this picture? This is naturally too large a subject for more than a few suggestions.

That evolution involves nonadaptive differentiation to a large extent at the subspecies, and even the species level is indicated by the kinds of differences by which such groups are actually distinguished by systematists. It is only at the subfamily and family levels that clear-cut adaptive differences become the rule (Robson, 1928; Jacot, 1932). The principal evolutionary mechanism in the origin of species must thus be an essentially nonadaptive one.

That natural species often are subdivided into numerous local races is indi-cated by many studies. The case of the human species is most familiar. Aside from the familiar racial differences, recent studies indicate a distribution of frequencies relative to an apparently nonadaptive series of allelomorphs, that which determine blood groups, of just the sort discussed above. I scarcely need to labor the point that changes in the average of mankind in the historic period have come about more by expansion of some types and decrease and absorption of others than by uniform evolutionary advance. During the recent period, no doubt, the phases of intergroup competition and crossbreeding have tended to overbalance the process of local differentiation, but it is probable that in the hundreds of thousands of years of prehistory, human evolution was determined by a balance between these factors.

Subdivision into numerous local races whose differences are largely nonadaptive has been recorded in other organisms wherever a sufficiently detailed study has been made. Among the land snails of the Hawaiian Islands, Gulick (1905) found that each mountain valley, often each grove of trees, had its own characteristic type, differing from others in "nonutilitarian" respects. Gulick attributed this differentiation to inbreeding. More recently, Crampton (1925) found a similar situation in the land snails of Tahiti and followed over a period of years evolutionary changes which seem to be of the type here discussed. I may also refer to the studies of fishes by David Starr Jordan (1908), garter snakes by Ruthven (1908), bird lice by Kellogg (1908), deer mice by Osgood (1909), and gall wasps by Kinsey (1930) as others which indicate the role of local isolation as a differentiating factor. Many other cases are discussed by Osborn (1927), and especially by Rensch (1929) in recent summaries. Many of these authors insist on the nonadaptive character of most of the differences among local races. Others attribute all differences to the environment, but this seems to be more an expression of faith than a view based on tangible evidence.

An even more minute local differentiation has been revealed when the methods of statistical analysis have been applied. Schmidt (1917) demonstrated the existence of persistent mean differences at each collecting station in certain species of marine fish of the fjords of Denmark, and these differences were not related in any close way to the environment. That the differences were in part genetic was demonstrated in the laboratory. David Thompson (1931) has found a correlation between water distance and degree of differentiation within certain fresh water species of fish of the streams of Illinois. Sumner's (1932) extensive studies of subspecies of Peromyscus (deer mice) reveal genetic differentiations, often apparently nonadaptive, among local populations and demonstrate the genetic heterogeneity of each such group.

The modern breeds of livestock have come from selection among the products of local inbreeding and of crossbreeding between these, followed by renewed inbreeding, rather than from mass selection of species. The recent studies of the geographical distribution of particular genes in livestock and cultivated plants by Serebrovsky (1929), Philiptschenko (1927), and others are especially instructive with respect to the composition of such species.

The paleontologists present a picture that has been interpreted by some as irreconcilable with the Mendelian mechanism, but this seems to be due more to a failure to appreciate statistical consequences of this mechanism than to anything in the data. The horse has been the standard example of an orthogenetic evolutionary sequence preserved for us with an abundance of material. Yet Mathew's (1926) interpretation as one in which evolution has proceeded by extensive differentiation of local races, intergroup selection, and crossbreeding is as close as possible to that required under the Mendelian theory.

Summing up: I have attempted to form a judgment as to the conditions for evolution based on the statistical consequences of Mendelian heredity. The most general conclusion is that evolution depends on a certain balance among its factors. There must be gene mutation, but an excessive rate gives an array of freaks, not evolution; there must be selection, but too severe a process destroys the field of variability, and thus the basis for further advance; prevalence of local inbreeding within a species has extremely important evolutionary consequences, but too close inbreeding leads merely to extinction. A certain amount of crossbreeding is favorable but not too much. In this dependence on balance the species is like a living organism. At all levels of organization life depends on the maintenance of a certain balance among its factors.

More specifically, under biparental reproduction a very low rate of mutation balanced by moderate selection is enough to maintain a practically infinite field of possible gene combinations within the species. The field actually occupied is relatively small though sufficiently extensive that no two individuals have the same genetic constitution. The course of evolution through the general field is not controlled by direction of mutation and not directly by selection, except as conditions change, but by a trial and error mechanism consisting of a largely nonadaptive differentiation of local races (due to inbreeding balanced by occasional crossbreeding) and a determination of long-time trend by intergroup selection. The splitting of species depends on the effects of more complete isolation, often made permanent by the accumulation of chromosome aberrations, usually of the balanced type. Studies of natural species indicate that the conditions for such an evolutionary process are often present.

References

Crampton, H. E., 1925. "Contemporaneous organic differentiation in the species of *Partula* living in Moorea, Society Islands," *Amer. Nat.*, 59:5–35.

East, E. M., 1918. "The role of reproduction in evolution," *Amer. Nat.*, 52: 273–289.

Gulick, J. T., 1905. "Evolution, racial and habitudinal," *Pub. Carnegie Instn.*, 25:1–269.

Jacot, A. P., 1932. "The status of the species and the genus," *Amer. Nat.*, 66: 346–364.

Jordan, D. S., 1908. "The law of geminate species," *Amer. Nat.*, 42:73–80.

Kellogg, V. L., 1908. *Darwinism, Today*, New York: Henry Holt and Co., 403 pp.

Kinsey, A. C., 1930. "The gall wasp genus *Cynips*," *Indiana Univ. Studies*, 84–86:1–577.

Mathew, W. D., 1926. "The evolution of the horse: A record and its interpretation," *Quart. Rev. Biol.*, 1:139–185.

Osborn, H. F., 1927. "The origin of species: V. Speciation and mutation," *Amer. Nat.*, 49:193–239.

Osgood, W. H., 1909. "Revision of the mice of the genus *Peromyscus*," *North American Fauna*, 28:1–285.

Philiptschenko, J., 1927. *Variabilität und Variation*, Berlin, 101 pp.

Rensch, B., 1929. *Das Prinzip geographischer Rassenkreise und das Problem der Artbildung*, Berlin: Gebrüder Borntraeger, 206 pp.

Robson, G. C., 1928. *The Species Problem*, Edinburgh and London: Oliver and Boyd, 283 pp.

Ruthven, A. G., 1908. "Variation and genetic relationships of the garter snakes," *U.S. Nat. Mus. Bull.*, 61:1–301.

Schmidt, J., 1917. "Statistical investigations with *Zoarces viviparus* L.," *J. Genet.*, 7:105–118.

Serebrovsky, A. S., 1929. "Beitrag zur geographischen Genetic des Haushahns in Sowjet-Russland," *Arch. für Geflügelkunde*, 3:161–169.

Sumner, F. B., 1932. "Genetic, distributional, and evolutionary studies of the subspecies of deer mice (*Peromyscus*)," *Bibl. genet.*, 9:1–106.

Thompson, D. H., 1931. "Variation in fishes as a function of distance," *Trans. Ill. State Acad. of Sci.*, 23:276–281.

Wright, S., 1931. "Evolution in Mendelian populations," *Genetics*, 16:97–159.

3

Theories of Group Selection

Sewall Wright

There has probably been some confusion between the "intergroup selection" that I proposed in 1929 and 1931 with "group selection" for group advantage that has been the subject of lively controversy in recent years.

Haldane (1932) introduced the term "altruist" for a phenotype that contributes to group advantage at the expense of disadvantage to itself. I discussed this subject from a somewhat different viewpoint in 1945. We both concluded, however, that such group selection is possible but extremely fragile, always likely to be reversed by slight changes in conditions.

The subject attracted little attention until Wynne-Edwards in 1962 vigorously urged its evolutionary importance on grounds that were more intuitive than mathematical. There have been active discussions of variants of his model since then.

Hamilton (1963) has urged the importance of kin selection. Discussion of this goes back to Darwin in the case of the evolution of a sterile worker caste in social insects. There seems no doubt of the evolutionary importance of this sort of selection, but it is a very different matter from group selection for the uniform advantage of a group.

... Maynard Smith, Williams and Dawkins have all discussed group selection for group advantage at length, and all have rejected it as of little or no evolutionary significance. They seem to have concluded, however, that this warrants the conclusion that natural selection is practically wholly genic, as implied by Fisher's fundamental theorem. None of them discussed group selection for organismic advantage to individuals, the dynamic factor in the shifting balance process, although this process, based on irreversible local peak-shifts, is not fragile at all, in contrast with the fairly obvious fragility of group selection for group advantage, which they considered worthy of extensive discussion before rejection.

From pp. 840–841 of "Genic and Organismic Selection," *Evolution* (1980), 34:825–843.

References

Dawkins, R., 1976. *The Selfish Gene,* New York: Oxford University Press.

Haldane, J. B. S., 1932. *The Causes of Evolution,* London: Longmans Green.

Hamilton, W. D., 1963. "The evolution of altruistic behavior," *Amer. Natur.,* 97:354–356.

Maynard Smith, J., 1975. *The Theory of Evolution,* London: Penguin.

Williams, G. C., 1966. *Adaptation and Natural Selection: A Critique of Some Current Evolutionary Thought,* Princeton: Princeton University Press. Chapter 4 is reprinted in part in this volume.

Wright, S., 1929. "Evolution in a Mendelian population," *Anat. Rec.,* 44:287.

Wright, S., 1931. "Evolution in Mendelian populations," *Genetics,* 10:97–159.

Wright, S., 1945. "*Tempo and Mode in Evolution:* A critical review," *Ecology,* 26:415–419.

4

Intergroup Selection in the Evolution of Social Systems

V. C. Wynne-Edwards

Preface, July 1983

This controversy will shortly take a new turn, which I hope will lead to resolving it. In a book to be entitled *Animal Sociality and Group Selection,* which should appear in 1984 (Oxford, Blackwell), I am offering the following solution.

Social cooperation by animals for the purpose of conserving their food resources for the future does not, after all, demand any sacrifice of individual fertility or life expectation, as mistakenly assumed in the fourth paragraph of my 1963 article. I have recently realized the simple truth that, on the contrary, individuals belonging to species that efficiently husband their food resources are normally born into very productive habitats. This enables them to achieve far higher fitnesses than would be attainable by members of the same species who opted to exploit the food resources for selfish advantage instead, without regard to the future. After a generation or two, the noncooperators would find themselves in habitats chronically run down, if not devastated, as a result of overexploitation. Thus what is good for the cooperative group is good for the individual members of it.

For a parallel reason, regulating the population is equally beneficial to animals, such as detritivores, that depend on food resources that are not overexploitable. For them, given a finite food supply, there is an optimal number of consumers that will produce the highest individual and collective fitnesses, when all are able to obtain as much food as they can usefully metabolize, but leave no unconsumed excess.

In both situations, noncooperators who did not conform to the social code would be a liability to any group that contained them, because of the damage they did by not complying with the restriction on numbers. Groups containing many noncooperators would fail to prosper. Consequently animal social codes, once they have evolved, are stable and cannot be undermined by antisocial mutants.

Text of 1963 Article*

In a recent book[1] I advanced a general proposition which may be summarized in the following way: (1) Animals, especially in the higher phyla, are variously adapted to control their own population densities. (2) The mechanisms involved work homeostatically, adjusting the population density in relation to fluctuating levels of resources; where the limiting resource is food, as it most frequently is, the homeostatic system prevents the population from increasing to densities that would cause overexploitation and the depletion of future yields. (3) The mechanisms depend in part on the substitution of conventional prizes—namely, the possession of territories, homes, living space, and similar real property, or of social status as the proximate objects of competition among the members of the group concerned—in place of the actual food itself. (4) Any group of individuals engaged together in such conventional competition automatically constitutes a society, all social behavior having sprung originally from this source.

As I developed the theme, it soon became apparent that the greatest benefits of sociality arise from its capacity to override the advantage of the individual members in the interests of the survival of the group as a whole. The kind of adaptations which make this possible, as explained more fully here, belong to and characterize social groups as entities, rather than their members individually. This in turn seems to entail that natural selection has occurred between social groups as evolutionary units in their own right, favoring the more efficient variants among social systems wherever they have appeared, and furthering their progressive development and adaptation.

The general concept of intergroup selection is not new. It has been widely accepted in the field of evolutionary genetics, largely as a result of the classical analysis of Sewall Wright.[2-4] He has expressed the view that "selection between the genetic systems of local populations of a species . . . has been perhaps the greatest creative factor of all in making possible selection of genetic systems as wholes in place of mere selection according to the net effects of alleles."[4] Intergroup selection has been invoked also to explain the special case of colonial evolution in the social insects.[5-7]

In the context of the social group a difficulty appears, with selection acting simultaneously at the two levels of the group and the individual. It is that the homeostatic control of population density frequently demands sacrifices of the individual; and while population control is essential in the long-term survival of the group, the sacrifices impair fertility and survivorship in the individual. One may legitimately ask how two kinds of selection can act simultaneously when on fundamental issues they are working at cross-purposes. At

*From *Nature* (1963), Vol. 200, No. 4907:623–626.

first sight there seems to be no easy way of reconciling this clash of interests; and to some people consequently the whole idea of intergroup selection is unacceptable.

Before an attempt is made to resolve the problem, it is necessary to fill in some of the background and give it clearer definition. The survival of a local group or population naturally depends among other things on the continuing annual yield of its food resources. Typically, where the tissues of animals or plants are consumed as food, persistent excessive pressure of exploitation can rather quickly overtax the resource and reduce its productivity, with the result that yields are diminished in subsequent years. This effect can be seen in the overfishing of commercial fisheries which is occurring now in different parts of the world, and in the overgrazing of pastoral land, which in dry climates can eventually turn good grassland into desert. Damage to the crop precedes the onset and spread of starvation in the exploiting population, and may be further aggravated by it. The general net effect of overpopulation is thus to diminish the carrying capacity of the habitat.

In natural environments undisturbed by man this kind of degradation is rare and exceptional: the normal evolutionary trend is in the other direction, toward building up and sustaining the productivity of the habitat at the highest attainable level. Predatory animals do not in these conditions chronically depress their stocks of prey, nor do herbivores impair the regeneration of their food plants. Many animals, especially among the larger vertebrates (including man), have themselves virtually no predators or parasites automatically capable of disposing of a population surplus if it arises.

It is the absence or undependability of external destructive agencies that makes it valuable, if not in some cases mandatory, that animals should be adapted to regulate their own numbers. By so doing, the population density can be balanced around the optimum level, at which the highest sustainable use is made of food resources.

Only an extraordinary circumstance could have concealed this elementary conclusion and prevented our taking it immediately for granted. Some eight or more thousand years ago, as neolithic man began to achieve new and greatly enhanced levels of production from the land through the agricultural revolution, the homeostatic conventions of his hunting ancestors, developed there as in other primates to keep population density in balance with carrying capacity, were slowly and imperceptibly allowed to decay. We can tell this from the centrally important place always occupied by fertility-limiting and functionally similar conventions in the numerous stone-age cultures which persisted into modern times.[8] Since these conventions disappeared, nothing has been acquired in their place: growing skills in resource development have, except momentarily, always outstripped the demands of a progressively increasing population; there has consequently been no effective natural selection against a freely expanding economy. So far as the regulation of numbers is concerned, the human race provides a spectacular exception to the general rule.

A secondary factor, tending to obscure the almost universal powers possessed by animals for controlling their numbers, is our everyday familiarity with insect and other pests which appear to undergo uncontrolled and sometimes violent fluctuations in abundance. In fact, human land-use practices seldom leave natural processes alone for any length of time: vegetation is gathered, the ground is tilled, treated, or irrigated, single-species crops are planted and rotated, predators and competitors are destroyed, and the animals' regulating mechanisms are thereby, understandably, often defeated. In the comparably drastic environmental fluctuations of the polar and desert regions, similar population fluctuations occur without human intervention.

The methods by which natural animal populations curb their own increase and promote the efficient exploitation of food resources include the control of recruitment and, when necessary, the expulsion and elimination of unwanted surpluses. The individual member has to be governed by the homeostatic system even when, as commonly happens, this means his exclusion from food in the midst of apparent plenty, or detention from reproduction when others are breeding. The recruitment rate must be determined by the contemporary relation between population density and resources; under average conditions, therefore, only part of the potential fecundity of the group needs to be realized in a given year or generation.

This is a conclusion amply supported by the results of experiments on fecundity versus density in laboratory populations in a wide variety of animals, including Crustacea, insects, fish, and mammals; and also by field data from natural populations.[1] But it conflicts with the assumption, still rather widely made, that under natural selection there can be no alternative to promoting the fecundity of the individual, provided that this results in his leaving a larger contribution of surviving progeny to posterity.[9] This assumption is the chief obstacle to accepting the principle of intergroup selection.

One of the most important premises of intergroup selection is that animal populations are typically self-perpetuating, tending to be strongly localized and persistent on the same ground. This is illustrated by the widespread use of traditional breeding sites by birds, fishes, and animals of many other kinds; and by the subsequent return of the great majority of experimentally marked young to breed in their native neighborhood. It is true of nonmigratory species, for example the more primitive communities of man; and all the long-distance two-way migrants that have so far been experimentally tagged, whether they are birds, bats, seals, or salmon, have developed parallel and equally remarkable navigating powers that enable them to return precisely to the same point, and consequently preserve the integrity of their particular local stock. Isolation is normally not quite complete, however. Provision is made for an element of pioneering, and infiltration into other areas; but the gene-flow that results is not commonly fast enough to prevent the population from accumulating heritable characteristics of its own. Partly genetic and partly traditional, these differentiate it from other similar groups.

Local groups are the smallest racial units capable of continuous existence for long enough to undergo evolutionary differentiation. In the course of generations some die out; others survive, and have the opportunity to spread into new or vacated ground as it becomes available, themselves subdividing as they grow. Insofar as the successful ones take over the habitat left vacant by the unsuccessful, the groups are in a relation of passive competition. Their survival or extinction is partly a matter of chance, arising from various forms of *force majeure,* including secular changes in the environment; for the rest it is determined, in general terms, by heritable qualities of fitness.

Gene-frequencies within the group may alter as time passes, through gene-flow, drift (the Sewall Wright effect), and selection at the individual level. Through the latter, adaptations to local conditions may accumulate. Population fitness, however, depends on something over and above the heritable basis that determines the success as individuals of a continuing stream of independent members. It becomes particularly clear in relation to population homeostasis that social groups have highly important adaptive characteristics in their own right.

When the balance of a self-regulating population is disturbed, for example by heavy accidental mortality or by a change in food-resource yields, a restorative reaction is set in motion. If the density has dropped below the optimum, the recruitment rate may be increased in a variety of ways, most simply by drawing on the reserve of potential fecundity referred to earlier, and so raising the reproductive output. Immigrants appearing from surrounding areas can be allowed to remain as recruits also. If the density has risen too high, aggression between individuals may build up to the point of expelling the surplus as emigrants; the reproductive rate may drop; and mortality due to social stress (and in some species cannibalism) may rise. These are typical examples of density-dependent homeostatic responses.

Seven years of investigation of the population ecology of the red grouse (*Lagopus scoticus*) near Aberdeen, by the Nature Conservancy Unit of Grouse and Moorland Ecology, have revealed many of these processes at work.[10] Their operation in this case depends to a great extent on the fact that individual members of a grouse population living together on a moor, even of the same sex, are not equal in social status. Some of the cock birds are sufficiently dominant to establish themselves as territory owners, parceling out the ground among them and holding sway over it, with a varying intensity of possessiveness, almost the whole year round. From February to June their mates enjoy the same established status.

In the early dawn of August and September mornings, after a short and almost complete recess, the shape of a new territorial pattern begins to be hammered out. In most years this quickly identifies a large surplus of males, old and young, which are not successful in securing any part of the ground, and consequently assume a socially inferior status. They are grouped with the hens at this stage as unestablished birds; and day by day their security is so disturbed by the dawn-aggressive stress that almost at once some begin to get forced out, never to return. By about 8 A.M. each day the passion subsides in all but the most refractory territorial cocks, after which the moor reverts to communal ground on which the whole population can feed freely for the rest of the day. As autumn wears on and turns to winter, the daily period of aggression becomes fiercer and lasts longer; birds with no property rights have to feed at least part of the time on territorial ground defended by owners that may at any moment chase them off. More and more are driven out altogether; and since they can rarely find a safe nook to occupy elsewhere in the neighborhood, they become outcasts, and are easily picked up by hawks and foxes, or succumb to malnutrition. Females are included among those expelled; but about February the remaining ones begin to establish marital attachments; and at the same time, quite suddenly, territories are vigorously defended all day. Of the unestablished birds still present in late winter, some achieve promotion by filling the gaps caused by casualties in the establishment. Some may persist occasionally until spring; but unless a cock holds a territory exceeding a minimum threshold capacity, or a hen becomes accepted by a territorially qualified mate, breeding is inhibited.

Territories are not all of uniform size, and on average the largest are held by the most dominating cocks. More important still, the average size of territory changes from year to year, thus varying the basic population density, apparently in direct response to changes in productivity of the staple food-plant, heather (*Calluna vulgaris*). As yet this productivity has been estimated only by subjective methods; but significant mutual correlations have been established between annual average values of body-weight of adults, adult survival, clutch-size, hatching success, survival of young, and, finally, breeding density the following year. As would be expected with changing densities, the size of the autumn surplus, measured by the proportions of unestablished to established birds, also varies from year to year.

There are increasing grounds for concluding that this is quite a typical organization, so far as birds are concerned, and that social stratification into established and unestablished members, particularly in the breeding season, is common to many other species, and other classes of animals. In different circumstances the social hierarchy may take the form of a more or less linear series or peck-order. Hierarchies commonly play a leading part in regulating animal populations; not only can they be made to cut off any required proportion of the population from breeding, but also they have exactly the same effect in respect of food when it is in short supply. According to circumstances, the surplus tail of the hierarchy may either be disposed of or retained as a nonparticipating reserve if resources permit.

It is not necessary here to explore in detail the elaborate patterns of behavior by which the social hierarchy takes effect. The processes are infinitely varied and complex, though the results are simple and functionally always the same. The hierarchy is essentially an overflow mechanism, continuously variable in terms of population pressure on one hand, and habitat capacity on the other. In operation it is purely conventional, prescribing a code of behavior. When a more dominant individual exerts sufficient aggressive pressure, usually expressed as threat although frequently in some more subtle and sophisticated form, his subordinates yield, characteristically without physical resistance or even demur. It may cost them their sole chance of reproduction to do so, if not their lives. The survival of the group depends on their compliance.

This has been taken as an example to illustrate one type of adaptation possessed by the group, transcending the individuality of its members. It subordinates the advantage of particular members to the advantage of the group; its survival value to the latter is clearly very great. The hierarchy as a system of behavior has innumerable variants in different species and different phyla, analogous to those of a somatic unit like the nervous or vascular system. Like them, it must have been subject to adaptive evolutionary change through natural selection; yet it is essentially an "organ" of a social group, and has no existence if the members are segregated.

A simple analogy may possibly help to bring out the significance of this point. A football team is made up of players individually selected for such qualities as skill, quickness, and stamina, material to their success as members of the team. The survival of the team to win the championship, however, is determined by entirely distinct criteria, namely, the tactics and ability it displays in competition with other teams, under a particular code of conventions laid down for the game. There is no difficulty in distinguishing two levels of selection here, although the analogy is otherwise very imperfect.

The hierarchy is not the only characteristic of this kind. There are genetic mechanisms, such as those that govern the optimum balance between recombination and linkage, in which it is equally clear that the benefit is with the group rather than the individual. Without leaving the sphere of population regulation, however, we can find a wide range of vital parameters, the optima of which must similarly be determined by intergroup selection. Among those discussed at length in the book already cited [1] are (1) the potential life-span of individuals and, coupled with it, the generation turnover rate; (2) the relative proportions of life spent in juvenile or nonsexual condition (including diapause) and in reproduction; (3) monotely (breeding only for a single season) versus polytely; (4) the basal fecundity-level, including, in any one season, the question of one brood versus more than one.

These and similar parameters, differing from one species or class to another, are interconnected. Their combined effects are being summed over the whole population at any one time and over many generations in any given area. It is the scale of the operation in time and space that precludes an immediate experimental test of group selection. An inference that may justifiably be drawn, however, is that maladjustment sufficient to interfere persistently with the homeostatic mechanism must either cause a progressive decline in the population or, alternatively, a chronic overexploitation and depletion of food resources; in the end either will depopulate the locality.

There still remains the central question of how an immediate advantage to the individual can be suppressed or overridden when it conflicts with the interests of the group. What would be the effect of selection, for example, on individuals the abnormal and socially undesirable fertility of which enabled them and their hereditary successors to contribute an ever-increasing share to future generations?

Initially, groups containing individuals like this that reproduced too fast, so that the over-all recruitment rate persistently tended to exceed the death rate, must have repeatedly exterminated themselves in the manner just indicated, by overtaxing and progressively destroying their food resources. The earliest adaptations capable of protecting the group against such recurrent disasters must necessarily have been very ancient; they may even have been acquired only once in the whole of animal phylogeny, and in this respect be comparable to such basic morphological elements as the mesoderm or, perhaps, the coelom. Once acquired, the protective adaptations could be endlessly varied and elaborated. It is inherently difficult to reconstruct the origin of systems of this kind; but genetic mechanisms exist which could give individual breeding success a low heritability, or, in other words, make it resistant to selection. This could be relatively simply achieved, for example, if the greatest success normally attached to heterozygotes for the alleles concerned, creating the stable situation characteristic of genetic homeostasis. [11]

A more complex system can be discerned, as it has developed in many of the higher vertebrates where the breeding success of individuals is very closely connected with social status. This connection must necessarily divert an enormous additional force of selection into promoting social dominance, and penalizing the less fortunate subordinates in the population that are prevented from breeding or feeding, or get squeezed out of the habitat. Yet it is self-evident that the conventional codes under which social competition is conducted are in practice not jeopardized from this cause: selection pressure, however great, does not succeed in promoting a general recourse to deadly combat or treachery between rivals, nor does it, in the course of generations, extinguish the patient compliance of subordinates with their lot.

The reason appears to be that social status depends on a summation of diverse traits, including virtually all the hereditary and environmental factors that predicate health, vigor, and survivorship in the individual. While this is favorable to the maintenance of a high-grade breeding stock, and can result in the enhancement through selection of the weapons and conventional adornments by which social dominance is secured, dominance itself is again characterized by a low heritability, as experiments have shown. In many birds and mammals, moreover, individual status, quite apart from its genetic basis, advances progressively with the individual's age. Not only are the factors that determine social and breeding success numerous and involved, therefore, but the ingredients can vary from one successful individual to the next. A substantial part of the gene pool of the population is likely to be involved and selection for social dominance or fertility at the individual level correspondingly dissipated and ineffective, except in eliminating the substandard fringe.

Such methods as these which protect group adaptations, including both population parameters and social structure, from short-term changes, seem capable of preventing the rise of any hereditary tendency toward antisocial self-interest among the members of a social group. Compliance with the social code can be made obligatory and automatic, and it probably is so in almost all animals that possess social homeostatic systems at all. In at least some of the mammals, on the contrary, the individual has been released from this rigid compulsion, probably because a certain amount of intelligent individual enterprise has proved advantageous to the group. In man, as we know, compliance with the social code is by no means automatic, and is reinforced by conscience and the law, both of them relatively flexible adaptations.

There appears, therefore, to be no great difficulty in resolving the initial problem of how intergroup selection can override the concurrent process of selection for individual advantage. Relatively simple genetic mechanisms can be evolved whereby the door is shut to one form of selection and open to the other, securing without conflict the maximum advantage from each; and since neighboring populations differ not only in genetic system but in population parameters (for example, mean fecundity[12]) and in social practices (for example, local differences in migratory behavior in birds, or in tribal conventions among primitive men), there is no lack of variation on which intergroup selection can work.

Notes

1 V. C. Wynne-Edwards, *Animal Dispersion in Relation to Social Behaviour,* Edinburgh and London, 1962.

2 S. Wright, *Anat. Rec.* (1929), 44:287.

3 S. Wright, *Genetics* (1930), 16:97.

4 S. Wright, *Ecology* (1945), 26:415.

5 J. B. S. Haldane, *The Causes of Evolution,* London, New York, and Toronto, 1932.

6 A. H. Sturtevant, *Quart. Rev. Biol.* (1938), 13:74.

7 G. C. and D. C. Williams, *Evolution* (1957), 11:32.

8 A. M. Carr-Saunders, *The Population Problem: A Study in Human Evolution,* Oxford University Press, 1922.

9 D. Lack, *The Natural Regulation of Animal Numbers,* Oxford University Press, 1954.

10 D. Jenkins, A. Watson, and G. R. Miller, *J. Anim. Ecol.* (1963), 32:317.

11 I. M. Lerner, *Genetic Homeostasis,* Edinburgh and London, 1954.

12 T. B. Bagenal, *J. Mar. Biol. Assoc.* (1962), 42:105.

5

Group Selection

George C. Williams

This book is a rejoinder to those who have questioned the adequacy of the traditional model of natural selection to explain evolutionary adaptation. The topics considered in the preceding chapters relate mainly to the adequacy of this model in the realms of physiological, ecological, and developmental mechanisms, matters of primary concern to individual organisms. At the individual level the adequacy of the selection of alternative alleles has been challenged to only a limited degree. Many more doubts on the importance of such selection have been voiced in relation to the phenomena of interactions among individuals. Many biologists have implied, and a moderate number have explictly maintained, that groups of interacting individuals may be adaptively organized in such a way that individual interests are compromised by a functional subordination to group interests.

It is universally conceded by those who have seriously concerned themselves with this problem (e.g., Allee et al., 1949; Haldane, 1932; Lewontin, 1958, 1962; Slobodkin, 1954; Wynne-Edwards, 1962; Wright, 1945) that such group-related adaptations must be attributed to the natural selection of alternative *groups* of individuals and that the natural selection of alternative alleles within populations will be opposed to this development. I am in entire agreement with the reasoning behind this conclusion. Only by a theory of between-group selection could we achieve a scientific explanation of group-related adaptations. However, I would question one of the premises on which the reasoning is based. Chapters 5 to 8 [of *Adaptation and Natural Selection*] will be primarily a defense of the thesis that group-related adaptations do not, in fact, exist. A *group* in this discussion should be understood to mean something other than a family and to be composed of individuals that need not be closely related.

The present chapter examines the logical structure of the theory of selection

From chapter 4 of *Adaptation and Natural Selection*, Princeton: Princeton University Press, 1966, pp. 92–101, 108–124.

between groups, but first I wish to consider an apparent exception to the rule
that the natural selection of individuals cannot produce group-related adaptations. This exception may be found in animals that live in stable social groups
and have the intelligence and other mental qualities necessary to form a system
of personal friendships and animosities that transcend the limits of family relationship. Human society would be impossible without the ability of each of
us to know, individually, a variety of neighbors. We learn that Mr. X is a noble
gentleman and that Mr. Y is a scoundrel. A moment of reflection should convince anyone that these relationships may have much to do with evolutionary
success. Primitive man lived in a world in which stable interactions of person-
alties were very much a part of his ecological environment. He had to adjust
to this set of ecological factors as well as to any other. If he was socially
acceptable, some of his neighbors might bring food to himself and his family
when he was temporarily incapacitated by disease or injury. In time of dearth,
a stronger neighbor might rob our primitive man of food, but the neighbor
would be more likely to rob a detestable primitive Mr. Y and his troublesome
family. Conversely, when a poor Mr. X is sick, our primitive man will, if he
can, provide for him. Mr. X's warm heart will know the emotion of gratitude
and, since he recognizes his benefactor and remembers the help provided, will
probably reciprocate some day. A number of people, including Darwin (1896,
chap. 5), have recognized the importance of this factor in human evolution.
Darwin speaks of it as the "lowly motive" of helping others in the hope of
future repayment. I see no reason why a conscious motive need be involved.
It is necessary that help provided to others be occasionally reciprocated if it is
to be favored by natural selection. It is not necessary that either the giver or
the receiver be aware of this.

Simply stated, an individual who maximizes his friendships and minimizes
his antagonisms will have an evolutionary advantage, and selection should favor those characters that promote the optimization of personal relationships.
I imagine that this evolutionary factor has increased man's capacity for altruism and compassion and has tempered his ethically less acceptable heritage of
sexual and predatory aggressiveness. There is theoretically no limit to the extent and complexity of group-related behavior that this factor could produce,
and the immediate goal of such behavior would always be the well-being of
some other individual, often genetically unrelated. Ultimately, however, this
would not be an adaptation for group benefit. It would be developed by the
differential survival of individuals and would be designed for the perpetuation
of the genes of the individual providing the benefit to another. It would involve only such immediate self-sacrifice for which the probability of later repayment would be sufficient justification. The natural selection of alternative

alleles can foster the production of individuals willing to sacrifice their lives for their offspring, but never for mere friends.

The prerequisites for the operation of this evolutionary factor are such as to confine it to a minor fraction of the Earth's biota. Many animals form dominance hierarchies, but these are not sufficient to produce an evolutionary advantage in mutual aid. A consistent interaction pattern between hens in a barnyard is adequately explained without postulating emotional bonds between individuals. One hen reacts to another on the basis of the social releasers that are displayed, and if individual recognition is operative, it merely adjusts the behavior towards another individual according to the immediate results of past interactions. There is no reason to believe that a hen can harbor grudges against or feel friendship toward another hen. Certainly the repayment of favors would be out of the question.

A competition for social good will cannot fail to have been a factor in human evolution, and I would expect that it would operate in many of the other primates. Altman (1962) described the formation of semipermanent coalitions between individuals within bands of wild rhesus monkeys and cited similar examples from other primates. Members of such coalitions helped each other in conflicts and indulged in other kinds of mutual aid. Surely an individual that had a better than average ability to form such coalitions would have an evolutionary advantage over its competitors. Perhaps this evolutionary factor might operate in the evolution of porpoises. This seems to be the most likely explanation for the very solicitous behavior that they sometimes show toward each other (Slijper, 1962, pp. 193-197). I would be reluctant, however, to recognize this factor in any group but the mammalia, and I would imagine it to be confined to a minority of this group. For the overwhelming mass of the Earth's biota, friendship and hate are not parts of the ecological environment, and the only way for socially beneficial self-sacrifice to evolve is through the biased survival and extinction of populations, not by selective gene substitution within populations.

To minimize recurrent semantic difficulties, I will formally distinguish two kinds of natural selection. The natural selection of alternative alleles in a Mendelian population will henceforth be called *genic selection.* The natural selection of more inclusive entities will be called *group selection,* a term introduced by Wynne-Edwards (1962). *Intrademic* and *interdemic,* and other terms with the same prefixes, have been used to make the same distinction. It has been my experience, however, that the repeated use in the same discussion of "inter" and "intra" for specifically contrasted concepts is a certain cause of confusion, unless a reader exerts an inconvenient amount of attention to spelling, or a speaker indulges in highly theatrical pronunciation.

The definitions of other useful terms, and the conceptual relations between the various creative evolutionary factors and the production of adaptation are indicated in Figure 1. Genic selection should be assumed to imply the current conception of natural selection often termed *neo-Darwinian*. An *organic adaptation* would be a mechanism designed to promote the success of an individual organism, as measured by the extent to which it contributes genes to later generations of the population of which it is a member. It has the individual's *inclusive fitness* (Hamilton, 1964) as its goal. Biotic evolution is any

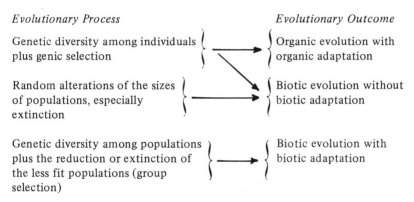

Evolutionary Process   *Evolutionary Outcome*

Genetic diversity among individuals plus genic selection → Organic evolution with organic adaptation

Random alterations of the sizes of populations, especially extinction → Biotic evolution without biotic adaptation

Genetic diversity among populations plus the reduction or extinction of the less fit populations (group selection) → Biotic evolution with biotic adaptation

Figure 1. Summary comparison of organic and biotic evolution, and of organic and biotic adaptation.

change in a biota. It can be brought about by an evolutionary change in one or more of the constituent populations, or merely by a change in their relative numbers. A *biotic adaptation* is a mechanism designed to promote the success of a biota, as measured by the lapse of time to extinction. The biota considered would have to be restricted in scope so as to allow comparison with other biotas. It could be a single biome, or community, or taxonomic group, or, most often, a single population. A change in the fish-fauna of a lake would be considered biotic evolution. It would come about through some change in the characters of one or more of the constituent populations or through a change in the relative numbers of the populations. Either would result in a changed fish-fauna, and such a change would be biotic evolution. A biotic adaptation could be a mechanism for the survival of such a group as the fish-fauna of a lake, or of any included population, or of a whole species that lives in that lake and elsewhere.

I believe that it is useful to make a formal distinction between biotic and organic evolution, and that certain fallacies can be avoided by keeping the distinction in mind. It should be clear that, in general, the fossil record can be a direct source of information on organic evolution only when changes in single populations can be followed through a continuous sequence of strata. Ordinarily the record tells us only that the biota at time t' was different from that at time t and that it must have changed from one state to the other during the interval. An unfortunate tendency is to forget this and to assume that the biotic change must be ascribed to appropriate organic change. The horse-fauna of the Eocene, for instance, was composed of smaller animals than that of the Pliocene. From this observation, it is tempting to conclude that, at least most of the time and on the average, a larger than mean size was an advantage to an individual horse in its reproductive competition with the rest of its population. So the component populations of the Tertiary horse-fauna are presumed to have been evolving larger size most of the time and on the average. It is conceivable, however, that precisely the opposite is true. It may be that at any given moment during the Tertiary, most of the horse populations were evolving a smaller size. To account for the trend towards larger size it is merely necessary to make the additional assumption that group selection favored such a tendency. Thus, while only a minority of the populations may have been evolving a larger size, it could have been this minority that gave rise to most of the populations of a million years later. Figure 2 shows how the

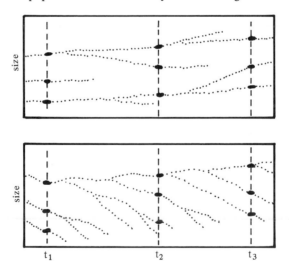

Figure 2. Alternative ways of interpreting the same observations of the fossil record. Average sizes in hypothetical horse species at three different times are indicated by boldface marks on the vertical time-scale at times t_1, t_2, and t_3. Upper and lower diagrams show the same observations. In the upper, hypothetical phylogenies explain the observations as the result of the organic evolution of increased size and of occasional chance extinction. In the lower, the hypothetical phylogenies indicate the organic evolution mainly of decreased size, but with effective counteraction by group selection so that the biota evolves a larger average size.

same observations on the fossil record can be rationalized on two entirely different bases. The unwarranted assumption of organic evolution as an explanation for biotic evolution dates at least from Darwin. In *The Origin of Species* he dealt with a problem that he termed "advance in organization." He interpreted the fossil record as indicating that the biota has evolved progressively "higher" forms from the Cambrian to Recent, clearly a change in the biota. His explanation, however, is put largely in terms of the advantage that an individual might have over his neighbors by virtue of a larger brain, greater histological complexity, etc. Darwin's reasoning here is analogous to that of someone who would expect that if the organic evolution of horses proceeded toward larger size during the Tertiary, most equine mutations during this interval must have caused larger size in the affected individuals. I suspect that most biologists would tend toward the opposite view, and expect that random changes in the germ plasm would be more likely to curtail growth than to augment it. Organic evolution would normally run counter to the direction of mutation pressure. There is a formally similar relation between organic evolution and group selection. Organic evolution provides genetically different populations, the raw material on which group selection acts. There is no necessity for supposing that the two forces would normally be in precisely the same direction. It is conceivable that at any given moment since the Cambrian, the majority of organisms were evolving along lines that Darwin would consider retrogression, degeneration, or narrow specialization, and that only a minority were progressing. If the continued survival of populations were sufficiently biased in favor of this minority, however, the biota as a whole might show "progress" from one geologic period to the next. I expect that the fossil record is actually of little use in evaluating the relative potency of genic and group selection.

In another respect the analogy between mutation and organic evolution as sources of diversity may be misleading. Mutations occur at random and are usually destructive of any adaptation, whereas organic evolution is largely concerned with the production or at least the maintenance of organic adaptation. Any biota will show a system of adaptations. If there is no group selection, i.e., if extinction is purely by chance, the adaptations shown will be a random sample of those produced by genic selection. If group selection does operate, even weakly, the adaptations shown will be a biased sample of those produced by genic selection. Even with such bias in the kinds of adaptations actually represented, we would still recognize genic selection as the process that actually produced them. We could say that the adaptations were produced by group selection only if it was so strong that it constantly curtailed organic evolution in all but certain favored directions and was thus able, by its own influence, to accumulate the functional details of complex adaptations. This distinction between the production of a biota with a certain set of organic adaptations and the production of the adaptations of a biota will be emphasized again in a number of contexts.

. . .

It is essential, before proceeding further with the discussion, that the reader firmly grasp the general meaning of biotic adaptation. He must be able to make a conceptual distinction between a population of adapted insects and an adapted population of insects. The fact that an insect population survives through a succession of generations is not evidence for the existence of biotic adaptation. The survival of the population may be merely an incidental consequence of the organic adaptations by which each insect attempts to survive and reproduce itself. The survival of the population depends on these individual efforts. To determine whether this survival is the proper function or merely an incidental by-product of the individual effort must be decided by a critical examination of the reproductive processes. We must decide: Do these processes show an effective design for maximizing the number of descendants of the individual, or do they show an effective design for maximizing the number, rate of growth, or numerical stability of the population or larger system? Any feature of the system that promotes group survival and cannot be explained as an organic adaptation can be called a biotic adaptation. If the population has such adaptations, it can be called an adapted population. If it does not, if its continued survival is merely incidental to the operation of organic adaptations, it is merely a population of adapted insects.

. . .

Like the theory of genic selection, the theory of group selection is logically a tautology and there can be no sane doubt about the reality of the process. Rational criticism must center on the importance of the process and on its adequacy in explaining the phenomena attributed to it. An important tenet of evolutionary theory is that natural selection can produce significant cumulative change only if selection coefficients are high relative to the rates of change of the selected entity. Since genic selection coefficients are high relative to mutation rates, it is logically possible for the natural selection of alternative alleles to have important cumulative effects. It was pointed out on pp. 22-23 [of Williams, 1966] that there can be no effective selection of somata. They have limited life spans and (often) zero biotic potential. The same considerations apply to populations of somata. I also pointed out that genotypes have limited lives and fail to reproduce themselves (they are destroyed by meiosis and recombination), except where clonal reproduction is possible. This is equally true of populations of genotypes. All of the genotypes of fruit-fly populations now living will have ceased to exist in a few weeks. Within a population, only the gene is stable enough to be effectively selected.

Likewise in selection among populations, only populations of genes (gene pools) seem to qualify with respect to the necessary stability. Even gene pools will not always qualify. If populations are evolving rapidly and have a low rate of extinction and replacement, the rate of endogenous change might be too great for group selection to have any cumulative effect. This argument precisely parallels that which indicates that mutation rates must be low relative to selection coefficients for genic selection to be effective.

If a group of adequately stable populations is available, group selection can theoretically produce biotic adaptations, for the same reason that genic selection can produce organic adaptations. Consider again the evolution of size among Tertiary horses. Suppose that at one time there was a genus of two species, one that averaged 100 kilograms when full grown and another that averaged 150 kilograms. Assume that genic selection in both species favored a smaller size so that a million years later the larger of the two averaged only 130 kilograms and the smaller had become extinct, but had lost 20 kilograms before it did so. In this case we could say that the genus evolved an increased size, even though both of the included species evolved a decreased size. If the extinction of the smaller species is not just a chance event but is attributable to its smaller size, we might refer to large size as a biotic adaptation of a simple sort. However, it is the origin of complex adaptations, for which the concept of functional design would be applicable, that is the important consideration.

If alternative gene pools are not themselves stable, it is still conceivable that group selection could operate among more or less constant rates of change. A system of relatively stable rates of change in the gene frequencies of a population might be called an evolutionary trajectory. It could be described as a vector in n-dimensional space, with n being the number of relevant gene frequencies. In a given sequence of a few generations a gene pool may be undergoing certain kinds of change at a certain rate. This is only one of an infinite number of other evolutionary trajectories that might conceivably be followed. Some trajectories may be more likely to lead to extinction than others, and group selection will then operate by allowing different kinds of evolutionary change to continue for different average lengths of time. There is paleontological evidence that certain kinds of evolutionary change may continue for appreciable lengths of time on a geological scale. Some of the supposed examples disappear as the evidence accumulates and shows that actual courses of evolution are more complex than they may have seemed at first. Other examples are apparently real and are attributed by Simpson (1944, 1953) to continuous genic selection in certain directions, a process he terms "orthoselection."

Wright (1945) proposed that group selection would be especially effective in a species that was divided up into many small populations that were almost but not quite isolated from each other. Most of the evolutionary change in such a species would be in accordance with genic selection coefficients, but the populations are supposed to be small enough so that genes would occasionally be fixed by drift in spite of adverse selection within a population. Some of the genes so fixed might benefit the population as a whole even though they were of competitive disadvantage within the population. A group so favored would increase in size (regarded as a benefit in Wright's discussion) and send out an augmented number of emigrants to neighboring populations. These migrants would partly or wholly counteract the adverse selection of the gene in neighboring populations and give them repeated opportunity for the chance fixation of the gene. The oft-repeated operation of this process eventually would produce complex adaptations of group benefit, but of competitive disadvantage to an individual. According to this theory, selection not only can act on preexisting variation, but also can help to produce the variation on which it acts, by repeatedly introducing the favored gene into different populations.

Wright formally derived this model in a review of a book by G. G. Simpson. Later, Simpson (1953, pp. 123, 164-165) briefly criticized Wright's theory by pointing out that it leaves too much to a rather improbable concatenation of the population parameters of size, number, degree of isolation, and the balance of genic and group selection coefficients. The populations have to be small enough for genetic drift to be important, but not so small that they are in danger of extinction, and they have to be big enough for certain gene substitutions to be more important than chance factors in determining size and rate of emigration. The unaugmented rates of immigration must be too small to reestablish the biotically undesirable gene after it is lost by drift. The populations must be numerous enough for the postulated process to work at a variety of loci, and each of the populations must be within the necessary size range. Lastly, the balance of these various factors must persist long enough for an appreciable amount of evolutionary change to take place. At the moment, I can see no hope of achieving any reliable estimate of how frequently the necessary conditions have been realized, but surely the frequency of such combinations of circumstances must be relatively low and the combinations quite temporary when they do occur. Simpson also expressed doubts on the reality of the biotic adaptations that Wright's theory was proposed to explain.

A number of writers have since postulated a role for the selection of alternative populations within a species in the production of various supposed "altruistic" adaptations. Most of these references, however, have completely ignored the problem that Wright took such pains to resolve. They have ignored the problem of how whole populations can acquire the necessary genes in high frequency in the first place. Unless some do and some do not, there is no set of alternatives for group selection to act upon. Wright was certainly aware, as some later workers apparently were not, that even a minute selective disadvantage to a gene in a population of moderate size can cause an almost deterministic reduction of the gene to a negligible frequency. This is why he explicitly limited the application of his model to those species that are subdivided into many small local populations with only occasional migrants between them. Others have postulated such group selection as an evolutionary factor in species that manifestly do not have the requisite population structures. Wynne-Edwards (1962), for example, postulated the origin of biotic adaptations of individual disadvantage, by selection among populations of smelts, in which even a single spawning aggregation may consist of tens of thousands of individuals. He envisioned the same process for marine invertebrates that may exist as breeding adults by the million per squre mile and have larval stages that may be dispersed many miles from their points of origin.

A possible escape from the necessity of relying on drift in small populations to fix the genes that might contribute to biotic adaptation is to assume that such genes are not uniformly disadvantageous in competitive individual relationships. If such a gene were, for some reason, individually advantageous in one out of ten populations, group selection could work by making the descendants of that population the sole representatives of the species a million years later. However, this process also loses plausibility on close examination. Low rates of endogenous change relative to selection coefficients are a necessary precondition for any effective selection. The necessary stability is the general rule for genes. While gene pools or evolutionary trajectories can persist little altered through a long period of extinction and replacement of populations, there is no indication that this is the general rule. Hence the effectiveness of group selection is open to question at the axiomatic level for almost any group of organisms. The possibility of effective group selection can be dismissed for any species that consists, as many do, of a single population. Similarly the group selection of alternative species cannot direct the evolution of a monotypic genus, and so on.

Even in groups in which all of the necessary conditions for group selection might be demonstrated, there is no assurance that these conditions will continue to prevail. Just as the evolution of even the simplest organic adaptation requires the operation of selection at many loci for many generations, so also would the production of biotic adaptation require the selective substitution of many groups. This is a major theoretical difficulty. Consider how rapid is the turnover of generations in even the slowest breeding organism, compared to the rate at which populations replace each other. The genesis of biotic adaptation must for this reason be orders of magnitude slower than that of organic adaptation. Genic selection may take the form of the replacement of one allele by another at the rate of 0.01 per generation, to choose an unusually high figure. Would the same force of group selection mean that a certain population would be 0.01 larger, or be growing 0.01 faster, or be 0.01 less likely to become extinct in a certain number of generations, or have a 0.01 greater emigration rate than another population? No matter which meaning we assign, it is clear that what would be a powerful selective force at the genic level would be trivial at the group level. For group selection to be as strong as genic selection, its selection coefficients would have to be much greater to compensate for the low rate of extinction and replacement of populations.

The rapid turnover of generations is one of the crucial factors that makes genic selection such a powerful force. Another is the large absolute number of individuals in even relatively small populations, and this brings us to another major difficulty in group selection, especially at the species level. A species of a hundred different populations, sufficiently isolated to develop appreciable genetic differences, would be exceptional in most groups of organisms. Such a complexly subdivided group, however, might be in the same position with respect to a bias of 0.01 in the extinction and replacement of groups, as a population of 50 diploid individuals with genic selection coefficients that differ by 0.01. In the population of 50 we would recognize genetic drift, a chance factor, as much more important than selection as an evolutionary force. Numbers of populations in a species, or of taxa in higher categories, are usually so small that chance would be much more important in determining group survival than would even relatively marked genetic differences among the groups. By analogy with the conclusions of population genetics, group selection would be an important creative force only where there were at least some hundreds of populations in the group under consideration.

Obviously the comments above are not intended to be a logically adequate evaluation of group selection. Analogies with the conclusions on genic selection are only analogies, not rigorously reasoned connections. I would suggest, however, that they provide a reasonable basis for skepticism about the effectiveness of this evolutionary force. The opposite tendency is frequently evident. A biologist may note that, logically and empirically, the evolutionary process is capable of producing adaptations of great complexity. He then assumes that these adaptations must include not only the organic but also the biotic, usually discussed in such terms as "for the good of the species." A good example is provided by Montagu (1952), who summarized the modern theory of natural selection and in so doing presented an essentially accurate picture of selective gene substitution by the differential reproductive survival of individuals. Then in the same work he states, "We begin to understand then, that evolution itself is a process which favors cooperating rather than disoperating groups and that 'fitness' is a function of the group as a whole rather than separate individuals." This kind of evolution and fitness is attributed to the previously described natural selection of individuals. Such an extrapolation from conclusions based on analyses of the possibilities of selection gene substitutions *in* populations to the production of biotic adaptations *of* populations is entirely unjustified. Lewontin (1961) has pointed out that population genetics as it is known today relates to genetic processes in populations, not of populations.

Lewontin (1962; Lewontin and Dunn, 1960) has produced what seems to me to be the only convincing evidence for the operation of group selection. There is a series of alleles symbolized by *t* in house-mouse populations that produces a marked distortion of the segregation ratio of sperm. As much as 95 per cent of the sperm of a heterozygous male may bear such a gene, and only 5 per cent bear the wild-type allele. This marked selective advantage is opposed by other adverse effects in the homozygotes, either an embryonic lethality or male sterility. Such characters as lethality, sterility, and measurable segregation ratios furnish an excellent opportunity for calculating the effect of selection as a function of gene frequency in hypothetical populations. Such calculations, based on a deterministic model of selection, indicate that these alleles should have certain equilibrium frequencies in the populations in which they occur. Studies of wild populations, however, consistently give frequencies below the calculated values. Lewontin concludes that the deficiency must be ascribed to some force in opposition to genic selection, and that group selection is the likely force. He showed that by substituting a stochastic model of natural selection, so as to allow for a certain rate of fixation of one or another allele in family groups and small local populations, he could account for the observed low frequencies of the *t*-alleles.

It should be emphasized that this example relates to genes characterized by lethality or sterility and extremely marked segregation distortions. Selection of such genes is of the maximum possible intensity. Important changes in frequency can occur in a very few generations as a result of genic selection, and no long-term isolation is necessary. Populations so altered would then be subject to unusually intense group selection. A population in which a segregation distorter reaches a high frequency will rapidly become extinct. A small population that has such a gene in low frequency can lose it by drift and thereafter replace those that have died out. Only one locus is involved. One cannot argue from this example that group selection would be effective in producing a complex adaptation involving closely adjusted gene frequencies at a large number of loci. Group selection in this example cannot maintain very low frequencies of the biotically deleterious gene in a population because even a single heterozygous male immigrant can rapidly "poison" the gene pool. The most important question about the selection of these genes is why they should produce such extreme effects. The segregation distortion makes the genes extremely difficult to keep at low frequency by either genic or group selection. Why has there not been an effective selection of modifiers that would reduce this distortion? Why also has there not been effective selection for modifiers that would abolish the lethality and sterility? The *t*-alleles certainly must constitute an important part of the genetic environment of every other gene in the population. One would certainly expect the other genes to become adapted to their presence.

Segregation distortion is something of a novelty in natural populations. I would be inclined to attribute the low frequency of such effects to the adjustment of each gene to its genetic environment. When distorter genes appear, they would be expected to replace their alleles unless they produced, like the *t*-alleles, drastic reductions in fitness at some stage of development. When such deleterious effects are mild, the population would probably survive and would gradually incorporate modifiers that would reduce the deleterious effects. In other words, the other genes would adjust to their new genetic environment. It is entirely possible, however, that populations and perhaps entire species could be rendered extinct by the introduction of such genes as the *t*-alleles of mice. Such an event would illustrate the production, by genic selection, of characters that are highly unfavorable to the survival of the species. The gene in question would produce a high phenotypic fitness in the gamete stage. It might have a low effect on some other stage. The selection coefficient would be determined by the mean of these two effects relative to those of alternative alleles, regardless of the effect on population survival. I wonder if anyone has thought of controlling the mouse population of an area by flooding it with *t*-carriers.

I am entirely willing to concede that the kinds of adaptations evolved by a population, for instance segregation distortion, might influence its chance for continued survival. I question only the effectiveness of this extinction-bias in the production and maintenance of any adaptive mechanisms worthy of the name. This is not the same as denying that extinction can be an important factor in biotic evolution. The conclusion is inescapable that extinction has been extremely important in producing the Earth's biota as we know it today. Probably only on the order of a dozen Devonian vertebrates have left any Recent descendants. If it had happened that some of these dozen had not survived, I am sure that the composition of today's biota would be profoundly different.

Another example of the importance of extinction can be taken from human evolution. The modern races and various extinct hominids derive from a lineage that diverged from the other Anthropoidea a million or perhaps several million years ago. There must have been a stage in which man's ancestors were congeneric with, but specifically distinct from, the ancestors of the modern anthropoid apes. At this time there were probably several and perhaps many other species in this genus. All but about four, however, became extinct. One that happened to survive produced the gibbons, another the orang, another the gorilla and chimpanzee, and another produced the hominids. These were only four (or perhaps three or five) of an unknown number of contemporary Pliocene alternatives. Suppose that the number had been one less, with man's ancestor being assigned to the group that became extinct! We have no idea how many narrow escapes from extinction man's lineage may have experienced. There would have been nothing extraordinary about his extinction; on the contrary, this is statistically the most likely development. The extinction of this lineage would, however, have provided the world today with a strikingly different biota. This one ape, which must have had a somewhat greater than average tendency toward bipedal locomotion and, according to recent views, a tendency towards predatory pack behavior, was transferred by evolution from an ordinary animal, with an ordinary existence, to a cultural chain reaction. The production and maintenance of such tributary adaptations as an enlarged brain, manual dexterity, the arched foot, etc. was brought about by the gradual shifting of gene frequencies at each genetic locus in response to changes in the genetic, somatic, and ecological environments. It was this process that fashioned a man from a beast. The fashioning was not accomplished by the survival of one animal type and the extinction of others.

I would concede that such matters of extinction and survival are extremely important in biotic evolution. Of the systems of adaptations produced by organic evolution during any given million years, only a small proportion will still be present several million years later. The surviving lines will be a somewhat biased sample of those actually produced by genic selection, biased in favor of one type of adaptive organization over another, but survival will always be largely a matter of historical accident. It may be that some people would not even recognize such chance extinction as important in biotic evolution. Ecologic determinists might attribute more of a role to the niche factor; man occupies an ecologic niche, and if one ancestral ape had failed to fill it, another would have. This sort of thinking probably has some validity, but surely historical contingency must also be an important factor in evolution. The Earth itself is a unique historical phenomenon, and many unique geological and biological events must have had a profound effect on the nature of the world's biota.

There is another example that should be considered, because it has been used to illustrate a contrary point of view. The extinction of the dinosaurs may have been a necessary precondition to the production of such mammalian types as elephants and bears. This extinction, however, was not the creative force that designed the locomotor and trophic specializations of these mammals. That force can be recognized in genic selection in the mammalian populations. There are analogies in human affairs. In World War II there was a rubber shortage due to the curtailment of imports of natural rubber. Scientists and engineers were thereby stimulated to develop suitable substitutes, and today we have a host of their inventions, some of which are superior to natural rubber for many uses. Necessity may have been the mother of invention, but she was not the inventor. I would liken the curtailment of imports, surely not a creative process, to the extinction of the dinosaurs, and the efforts of the scientists and engineers, which certainly were creative, to the selection of alternative alleles within the mammalian populations. In this attitude I ally myself with Simpson (1944) and against Wright (1945), who argued that the extinction of the dinosaurs, since it may have aided the adaptive radiation of the mammals, should be regarded as a creative process.

Group selection is the only conceivable force that could produce biotic adaptation. It was necessary, therefore, in this discussion of biotic adaptation to examine the nature of group selection and to attempt some preliminary evaluation of its power. The issue, however, cannot be resolved on the basis of hypothetical examples and appeals to intuitive judgments as to what seems likely or unlikely. A direct assessment of the importance of group selection would have to be based on an accurate knowledge of rates of genetic change, due to different causes, within populations; rates of proliferation and extinction of populations and larger groups; relative and absolute rates of migration and interbreeding; relative and absolute values of the coefficients of genic and group selection; etc. We would need such information for a large and unbiased sample of present and past taxa. Obviously this ideal will not be met, and some indirect method of evaluation will be necessary. The only method that I can conceive of as being reliable is an examination of the adaptations of animals and plants to determine the nature of the goals for which they are designed. The details of the strategy being employed will furnish indications of the purpose of its employment. I can conceive of only two ultimate purposes as being indicated, genic survival and group survival. All other kinds of survival, such as that of individual somata, will be of the nature of tactics employed in the grand strategy, and such tactics will be employed only when they do, in fact, contribute to the realization of a more general goal.

The basic issue then is whether organisms, by and large, are using strategies for genic survival alone, or for both genic and group survival. If both, then which seems to be the predominant consideration? If there are many adaptations of obvious group benefit which cannot be explained on the basis of genic selection, it must be conceded that group selection has been operative and important. If there are no such adaptations, we must conclude that group selection has not been important, and that only genic selection—natural selection in its most austere form—need be recognized as the creative force in evolution. We must always bear in mind that group selection and biotic adaptation are more onerous principles than genic selection and organic adaptation. They should only be invoked when the simpler explanation is clearly inadequate. Our search must be specifically directed at finding adaptations that promote group survival but are clearly neutral or detrimental to individual reproductive survival in within-group competition. The criteria for the recognition of these biotic adaptations are essentially the same as those for organic adaptations. The system in question should produce group benefit in an economical and efficient way and involve enough potentially independent elements that mere chance will not suffice as an explanation for the beneficial effect.

References

Allee, W. C., Alfred E. Emerson, Orlando Park, Thomas Park, Karl P. Schmidt, 1949. *Principles of Animal Ecology,* Philadelphia: W. B. Saunders, xii + 837 pp.

Altman, Stuart A., 1962. "A field study of the sociobiology of rhesus monkeys, *Macaca mulatta,*" *Ann. N. Y. Acad. Sci.,* 102:338–435.

Ashley Montagu. *See* Montagu.

Darwin, Charles R., 1896. *The Descent of Man and Selection in Relation to Sex,* New York: D. Appleton, xvi + 688 pp.

Haldane, J. B. S., 1932. *The Causes of Evolution,* London: Longmans, vii + 235 pp.

Hamilton, W. D., 1964. "The genetical evolution of social behaviour, I," *J. Theoret. Biol.,* 7:1–16.

Lewontin, R. C., 1958. "The adaptations of populations to varying environments," *Cold Spring Harbor Symp. Quant. Biol.,* 22:395–408.

Lewontin, R. C., 1961. "Evolution and the theory of games," *J. Theoret. Biol.,* 1:382–403.

Lewontin, R. C., 1962. "Interdeme selection controlling a polymorphism in the house mouse," *Am. Naturalist,* 96:65–78.

Lewontin, R. C., L. C. Dunn, 1960. "The evolutionary dynamics of a polymorphism in the house mouse," *Genetics,* 45:705–722.

Montagu, M. F. Ashley, 1952. *Darwin, Competition and Cooperation,* New York: Henry Schuman, 148 pp.

Simpson, George Gaylord, 1944. *Tempo and Mode in Evolution*, New York: Columbia University Press, xii + 237 pp.

Simpson, George Gaylord, 1953. *The Major Features of Evolution*, New York: Columbia University Press, xx + 434 pp.

Slijper, E. J., 1962. *Whales*, trans. A. J. Pomerans, New York: Basic Books, 475 pp.

Slobodkin, L. Basil, 1954. "Population dynamics of *Daphnia obtusa* Kurz," *Ecol. Monog.*, 24:69–88.

Williams, George C., 1966. *Adaptation and Natural Selection*, Princeton: Princeton University Press, x + 307 pp.

Wright, Sewall, 1945. "*Tempo and mode in evolution:* A critical review," *Ecology*, 26:415–419.

Wynne-Edwards, V. C., 1962. *Animal Dispersion in Relation to Social Behaviour*, Edinburgh and London: Oliver and Boyd, xi + 653 pp.

6

The Unity of the Genotype

Ernst Mayr

Preface, August 1983

Like anyone who fully understands the difference between genotype and phenotype, I have long realized that there must be a complex interaction of genes and gene products in the production of the phenotype. The atomistic approach so favored by mathematically inclined geneticists, who tend to treat each gene as if it acted independently of all other genes, ignores or at least minimizes gene interaction. My disagreement with this approach was vigorously expressed ("beanbag genetics") in my essay "Where Are We?" (1959). For me, what was most important was the "unity of the genotype," a theme to which I devoted chapter 10 in the 1963 and 1970 editions of my evolution book. I am afraid this somewhat holistic approach had only a limited impact, and for this reason, in the journal article here reprinted, I reiterated my plea for a greater consideration of the internal cohesion of the genotype.

As research in the factors of evolution progresses, more facts are found all the time—or long-known facts remembered—which confirm my basic thesis. The first tetrapods became terrestrial some 400 million years ago and yet mammal and bird embryos still pass through the gill-arch stage, not having been able during this immense time span to evolve a more direct ontogeny of the neck region. Selection pressure on individual genes has been unable to break down the cohesion of the gill-arch genotype. This is true for almost all the phenomena usually cited under the heading of "recapitulation."

Paleontologists, most recently S. J. Gould, have pointed out how lavishly the drastically different types of metazoans evolved during the late Precambrian and Cambrian (immediately after the origin of the metazoans), but once their genotypes had, so to speak, "congealed," all subsequent variation took place within the well established 24 or 25 structural types of living animals. Not a single new phylum evolved in more than 400 million years. One gets the impression that the cohesion of the genotype becomes stronger and stronger with time and that this process can be reversed only under rather special circumstances. The "genetic revolutions" that seem to take place, sometimes during peripatric speciation, qualify as such a special circumstance. The highly one-sided selection (combined with inbreeding) which accompanies domestication is another such "destabilizing" process, as the Soviet geneticist D. K. Belyaev has rightly emphasized recently.

Just exactly what controls this cohesion is still puzzling. When the genotype was thought to resemble a string of beads with, on the whole, unlimited crossing over, only allelic and simple epistatic interactions (together with temporary linkage) were available to explain cohesion. Some of the recent findings of molecular biology which have revealed how many different kinds of DNA there are (structural genes, regulator genes, middle repetitive DNA, highly repetitive DNA, copia like genes, transposons, etc.), raise the hope that one will soon have a better understanding of the structure of the genotype.

Under this view, evolution is not merely a change of allelic frequencies, but rather of unequal sized chunks of DNA that may differ in the function they fulfill in the genotype. Although this interpretation will not affect the role of the individual as the principal target of selection, it will nevertheless make the consequences of selection less atomistic than the traditional concept of the structure of the genotype.

Text of 1975 Article*

The historian of science often finds that a particular area of research alternates, in its interests and interpretations, between two extremes. This is certainly true for the attitude of geneticists toward the genotype. The pre-Mendelian breeders and hybridizers had discovered many striking manifestations of segregation, including 3 to 1 ratios, without coming even near to a Mendelian interpretation. One of the reasons for their blindness is now obvious. These forerunners considered the essence of the species an indivisible whole. Questions about individual genetic factors simply made no sense to an essentialist.

After the rediscovery of the Mendelian rules the pendulum swung to the other extreme. The approach now became entirely atomistic and, for the sake of convenience, each gene was treated as if it were quite independent of all the others. In due time all sorts of phenomena were discovered which contradicted *this* interpretation, such as the linkage of genes, epistasis, pleiotropy, and polygeny, and yet in evolutionary discussions only lip service was paid to these complications. Differences among populations and species continued to be simply described in terms of gene frequencies. Evolution, as recently as the 1950's, was defined as a change in gene frequencies, the replacement of one allele by another; thus it was treated as a purely additive phenomenon.

As useful as this approach was, and as magnificent as the results which it

*From *Biologisches Zentralblatt* (1975), 94:377–388.

produced, it did not provide the whole answer. Almost as far back as the rediscovery of Mendel's work there was a minority of authors who stressed interaction among genes, the integration of the genotype. The purely analytical school thought that such an integrative attitude was incompatible with a meaningful analysis and dangerously close to such a stultifying concept as holism. Chetverikov (1926), with his concept of the genetic milieu, was perhaps the first author to stress constructive aspects of the study of the interaction of genes, and through him and his school the study of the cohesion of the genotype has become an increasingly important branch of evolutionary genetics. Progress, however, was slow. If we want to single out a definite year that signalizes the new interest in the interactions of the genotype, it is the year 1954, in which Lerner's *Genetic Homeostasis* was published as well as my own paper on the importance of the genetic environment in evolution (Mayr, 1954). The newer views can be summarized as follows: Free variability is found only in a limited portion of the genotype. Most genes are tied together into balanced complexes that resist change. The fitness of genes tied up in these complexes is determined far more by the fitness of the complex as a whole than by any functional qualities of individual genes.

What is the Evidence for This Unity of the Genotype?

Even though this problem was grossly neglected for nearly 100 years, naturalists and breeders had long been aware of it. It is involved in what morphologists and systematists had in mind when they spoke of the mammalian or chordate type. Darwin and others spoke of "the mysterious laws of correlation." When referring to *correlation of growth,* Darwin said: "I mean by this expression that the whole organization is so tied together during its growth and development, that when slight variations in any part occur, and are accumulated through natural selection, other parts become modified" (1859: 143). E. Geoffroy St. Hilaire's *loi de balancement* is an indication of similar ideas.

Other aspects of the unit of the genotype became apparent already rather early in the history of genetics. The phenomenon of pleiotropy, the capacity of a gene to affect several different aspects of the phenotype, led Chetverikov (1926) "to the idea of the genetic milieu which acts from the inside on the manifestation of every gene in its character. An individual is indivisible not only in its soma but also in the manifestation of every gene it has."

Evidence for interaction among genes is manifold. Most convincing are the consequences of *artificial selection.* Darwin already had stated that: "If man goes on selecting, and thus augmenting any peculiarity, he will almost certainly modify unconsciously other parts of the structure, owing to the mysterious laws of the correlation of growth." Dog fanciers and the breeders of race horses are sadly aware of the undesirable side effects of a breeder's concentration on a particular character. In almost all recent experiments on maximizing a particular character in *Drosophila,* such as bristle number, some selected lines died out because of sterility. I do not know of a single intensive selection experiment during the past 50 years during which some such undesirable side effects have not appeared.

The phenomenon which Lerner has designated as *genetic homeostasis* is additional evidence for the organization of genes into co-adapted systems. When selection directed toward the maximization of one particular character is terminated after a series of generations and the population is permitted to reach its own genetic equilibrium, the strongly selected character very often loses part, if not most, of the phenotypic advance it had achieved during the preceding period of intense selection. There is, as it were, an internal balance of selection pressures, restoring the co-adapted system to its previous balance. One can infer from this phenomenon of genetic homeostasis that genes, which are tied up in a co-adapted complex, participate in a number of independent metabolic operations (or ontogenetic processes), and that a rather specific frequency of the various interacting genes is needed for the optimal performance of these physiological processes. If this frequency has been distorted by the one-sided selection, internal selection pressures will tend to restore it to the original optimal frequency. The original fitness will be restored by this return to the original balance of genes.

I will refrain, at this point, from becoming specific on the nature of the interaction among genes because we are skating here on thin ice. We have become dimly aware that structural genes, the material mainly studied by the geneticist, may well be only a small minority of all the genes, let us say 50,000 among 5 million. What percentage of the other genes are regulator genes of all sorts and what else the remaining DNA does are subjects of intense current research. When one studies long-term evolution, one has the uncomfortable feeling that it is no longer sufficient to interpret it entirely in terms of the traditional genes. Britten and Davidson (1969: 356) might well be right when saying: "At higher grades of organization, evolution might indeed be considered in terms of changes in the regulatory systems." Much that is now explained as "epistatic interactions between different loci" might well be due to the activities of regulatory genes. Fortunately, this possibility does not affect very greatly what I am now attempting to present.

Among the many manifestations of the cohesion of the genotype encountered by the naturalist, I will discuss here only one, the narrowness of hybrid zones. When the geographic barrier between two incipient species breaks down after they had been isolated for a lengthy period of time, either they will have completed the acquisition of isolating mechanisms or they will hybridize. One would expect that such hybridization would lead to a free introgression of genes of either population into the other one. This, in turn, should lead to a rapid widening of the hybrid zone until the introgressing genes have reached the opposite species border. But this is not at all what happens in most cases of hybrid zones. The hooded and the carrion crows met in Central Europe at the end of the Ice Age some 8,000 years ago and hybridized freely. Yet, as Meise (1928) pointed out, this hybrid belt is still only about 100 miles wide. This was correctly interpreted by Dobzhansky as early as 1941 to mean that the introgressing genes of the hooded crow are selected against in the genotype of the carrion crow and vice versa.

A far more precise analysis of the same phenomenon was recently provided by Hunt and Selander (1973) for the hybrid zone between *Mus m. musculus* and *M. m. domesticus* in Denmark. Allozymic variation in 13 proteins controlled by 41 loci was studied and 7 polymorphic enzymes were selected for detailed analysis. As in the case of the crows the width of the hybrid zone is still relatively narrow, even though the two kinds of mice must have first met many thousands of years ago. The rate of introgression is distinctive for each locus. Some alleles have penetrated into the alien genotype for a much larger distance than others. Although several additional factors, such as a slow dispersal rate of the mice and local climatic fluctuations, affect the rate of introgression, there can be little doubt that selection against the alien genes is an important if not the major factor for the slowness of the introgression. The fact that the width of the hybrid belt is asymmetrical—that is, that introgression into *musculus* is more extensive than into *domesticus*—also shows that the dispersal of genes is not simply a "mechanical" phenomenon.

A particularly elegant demonstration for the unity of the genotype is provided for by the so-called "lethal chromosomes," chromosomes that are lethal when homozygous. As summarized in his *Topics in Population Genetics* (1968), Wallace has shown how often such chromosomes are normal or superior in heterozygous condition when placed in the gene pool of their own population. Furthermore the "lethality" of a newly arisen lethal chromosome becomes steadily less through natural selection when maintained in its population. Anderson (1969) showed in an analysis of data provided by Dobzhansky and Spassky that among 45 lethal chromosomes tested on the genetic background of their own populations, none was significantly deleterious in heterozygous conditions, but 5 were significantly heterotic. When tested on foreign genetic backgrounds, however, 10 of these chromosomes were significantly deleterious and one was significantly heterotic.

The Mechanisms of Cohesion

Nothing is explained, however, by simply saying that such and such a phenomenon is due to the unity of the genotype. We also want to know by what mechanisms this unity of the genotype is accomplished. Why is it that not all genes are entirely independent during recombination? What holds them together in the face of the centrifugal forces of recombination? To be frank, our answers to these questions are still incomplete. Until rather recently genetic analysis was able to focus on only one locus or at best one gene arrangement at a time. But this has been changed by technological advances. The method of gel-electrophoresis and the availability of large computers for linkage studies have greatly enlarged the power of the analysis. The literature is expanding rapidly and I will give only a short résumé, since I want to concentrate on the evolutionary consequences of this cohesion.

To summarize it in a single sentence, the interaction of macromolecules at the cellular level produces individual phenotypes of different fitness, and natural selection will therefore tend to hold together those alleles at different loci that produce individuals of the greatest selective value.

Let me now present some evidence for the individual links of this causal chain.

Interaction of Macromolecules

I am not a molecular biologist and am not at all qualified to talk about this subject. But let me remind you that the "morphology" of a macromolecule—that is, its structural contour, caused by the folding of its protein chain (or other constituents) must match the structure of the membranes to which it is attached or of other macromolecules with which it interacts. Furthermore, a single enzyme is often involved in several reasonably different functions (O'Brien, et al., 1972) and must have the optimal constitution for each of these separate demands. The literature of molecular biology reports numerous cases where even a seemingly very slight change had a drastic effect on the efficient interaction of such a molecule.

Also, let us remember that the products of one locus may serve as repressors or inducers at other loci. Finally, the activity of regulator genes provides almost unlimited scope for the interaction of genes. These are merely reminders of the importance of macromolecules for cohesion.

Selection

How does selection cope with this situation? Let us say allele I at locus A gives superior fitness when in epistatic balance with allele 3 at locus B, but that there is simultaneously a selective premium for heterozygosity at each of these loci. Free recombination in such a system would, obviously, produce a tremendous genetic load, through inferior recombinants. If I would ask you how many such gene pairs a population could maintain without accumulating an intolerable genetic load, you would probably give some figure between 5 and 10. Actually the figure is much larger than one might think at first sight (Mayr, 1963: 261). On the average only 2 offspring need to be successful in an animal pair that produces 1,000 or 100,000 zygotes. This means that well over 99 percent of these zygotes are expendable, and the genetic load can, so to speak, be charged against the surplus, provided that the few survivors carry the superior gene combinations.

The production of a large number of offspring so that an inevitable genetic load of inferior gene combinations can be charged to this reproductive surplus is one possible evolutionary strategy.

Linkage

An alternative strategy is to prevent free recombination. Cytogeneticists, from the earliest times on, have emphasized that the organization of the genetic material into chromosomes is a powerful mechanism for keeping superior gene combinations together. Yet chromosomes are not permanently inviolable structures, because genes are separated from each other in every generation owing to the process of crossing-over during meiosis. Linkage, for this reason, was for a long time considered a rather inefficient mechanism for a long-term tying together of specific alleles at different loci of the same chromosome, unless reinforced by special cross-over inhibitors. It would indeed be highly advantageous if favorable gene combinations could be tied together into unbreakable linkage groups, as has been stressed by R. A. Fisher and others since the 1920's. The great advantage of such "supergenes" is that their existence drastically reduces the frequency of deleterious recombinants, and with it the genetic load.

There are two lines of evidence to indicate that chromosomes and chromosome arms are far more permanent structures than had been envisioned by the earlier students of linkage and of crossing-over. One of these are detailed studies of chromosome structure in insects, amphibians, mammals and other animals. They show that the chromosomes contain balanced gene combinations and that speciation, in a high proportion of cases, involves a more or less extensive repatterning of the chromosome (White, 1973). We shall come back to these speciational aspects later.

The other evidence is provided by Franklin and Lewontin's linkage simulation studies (1970). These show that linkage is far more powerful than had been previously imagined and that superior chromosomes go through meiosis from generation to generation virtually untouched.

Although this conclusion was at first largely conjectural, concrete evidence for it has now been found in several cases, again through the gel-electrophoresis method. Clegg and Allard (1972) for a number of cases in *Avena* and Preston

Webster (1973) for one case in the salamander *Plethodon cinereus* have demonstrated that certain alleles at different loci go always (or preferably) together. Cytogeneticists refers to this occurrence by the quaint term "linkage disequilibrium."

A tight linkage of alleles at two different loci, like that of *Avena* and *Plethodon*, has so far been found in *Drosophila only* for inversions or near breakage points. How widespread and important linkage disequilibrium in other organisms is still remains to be determined.

There are, of course, various chromosomal mechanisms which can induce an increase or decrease in the level of recombination and in chiasma localization.

I am afraid I have barely scratched the surface, because there are surely numerous other mechanisms either to tighten or loosen the cohesion of the genotype.

Consequences of the Cohesion of the Genotype

As long as genes were considered to be independent of each other, it was difficult to explain certain evolutionary phenomena. Indeed some of the anti-Darwinian arguments arose from such an inability to explain the "mysterious laws of correlation" and other phenomena that we shall presently mention. However, as soon as it is realized that the genotype consists of a number of co-adapted gene complexes and that even the gene pool of a population as a whole is well integrated and co-adapted, such arguments lose their validity.

Let us now look in more detail at what kind of consequences one may derive from the concept of the unity of the genotype:

(1) Since the fitness of a gene depends in part on the success of its interaction with its genetic background, it is no longer possible to assign an absolute selective value to a gene. A gene has potentially as many selection values as it has possible genetic backgrounds.

(2) The target of selection does not consist of single genes but rather of such components of the phenotype as the eye, the legs, the flower, the thermo-regulatory or photo-synthetic apparatus, etc. As a result any given selection pressure affects simultaneously whole packages of genes which may or may not be tied together by special devices, such as linkage, epistatic balances, etc.

(3) At no stage in the life of an individual is the interaction of genes more obvious than during ontogeny. The adult individual is the end-product of the entire epigenetic process. The endeavor to dissect this into the effects of individual genes can only rarely be successful.

(4) The genetic structure of the species. The climatic adaptations of species are conspicuous and have been described through the study of climatic rules, clines, ecotypes, and the many other manifestations of local or regional

selection pressures. Much of geographic variation is conspicuously adaptive and has supplied some of the most convincing evidence for Darwinian selection. Yet as I pointed out some 20 years ago, pronounced geographic variation of the phenotype is far less universal, or at least far less conspicuous, than is usually assumed. When I first encountered the phenomenon of a seeming uniformity of a species over wide areas in spite of drastic environmental differences, I attempted to explain it as the result of gene flow. Gene flow indeed is an important factor, more so than admitted by some contemporary critics, but when the phenotypic uniformity of a species extends across all of North America from the Pacific to the Atlantic or across the entire Eurasian continent, it becomes obvious that additional factors must be involved.

At one time it was suggested that the seeming phenotypic uniformity of such species is only apparent, being of the type of similarity found in sibling species while concealing great cryptic variation of the genotype under this superficial cloak. The method of gel-electrophoresis has refuted this assumption. Prakash and Lewontin (1968) for *D. pseudoobscura* were the first to show—and this was later confirmed by Ayala et al. (1972) for *D. willistoni*—that rare allozymes are often found throughout the range of these species at very similar low frequencies. If these genes were either neutral or serving strictly local adaptation, one would expect stochastic processes or selection pressures to produce strong geographic variation in their frequencies. Nor can gene flow be responsible for this universally even frequency, as Ayala et al. demonstrate convincingly. Admittedly the universal distribution of certain alleles at the same low frequencies is not explained easily. The interpretations that make the most sense are (1) that these alleles are normally inferior but sufficiently valuable in certain epistatic interactions or in certain subniches, to be retained in the gene pool of the population as a necessary component of the co-adapted gene complex, or (2) that frequency dependent selection is involved.

If we make the assumption that the frequency of these alleles is neither the result of stochastic processes nor the result of ecotypic selection but is determined by the unity of the genotype, then we must postulate that a different set of such alleles will be favored in every species because speciation entails a thorough reorganization of the genotype, and new balances of interacting genes will result from such a genetic revolution. Ayala and Anderson (1973) have shown that this is indeed the case for a certain enzyme in the three closely related sibling species, *Drosophila willistoni*, *D. equinoxialis*, and *D. tropicalis*. Experimental evidence indicates that selection favors that allele which is most common ("wild type") in the particular species. Since these three species are largely sympatric, it is clearly not the absolute activity of the allele which is selected but rather how the particular allozyme fits with the physiological and genetic background of the particular species in which it finds itself.

The uniformity of the frequency of rare alleles and many of the other phenomena just discussed demonstrate what a conservative influence the unity of the genotype is. As soon as one has fully grasped this point, the whole problem of speciation appears in a new light.

Speciation

The classical theory of geographic speciation postulates the following sequence of events. Some newly arisen geographical barrier divides the range of a species in two; the two subdivisions of the species acquire isolating mechanisms during their period of isolation and are able to coexist after the break-down of the barrier. Massive evidence has accumulated in recent decades to indicate that this is probably the exceptional rather than the standard case of geographic speciation. What apparently happens far more frequently is that a founder population becomes peripherally isolated and undergoes a genetic revolution (Mayr, 1954) during which it rather rapidly acquires isolating mechanisms and species status. The evidence for this thesis is far too massive to be presented here in detail, and all I can do is to outline it and to give a few striking examples.

It has long been known that in addition to the conventional species with wide-ranging, continental distribution patterns, there is a second category of species with an "insular" or "colonial" population structure (Kinsey, 1937; Mayr, 1942). Wingless grasshoppers and subterranean mammals provide particularly instructive examples. The pocket gophers (*Thomomys*), the mole rats (*Spalax*) of eastern Europe and the Near East, and the tuco-tucos (*Ctenomys*) of Argentina all have a distribution pattern consisting of numerous isolated populations. We used to make fun of the pocket gopher specialists for describing hundreds of new subspecies, but—up to a point—they now have the last laugh. The work of Patton and others has shown, at least for some groups of pocket gophers, that there is strong variation in chromosome number and chromosome repatterning from colony to colony. In spite of minimal morphological differences, some of the populations seem to have reached species level.

In the case of species with an insular distribution pattern, new outposts are established by founders, and this provides an opportunity either for genic or for chromosomal genetic revolutions. If the colonization of a *terra nova* is successful owing to the greatly increased opportunity for the incorporation of new adaptive gene combinations (H. Lewis, 1973), this will place a selective premium on any and all genic or chromosomal mechanisms that facilitate genetic revolutions.

At this point I would like to call attention to the history of our thinking about speciation. The early Mendelians thought that a single mutation could create a new species. This was replaced in the early days of population genetics by the postulate that a relatively small number of genes was involved in speciation, geographic or otherwise. I recall a report in an early issue of *Evolution* in which the author postulated a number of less than 10 gene fixations for speciation in beetles. In recent decades it has become quite apparent that a purely additive approach to this problem is misleading. Perhaps one can go to the opposite extreme and postulate that successful speciation always requires the acquisition of a new balance, or, to describe it more appropriately, it requires the breaking up, the dissolution, of the previous cohesion and its replacement by a new cohesion.

Carson (1970) has demonstrated through his discovery of homosequential species of Hawaiian *Drosophilae* that such a reorganization can be accomplished purely on the gene level. The same has been demonstrated by the genetic revolution in the founder population of *Drosophila pseudoobscura* at Bogota. This population is still remarkably similar to the Central and North American populations of the species, and no behavioral isolation of either males or females of the Bogota population from North American flies was found. Yet, F_1 males obtained from the cross of *D. pseudoobscura* females from Bogota with males of this species from the North American mainland (from Guatemala north) are sterile. This sterility is due to about two genes located on the X chromosome and one each on two of the other chromosomes (Prakash, 1972). The most likely explanation is that the reproductive isolation is due to the incorporation of new genes on the four stated loci to improve the fertility of the males in the highly inbred Bogota founder population. Additional fixation at other loci is, of course, also possible, since only 24 of approximately 10,000 enzyme loci were tested.

An increasing amount of evidence is now accumulating to indicate that purely genic speciation, such as that found by Carson, not involving chromosome repatterning, is comparatively rare. There has been a gradual return in recent years to earlier views of the great importance of karyotypic events in speciation. In contrast to the earlier view, however, the concepts of chromosomal reorganization are now integrated into the biological species concept and combined with population thinking. Harlan Lewis (1966, 1973) and his school for plants and M. J. D. White, in a series of papers for animals (summarized in White 1973), have demonstrated two facts:

(1) That closely related species differ in the majority of cases by chromosomal rearrangements, while such differences are rarely found among contiguous populations of the same species.

(2) That in cases of incipient speciation, for instance peripherally isolated

populations, and in cases of recently separated parapatric species, one can usually demonstrate a lowered fitness of genotypes heterozygous for the chromosomal rearrangements. It is highly probable that the passing through the bottleneck of deleterious heterozygosity cannot occur in a populous widespread population but only during the genetic revolution in a founder population.

Macroevolutionary Consequences

Recognition of the fact that there is a strong cohesion of the genotype has greatly helped in the understanding of certain previously puzzling macro-evolutionary phenomena. These had caused the early Darwinians a good deal of trouble and had induced certain evolutionists, particularly many paleontologists between 1880 and 1930, to reject the Darwinian interpretation of macroevolution.

(1) Rudimentary organs. Why, for example, do the embryos of terrestrial vertebrates still go through the gill-arch stage? Or, more broadly, why are all those ancestral conditions maintained in ontogeny which at one time were interpreted as evidence for recapitulation?

(2) What is the explanation for the extreme evolutionary inertia (stagnation) of certain evolutionary lines, as indicated by such types as *Gingko, Equisetum, Limulus, Lingula, Triops,* and *Nautilus* (Mayr, 1970:367)?

(3) What is the explanation for the sudden flowering ("explosive evolution") of certain previously long-stagnant evolutionary lines?

(4) What is the explanation for the conservative nature of the "Baupläne" of the major animal types? The basic mammalian Bauplan, for instance, is maintained in elephants, bats, man, and whales. Why do all terrestrial vertebrates develop as tetrapods, all insects as hexapods? Obviously it would be absurd to claim that the type of locomotion of insects requires three pairs of legs and that of terrestrial vertebrates two pairs of extremities.

In terms of the cohesion of the genotype the situation is no longer a puzzle. A restructuring of the major morphogenetic pathways (resulting in a different number of pairs of extremities) would require such a drastic interference with the cohesion of the genotype—as a whole—that it would be selected against quite vigorously. That it is not the characters themselves but their integration into the total genotype that is important is obvious when we compare the stability of certain wing veins and bristle patterns in insects from one genus or family to another.

The most difficult feat of evolution is to break out of the strait jacket of this cohesion. This is the reason why only so relatively few new structural types have arisen in the last 500 million years, and this may well also be the reason why 99.999% of all evolutionary lines have become extinct. They did so because the cohesion prevented them from responding quickly to sudden new demands by the environment.

We recognize about 24 distinct phyla among the recent animals. There is much evidence to indicate that the basic features of the structural plan of these phyla is derived from that of the founders of these types. If the founder crawled on the surface, there was a premium on the development of metamerism; if he tunneled through the soft substrate, the development of a compressible coelom was favored. The same basic adaptation could evolve independently in different founders. Once established and properly consolidated in the genotype, such a Bauplan remained remarkably stable regardless of subsequent developments. The metamerism of the annelids is still apparent in the tube-living sessile polychaetes, and coeloms are retained by most of the coelomates that have long since given up tunneling.

The same phenomenon is illustrated by the gill arches that still dominate the ontogeny of land-living vertebrates. It is obvious in all these cases that development is controlled by such a large number of interacting genes that the selection pressure to eliminate vestigial structures is less effective than the selection to maintain the efficiency of well established developmental pathways. This is, of course, not a new explanation, but it has been remarkably little explored by the students of developmental physiology.

Two other sets of phenomena confirm this conclusion.

Evolutionary Trends

In many, if not most, phyletic lines there is an indication of trends. Many evolutionists prior to 1940 considered such "orthogenetic" trends as a refutation of "Darwinian evolution by chance," as they phrased it. It is now quite obvious that such trends are the necessary consequence of the unity of the genotype which greatly restricts evolutionary potential. Each family or order of animals and plants has its special potential, such as that of the ungulates for horns or of the drongos (*Dicruridae*) for elaborations of the tail feathers.

Evolutionary Rates

Evolutionary rates are highly dissimilar at the species level. Large, populous species with wide distribution show great evolutionary inertia, not so much, as was once said, because it takes so long for an allele to disperse through the entire species range, but rather because the co-adapted gene complex is highly resistant to the incorporation of new genes. On the other hand, founder populations may undergo a genetic evolution within an extremely short time and may possibly replace alleles at 30 to 50 percent of the loci within 5,000 to 10,000 years. Such cases as the Bogota population of *D. pseudoobscura* or the five new species of *Haplochromis* fishes in Lake Nabugabo, which is less than 4,000 years old, and the rapid speciation of subterranean mammals all indicate exceedingly rapid rates of speciation.

Considering these drastic differences at the species level, it is difficult to advance generalizations as far as phyletic evolution is concerned. There is little doubt, however, that those who enter biology from the physical sciences make rather unrealistic assumptions on the evolutionary rate of changes in macromolecules. From the fact that some molecules like the histones evolve very slowly while others have intermediate or very rapid evolution, some authors have drawn the conclusion that such molecules have a, so to speak, built-in orthogenetic rate of evolution. Depending on the particular macromolecule, they assume that there will be an amino-acid replacement every 2 million, 5 million, or 10 million years. All the known facts contradict this naive assumption.

Certain biochemists, on the basis of the assumption of standard rates in the evolution of molecules, postulated that the splitting of the hominid line from that of the African apes occurred as recently as 3 to 5 million years ago. The fossil record demonstrates conclusively, however, that the split happened at least 14 million years ago.

It seems to me that a far more realistic interpretation of evolutionary rates results if we assume that the evolutionary change of a given type of macromolecule is due not to a built-in rate but rather to the need for coadaptation with other molecules with which it has to interact. As the other molecules change in the course of time in response to ad hoc selection pressures, every molecule occasionally has to adjust to its changed molecular environment; it must adjust to the cohesion of the genotype. This, undoubtedly, is the reason for the continuous evolutionary change of molecules, even of those in which the active site has not changed since the days of the most primitive eukaryotes or even prokaryotes.

Let me now summarize:

The genes are not the units of evolution, nor are they, as such, the targets of natural selection. Rather, genes are tied together into balanced adaptive complexes, the integrity of which is favored by natural selection.

The study of the mechanisms by which the cohesion of the genotype is achieved is a promising area of evolutionary research.

It is important to understand this cohesion of the genotype, because it permits the explanation of many previously puzzling phenomena of speciation and macroevolution.

References

Anderson, W. W., 1969. "The selection coefficients of heterozygotes for lethal chromosomes in *Drosophila* on different genetic backgrounds," *Genetics*, 62: 827–836.

Ayala, F. J., et al., 1972. "Genic variation in natural populations of *Drosophila willistoni,*" *Genetics,* 70:113–139.

Ayala, F. J., and W. W. Anderson, 1973. "Evidence of natural selection in molecular evolution," *Nature* (New Biology), 241:274–276.

Britten, R. J., and E. H. Davidson, 1969. "Gene regulation for higher cells: A theory," *Science,* 165:349–357.

Carson, H. L., 1970. "Chromosome tracers of the origin of species," *Science,* 168:1414–1418.

Chetverikov, S. S., 1926. "On certain aspects of the evolutionary process from the standpoint of modern genetics," *J. Expltl. Biol.* (Russian), A2:3–54; English trans. (1961), *Proc. Amer. Phil. Soc.,* 105:167–195.

Clegg, M. T., and R. W. Allard, 1972. "Patterns for genetic differentiation in the slender wild oat species *Avena barbata,*" *Proc. Nat. Acad. Sci.* 69:1820–1824.

Darwin, C., 1859. *On the Origin of Species by Means of Natural Selection,* London, John Murray.

Dobzhansky, Th., 1941. *Genetics and the Origin of Species,* 2nd ed., New York, Columbia University Press.

Fisher, R. A., 1930. *The Genetical Theory of Natural Selection,* Oxford, Clarendon Press.

Franklin, J., and R. C. Lewontin, 1970. "Is the gene the unit of selection?" *Genetics,* 65:707–734.

Geoffroy St. Hilaire, E., 1818. *Philosophie anatomique,* Paris, Vol. 1.

Hunt, W. G., and R. K. Selander, 1973. "Biochemical genetics of hybridization in European house mice," *Heredity,* 31:11–33.

Kinsey, A. C., 1937. "An evolutionary analysis of insular and continental species," *Proc. Nat. Acad. Sci.* 23:5–11.

Lerner, I. M., 1954. *Genetic Homeostasis,* Edinburgh, Oliver and Boyd.

Lewis, H., 1966, "Speciation in flowering plants," *Science,* 152:167–172.

Lewis, H., 1973. "The origin of diploid neospecies in *Clarkia,*" *Amer. Nat.,* 107:161–170.

Mayr, E., 1942. *Systematics and the Origin of Species,* New York, Columbia University Press.

Mayr, E., 1954. "Change of genetic environment and evolution," in J. Huxley, A. C. Hardy, and E. B. Ford, eds., *Evolution as a Process,* London, Allen and Unwin, pp. 157–180.

Mayr, E., 1963. *Animal Species and Evolution,* Cambridge (Mass.), Harvard University Press.

Mayr, E., 1970. *Populations, Species, and Evolution,* Cambridge (Mass.), Harvard University Press.

Meise, W., 1928. "Die Verbreitung der Aaskrähe (Formenkreis *Corvus corone* L.)," *J. Ornith.,* 76:1–203.

Nevo, E., J. K. Yung, C. R. Shaw, and C. S. Thaeler, Jr., 1974. "Genetic variation, selection and speciation in *Thomomys talpoides* pocket gophers," *Evolution*, 28:1–23.

O'Brien, S. J., D.Wallace, and R. J. MacIntyre, 1972. "The x-Glycerophosphate cycle in *Drosophila melanogaster* III," *Amer. Nat.*, 106:767–771.

Patton, J. L., 1973, "Patterns of geographic variation in karyotype in the pocket gopher, *Thomomys bottae*," *Evolution*, 26:574–586.

Prakash, S., 1972, "Origin of reproductive isolation in the absence of apparent genic differentiation in a geographic isolate of *Drosophila pseudoobscura*," *Genetics*, 72:143–155.

Prakash, S., 1972, and R. C. Lewontin, 1968. "Direct evidence of coadaptation in gene arrangements of Drosophila," *Proc. Nat. Acad. Sci.* 59:398–405.

Wallace, B., 1968. *Topics in Population Genetics*, New York, W. W. Norton.

Webster, T. P., 1973. "Adaptive linkage disequilibrium between two esterase loci of a salamander," *Proc. Nat. Acad. Sci.*, 70:1156–1160.

White, M. J. D., 1973. *Animal Cytology and Evolution*, 3rd ed., London, Cambridge University Press.

II

Levels and Units of Selection: Conceptual Analyses

As indicated in the previous introductions, *genic selectionism* treats genes as the ultimate units of selection. The first two articles in this section deny such exclusivity. Both articles elaborate on the influential analysis of Lewontin (1970), according to which all entities that exhibit heritable variance in fitness are, in fact, units of selection. This position accommodates a hierarchy of units, including prebiotic molecules, cell organelles, cells, gametes, individuals, kin-groups, whole populations, and even higher-level units.

Wimsatt (this volume) argues that heritable variation in fitness is a necessary, but not sufficient condition for an entity to be a unit of selection. In order to specify such conditions Wimsatt introduces the notion of *context-independence*. This turns out to be a special application of a more general form of analysis of selection due to Price (1970 and 1972), which will be discussed at greater length in the next part of this book. Basically, Wimsatt argues that genic selectionism is false because interaction between genes (epistasis) and gene linkage tend to make the variation in fitness at the genic level context-dependent. The importance of context-independence is that only the context-independent variation will be heritable. For instance, in standard population genetic models the only part of the total variation that is heritable is the additive part. Wimsatt points out that additivity is a special case of context independence. Thus, Wimsatt argues, where there is epistasis and gene linkage, genes are at too low a level of organization to be units of selection; he maintains that in standard cases of organismic selection a larger part of the genome, in the limit the entire genome, is the unit of selection.

Wimsatt considers genic selectionism a mistake that is brought about by the biases inherent in certain reductionistic research strategies. He analyzes these strategies to show how these biases arise and how they relate to the group selection controversy (see also Wade, this volume). Wimsatt develops a hierarchical picture of units of selection similar to that of Arnold and Fristrup (this volume).

Sober and Lewontin are less interested in developing an account of units of selection than in detailing the inadequacies of genic selectionism. One of their main lines of argumentation is that the computational or predictive adequacy of models is not, or should not be, the sole criterion by which we judge them. A good model should also accurately represent the relevant causal processes of the system being modeled. They argue that insofar as one is only concerned with computational adequacy, one can model any selection process using only genic selection coefficients. (This point is correct only under certain conditions; we will discuss this further in our introduction to part III.) But, they continue, this is of no biological significance, since in most cases the genic selection coefficients are mathematical artifacts having little to do with the causal process of selection. On this point they are in agreement with Wimsatt.

Like Wimsatt, Sober and Lewontin illustrate their point by reference to gene linkage and genic interaction. Because of these features of genetic systems, the fitnesses of genes will be *context sensitive*. For example, in cases of heterozygote superiority the fitness of allele *a* depends on its partner at that locus. They suggest that "if the fitness of X is context sensitive, then there is not selection for X; rather, there is selection at a level of organization higher than X." Thus in the case of heterozygote superiority, one must go at least to the level of the diploid genotype. On their view in order for there to be selection for X, "every object which has X has its reproductive chances augmented by its possessing X." Thus like Wimsatt, and Mayr (1963 and this volume) and Lewontin (1974) before him, Sober and Lewontin argue that fairly large chunks of the genome (in the limit, the entire genome) will be the units of selection in standard cases of organismic selection. They also think that their analysis can be extended in fairly straightforward ways to adjudicate questions concerning higher levels of selection.

The last three articles in this section mark an important break from the first two and from the entire earlier literature on the units of selection. Brandon states: "It is a mistake to suppose that the units of selection controversy in biology centers around a single question." Hull says that "the phrase 'unit of selection' is inherently ambiguous. Sometimes it means those entities which differentially replicate themselves, sometimes those which interact with their environments in ways which are responsible for the replication being differential." Dawkins, in discussing Lewontin's seminal paper (Lewontin, 1970), says, "his paper, like my own first discussion of the matter (Dawkins, 1976), suffers from its failure to make a clear distinction between replicators and vehicles." All three authors agree that there is no simple hierarchy of units of selection, including genes, organisms, groups, etc. Genes and organisms are importantly different in that they play quite disparate roles in selective processes.

Before discussing these articles further, we should offer a brief guide to their terminological differences. Brandon distinguishes *levels of selection* from *units of selection* (*sensu* Wimsatt). Hull distinguishes *replicators* from *interactors*. Dawkins, attempting to capture nearly the same distinction, uses almost the same terms—*replicators* and *vehicles*.

A replicator is any entity which reproduces its structure directly. Genes are paradigm examples of replicators. Both for germ-line replication (meiosis) and soma-line replication (mitosis), reproduction is physically quite direct and is also highly accurate, though not perfect; mutations do occur. There is an important difference between sexual and asexual reproduction here. In asexual organisms the entire genome is a replicator, whereas in sexual organisms the recombination breaks up the genome so that smaller units, "genes" (*sensu* Williams), are the replicators. An interactor (Hull) or vehicle (Dawkins) is any entity that interacts directly with its environment; differences in these interactions result in the differential reproduction of replicators. Organisms are paradigm examples of such entities, whatever we decide to call them. On the whole we prefer Hull's term, "interactor." The term "vehicle," by conjuring up images of little genes riding around in splendid isolation, seems to us to prejudice the case as to what sorts of entities are of primary importance in accounting for evolution by natural selection. Brandon's analysis of levels of selection applies only to interactors. Wimsatt's analysis of units of selection (and, we think, those of all earlier authors) has been applied, whether appropriately or not, to both interactors and replicators, often at the cost of considerable ambiguity.

Brandon explicates Mayr's statement that "natural selection favors (or discriminates against) phenotypes, not genes or genotypes" (1963, p. 184) by using the Salmon-Reichenbach notion of *screening off* (see Salmon, 1971). By definition, A screens off B from E if and only if: $P(E,A \cdot B) = P(E,A) \neq P(E,B)$. (Read "$P(E,A \cdot B)$" as the probability of E given A and B.) If A screens off B from E then, in the presence of A, B is statistically irrelevant to E, i.e., $P(E,A) = P(E,A \cdot B)$. But this relation between A and B is not symmetric. Given B, A is still statistically relevant to E, i.e., $P(E,B) \neq P(E,A \cdot B)$. This device enables him to resolve a problem which Sober and Lewontin had despaired of solving: identifying an asymmetry between phenotype and genotype strong enough to allow Mayr to make his point. Brandon argues that by using the probabilistically defined notion of screening off, we can see that there is just such an asymmetry. Since proximate causes screen off (that is, act irrespective of) remote causes, and since interactors are proximate causes of differential reproduction while replicators are remote causes, interactors will always screen off replicators from differential reproductive success. (Note that in cases of meiotic drive, chromosomes, or parts of chromosomes, are interactors.) In other words, according to Brandon, in order to give a causal explanation of differential reproduction, one must refer to differences between interactors. This apparatus allows Brandon to offer a general definition of levels of selection from which one can provide a coherent account of a hierarchy of interactors in many of the cases under investigation.

Hull and Dawkins are, for the most part, in agreement. They agree that both interactor selection and the differential reproduction of replicators are essential processes for evolution by natural selection to occur. Thus there is no conflict between those stressing the importance of the one process and those stressing the importance of the other. Hull and Dawkins also agree that one and the same entity can be both an interactor and a replicator. In the early stages of evolution on this planet probably most entities involved in the selection process were both. But—and again they agree on this point—these roles are at present usually played by different entities.

Hull parts company with Dawkins over the use of the term "replicator." He argues for a more liberal usage. Directness and accuracy of replication are the hallmarks of replicators. But both directness and accuracy are degree terms, and in some circumstances an organism can replicate fairly directly and fairly accurately. In such cases Hull would call the organism a replicator (which does *not* preclude it from being an interactor as well). Dawkins would dissent. He holds that any change in replicator structure is passed on in the process of replication. Thus, given the truth of Weismannism (i.e. the doctrine that there is a one-way causal influence from germ line to body), replicators (*sensu* Dawkins) are importantly different from *most* interactors.

References

Lewontin, R. C., 1970. "The units of selection," *Ann. Rev. Ecol. Syst.*, 1: 1–18.

Lewontin, R. C., 1974. *The Genetic Basis of Evolutionary Change*, New York: Columbia University Press.

Mayr, E., 1963. *Animal Species and Evolution*, Cambridge, Mass.: Harvard University Press.

Price, G. R., 1970. "Selection and covariance," *Nature*, 227:520–21.

Price, G. R., 1972. "Extension of covariance selection mathematics," *Ann. Hum. Genet.*, 35:485–90.

Salmon, W. C., 1971. *Statistical Explanation and Satistical Relevance*, Pittsburgh: University of Pittsburgh Press.

7

Reductionistic Research Strategies and Their Biases in the Units of Selection Controversy

William C. Wimsatt

Williams's "In Principle" Reductionism and the Case of Two Loci

A problem-solving heuristic which Simon (1966) has called "factoring into subproblems" appears in a variety of guises in reductionistic modeling. Simon illustrates the heuristic and its advantages using the problem of finding the right combination for a combination lock. Imagine a bicycle lock with ten wheels of ten positions each. If there is only one combination which will work, one would expect to look through about half of the possible 10^{10} combinations on the average before finding it. On the other hand, suppose that the lock is cheap or defective and one can tell individually for each wheel when it is in the right position. Then an average of 5 tries on each wheel, for a total of 50 tries, would be expected to find the right combination. The advantage that accrues from being able to break the problem down into subproblems, being able to find out parts of the combination, rather than having to solve the whole problem at once, is given by the ratio of the number of alternatives which must be inspected. This is, in this case, $(5 \times 10^9)/(5 \times 10) = 10^8$.

Similar advantages accrue for similar combinatorial reasons if problems of evolutionary dynamics can be treated in terms of the frequencies of individual alleles, with no epistatic interactions and no probabilistic associations between alleles at different loci due to linkage or assortative mating rather than in terms of the gametic or zygotic genotype frequencies required if these assumptions do not hold. Here the simplification occurs in the number of dimensions in the phase space required to describe and predict evolutionary changes adequately, and, correlatively, in the number of state variables in the equations required to describe and predict the dynamics of evolutionary change. Table 1, derived and extended from Table 56 of Lewontin (1974, p. 283), summarizes the dimensionality of the problem under different simplifying assumptions. It is worth noting that if *no* simplifying assumptions are made,

From pp. 222–238 and 253–259 of T. Nickles, ed., *Scientific Discovery: Case Studies,* Dordrecht: Reidel, 1980. Original article: pp. 213–259.

Table 1
Sufficient dimensionality required for the prediction of evolution of a single
locus with a alleles where there are n segregating loci in the system

Level of Description:	Zygotic Classes	Gametic Classes	Allele Frequencies	Allele Frequencies
Dimensionality:	$\dfrac{a^n(a^n+1)}{2} - 1$	$a^n - 1$	$n(a-1)$	$(a-1)$
Assumptions:	none	1	1,2	1,2,3
n: a:				
2 2	9	3	2	1
3 2	35	7	3	1
3 3	377	26	6	2
5 2	527	31	5	1
10 2	524799	1023	10	1
32 2	9.22×10^{18}	4.29×10^9	32	1

Assumptions:
   (1) random union of gametes (no sex linkage, no assortative mating).
   (2) random statistical association of genes at different loci (linkage equilibrium).
   (3) no epistatic interaction (inter-locus effects are totally additive).
(Table is adapted and extended from Table 56 of Lewontin, 1974, p. 283.)

even the simplest multi-locus case of two alleles at each of two loci is analytically intractable. This should not be surprising: the problem of dimensionality nine (there are nine possible genotypes, with independently specifiable
fitness parameters) is already more complicated than the three-body problem
of classical mechanics. Like the three-body problem, it has been solved for a
variety of special cases (see Roughgarden, 1979, chapter 8, pp. 111–133) but
has not been solved in general.

   In the light of this, G. C. Williams makes a claim which gives substantial
hope, for it appears to promise that the problem can be treated as one of the
lowest dimensionality. His view is that since the operation of any higher-
level selection processes can be mathematically expressed as resulting from
the operation of selection coefficients acting independently at each locus to
change the frequency of individual alleles or genes, there is no need to postulate the existence of any higher-level units of selection or selection forces.
This view will look most familiar to philosophers, since it bears the strongest
resemblance to traditional philosophical accounts of theory reduction. Williams expresses it as follows:

Obviously it is unrealistic to believe that a gene actually exists in its own
world with no complications other than abstract selection coefficients and
mutation rates. The unity of the genotype and the functional subordination

of the individual genes to each other and to their surroundings would seem, at first sight, to invalidate the one-locus model of natural selection. Actually these considerations do not bear on the basic postulates of the theory. No matter how functionally dependent a gene may be, and no matter how complicated its interactions with other genes and environmental factors, it must always be true that a given gene substitution will have an arithmetic mean effect on fitness in any population. One allele can always be regarded as having a certain selection coefficient relative to another at the same locus at any given point in time. Such coefficients are numbers that can be treated algebraically, and conclusions inferred from one locus can be iterated over all loci. Adaptation can thus be attributed to the effect of selection acting independently at each locus. (Williams, 1966, pp. 56–57)

Williams goes on, in the next two pages, to illustrate how this algebraic manipulation can be accomplished in a simplified genetic environment of two alleles at each of two loci, and we are to imagine the extrapolation to cases of many alleles at many loci. Complicated it would be, but *in principle*, of course (we are told), it could be done, "by iterating over all loci."

This claim might appear to involve another variant of the "factoring into subproblems" heuristic which Simon has studied and written upon at length and which he has called "the hypothesis of near decomposability" (see Simon, 1968, pp. 99ff. in Ando et al., 1963, and further references given there; also Wimsatt, 1974, for further discussion).

The hypothesis of near decomposability involves the assumption that a complex system can be decomposed into a set of subsystems such that all strong interactions are contained within subsystems' boundaries, and interactions between variables or entities in different subsystems are appreciably weaker than those relating variables or entities in the same subsystem. In this case, an approximation to the behavior of the system, in the short run, can be gotten by ignoring the intersystemic interactions and analyzing each subsystem as if it were isolated, studying only internal variables in their common approach to equilibrium. Its behavior in the long run can be approximated by ignoring the intrasystemic interactions of the subsystems (assuming that there is intrasystemic equilibrium), representing each subsystem by a single index, and considering the equilibration of the various subsystems with one another as a system involving the interaction only of these lumped index variables.

There are thus two different approximations involved in studying the short-run and the long-run behavior of the system. Each substantially reduces the complexity of the problem if the assumptions allowing the approximation are justified.

Indeed the hypothesis of near decomposability *is* used in this way in a number of multi-locus models—in particular when it is assumed: (1) that the system starts at or near linkage equilibrium. (This is the condition when all genotypes occur at frequencies given by the products of the frequencies of their constituent genes, a condition equivalent to the assumption of a multi-locus Hardy-Weinberg equilibrium.) (2) That selection between genotypes is relatively weak (a condition that guarantees that the population never deviates far from the multi-locus Hardy-Weinberg equilibrium). Indeed, these assumptions (as well as that of random association of gametes, implying no assortative mating) are made in the original model (Lewontin and White, 1960) for which the two-locus fitness surfaces, which provide below a counterexample to Williams's claim, originally were derived. Under these conditions, recombination can be neglected as a significant contributor to genotype frequencies, and the dynamics can be treated as if they are affected by segregation and selection only. This is equivalent to using the "long range" approximation in studying the behavior of a nearly decomposable system, since if the system is far from linkage-equilibrium, recombination may be a far greater contributor to genotype frequency of some genotypes than either segregation or selection, and thus behaves like an intra-systemic "strong" interaction that goes relatively rapidly to equilibrium.[1] The observation that under some conditions there can be permanent and substantial linkage disequilibrium (see Lewontin, 1974; Roughgarden, 1979; and also Maynard Smith, 1978, chapter 5) is equivalent, then, to saying that the system cannot be treated as nearly decomposable.

In fact, however, Williams's claim in the above quote appears to be far stronger than a near decomposability claim and is not made on the basis of these assumptions about linkage equilibrium and random assortment of gametes produced by random mating. He claims that the problem can be solved one locus at a time and then extended to a global solution by "iterating over all loci." His claim is thus not that the genetic system is nearly decomposable, but that it is simply decomposable, like the simpler of Simon's two locks. Without all of the qualifications in Lewontin's table, this claim is simply incorrect, and can be shown to be so for the simplest case involving more than one locus—that of two alleles at each of two loci. The reasons for the failure of Williams's claim can best be seen after a discussion of this case.

A claim that evolutionary processes can be analyzed in the manner Williams suggests, as being of the lowest possible dimensionality, involves at least the claim that a deterministic theory of the change of gene frequencies at a given locus can be constructed using only the frequencies of the alternative alleles of that locus. In the simplest case of two alleles at one locus, this involves saying that it is a function only of the frequency of a single gene, since if q is the frequency of gene a, then $1-q$ must be the frequency of the other gene, A, because there are no other genes at that locus. (It is a function also of the fitnesses, W_{11}, W_{12}, and W_{22} of the genotypes AA, Aa, and aa, but these are assumed to be constant parameters of the system in this discussion.)

Consider Figure 1 as a graph of gene frequency from different initial points (.05 for the bottom curve, .95 for the top curve) as it changes in successive generations. If this were the graph of an actual case (Lewontin describes it as of a "hypothetical laboratory population"), it would falsify Williams's claim. Why? Consider the topmost curve. At all points between the initial high value of gene frequency of .95 and the minimum value (of about .7, reached in generation 4), a population which is decreasing in gene frequency at that value (between generations 0 and 4) is later increasing in gene frequency at that value (in generations 5 and later). *But if gene frequency can either increase or decrease from a given value, then gene frequency* (of that gene or its allele) *alone is not an adequate basis for a deterministic theory of evolutionary change.*

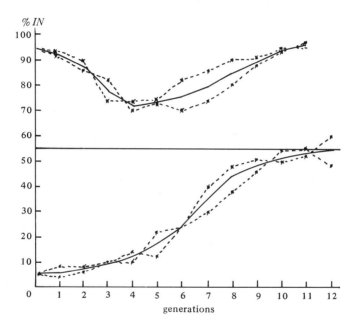

Figure 1. The frequency of an inversion, IN, in hypothetical laboratory populations. The heavy lines represent the average behavior of replicates, while the X's represent individual data points. (Reprinted from Lewontin, 1974, Figure 23, p. 274, with permission of Columbia University Press.)

Williams gets into trouble at this point because his claim is neither a theory of evolution in terms of gene frequencies, nor even a schematic description of the form of such a theory. His statement that "it must always be true that a given gene substitution will have an arithmetic mean effect on fitness in any population" (1966, p. 56) suggests the following procedure for evaluating this effect on fitness. Imagine a gigantic (noninterventive) DNA sequencer that, given a population, will determine all of the genes in that population and their frequencies. Perform this genetic census at two points in time—or perhaps in each generation. For each gene, its frequency in the interval will either increase (in which case it is being selected for), decrease (it is selected against), or remain constant (it is neutral).

These data can then be used in one of two ways. They can be used to describe the evolutionary trajectory of the population in its phase space; but then this is not a *theory* of evolutionary change but a description. The fitnesses W_{11}, W_{12}, and W_{22} inferred from this are merely biological redescriptions of what is happening in successive generations[2] and may undergo arbitrary changes as the "curve-fitting" parameters that they are. Or the changes observed in one generation may be used to estimate fitness values which are then used to predict future changes. This is more of a process of trend extrapolation using an assumed model than a theory itself, but it is at least not totally tautological. To have a predictive tool or theory, then, Williams must intend his remarks to describe a process of trend extrapolation.

But here is where the trouble arises. The graph of Figure 1 indicates that local estimates of fitness values *cannot* be used in this way to extrapolate evolutionary trends. After all, gene *a* is apparently being selected *against* in generations 0-4, but subsequently it must be being selected *for*, as its frequency is then *increasing*. To put it more generally, local estimates of fitness or selective value are not valid globally for other values of the frequency of that and other genes.

The reason why this is not the case becomes apparent in Figure 2. Indeed, Lewontin's hypothetical laboratory population of Figure 1 was not hypothetical at all, but a description of changes that would be expected in a field population of the grasshopper, *Moraba scurra*, whose mean Darwinian fitness, $\bar{W}$, is given as a function of the frequency of two alleles at each of two loci in the adaptive topography of Figure 2. An adaptive topography is a plot of contours of equal mean population fitness, $\bar{W}$, as a function of the gene frequencies (in this case, at two loci). Since in many simpler models (particularly where the genotypic fitnesses are constant) a population will tend to evolve in directions of increasing $\bar{W}$, the adaptive topography gives a visual means of making qualitative predictions about the direction and relative rates of local evolutionary change.

Indeed, the lower curve of Figure 1 is just trajectory 1 of Figure 2, and the upper (problematic) curve of Figure 1 is trajectory 4 of Figure 2. And the results that appeared as indeterministic in terms of the trajectory of gene frequencies of a single locus are seen to be deterministic once the frequencies of each of two loci are specified. Thus the initial points of trajectories 1 and 4 should not have been specified as .05 and .95, the frequency of a gene at the

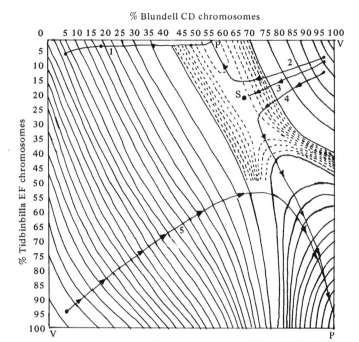

Figure 2. Projected changes in the frequency of two polymorphic inversion systems in *Moraba scurra* from different initial compositions, based on fitness estimates from nature. The trajectories, shown by arrow-marked lines, are calculated by the solution of differential equations of gene frequency change. Lines crossing the trajectories are contours of equal mean population fitness, $\overline{W}$. (Reprinted from Lewontin, 1974, Figure 24, p. 280, with permission of Columbia University Press.)

first locus, as is implicit in Figure 1, but as (.05, .05) and as (.95, .12), the freqencies of the genes at both loci as in Figure 2. Note also that trajectory 2, with initial point (.95, .07)—in which the frequency at the first locus is the same as for trajectory 4, but that at the second locus is different—also shows a violation of the deterministic assumption if only the first locus frequency is looked at when the two trajectories are compared. Trajectory 2 is not by itself evidence of a violation, as is trajectory 4, however.

It is quite clear from this adaptive topography that what will happen in evolution is a function of the joint values of gene frequency at two loci, and no set of measurements or extrapolations looking at frequencies of just one locus at a time can provide an adequate basis for prediction. This is true in this case because of epistatic interactions between loci, which is a sufficient condition for having to go to a phase space of greater dimensionality for prediction.

Williams's proposal, then, fails in this case, in 3 ways:

(1) It does not result in a deterministic theory of evolutionary change in terms of the gene frequencies of individual loci which can be "iterated over all loci" to produce a global solution.

(2) It fails to do so because epistatic interactions among loci prevent local estimates of fitness at single loci from being projectable or extrapolatable *if gene frequencies at other loci are free to change simultaneously.* (The appearance of projectability usually arises when estimates are only done locally under conditions in which there *is* no change or no significant change at other loci. But this cannot be assumed in general.) Williams in effect errs by assuming that single locus fitnesses are independent of context, when in fact they are functions of the context of other loci. Illegitimate assumptions of context-independence are a frequent error in reductionistic analyses. See Wimsatt, 1976b, p. 688, and 1980 for further discussion.

(3) In fact, Lewontin's data on *Moraba scurra* represent no gene frequency changes at single loci, but the frequencies of chromosomal inversions involving *many* loci. For reasons which I will not detail here, inversions can often act as units of selection, and Lewontin has devoted much of the earlier portions of his book to arguing that Williams's aim of measuring the fitness effects of single gene substitutions is bedeviled with a host of practical and theoretical problems. So Lewontin's one-chromosome example of Figure 1 and the two-chromosome counterexample of Figure 2 are already at a higher level of organization than that supposed by Williams's single locus genetic reductionism.

What goes for two loci or chromosomes goes as well for many. In this light Williams's remarks suggesting genetic reductionism are better seen as having more import as a kind of genetic bookkeeping than as promising a reductionistic theory of evolutionary change in terms of gene frequencies. The latter is a tempting mirage which vanishes upon closer inspection of the complexities and heuristics of the actual theory.

A General Class of Reductionistic Research Heuristics and Their Biases

The kind of mistake implicit in the reductionistic argument discussed in the preceding sections seems so straightforward yet is so pervasive and is made by so many leading practitioners of the discipline that it cries out for a deeper explanation. Any engineer knows that systematic failures in a mechanism indicate a design problem, which he then tries to locate and eliminate. This procedure is so important (and so often ignored in the traditional education of engineers) that at least one company holds seminars for the engineers of its various divisions to teach approaches and methods for doing it, as described in Moss (1979). The heuristics in our reasoning processes have similar possibilities for systematic error, and we should similarly try to analyze these failures to get an understanding of where they are likely to occur and, where possible, eliminate or moderate their effects through redesign. If redesign (through teaching different or modified heuristics) is impossible or impractical, we can at least, through an understanding of the causes of failure, be warned when they are likely to lead us into error, so that our troubleshooting efforts may be concentrated there.

I will describe here a general class of heuristics and their biases which have a common origin in the nature of reductionistic analyses, thus providing the appropriate warnings. After defining the notion of a unit of selection, I will describe some of the results of Wade's review of the models of group selection (1978), which nicely illustrates several of these biases with systematic failures in the literature. I will then discuss a design modification in our heuristic which should serve to eliminate or at least moderate the effects of several of these biases.

(1) Any analysis of a system presupposes a division of the world, however tentatively, into the system being studied and its environment. This division may be made on grounds of interest, which will in turn often be determined by judgments of the scope of one's field (a molecular geneticist is unlikely, at least initially, to consider social forces as part of the subject matter of his discipline), other jurisdictional criteria, and, probably most frequently, intuitive judgments about the natural chunks and boundaries in his area.[3] Judgments of what can be manipulated relatively independently of "outside" forces are likely to enter into any of these, and this in turn implies judgments of near decomposability or near isolatability in the individuation of systems.

(2) A reductionist adds to this a further consideration: by his description as a reductionist he is interested in understanding the behavior of his system in terms of the interaction of its parts. This means that his *interest* at least (though not necessarily his scope of investigation) will be focused on the entities and interrelations between them *internal* to the system he is studying.

(3) The third and last constraint is to recognize the practical impossibility of generating an exhaustive, quasi-algorithmic, or exact analysis of the behavior of the system in its environment. This is an application of Simon's "principle of bounded rationality" discussed earlier. So the reductionist must start simplifying. In general, simplifying assumptions will have to be made everywhere, but given his interest in studying relations *internal* to the system, he will tend to order his list of economic priorities so as to simplify, first and more extremely, in his description, observation, control, and analysis of the environment than in the system he is studying. After all, simplifications internal to the system face the danger of simplifying out of existence the very phenomena and mechanisms he wishes to study.

This fact alone, derived just from these three very general assumptions, is sufficient to generate and explain a wealth of heuristics and their attendant biases arising in the reductionistic analysis of systems. These heuristics and biases can be classified roughly as biases of conceptualization, biases of model building and theory construction, and biases of observation and experimental design, though any rigid classification would fail because of the interdependence and intercalation of these activities in the course of a scientific investigation.

I will here describe them only relatively cursorily, leaving their further elaboration for other occasions. (I have already discussed item 2 in 1976a, pp. 244–245, and in 1978. Extensive discussions of items 1, 3, and 4 are forthcoming in Wimsatt, 1980a. Wade's work, and the work I have done so far in population biology relates most strongly to items 4, 5, and 6, though 1, 7, 8, and 9 are also implicated.) This is possible because even a statement of the heuristic naturally suggests the pervasiveness of their use and multiplicity of their possible effects, and it is in any case necessitated by space limitations.

These heuristics and/or biases are as follows:

A. *Conceptualization:*

1. *Descriptive Localization.* Describe a relational property as if it were monadic, or a lower-order relational property; thus, e.g., fitness as a property of phenotype (or even of genes) rather than phenotype-environmental relation.

2. *Meaning Reductionism.* Assume lower-level redescriptions to change meanings of scientific terms; higher-level redescriptions not. Result: philosophers (who view themselves as concerned with meaning relations) are inclined to a reductionistic bias.

3. *Interface Determinism.* Assume that all that counts in analyzing the nature and behavior of a system is what comes or goes across the system-environment interface. This has two versions: (a) black-box behaviorism: all that matters about a system is how it responds to given inputs; (b) black-world perspectivalism: all that matters about the environment is what comes in across the system boundaries and how it responds to system inputs. Either can introduce reductionistic biases when conjoined with the assumption of white box analysis . . . that the order of study is from a system, with its input-output relations, to its subsystems, with theirs, and so on. The analysis of functional properties, in particular, is rendered incoherent and impossible by these assumptions.

B. *Model Building and Theory Construction:*

4. *Modeling Localization.* Look for an intrasystemic mechanism to explain a systemic property, rather than an intersystemic one. Structural properties are regarded as more important than functional ones, and mechanisms as more important than context.

5. *Simplification.* In reductionistic model building, simplify environment before simplifying system. This strategy often legislates higher-level systems out of existence or leaves no way of describing systemic phenomena appropriately.

6. *Generalization.* When starting out to improve a simple model of system environment: focus on generalizing or elaborating the internal structure at the cost of ignoring generalizations of elaborations of the external structure.

Corollary. If the model doesn't work, it must be because of simplifications in description of internal structure, not because of simplified descriptions of external structure.

C. *Observation and Experimental Design:*

7. Observation. Reductionists will tend not to monitor environmental variables, and thus will often tend not to record data necessary to detect interactional or larger-scale patterns.

8. Control. Reductionists will tend to keep environmental variables constant, and will thus often tend to miss dependencies of system variables on them. (*"Ceteris paribus"* is viewed as a qualifier on environmental variables.)

9. Testing. Make sure that a theory works out only locally (or only in the laboratory) rather than testing it in appropriate natural environments, or doing appropriate robustness analyses to suggest what are important environmental variables and/or parameter ranges.

These heuristics and their biases can be particularly powerful for two reasons: (1) There is, on the face of it, no way to correct for their effects—at best not in the most obvious way by producing the exact and general analysis of the behavior of the system in its environment to use as a check against the models produced. That may be all right in theory, but it won't work out in practice, as I have tried to suggest in section 3. Nonetheless, there are at least two possible corrective measures that will be discussed later. The first is robustness analysis—a term and procedure first suggested by Richard Levins in his (1966). The second, which I will call "multilevel reductionistic analysis," involves using these heuristics simultaneously at more than one level of organization—a procedure that allows discovery of errors and their correction in at least some circumstances, and that in fact implicitly followed as a species of "means-end analysis" (see Simon, 1966) in the construction of interlevel theories involving compositional identities (see Wimsatt, 1976a, pp. 230–237, and 1976b, Section 8).

(2) Secondly, it should be clear that *these heuristics are mutually supporting,* not only in their effective use in structuring and in solving problems, but also *in reinforcing, in multiplying, and, above all, in hiding the effects of their respective biases.* This effect of bias amplification is very serious, and one of the biggest reasons why the effects of these biases are so hard to detect and why the proponents of extreme reductionistic positions can be so resistant to recognizing potential counterexamples to their position. Whatever can be said for theories or paradigms as self-confirming entitites (and much that has been said is too excessive and would render progressive science impossible), as much and perhaps more can be said similarly for heuristics. Indeed, I suspect that most of the blame and criticism of theories in this regard is more accurately

laid at the doorstep of the heuristics used by those applying these theories and extending these paradigms.

Consider how this could work. Heuristics 1 and 4, applied in the early stage of an investigation, give apparent conceptual and theoretical reasons for locating a phenomenon of interest (say, that an organism has a given fitness in a given environment) as having causes primarily or wholly within the system under study. In the process of model building, the environment may be simply described (e.g., as totally constant in space and time, a frequent assumption in population genetics) that relevant variables (and the possibility of their variation) are ignored (bias 5), further leading to and being reinforced by tendencies not to observe variation in relevant environmental variables (bias 7) and to make efforts to assure (or, too often, merely to assume) that they are constant as controls in the experimental analysis of the system (bias 8). Any failures in the model are then assumed to be caused by a failure to model intrasystemic interactions in sufficient detail (bias 6), leading to another cycle, beginning with biases 1 and 4 applied to the properties and phenomena which were anomalous for the first model. This may result in further simplifications in the environment to offset the loss in analytical tractability arising from the increased internal complexity now assumed, or it may result in focusing in on a particular subsystem to be modeled in further detail, with much of the rest of the system now becoming part of the systematically simplified, ignored, and controlled environment. If even a part of this scenario or one like it is correct, we should not be surprised if quite remarkable failures went undetected for appreciable lengths of time. At present this remains just a hypothetical scenario, probably only one of many possible scenarios for producing this result. It would be very difficult to establish that the whole scenario, or one like it, was played out in any given case, in part because of the practice of not describing chains of hypothetical reasoning or discovery in scientific papers. Moreover, the practitioners are usually not themselves aware of the microstructure and background presuppositions of their reasoning processes, a fact that has bedeviled attempts to use protocols in which experimental subjects try to describe their reasoning processes as a basis for constructing theories of problem-solving behavior even for much simpler tasks (see Newell and Simon, 1972). Nonetheless, the scientific literature does contain suggestive evidence of several of these heuristics in operation, and it could be hoped that future research would turn up more. A remarkable example of cumulative and systematic biases was unearthed by the work of Michael Wade on the models of group selection, which will be discussed after some preliminary discussion of the notion of a unit of selection in the next section.

Darwin's Principles and the Definition of a Unit of Selection

Charles Darwin's argument in *The Origin of Species* is adumbrated[4] by R. C. Lewontin (1970, p. 1) as a scheme involving three essential principles:

1. Different individuals in a population have different morphologies, physiologies, and behaviors (*phenotypic variation*).

2. Different phentoypes have different rates of survival and reproduction in different environments (*differential fitness*).

3. There is a correlation between parents and offspring in the contribution of each to future generations (*fitness is heritable*).

Where (and while)[5] these three principles hold, evolutionary change will occur. Lewontin argues not only that these requirements are necessary for evolution to occur, but also that they are sufficient. They also embody what is generally regarded as Darwin's major contribution over prior evolutionists in that they specify a mechanism, natural selection, which produces this change.

Mechanism or not, these principles specify very little about the units which must meet these conditions. Although they are specified in terms of phenotypes and their properties (a form appropriate to Darwin's original theory and one to which modern evolutionists still pay lip service), Lewontin immediately applies them to genes (the units of the neo-Darwinian theory, under the impetus of Weismannism). Lewontin exploits the fact that these requirements say little about the units that must meet them, to argue that selection can operate—simultaneously and in different directions—on a variety of units (the unspecified individuals) at a number of levels of organization. In his view, he discusses selection processes at the micro- and macromolecular levels, and as operating on cell organelles, cells (in the immune system, in developmental processes, and, he could have added, in cancer), gametes, individual organisms, varieties of kin groups, populations, species, and even ecological communities.

These principles give necessary conditions for an entity to act as a unit of selection, as well as necessary and sufficient conditions for evolution to occur. The three conditions must all be met by the same entity, in a way that can be summarized by saying that entities of that kind must show *heritable variance in fitness*.[6]

These conditions fail to be sufficient for the entity to be a unit of selection, however, for they guarantee only that the entity in question is either a unit of selection *or is composed of units of selection*. A further condition, which is sufficient, is given in the following definition:

A *unit of selection* is any entity for which there is heritable *context-independent* variance in fitness among entities at that level which does not appear as heritable context-independent variance in fitness (and, thus, for which the variance in fitness is *context-dependent*) at any lower level of organization.

Much of population genetic theory involves the notion of additive variance in fitness. It is this quantity which, in Fisher's fundamental theorem of natural selection (Fisher, 1930), determines the rate of evolution. To say that variance in fitness is totally additive is to say that the fitness increase in a genotype is a linear function of the number of genes of a given type present in it. But this entails that the contribution to fitness of a given gene whose effect on fitness is totally additive is independent of the genetic background in which it occurs, which is to say that the variance in fitness is context-independent. Additivity is thus a special case of context-independence. It is assumed for reasons of analytical tractability, but the properties that flow from this assumption derive from its relation to context-independence.

One very important result follows when this assumption holds at a given level of organization. *If variance in fitness is totally additive at a given level of organization over a given range of conditions on the environment and the system, then under those conditions there are no higher-level units of selection!* This is true because fitness of any higher-level unit is then a totally aggregative or mass effect of the fitnesses of the individual entities at that level of organization. With no context-dependence of fitness, the *organization* of these units into higher-level units does not matter. There are no epistatic interactions to tie complexes of these entities together as units of selection. The higher-level unit is totally reducible in its effects to the action of various lower-level units, acting in a context-independent manner.[7]

It may be that this assumption (a product of bias 4 or 5 applied at the level of the gene to increase the analytical tractability of the model) is one of the major reasons contributing to the plausibility of Williams's reductionistic vision. It is clear that once this assumption is made, it becomes plausible to attribute adaptation (and thus fitness) "to the effect of selection acting independently at each locus" (Williams, 1966, p. 57) and leads naturally to regarding fitness as a property of genes (a case of bias 1). It is also true that many or most population geneticists believe and argue (as James Crow has, in personal conversation) that most variance in fitness is additive—presumably, at the level of the contributions of individual genes. This is an empirical claim and represents a view not shared by all population geneticists. Sewall Wright has systematically argued throughout his professional life and in his magisterial four-volume treatise that the opposite is true, that epistatic interactions are all-pervasive and important (personal conversation; see, e.g., Wright, 1968, chapter 5, especially pp. 71–105). Michael Wade's current research indicates the importance of epistatic interactions at the *individual* level (that is, between individuals in populations) in group selection (personal conversation; see Wade and McCauley, 1980, and McCauley and Wade, 1980). What is clearly true is that biases 7, 8, and 9 would in general contribute substantially to failures to detect nonadditive variance if it exists because of artificially induced constancies in or ignorance of environmental conditions capable of producing nonadditive components of variance in fitness.

To summarize, then, if variance in fitness at a given level is totally additive, the entities of that level are composed of units of selection, and there are no higher-level units of selection. If the additive variance in fitness at that level is totally analyzable as additive variance in fitness at lower levels, then the entities at that level are composed of units of selection at these lower levels, rather than being units of selection themselves. To put it in terms of Salmon's (1971) analysis of statistical explanation, the higher-level units of selection as causal factors are then "screened off" by the lower-level units of selection. In their causal effects, they are then "nothing more than" collections of the lower-level entities, and any independent causal efficacy is illusory. This is a necessary and sufficient condition for the truth of Williams's genetic reductionism.

But, in general, we would expect this partitioning of variance in fitness into additive and nonadditive components at different levels to show a number of levels—genes, gene complexes, chromosomes, individuals, even groups—at which additive variance at that level appears only as nonadditive variance at lower levels. There are units of selection at each level at which this occurs, and if it does, genetic reductionism and determinism are false.

Acknowledgment

This work owes a great deal more to many people than is reflected in the footnotes: To Richard Lewontin for his leading me past the most elemental understandings (and sometimes misunderstandings) I brought to my study of population genetics as a postdoctoral fellow in his lab, and for his early advocacy of the importance of gene interactions and higher-level units of selection in evolution, which, as with many other things he has taught me, had a formative effect on my present views. To Richard Levins I owe a similar debt, for his tutelage in mathematical ecology and the analysis of complex systems, for his friendly tolerance of my early naive and principled reductionism, while he gradually taught me elements of a richer vision. To George Williams, whose book was an education to me and to many others, formulating for the first time a clear reductionistic vision and many arguments supporting that view, which I continue to respect, even though I now believe it to be mistaken. More recently, I have learned a great deal from discussions with Ross Kiester and Mike Wade about model building and experimental design, as well as a lot of fascinating and useful biology, and Wade in particular has done a lot to shape my views on group selection. I have profited also in particular from discussions with David Hull, but also with Bob McCauley, Bill Bechtel, Bob Richardson, Elliott Sober, and Mary Jane West-Eberhard, the participants of a Midwest Faculty Seminar on Evolution at Chicago, and seminar or conference participants at the Leonard Conference at Reno, Denison University, Ohio

State, the University of Wisconsin at Madison, and the University of Colorado at Boulder, where versions of this work were presented in 1978–79.

I would like to thank Columbia University Press for permission to reprint Figures 23 and 24 from Lewontin (1974), pp. 274 and 280, and to adapt Table 56 from p. 283. Finally, all of this would have occurred substantially later or perhaps not at all without the support of the National Science Foundation (Grant SOC78–07310 research).

Notes

1 On the most obvious reading, in which genotypes are the subsystems containing genes, which interact to produce fitness, which is a property of genotypes, which affects the multiplication ratios of the genes they contain, selection and mating would be treated as an intersystemic interaction, with segregation and recombination as intrasystemic interactions. Thus the analogy is not quite exact. In this case, with mating assumed to be at random and the genotypic frequencies in linkage equilibrium, the long-range behavior of the system involves the interaction of an intrasystemic force (segregation) and an intersystemic one (selection). This particular decomposition into subsystems (at variance with that required for easy analysis of near decomposability) is necessitated by the particular structure of Mendelian genetics, which, through mating and differential reproduction, inextricably combines inter- and intra-organismic forces.

Other ways of breaking up the system (e.g., into loci as subsystems, which might be suggested by Williams's remarks) produce similar problems: then recombination (a strong force if there is substantial linkage disequilibrium) is intersystemic, rather than intrasystemic, as it "should" be. Nonetheless, the partitioning of forces into strong and weak, characteristic of near decomposability analysis, is found here also; so there remains an important (and probably the most important) ground of analogy.

2 The biologist's use of "tautology" here is looser than the philosopher's, and means roughly a relation that has no empirical content because of the way in which it is used. As such it is related to the vernacular use of "tautology" as in "covert tautology," rather than to the logician's sense. I will here use the term as the biologist does.

3 These judgments are themselves an important source of error, associated with heuristics for cutting the world up into entities, using the robustness or overdetermination of boundaries. These heuristics and examples of their application and misapplication are discussed at length in Wimsatt (1980b), where they are particularly relevant in understanding the nature and origin of functional localization fallacies.

4 These make no mention of the geometric rate of natural increase of organisms and the consequent inevitability of competition for resources (Malthus's observation). But this was a subsidiary argument employed by Darwin to establish the second principle—that different types of organism had different fitnesses. Darwin needed this a priori argument because he had no direct observations of the occurrence of natural selection in nature.

5 Lewontin applies these principles on a genetic micro-evolutionary scale, and points out that for a population in equilibrium of gene frequencies, however temporary, conditions 2, 3, or both are not met (1970, p. 1). And obviously, if there is only a single allele at a given locus in a population (violating condition 1), no change in gene frequency (or micro-evolution) is possible at that locus.

6 I have analyzed these conditions and their ramifications in much greater detail in a book manuscript now in process and tentatively to be called *Reductionism, Sociobiology, and the Units of Selection.* Further excellent discussions of related issues can be found in Hull (1981), Sober (1979), and less directly, Cassidy (1978).

7 Mike Wade felt that this did not emphasize sufficiently strongly that whether an interaction was additive or epistatic is a function of the relation of the system to the environments in which it is studied. He feels that many studies purporting to show that variance in fitness is additive rather than epistatic suffer from looking at a restricted environment (usually in the laboratory) or range of environments, and that investigation of the system in a wide range of environments would show that many or most of the supposedly additive interactions are, in fact, epistatic.

It is worth pointing out that the term "epistasis" is traditionally reserved for interactions between genes *within a given genotype.* But the discussion here naturally suggests an extension to interactions between higher-level complexes of genes. Thus when one speaks, as Wade does, of a *group* phenotype, it becomes natural to describe nonadditive interactions between individuals in the group as epistatic.

References

Ando, A., F. M. Fisher, and H. A. Simon, 1963. *Essays on the Structure of Social Science Models,* Cambridge (Mass.), MIT Press.

Cassidy, John, 1978. "Philosophical aspects of the group selection controversy," *Philosophy of Science,* 45:575–594.

Fisher, R. A., 1930. *The Genetical Theory of Natural Selection,* London, Oxford University Press.

Hull, D. L., 1981. "The units of evolution: A metaphysical essay," in U. L. Jensen and R. Harre, eds., *The Philosophy of Evolution,* Brighton (Eng.), Harvester, pp. 23–44. Reprinted in this volume.

Levins, R., 1966. "The strategy of model building in population biology," *American Scientist,* 54:421–431.

Lewontin, R. C., 1970. "The units of selection," *Annual Review of Ecology and Systematics,* 1:1–18.

Lewontin, R. C., 1974. *The Genetic Basis of Evolutionary Change,* New York, Columbia University Press.

Lewontin, R. C., and M. J. D. White, 1960. "Interaction between inversion polymorphisms of two chromosome pairs in the grasshopper, *Moraba scurra,*" *Evolution,* 14:116–129.

Maynard Smith, J., 1978. *The Evolution of Sex,* London, Cambridge University Press.

McCauley, D. E., and M. J. Wade, 1980. "Group selection: The genetic and demographic basis for the phenotypic differentiation of small populations of *Tribolium castaneum,*" *Evolution,* 34:813–821.

Moss, R. Y., 1979. "Designing reliability into electronic components," Palo Alto, California, Hewlett-Packard.

Newell, A., and H. A. Simon, 1972. *Human Problem Solving,* Englewood Cliffs, New Jersey, Prentice-Hall.

Roughgarden, J., 1979. *Theory of Population Genetics and Evolutionary Ecology: An Introduction,* New York, Macmillan.

Salmon, W. C., 1971. *Statistical Explanation and Statistical Relevance,* Pittsburgh, University of Pittsburgh Press.

Simon, H. A., 1966a. "Thinking by computers," in R. G. Colodny, ed., *Mind and Cosmos,* Pittsburgh, University of Pittsburgh Press, pp. 3–21.

Simon, H. A., 1966b. "Scientific discovery and the psychology of problem solving," in R. G. Colodny, ed., *Mind and Cosmos,* Pittsburgh, University of Pittsburgh Press, pp. 22–40.

Simon, H. A., 1968. *The Sciences of the Artificial,* Cambridge (Mass.), MIT Press.

Sober, E., 1979. "Significant units and the group selection controversy," MS. A later version, entitled "Holism, individualism, and the units of selection," was published in P. Asquith and R. Giere, eds., *PSA 1980,* Vol. 2, East Lansing, Mich., Philosophy of Science Association, 1982, pp. 93–121.

Wade, Michael J., 1978. "A critical review of the models of group selection," *Quarterly Review of Biology,* 53:101–114. Reprinted in this volume.

Wade, Michael J., and D. E. McCauley, 1980. "Group selection: The phenotypic and genotypic differentiation of small populations," *Evolution,* 34: 799–812.

Williams, G. C., 1966. *Adaptation and Natural Selection,* Princeton, Princeton University Press.

Wilson, E. O., 1975. *Sociobiology: The New Synthesis,* Cambridge (Mass.), Harvard University Press.

Wimsatt, W. C., 1974. "Complexity and organization," in K. F. Schaffner and R. S. Cohen, eds., *PSA 1972,* Boston Studies in the Philosophy of Science, Vol. 20, Dordrecht, Holland: Reidel, pp. 67–86.

Wimsatt, W. C., 1976a. "Reductionism, levels of organization, and the mind-body problem," in G. Globus et al., eds., *Brain and Consciousness: Scientific and Philosophic Strategies,* New York, Plenum Press, pp. 199–267.

Wimsatt, W. C., 1976b. "Reductive explanation: A functional account," in Cohen et al., eds., *PSA 1974,* Boston Studies in the Philosophy of Science, Vol. 32, Dordrecht, Holland: Reidel, pp. 671–710.

Wimsatt, W. C., 1978. "Reduction and reductionism," in H. Kyburg, Jr., and P. D. Asquith, eds., *Current Problems in Philosophy of Science,* East Lansing, Mich., Philosophy of Science Association.

Wimsatt, W. C., 1980a. "Randomness and perceived-randomness in evolutionary biology," *Synthese,* 43:287–329.

Wimsatt, W. C., 1980b. "Robustness and functional localization, heuristics for determining the boundaries of systems and their biases," in M. Brewer and B. Collins, eds., *Knowing and Validating in the Social Sciences: A Tribute to Donald T. Campbell,* San Francisco, Jossey-Bass.

Wright, Sewall, 1968. *Evolution and the Genetics of Populations,* Vol. 1, Chicago, University of Chicago Press.

8

Artifact, Cause and Genic Selection

Elliott Sober and Richard C. Lewontin

Introduction

Although predicting an event and saying what brought it about are different, a science may yet hope that its theories will do double duty. Ideally, the laws will provide a set of parameters which facilitate computation and pinpoint causes; later states of a system can be predicted from its earlier parameter values, where these earlier parameter values are the ones that cause the system to enter its subsequent state.

In this paper we argue that these twin goals are not jointly attainable by some standard ideas used in evolutionary theory. The idea that natural selection is always, or for the most part, selection for and against single genes has been vigorously defended by George C. Williams (*Adaptation and Natural Selection*) and Richard Dawkins (*The Selfish Gene*). Although models of evolutionary processes conforming to this view of genic selection may permit computation, they often misrepresent the causes of evolution. The reason is that genic selection coefficient are *artifacts*, not causes, of population dynamics. Since the gene's eye point of view exerts such a powerful influence both within biology and in popular discussions of sociobiology, it is important to show how limited it is. Our discussion will not focus on cultural evolution or on group selection, but rather will be restricted to genetic cases of selection in a single population. The selfish gene fails to do justice to standard textbook examples of Darwinian selection.

The philosophical implications and presuppositions of our critique are various. First, it will be clear that we reject a narrowly instrumentalist interpretation of scientific theories; models of evolutionary processes must do more than correctly predict changes in gene frequencies. In addition, our arguments

From *Philosophy of Science* (1982), 49:157–180. This paper was written while the authors held grants, respectively, from the University of Wisconsin Graduate School and the John Simon Guggenheim Foundation and from the Department of Energy (DE-AS02-76EV02472). We thank John Beatty, James Crow, and Steven Orzack for helpful suggestions.

go contrary to certain regularity and counterfactual interpretations of the concepts of causality and force. To say that *a* caused *b* is to say more than just that any event that is relevantly similar to *a* would be followed by an event that is relevantly similar to *b* (we ignore issues concerning indeterministic causation); and to say that a system of objects is subject to certain forces is to say more than just that they will change in various ways, as long as nothing interferes. And lastly, our account of what is wrong with genic selection coefficients points to a characterization of the conditions under which a predicate will pick out a real property. Selfish genes and grue emeralds bear a remarkable similarity.

1. The "Canonical Objects" of Evolutionary Theory

The Modern Synthesis received from Mendel a workable conception of the mechanism of heredity. But as important as this contribution was, the role of Mendelian "factors" was more profound. Not only did Mendelism succeed in filling in a missing link in the three-part structure of variation, selection, and transmission; it also provided a canonical form in which *all* evolutionary processes could be characterized. Evolutionary models must describe the interactions of diverse forces and phenomena. To characterize selection, inbreeding, mutation, migration, and sampling error in a single predictive theoretical structure, it is necessary to describe their respective effects in a common currency. Change in gene frequencies is the "normal form" in which all these aspects are to be represented, and so genes might be termed the canonical objects of evolutionary theory.

Evolutionary phenomena can be distilled into a tractable mathematical form by treating them as preeminently genetic. It by no means follows from this that the normal form characterization captures everything that is biologically significant. In particular, the computational adequacy of genetic models leaves open the question of whether they also correctly identify the causes of evolution. The canonical form of the models has encouraged many biologists to think of all natural selection as genic selection, but there has always been a tradition within the Modern Synthesis which thinks of natural selection differently and holds this gene's eye view to be fundamentally distorted.

Ernst Mayr perhaps typifies this perspective. Although it is clear that selection has an *effect* on gene frequencies, it is not so clear that natural selection is always selection for or against particular genes. Mayr has given two reasons for thinking that the idea of genic selection is wrong. One of the interesting things about his criticisms is their simplicity; they do not report any recondite facts about evolutionary process, but merely remind evolutionary theorists of what they already know (although perhaps lose sight of at times). As we will see, genic selectionists have ready replies for these criticisms.

The first elementary observation is that "natural selection favors (or discriminates against) phenotypes, not genes or genotypes" (1963, p. 184). Protective coloration and immunity from DDT are phenotypic traits. Organisms differ in their reproductive success under natural selection because of their phenotypes. If those phenotypes are heritable, then natural selection will produce evolutionary change (*ceteris paribus,* of course). But genes are affected by natural selection only indirectly. So the gene's eye view, says Mayr, may have its uses, but it does not correctly represent how natural selection works.

Mayr calls his second point *the gentic theory of relativity* (1963, p. 296). This principle says that "no gene has a fixed selective value, the same gene may confer high fitness on one genetic background and be virtually lethal on another." Should we conclude from this remark that there is never selection for single genes or that a single gene simultaneously experiences different selection pressures in different genetic backgrounds? In either case, the lesson here seems to be quite different from that provided by Mayr's first point— which was that phenotypes, not genotypes, are selected for. In this case, however, it seems to be gene complexes, rather than single genes, which are the objects of selection.

Mayr's first point about phenotypes and genotypes raises the following question: if we grant that selection acts "directly" on phenotypes and only "indirectly" on genotypes, why should it follow that natural selection is not selection for genetic attributes? Natural selection is a causal process; to say that there is selection for some (genotypic or phenotypic) trait X is to say that having X causes differential reproductive success (*ceteris paribus*).[1] So, if there is selection for protective coloration, this just means that protective coloration generates a reproductive advantage. But suppose that this phenotype is itself caused by one or more genes. Then having those genes causes a reproductive advantage as well. Thus, if selection is a causal process, in acting on phenotypes it also acts on the underlying genotypes. Whether this is "direct" or not may be important, but it doesn't bear on the question of what is and what is not selected for. Selection, in virtue of its causal character and on the assumption that causality is transitive, seems to block the sort of asymmetry that Mayr demands. Asking whether phenotypes or genotypes are selected for seems to resemble asking whether a person's death was caused by the entry of the bullet or by the pulling of the trigger.

Mayr's second point—his genetic principle of relativity—is independent of the alleged asymmetry between phenotype and genotype. It is, of course, not in dispute that a gene's fitness depends on its genetic (as well as its extra-somatic) environment. But does this fact show that there is selection for gene complexes and not for single genes? Advocates of genic selection tend to acknowledge the relativity but to deny the conclusion that Mayr draws. Williams (1966, pp. 56-57) gives clear expression to this common reaction when he writes:

Obviously it is unrealistic to believe that a gene actually exists in its own world with no complications other than abstract selection coefficients and mutation rates. The unity of the genotype and the functional subordination of the individual genes to each other and to their surroundings would seem, at first sight, to invalidate the one-locus model of natural selection. Actually these considerations do not bear on the basic postulates of the theory. No matter how functionally dependent a gene may be, and no matter how complicated its interactions with other genes and environmental factors, it must always be true that a given gene substitution will have an arithmetic mean effect on fitness in any population. One allele can always be regarded as having a certain selection coefficient relative to another at the same locus at any given point in time. Such coefficients are numbers that can be treated algebraically, and conclusions inferred for one locus can be iterated over all loci. Adaptation can thus be attributed to the effect of selection acting independently at each locus.

Dawkins (1976, p. 40) considers the same problem: how can single genes be selected for, if genes build organisms only in elaborate collaboration with each other and with the environment? He answers by way of an analogy:

One oarsman on his own cannot win the Oxford and Cambridge boat race. He needs eight colleagues. Each one is a specialist who always sits in a particular part of the boat—bow or stroke or cox, etc. Rowing the boat is a cooperative venture, but some men are nevertheless better at it than others. Suppose a coach has to choose his ideal crew from a pool of candidates, some specializing in the bow position, others specializing as cox, and so on. Suppose that he makes his selection as follows. Every day he puts together three new trial crews, by random shuffling of the candidates, for each position, and he makes the three crews race against each other. After some weeks of this it will start to emerge that the winning boat often tends to contain the same individual men. These are marked up as good oarsmen. Other individuals seem consistently to be found in slower crews, and these are eventually rejected. But even an outstandingly good oarsman might sometimes be a member of a slow crew, either because of the inferiority of the other members, or because of bad luck—say a strong adverse wind. It is only *on average* that the best men tend to be in the winning boat.

The oarsmen are genes. The rivals for each seat in the boat are alleles potentially capable of occupying the same slot along the length of a chromosome. Rowing fast corresponds to building a body which is successful at surviving. The wind is the external environment. The pool of alternative candidates is the gene pool. As far as the survival of any one body is concerned, all its genes are in the same boat. Many a good gene gets into bad company, and finds itself sharing a body with a lethal gene, which kills the body off in childhood. Then the good gene is destroyed along with the rest. But this is only one body, and replicas of the same good gene live on in other bodies which lack the lethal gene. Many copies of good genes are dragged under because they happen to share a body with bad genes, and many perish through other forms of ill luck, say when their body is struck by lightning. But by definition luck, good and bad, strikes at random, and a gene which is consistently on the losing side is not unlucky; it is a bad gene.

Notice that this passage imagines that oarsmen (genes) are good and bad pretty much *in*dependently of their context. But even when fitness is heavily influenced by context, Dawkins still feels that selection functions at the level of the single gene. Later in the book (pp. 91-92), he considers what would happen if a team's performance were improved by having the members communicate with each other. Suppose that half of the oarsmen spoke only English and the other half spoke only German:

What will emerge as the overall best crew will be one of the two stable states —pure English or pure German, but not mixed. Superficially it looks as though the coach is selecting whole language groups *as units.* This is not what he is doing. He is selecting individual oarsmen for their apparent ability to win races. It so happens that the tendency for an individual to win races depends on which other individuals are present in the pool of candidates.

Thus Dawkins follows Williams in thinking that genic selectionism is quite compatible with the fact that a gene's fitness depends on context.

Right after the passage just quoted, Dawkins says that he favors the perspective of genic selectionism because it is more "parsimonious." Here, too, he is at one with Williams (1966), who uses parsimony as one of two main lines of attack against hypotheses of group selection. The appeal to simplicity may confirm a suspicion that already arises in this context: perhaps it is a matter of taste whether one prefers the single gene perspective or the view of selection processes as functioning at a higher level of organization. As long as we agree that genic fitnesses depend on context, what difference does it make how we tell the story? As natural as this suspicion is in the light of Dawkins' rowing analogy, it is mistaken. Hypotheses of group selection can be genuinely incompatible with hypotheses of organismic selection (Sober, 1980), and, as we will see in what follows, claims of single gene selection are at times incompatible with claims that gene complexes are selected for and against. Regardless of one's aesthetic inclinations and regardless of whether one thinks of parsimony as a "real" reason for hypothesis choice, the general perspective of genic selectionism is mistaken for biological reasons. [2]

Before stating our objections to genic selectionism, we want to make clear one defect that this perspective does *not* embody. A quantitative genetic model that is given at any level can be recast in terms of parameters that attach to genes. This genic representation will correctly trace the trajectory of the population as its gene frequencies change. In a minimal sense (to be made clear in what follows), it will be "descriptively adequate." Since the parameters encapsulate information about the environment, both somatic and extrasomatic, genic selectionism cannot be accused of ignoring the complications of linkage or of thinking that genes exist in a vacuum. The defects of genic selectionism concern its distortion of causal processes, not whether its models allow one to predict future states of the population.[3]

The causal considerations which will play a preeminent role in what follows are not being imposed from without, but already figure centrally in evolutionary theory. We have already mentioned how we understand the idea of *selection for X*. Our causal construal is natural in view of how the phenomena of linkage and pleiotropy are understood (see Sober, 1981a). Two genes may be linked together on the same chromosome, and so selection for one may cause them both to increase in frequency. Yet the linked gene—the "free rider"—may be neutral or even deleterious; there was no selection *for it*. In describing pleiotropy, the same distinction is made. Two phenotypic traits may be caused by the same underlying gene complex, so that selection for one leads to a proliferation of both. But, again, there was no selection for the free rider. So it is a familiar idea that two traits can attach to exactly the same organisms and yet differ in their causal roles in a selection process. What is perhaps less familiar is that two sets of selection coefficients may both attach to the same population and yet differ in their causal roles—the one causing change in frequencies, the other merely reflecting the changes that ensue.

2. Averaging and Reification

Perhaps the simplest model exhibiting the strategy of averaging recommended by Williams and Dawkins is used in describing heterozygote superiority. In organisms whose chromosomes come in pairs, individuals with different genes (or alleles) at the same location on two homologous chromosomes are called heterozygotes. When a population has only two alleles at a locus, there will be one heterozygote form (Aa) and two homozygotes (AA and aa). If the heterozygote is superior in fitness to both homozygotes, then natural selection may modify the frequencies of the two alleles A and a but will not drive either to fixation (i.e., 100 percent), since reproduction by heterozygotes will inevitably replenish the supply of homozygotes, even when homozygotes are severely selected against. A textbook example of this phenomenon is the sickle cell trait in human beings. Homozygotes for the allele controlling the trait develop severe anemia that is often fatal in childhood. Heterozygotes, however, suffer no deleterious effects, but enjoy a greater than average resistance to malaria. Homozygotes for the other allele have neither the anemia nor the immunity, and so are intermediate in fitness. Human populations with both alleles that live in malarial areas have remained polymorphic, but with the eradication of malaria, the sickle cell allele has been eliminated.

Population genetics provides a simple model of the selection process that results from heterozygotes' having greater viability than either of the homozygotes (Li 1955). Let p be the frequency of A and q be the frequency of a (where $p + q = 1$). Usually, the maximal fitness of Aa is normalized and set equal to 1. But for clarity of exposition we will let w_1 be the fitness of AA, w_2 be the fitness of Aa, and w_3 be the fitness of aa. These genotypic fitness values play the mathematical role of transforming genotype frequencies before selection into genotype frequencies after selection:

	AA	Aa	aa
Proportion before selection	p^2	$2pq$	q^2
Fitness	w_1	w_2	w_3
Proportion after selection	$\dfrac{p^2 w_1}{\overline{W}}$	$\dfrac{2pq w_2}{\overline{W}}$	$\dfrac{q^2 w_3}{\overline{W}}$

Here, $\overline{W}$, the average fitness of the population, is $p^2 w_1 + 2pq w_2 + q^2 w_3$. Assuming random mating, the population will move towards a stable equilibrium frequency $\hat{p}$ where

$$\hat{p} = \frac{w_3 - w_2}{(w_1 - w_2) + (w_3 - w_2)} .$$

It is important to see that this model attributes fitness values and selection coefficients to diploid genotypes and not to the single genes A and a. But, as genic selectionists are quick to emphasize, one can always define the required parameters. Let us do so.

We want to define W_A, which is the fitness of A. If we mimic the mathematical role of genotype fitness values in the previous model, we will require that W_A obey the following condition:

$W_A \times$ frequency of A before selection = frequency of A after selection $\times \overline{W}$.

Since the frequency of A before selection is p and the frequency of A after selection is

$$\frac{w_1 p^2 + w_2 pq}{\overline{W}} ,$$

it follows that

$$W_A = w_1 p + w_2 q.$$

By parity of reasoning,

$$W_a = w_3 q + w_2 p.$$

Notice that the fitness values of single genes are just weighted averages of the fitness values of the diploid genotypes in which they appear. The weighting is provided by their frequency of occurrence in the genotypes in question. The genotypic fitnesses specified in the first model are *constants;* as a population moves toward its equilibrium frequency, the selection coefficients attaching to the three diploid genotypes do not change. In contrast, the expression we have derived for allelic fitnesses says that allelic fitnesses change as a function of their own frequencies; as the population moves toward equilibrium, the fitnesses of the alleles must constantly be recomputed.

Heterozygote superiority illustrates the principle of genetic relativity. The gene *a* is maximally fit in one context (namely, when accompanied by *A*) but is inferior when it occurs in another (namely, when it is accompanied by another copy of itself). In spite of this, we can average over the two different contexts and provide the required representation in terms of genic fitness and genic selection.

In the diploid model discussed first, we represented the fitness of the three genotypes in terms of their *viability*—that is, in terms of the proportion of individuals surviving from egg to adult. It is assumed that the actual survivorship of a class of organisms sharing the same genotype precisely represents the fitness of that shared genotype. This assumes that random drift is playing no role. Ordinarily, fitness *cannot* be identified with actual reproductive success (Brandon, 1978; Mills and Beatty, 1979; Sober, 1981a). The same point holds true, of course, for the fitness coefficients we defined for the single genes.[4]

Of the two descriptions we have constructed of heterozygote superiority, the first model is the standard one; in it, *pairs* of genes are the bearers of fitness values and selection coefficients. In contrast to this diploid model, our second formulation adheres strictly to the dictates of genic selectionism, according to which it is *single genes* which are the bearers of the relevant evolutionary properties. We now want to describe what each of these models will say about a population that is at its equilibrium frequency.

Let's discuss this situation by way of an example. Suppose that both homozygotes are lethal. In that case, the equilibrium frequency is .5 for each of the alleles. Before selection, the three genotypes will be represented in proportions 1/4, 1/2, 1/4, but after selection the frequencies will shift to 0, 1, 0. When the surviving heterozygotes reproduce, Mendelism will return the population to its initial 1/4, 1/2, 1/4 configuration, and the population will continue to zig-zag between these two genotype configurations, all the while maintaining each allele at .5. According to the second, single gene, model, at equilibrium the fitnesses of the two genes are both equal to 1 and the selection coefficients are therefore equal to zero. At equilibrium, no selection occurs, on this view. Why the population's *genotypic configuration* persists in zig-zagging, the gene's eye point of view is blind to see; it must be equally puzzling why $\bar{W}$, the average fitness of the population, also zig-zags. However, the standard diploid model yields the result that selection occurs when the population is at equilibrium, just as it does at other frequencies, favoring the heterozygote at the expense of the homozygotes. Mendelism *and selection* are the causes of the zig-zag. Although the models are computationally equivalent in their prediction of gene frequencies, they are not equivalent when it comes to saying whether or not selection is occurring.

It is hard to see how the adequacy of the single gene model can be defended in this case. The biological term for the phenomenon being described is apt. We are talking here about *heterozygote superiority,* and both terms of this label deserve emphasis. The heterozygote—i.e., the diploid genotype (not a single gene)—is superior *in fitness* and, therefore, enjoys a selective advantage. To insist that the single gene is always the level at which selection occurs obscures this and, in fact, generates precisely the wrong answer to the question of what is happening at equilibrium. Although the mathematical calculations can be carried out in the single gene model just as they can in the diploid genotypic model, the phenomenon of heterozygote superiority cannot be adequately "represented" in terms of single genes. This model does not tell us what is patently obvious about this case: even at equilibrium, what happens to gene frequencies is an artifact of selection acting on diploid genotypes.

One might be tempted to argue that, in the heterozygote superiority case, the kind of averaging we have criticized is just an example of frequency dependent selection and that theories of frequency dependent selection are biologically plausible and also compatible with the dictates of genic selectionism. To see where this objection goes wrong, one must distinguish genuine from spurious cases of frequency dependent selection. The former occurs when the frequency of an allele has some *biological impact* on its fitness; an example would be the phenomenon of mimicry in which the rarity of a mimic enhances its fitness. Here one can tell a biological story explaining why the fitness values have the mathematical form they do. The case of heterozygote superiority is altogether different; here frequencies are taken into account simply as a mathematical contrivance, the only point being to get the parameters to multiply out in the right way.

The diploid model is, in a sense, more contentful and informative than the single gene model. We noted before that from the *constant* fitness values of the three genotypes we could obtain a formula for calculating the fitnesses of the two alleles. Allelic fitnesses are implied by genotype fitness values and allelic frequencies; since allelic frequencies change as the population moves toward equilibrium, allelic fitnesses must constantly be recomputed. However, the derivation in the opposite direction cannot be made:[5] one cannot deduce the fitnesses of the genotypes from allelic fitnesses and frequencies. This is especially evident when the population is at equilibrium. At equilibrium, the allelic fitnesses are identical. From this information alone, we cannot tell whether there is no selection at all or whether some higher-level selection process is taking place. Allelic frequencies plus genotypic fitness imply allelic fitness values, but allelic frequencies plus allelic fitness values do not imply genotypic fitness values. This derivational asymmetry suggests that the genotypic description is more informative.

Discussions of reductionism often suggest that theories at lower levels of organization will be more detailed and informative than ones at higher levels. However, here the more contentful, constraining model is provided at the higher level. The idea that genic selection models are "deeper" and describe the fundamental level at which selection "really" occurs is simply not universally correct.

The strategy of averaging fosters the illusion that selection is acting at a lower level of organization than it in fact does. Far from being an idiosyncratic property of the genic model of heterozygote superiority just discussed, averaging is a standard technique in modeling a variety of selection processes. We will now describe another example in which this technique of representation is used—the example of heterozygote superiority focused on differences in genotypic *viabilities*. Let us consider the way differential fertilities can be modeled for one locus with two alleles. In the fully general case, fertility is a property of a mating pair, not of an individual. It may be true that a cross between an *AA* male and *aa* female has an expected number of offspring different from a cross between an *AA* female and an *aa* male. If fitnesses are a unique function of the pair, the model must represent nine possible fitnesses, one for each mating pair. Several special cases permit a reduction in dimensionality. If the sex of a genotype does not affect its fertility, then only six fitnesses need be given; and if fertility depends only on one of the sexes, say the females, the three female genotypes may be assigned values which fix the fertilities of all mating pairs.

But even when these special cases fail to obtain, the technique of averaging over contexts can nevertheless provide us with a fitness value for each genotype. Perhaps an *aa* female is highly fertile when mated with an *Aa* male but is much less so when mated with an *AA* male; perhaps *aa* females are quite fertile on average, but *aa* males are uniformly sterile. No matter—we can merely average over all contexts and find the average effect of the *aa* genotype. This number will fluctuate with the frequency distributions of the different mating pairs. Again, the model appears to locate selection at a level lower than what might first appear to be the case. Rather than assigning fertilities to mating pairs, we now seem to be assigning them to genotypes. This mathematical contrivance is harmless as long as it does not lead us to think that selection really acts at this lower level of organization.[6]

Our criticism of genic selectionism has so far focused on two forms of selection at a single locus. We now need to take account of how a multilocus theory can imply that selection is not at the level of the selfish gene. The pattern of argument is the same. Even though the fitness of a pair of genes at one locus may depend on what genes are found at other loci, the technique of averaging may still be pressed into service. But the selection values thereby assigned to the three genotypes at a single locus will be artifacts of the fitnesses of the nine genotype complexes that exist at the two loci. As in the examples we already described, the lower-level selection coefficients will change as a function of genotype frequencies, whereas the higher-level selection coefficients will remain constant. An example of this is provided by the work of Lewontin and White (reported in Lewontin, 1974) on the interaction of two chromosome inversions found in the grasshopper *Moraba scura*. On each of the chromosomes of the EF pair, Standard (ST) and Tidbinbilla (TD) may be found. On the CD chromosome pair, Standard (ST) and Blundell (BL) are the two alternatives. The fitness values of the nine possible genotypes were estimated from nature as follows:

	Chromosome CD		
Chromosome EF	ST/ST	ST/BL	BL/BL
ST/ST	0.791	1.000	0.834
ST/TD	0.670	1.006	0.901
TD/TD	0.657	0.657	1.067

Notice that there is heterozygote superiority on the CD chromosome if the EF chromosome is either ST/ST or ST/TD, but that BL/BL dominance ensues when the EF chromosome is homozygous for TD. Moreover, TD/TD is superior when in the context BL/BL but is inferior in the other contexts provided by the CD pair. These fitness values represent differences in viability, and again the inference seems clear that selection acts on multilocus genotypic configurations and not on the genotype at a single locus, let alone on the separate genes at that locus.

3. Individuating Selection Processes

The examples in the previous section have a common structure. We noted that the fitness of an object (a gene, a genotype) varied significantly from context to context. We concluded that selection was operating at a level higher than the one posited by the model—at the level of genotypes in the case of heterozygote superiority, at the level of the mating pair in the fertility model, and at the level of pairs of chromosome inversions in the *Moraba scura* example.

These analyses suggest the following principle: *if the fitness of X is context sensitive, then there is not selection for X; rather, there is selection at a level of organization higher than X.*

We believe that this principle requires qualification. To see why context sensitivity is not a *sufficient* condition for higher-level selection, consider the following example. Imagine a dominant lethal gene; it kills any organisms in which it is found unless the organism also has a suppressor gene at another locus. Let's consider two populations. In the first population, each organism is homozygous for a suppressor gene which prevents copies of the lethal gene from having any effect. In the second population, no organism has a suppressor; so, whenever the lethal gene occurs, it is selected against. A natural way of describing this situation is that there is selection against the lethal gene in one population, but in the other there is no selection going on at all. It would be a mistake (of the kind we have already examined) to think that there is a single selection process at work here against the lethal gene, whose magnitude we calculate by averaging over the two populations. However, we do not conclude from this that there is a selection process at work at some higher level of organization than the single gene. Rather, we conclude that there are *two* populations; in one, *genic* selection occurs, and in the other *nothing* occurs. So the context sensitivity of fitness is an ambiguous clue. If the fitness of *X* depends on genetic context, this may mean that there is a single selection process at some higher level, *or* it may mean that there are several different selection processes at the level of *X*. Context sensitivity does not suffice for there to be selection at a higher level.[7]

Thus the fitness of an object can be sensitive to genetic context for at least two reasons. How are they to be distinguished? This question leads to an issue at the foundation of *all* evolutionary models. What unites a set of objects as all being subject to a single selection process? Biological modeling of evolution by natural selection is based on three necessary and sufficient conditions (Lewontin, 1970): a given set of objects must exhibit variation; some individuals must be fitter than others; and there must be correlation between the fitness of parents and the fitness of offspring. Here, as before, we will identify fitness with actual reproductive success, subject to the proviso that these will coincide only in special cases. Hence, evolution by natural selection exists when and only when there is heritable variation in fitness.

Using these conditions presupposes that some antecedent decision has been made about which objects can appropriately be lumped together as participating in a single selection process (or, put differently, the conditions are not sufficient after all). Biologists do not talk about a *single* selection process subsuming widely scattered organisms of different species which are each subject to quite different local conditions. Yet such a gerrymandered assemblage of objects may well exhibit heritable variation in fitness. And even within the same species, it would be artificial to think of two local populations as participating in the same selection process because one encounters a disease and the other experiences a food shortage as its principal selection pressure. Admittedly, the gene frequencies can be tabulated and pooled, but in some sense the relation of organisms to environments is too heterogeneous for this kind of averaging to be more than a mathematical contrivance.

It is very difficult to spell out necessary and sufficient conditions for when a set of organisms experience "the same" selection pressure. They need not compete with each other. To paraphrase Darwin, two plants may struggle for life at the edge of a desert, and selection may favor the one more suited to the stressful conditions. But it needn't be the case that some resource is in short supply, so that the amount expropriated by one reduces the amount available to the other. Nor need it be true that the two organisms be present in the same geographical locale; organisms in the semi-isolated local populations of a species may experience the same selection pressures. What seems to be required, roughly, is that some common causal influence impinge on the organisms. This sameness of causal influence is as much determined by the biology of the organisms as it is by the physical characteristics of the environment. Although two organisms may experience the same temperature fluctuations, there may be no selective force acting on both. Similarly, two organisms may experience the same selection pressure (for greater temperature tolerance, say) even though the one is in a cold environment and the other is in a hot one. Sameness of causal influence needs to be understood biologically.

For all the vagueness of this requirement, let us assume that we have managed to single out the class of objects which may properly be viewed as participating in a single selection process. To simplify matters, let us suppose that they are all organisms within the same breeding population. What, then, will tell us whether selection is at the level of the single gene or at the level of gene complexes? To talk about either of these forms of selection is, in a certain important but nonstandard sense, to talk about "group selection." Models of selection do not concern single organisms or the individual physical copies of genes (i.e., geno*tokens*) that they contain. Rather, such theories are about groups of organisms which have in common certain geno*types*. To talk about selection for X, where X is some single gene or gene cluster, is to say something about the effect of having X and of lacking X on the relevant subgroups of the breeding population. If there is selection for X, every object which has X has its reproductive chances augmented by its possessing X. This does not mean that every organism which has X has precisely the same overall fitness, nor does it mean that every organism must be affected in precisely the same way (down to the minutest details of developmental pathways). Rather, what is required is that the effect of X on each organism be in the same direction as far as its overall fitness is concerned. Perhaps this characterization is best viewed as a limiting ideal. To the degree that the population conforms to this requirement, it will be appropriate to talk about genic selection. To the degree that the population falls short of this, it will be a contrivance to represent matters in terms of genic selection.[8]

It is important to be clear on why the context sensitivity of a gene's effect on organismic fitness is crucial to the question of genic selection. Selection theories deal with groups of single organisms and not with organisms taken one at a time. It is no news that the way a gene inside of a single organism will affect that organism's phenotype and its fitness depends on the way it is situated in a context of background conditions. But to grant this fact of context sensitivity does not impugn the claim of causation; striking the match caused it to light, even though the match had to be dry and in the presence of oxygen for the cause to produce the effect.

Selection theory is about geno*types* not geno*tokens*. We are concerned with what properties are selected for and against in a population. We do not describe single organisms and their physical constituents one by one. It is for this reason that the question of context sensitivity becomes crucial. If we wish to talk about selection for a single gene, then there must be such a thing as *the* causal upshot of possessing that gene. A gene which is beneficial in some contexts and deleterious in others will have many *organismic* effects. But at *the population level,* there will be no selection for or against that gene.

It is not simply the averaging over contexts which reveals the fact that genic selection coefficients are pseudoparameters; the fact that such parameters *change* in value as the population evolves while the biological relations stay fixed also points to their being artifacts. In the case of heterozygote superiority, genotypic fitnesses remain constant, mirroring the fact that the three genotypes have a uniform effect on the viability of the organisms in which they occur. The population is thereby driven to its equilibrium value while genic fitness values are constantly modified. A fixed set of biological relationships fuels both of these changes; the evolution of genic fitness values is effect, not cause.[9]

Are there real cases of genic selection? A dominant lethal—a gene which causes the individual to die regardless of the context in which it occurs— would be selected against. And selection for or against a phenotypic trait controlled by a single locus having two alleles might also be describable in terms of genic selection, provided that the heterozygote is intermediate in fitness between the two homozygotes. In addition, meiotic drive, such as is found in the house mouse *Mus musculus,* similarly seems to involve genic selection (Lewontin and Dunn, 1960). Among heterozygote males, the proportion of t-alleles in the sperm pool is greater than $1/2$. Chromosomes with the t-allele have enhanced chances of representation in the gamete pool, and this directional effect seems to hold true regardless of what other genes are present at other loci.[10] At this level, but not at the others at which the t-allele affects the population, it is appropriate to talk about genic selection.

So far we have construed genic selection in terms of the way that having or lacking a gene can affect the reproductive chances of organisms. But there is another possibility—namely, that genes differentially proliferate even though they have *no* effect on the phenotypes of organisms. A considerable quantity of DNA has no known function; Orgel and Crick (1980) and Doolittle and Sapienza (1980) have suggested that this DNA may in fact be "junk." Such "selfish DNA," as they call it, could nonetheless undergo a selection process, provided that some segments are better replicators than others. Although these authors associate their ideas with Dawkins' selfish gene, their conception is far more restrictive. For Dawkins, *all* selection is genic selection, whereas for these authors selfish DNA is possible only when the differential replication of genes is not exhaustively accounted for by the differential reproductive success of organisms.

Standard ways of understanding natural selection rule out rather than substantiate the operation of genic selection. It is often supposed that much of natural selection is *stabilizing selection,* in which an intermediate phenotype is optimal (e.g., birth weight in human beings). Although the exact genetic bases of such phenotypes are frequently unknown, biologists often model this selection process as follows. It is hypothesized that the phenotypic value is a monotone increasing function of the number of "plus alleles" found at a number of loci. Whether selection favors the presence of plus genes at one locus depends on how many such genes exist at other loci. Although this model does not view heterozygote superiority as the most common fitness relation *at a locus,* it nevertheless implies that a *heterogeneous genome* is superior in fitness. Exceptions to this intermediate optimum model exist, and the exact extent of its applicability is still an open question. Still, it appears to be widely applicable. If it is generally correct, we must conclude that the conditions in which genic selection exists are extremely narrow. Genic selection is not impossible, but the biological constraints on its operation are extremely demanding.

Although it is just barely conceivable that a critique of a scientific habit of thought might be devoid of philosophical presuppositions, our strictures against genic selectionism are not a case in point. We have described selection processes in which genic selection coefficients are *reifications;* they are artifacts, not causes, of evolution. For this to count as a criticism, one must abandon a narrowly instrumentalist view of scientific theories; this we gladly do, in that we assume that selection theory ought to pinpoint causes as well as facilitate predictions.

But even assuming this broadly noninstrumentalist outlook, our criticisms are philosophically partisan in additional ways. In that we have argued that genic selection coefficients are often "pseudoproperties" of genes, our criticisms of the gene's-eye point of view are connected with more general metaphysical questions about the ontological status of properties. Some of these we take up in the following section. And in that we have understood "selection for" as a causal locution, it turns out that our account goes contrary to certain regularity analyses of causation. In populations in which selection generated by heterozygote superiority is the only evolutionary force, it is true that gene frequencies will move to a stable equilibrium. But this lawlike regularity does not imply that there is selection for or against any individual gene. To say that "the gene's fitness value caused it to increase in frequency" is not simply to say that "any gene with that fitness value (in a relevantly similar population) would increase in frequency," since the former is false and the latter is true. Because we take natural selection to be a force of evolution, these remarks about causation have implications (explored in section 5) for how the concept of force is to be understood.

4. Properties

The properties, theoretical magnitudes, and natural kinds investigated by science ought not to be identified with the meanings that terms in scientific language possess. Nonsynonymous predicates (like "temperature" and "mean kinetic energy" and like "water" and "H_2O") may pick out the same property, and predicates which are quite meaningful (like "phlogiston" and "classical mass") may fail to pick out a property at all. Several recent writers have explored the idea that properties are to be individuated by their potential causal efficacy (Achinstein, 1974; Armstrong, 1978; Shoemaker, 1980; and Sober, 1982b). Besides capturing much of the intuitive content of our informal talk of properties, this view also helps explicate the role of property-talk in science (Sober, 1981). In this section we will connect our discussion of genic selectionism with this metaphysical problem.

The definitional power of ordinary and scientific language allows us to take predicates each of which pick out properties, and to construct logically from these components a predicate that evidently does not pick out a property at all. An example is that old philosophical chestnut, the predicate "grue." We will say that an object is grue at a given time if it is green and the time is before the year 2000, or it is blue and the time is not before the year 2000. The predicate "grue" is defined from the predicates "green," "blue," and "time," each of which, we may assume for the purposes of the example, picks out a "real" property. Yet "grue" does not. A theory of properties should explain the basis of this distinction.

The difference between real and pseudo-property is not captured by the ideas that animate the metaphysical issues usually associated with doctrines of realism, idealism, and conventionalism. Suppose that one adopts a "realist" position toward color and time, holding that things have colors and temporal properties independently of human thought and language. This typical realist declaration of independence (Sober, 1982a) will then imply that objects which are grue are so independently of human thought and language as well. In this sense, the "reality" of grulers is ensured by the "reality" of colors and time. The distinction between real properties and pseudo-properties must be sought elsewhere.

Another suggestion is that properties can be distinguished from nonproperties by appeal to the idea of *similarity* or of *predictive power*. One might guess that green things are more similar to one another than grue things are to one another or that the fact that a thing is green is a better predictor of its further characteristics than that it is grue. The standard criticism of these suggestions is that they are circular. We understand the idea of similarity in terms of shared *properties*, and the idea of predictive power in terms of the capacity to facilitate inference of further *properties*. However, a more fundamental difficulty with these suggestions presents itself: even if grue things happened to be very similar to one another, this would not make grue a real property. If there were no blue things after the year 2000, then the class of grue things would simply be the class of green things before the year 2000. The idea of similarity and the idea of predictive power fail to pinpoint the *intrinsic* defects of nonproperties like grue. Instead, they focus on somewhat accidental facts about the objects which happen to exist.

Grue is not a property for the same reason that genic selection coefficients are pseudo-parameters in models of heterozygote superiority. The key idea is not that nonproperties are mind-dependent or are impoverished predictors; rather, they cannot be causally efficacious. To develop this idea, let's note a certain similarity between grue and genic selection coefficients. We pointed out before that genotype fitnesses plus initial genotype frequencies in the population causally determine the gene frequencies after selection. These same parameters also permit the mathematical derivation of genic fitness values. But, we asserted, these genic fitness values are artifacts; they do not cause the subsequent alteration in gene frequencies. The structure of these relationships is as follows.

genotype fitness values and → genic frequencies
frequencies at time t at $t + 1$
    ↓
genic fitness values at time t

Note that there are two different kinds of determination at work here. Genic fitness values at a given time are not *caused* by the genotypic fitness values at the same time. We assume that causal relations do not obtain between simultaneous events; rather, the relationship is one of logical or mathematical deducibility (symbolized by a broken line). On the other hand, the relation of initial genotype fitnesses and frequencies and subsequent gene frequencies is one of causal determination (represented by a solid line).

Now let's sketch the causal relations involved in a situation in which an object's being green produces some effect. Let the object be a grasshopper. Suppose that it matches its grassy background and that this protective coloration hides it from a hungry predator nearby. The relationships involved might be represented as follows.

the grasshopper is green at time t → the grasshopper evades
    ↓   the predator at time $t + 1$
the grasshopper is grue at time t

Just as in the above case, the object's color at the time *logically implies* that it is grue at that time but is the *cause* of its evading the predator at a subsequent time. And just as genic fitness values do not cause changes in gene frequencies, so the grasshopper's being grue does not cause it to have evaded its predator.

Our assessment of genic selectionism was not that genic fitness values are *always* artifactual. In cases other than that of heterozygote superiority—say, in the analysis of the t-allele—it may be perfectly correct to attribute causal efficacy to genic selection coefficients. So a predicate can pick out a real (causally efficacious) property in one context and fail to do so in another. This does not rule out the possibility, of course, that a predicate like "grue" is *globally artifactual*. But this consequence should not be thought to follow from a demonstration that grue is artifactual in a single kind of causal process.

The comparison of grue with genic selection is not meant to solve the epistemological problems of induction that led Goodman (1965) to formulate the example. Nor does the discussion provide any a priori grounds for distinguishing properties from nonproperties. Nor is it even a straightforward and automatic consequence of the truth of any scientific model that grue is artifactual, or that the idea of causal efficacy captures the metaphysical distinction at issue. Instead, the point is that a certain natural interpretation of a biological phenomenon helps to indicate how we ought to understand a rather abstract metaphysical issue.[11]

5. Forces

Our arguments against genic selectionism contradict a standard positivist view of the concept of force. Positivists have often alleged that Newtonian mechanics tells us that forces are not "things," but that claims about forces are simply to be understood as claims about how objects actually behave, or would behave, if nothing else gets in the way. An exhaustive catalog of the forces acting on a system is to be understood as simply specifying a set of counterfactuals that describe objects.[12]

A Newtonian theory of forces will characterize each force in its domain in terms of the changes it would produce, were it the only force at work. The theory will take pairwise combinations of forces and describe the joint effects that the two forces would have were they the only ones acting on a system. Then the forces would be taken three at a time, and so on, until a fully realistic model is constructed, one that tells us how real objects, which after all are subject to many forces, can be expected to behave. Each step in this program may face major theoretical difficulties, as the recent history of physics reveals (Cartwright, 1980b; Joseph, 1980).

This Newtonian paradigm is a hospitable home for the modeling of evolutionary forces provided in population genetics. The Hardy-Weinberg Law says what happens to gene frequencies when no evolutionary forces are at work. Mutation, migration, selection, and random drift are taken up one at a time, and models are provided for their effects on gene frequencies when no other forces are at work. Then these (and other) factors are taken up in combination. Each of these steps increases the model's realism. The culmination of this project would be a model that simultaneously represents the interactions of all evolutionary forces.

Both in physics and in population genetics, it is useful to conceive of forces in terms of their *ceteris paribus* effects. But there is more to a force than the truth of counterfactuals concerning change in velocity, or change in gene frequencies. The laws of motion describe the *effects* of forces, but they are supplemented by source laws which describe their *causes*. The standard genotypic model of heterozygote superiority not only says what will happen to a population, but also tells us what makes the population change.

It is quite true that when a population moves to an equilibrium value due to the selection pressures generated by heterozygote superiority, the alleles are "disposed" to change in frequency in certain ways.[13] That is, the frequencies *will* change in certain ways, as long as no other evolutionary forces impinge. Yet, there is no force of genic selection at work here. If this is right, then the claim that genic selection is occurring must involve more than the unproblematic observations that gene frequencies are disposed to change in certain ways.

There is something more to the concept of force because it involves the idea of *causality,* and there is more to the idea of causality than is spelled out by such counterfactuals as the ones cited above. Suppose that something pushes (i.e., causally interacts with in a certain way) a billiard ball due north, and something else pushes it due west. Assuming that nothing else gets in the way, the ball will move northwest. There are two "component" forces at work here, and, as we like to say, one "net" force. However, there is a difference between the components and the resultant. Although something pushes the ball due north and something else pushes it due west, nothing pushes it northwest. In a sense, the resultant force is not a force at all, if by force we mean a causal agency. The resultant force is an artifact of the forces at work in the system. For mathematical purposes this distinction may make no difference. But if we want to understand why the ball moves the way it does, there is all the difference in the world between component and net.[14]

The "force" of genic selection in the evolutionary process propelled by heterozygote superiority is no more acceptable than the resultant "force" which is in the northwesterly direction. In fact, it is much worse. The resultant force, at least, is defined from the same conceptual building blocks as the component forces are. Genic selection coefficients, however, are gerrymandered hodgepodges, conceptually and dynamically quite unlike the genotypic selection coefficients that go into their construction. For genic selection coefficients are defined in terms of genotypic selection coefficients *and* gene frequencies. As noted before, they vary as the population changes in gene frequency, whereas the genotypic coefficients remain constant. And if their uniform zero value at equilibrium is interpreted as meaning that no selection is going on, one obtains a series of false assertions about the character of the population.

The concept of force is richer than that of disposition. The array of forces that act on a system uniquely determine the disposition of that system to change, but not conversely. If natural selection is a force and fitness is a disposition (to be reproductively successful), then the concept of selection is richer than that of fitness. To say that objects differ in fitness is not yet to say *why* they do so. The possible causes of such differences may be various, in that many different combinations of selection pressures acting at different levels of organization can have the same instantaneous effect on gene frequencies. Although selection coefficients and fitness values are interdefinable mathematically (so that, typically, $s = 1 - w$), they play different conceptual roles in evolutionary theory (Sober, 1980).

Notes

1 The "*ceteris paribus*" is intended to convey the fact that selection for X can fail to bring about greater reproductive success for objects that have X, if countervailing forces act. Selection for X, against Y, and so on, are component forces that combine vectorially to determine the dynamics of the population.

2 In the passages quoted, Williams and Dawkins adopt a very bold position: any selection process which *can* be represented as genic selection *is* genic selection. Dawkins never draws back from this monolithic view, although Williams' more detailed argumentation leads him to hedge. Williams allows that group selection (clearly understood to be an alternative to genic selection) is possible and has actually been documented once (see his discussion of the t-allele). But *all* selection processes—including group selection—can be "represented" in terms of selection coefficients attaching to single genes. This means that the representation argument proves far too much.

3 Wimsatt (1980) criticizes genic selectionist models for being computationally inadequate and for at best providing a kind of "genetic bookkeeping" rather than a "theory of evolutionary change." Although we dissent from the first criticism, our discussion in what follows supports Wimsatt's second point.

4 We see from this that Dawkins' remark that a gene that is "consistently on the losing side is not unlucky; it's a bad gene" is not quite right. Just as a single genotoken (and the organism in which it is housed) may enjoy a degree of reproductive success that is not an accurate representation of its fitness, so a set of genotokens (which are tokens of the same genotype) may encounter the same fate. Fitness and actual reproductive success are guaranteed to be identical only in models that ignore random drift and thereby presuppose an infinite population.

5 If the heterozygote fitness is set equal to 1, the derivation is possible for the one-locus two-allele case considered. But if more than two alleles are considered, the asymmetry exists even in the face of normalization.

6 The averaging of effects can also be used to foster the illusion that a group selection process is really just a case of individual selection. But since this seems to be a relatively infrequent source of abuse, we will not take the space to spell out an example.

7 The argument given here has the same form as one presented in Sober (1980), which showed that the following is not a sufficient condition for group selection: there is heritable variation in the fitness of groups in which the fitness of an organism depends on the character of the group it is in.

8 The definition of genic selection just offered is structurally similar to the definition of group selection offered in Sober (1980). There the requirement was that for there to be selection for groups that are X, it must be the case that every organism in a group that is X has one component of its fitness determined by the fact that it is in a group that is X. In group selection, organisms within the same group are bound together by a common group characteristic, just as in genic selection, organisms with the same gene are influenced in the same way by their shared characteristic.

9 In our earlier discussion of Mayr's ideas, we granted that selection usually

acts "directly" on phenotypes and only "indirectly" on genotypes. But given the transitivity of causality, we argued that this fact is perfectly compatible with the existence of genotypic selection. However, our present discussion provides a characterization of when phenotypic selection can exist without any selection at the genotypic level. Suppose that individuals with the same genotype in a population end with different phenotypes, because of the different microenvironments in which they develop. Selection for a given phenotype may then cross-classify the genotypes, and by our argument there will be no such things as *the* causal upshot of a genotype. Averaging over effects will be possible, as always, but this will not imply genotypic selection. It is important to notice that this situation can allow evolution by natural selection to occur; gene frequencies can change in the face of phenotypic selection that is not accompanied by any sort of genotypic selection. Without this possibility, the idea of phenotypic selection is deprived of its main interest. There is no reason to deny that there can be selection for phenotypic differences that have no underlying genetic differences, but this process will not produce any change in the population (ignoring cultural evolution and the like).

10 Genes at other loci which modify the intensity of segregator distortion are known to exist in *Drosophila;* the situation in the house mouse is not well understood. Note that the existence of such modifiers is consistent with genic selection as long as they do not affect the *direction* of selection.

11 Another consequence of this analogy is that one standard diagnosis of what is wrong with "grue" fails to get to the heart of the matter. Carnap (1947) alleged that "green," unlike "grue," is purely qualitative, in that it makes no essential reference to particular places, individuals, or times. Goodman (1965) responded by pointing out that *both* predicates can be defined with reference to the year 2000. But a more fundamental problem arises: even if "grue" were, in some sense, not purely qualitative, this would not provide a fully general characterization of when a predicate fails to pick out a real property. Genic selection coefficients are "purely qualitative" if genotypic coefficients are, yet their logical relationship to each other exactly parallels that of "grue" to "green." Predicates picking out real properties can be "gruified" in a purely qualitative way: Let F and G be purely qualitative and be true of all the objects sampled (the emeralds, say). The predicate "$(F$ and $G)$ or $(-F$ and $-G)$" is a gruification of F and poses the same set of problems as Goodman's "grue."

12 Joseph (1980) has argued that this position, in treating the distribution of objects as given and then raising epistemological problems about the existence of forces, is committed to the existence of an asymmetry between attributions of quantities of *mass* to points in space-time and attributions of quantities of *energy* thereto. He argues that this idea, implicit in Reichenbach's (1958) classic argument for the conventionality of geometry, contradicts the relativistic equivalence of mass and energy. If this is right, then the positivistic view of force just described, far from falling out of received physical theory, in fact contradicts it.

13 For the purpose of this discussion, we will assume that attributions of dispositions and subjunctive conditionals of certain kinds are equivalent. That

is, we will assume that to say that x is disposed to F is merely to say that if conditions were such-and-such, x would F.

14 This position is precisely the opposite of that taken by Cartwright (1980a), who argues that net forces, rather than component forces, are the items that really exist. Cartwright argues this by pointing out that the billiard ball moves northwesterly and not due north or due west. However, this appears to conflate the *effect* of a force with the force or forces actually at work.

References

Achinstein, P., 1974. "The identity of properties," *American Philosophical Quarterly,* 11:257–75.

Armstrong, D., 1978. *Universals and Scientific Realism,* Cambridge (Eng.), Cambridge University Press.

Carnap, R., 1947. "On the application of inductive logic," *Philosophy and Phenomenological Research,* 8:133–47.

Cartwright, N., 1980a. "Do the laws of nature state the facts?" *Pacific Philosophical Quarterly,* 61:75–84.

Cartwright, N., 1980b. "The truth doesn't explain much," *American Philosophical Quarterly,* 17:159–63.

Dawkins, R., 1976. *The Selfish Gene,* Oxford, Oxford University Press.

Doolittle, W., and Sapienza, C., 1980. "Selfish genes, the phenotype paradigm, and genome evolution," *Nature,* 284:601–603.

Fisher, R., 1930. *The Genetical Theory of Natural Selection,* New York, Dover.

Goodman, N., 1965. *Fact, Fiction, and Forecast,* Indianapolis, Bobbs Merrill.

Joseph, G., 1979. "Riemannian geometry and philosophical conventionalism," *Australasian Journal of Philosophy,* 57:225–236.

Joseph, G., 1980. "The many sciences and the one world," *Journal of Philosophy,* 77:773–790.

Lewontin, R., 1970. "The units of selection," *Annual Review of Ecology and Systematics,* 1:1–18.

Lewontin, R., 1974. *The Genetic Basis of Evolutionary Change,* New York, Columbia University Press.

Lewontin, R., and Dunn, L., 1960. "The evolutionary dynamics of a polymorphism in the House Mouse," *Genetics,* 45:705–722.

Li, C., 1955. *Population Genetics,* Chicago, University of Chicago Press.

Mayr, E., 1963. *Animal Species and Evolution,* Cambridge (Mass.), Harvard University Press.

Mills, S., and Beatty, J., 1979. "The propensity interpretation of fitness," *Philosophy of Science,* 46:263–286.

Orgel, L., and Crick, F., 1980. "Selfish DNA, the ultimate parasite," *Nature,* 284:604–607.

Reichenbach, H., 1958. *The Philosophy of Space and Time,* New York, Dover.

Shoemaker, S., 1980. "Causality and properties," in *Essays in Honor of Richard Taylor,* ed., P. Van Inwagen, Dordrecht, Reidel.

Sober, E., 1980. "Holism, individualism, and the units of selection," in *PSA 1980,* Vol. 2, ed. P. Asquith and R. Giere, East Lansing, Michigan.

Sober, E., 1981. "Evolutionary theory and the ontological status of properties," *Philosophical Studies,* 40:147-176.

Sober, E., 1982a. "Realism and independence," *Nous,* 16:369-385.

Sober, E., 1982b. "Why logically equivalent predicates may pick out different properties," *American Philosophical Quarterly,* 19:183-189.

Williams, G., 1966. *Adaptation and Natural Selection,* Princeton, Princeton University Press. Chapter 4 is reprinted in part in this volume.

Wimsatt, W., 1980. "Reductionistic research strategies and their biases in the units of selection controversy," in *Scientific Discovery,* Vol. 2, *Case Studies,* ed. T. Nickles, Dordrecht, Reidel. Reprinted in part in this volume.

9

The Levels of Selection

Robert N. Brandon

It is a mistake to suppose that the *units of selection* controversy in biology centers on a single question. In this paper I will take Wimsatt's recent work (1980 and 1981) as defining the question "What are the units of selection?" I will show that there is another important question, what I will call the *levels of selection* question, separable from the first but easily confused with it. Finally, I will try to show why the levels of selection question is important.

First I must make a terminological point. In this paper I will adopt the distinction between fitness and adaptedness. I will not defend the distinction here, since that has been done elsewhere (Brandon, 1978 and 1981), but I will briefly indicate what the distinction is. "Fitness" in this usage refers to actual reproductive success. "Adaptedness" refers to an expected fitness value, in the mathematical sense of expected value.[1] The role of relative adaptedness in evolutionary theory is to explain differential fitness via the principle of natural selection. The distinction is not as simple as the above might indicate; some complications are relevant to the topic at hand, but exploring them goes beyond the scope of this paper.

I am going to distinguish levels of selection from units of selection. This distinction has not been made before, but the seeds of it may be found in Mayr (1963). There he marshaled two arguments against the view that adaptedness can and should be attributed to genes. First, he pointed out that the fitness— that is, reproductive success—of a gene depends as much on the surrounding genes (the genetic environment) as it does on the ecological environment. Thus he argued, "no gene has a fixed selective value, the same gene may confer high fitness on one genetic background and be virtually lethal on another" (1963, pp. 295-296). This he termed the *genetic theory of relativity*. (Also see Mayr, 1954.) Second, he pointed out that "natural selection favors (or discriminates against) phenotypes, not genes or genotypes" (1963, p. 184).

From *PSA 1982,* ed. P. Asquith and T. Nickles, East Lansing, Mich., Philosophy of Science Association (1982), 1:315–322.

One may, as I believe Mayr did, take both points as arguments against attributing adaptedness to genes, but they may also be taken as two distinguishable arguments for two closely related but importantly different conclusions. The first point, the genetic relativity point, addresses the units of selection question; the second, the levels of selection question.

Lewontin (1974) developed Mayr's genetic relativity point in a rigorous and convincing manner. In brief, he argued as follows: In standard cases of organismic selection (i.e., selection among organisms within an interbreeding population), genes do reproduce at different rates, and some alleles increase in frequency relative to others. Thus genes can be assigned fitness values (values which are just summaries of what has happened at the genic level). But because of interactive effects among genes and also gene linkage, these fitness values are mere statistical abstractions; they are of little or no predictive value. Thus, the argument goes, genes are not the units of organismic selection, since they are not the proper units of fitness. The proper unit of organismic selection is, in general, the genome.

Lewontin's work provides the foundation for Wimsatt's definition of units of selection, which is as follows:

A *unit of selection* is any entity for which there is heritable *context-independent* variance in fitness among entities at that level which does not appear as heritable context-independent variance in fitness (and thus, for which the variance in fitness is *context-dependent*) at any lower level of organization. (Wimsatt 1981, p. 144)[2]

So in standard cases of organismic selection where there are epistatic interactions among genes, genes are not the units of selection, because the variance in fitness is not context-independent at the genic level. Thus the units of selection in such cases are some higher-level entities, in the limit, the whole genome.

There is another important point one might make concerning organismic selection, a point corresponding to Mayr's dictum that selection acts directly on phenotypes, not genes or genotypes—that is, that what I have characterized as organismic selection is *in fact* selection at the organismic level. How and why might one argue for this point?

Most biologists would give lip-service to Mayr's dictum, yet many have not taken it seriously. Thus reductionistically inclined biologists will admit that the process I've called organismic selection has as its mechanism the differential reproduction of organisms, but will claim that organismic selection *really* acts directly on genes. Using the Salmon-Reichenbach (Salmon, 1971) notion of *screening off,* we can show that this claim is simply wrong.

The basic idea behind the notion of screening off is this: If *A* renders *B* statistically irrelevant with respect to outcome E but not vice versa, then A is a better causal explainer of E than is B. In symbols, A screens off B from E if and only if:

$$P(E, A \cdot B) = P(E, A) \neq P(E, B)$$

(Read "$P(E, A \cdot B)$" as the probability of E given A and B.) The screening-off relation is an asymmetric relation defined in terms of statistical relevance that is meant to capture causal relevancies. Salmon has argued that causes screen off symptoms from effects. For example, a sudden drop in atmospheric pressure screens off a drop in barometer reading from the occurrence of a storm, since $P(s, a \cdot b) = P(s, a) \neq P(s, b)$. (Where s, and a and b stand for the obvious.) Similarly, he has argued that common causes screen off common effects from one another. And most importantly for present purposes, more immediate causes screen off more remote causes.[3]

When concerned with the differential reproduction of organisms (which is the mechanism of organismic selection), phenotypes screen off genotypes (and so genes as well). That is, $P(n, g \cdot p) = P(n, p) \neq P(n, g)$ (where n stands for "having n offspring," g for "having genotype g," and p for "having phenotype p"). *Gedanken* experiments suffice to establish the relevant equality and inequality. Basically the idea is that tampering with the phenotype without changing the genotype can affect reproductive success (as my castrated cat testifies), while tampering with the genotype without changing the phenotype cannot affect reproductive success.[4] What is true of the relation between phenotype and genotype obviously holds for the relation between phenotype and gene.

I have argued that in episodes of organismic selection, phenotypes screen off both genotypes and genes from the reproductive success of organisms. This, I think, is a precise and systematic way to explicate the principle that organismic selection acts on phenotypes, not directly on genes or genotypes. Importantly, the screening-off relation between phenotype and genotype vis-à-vis organismic reproductive success is asymmetric. This is in spite of the fact that causality is, we may suppose, transitive. Schematically we may say that having genotype g causes phenotype p which causes reproductive success n. But that does not imply that the relation between phenotype and genotype is symmetric; as we have seen, it is not. Thus screening off provides us with the means for answering the question "At what level does the causal machinery of organismic selection really act?"

I have argued that the level of organismic selection is the organismic phenotype. Notice that this conclusion is different from the Lewontin-Wimsatt conclusion that the unit of organismic selection is, in general, the genome. To show that two arguments are different, it should suffice to show that they have different conclusions; but to be safe let me point out that the premises of the two arguments are different as well. The Lewontin-Wimsatt argument depends on certain genetic facts, most important among them that epistatic interactions do occur (epistasis) and that not all genes segregate independently (gene linkage). If the facts were different, their conclusion would be different. If the "bean-bag" picture of genetics were true—that is, if genes segregated independently and if the one-gene-one-trait hypothesis were true (and further if there were no interactive effects among traits at the phenotypic level), then genes would be the units of organismic selection. In Wimsatt's terms the variance in fitness at the genic level would be context-independent. None of those facts is relevant to my screening-off argument. Let the "bean-bag" picture be true; phenotypes would still screen off genotypes from the reproductive success of organisms, and so selection would still be the level of the organismic phenotype.

Have I argued that all selection must be at the level of the organismic phenotype? No. Selection may occur at many levels. Shortly I will offer a general definition of levels of selection, but first let us consider selection at the group level.

Natural selection is the differential reproduction of biological entities which is *due to* the differential adaptedness of those entities to a common environment (Brandon, 1978, 1981). Group selection, then, is the differential reproduction of biological groups which is due to the differential adaptedness of those groups to a common environment. Thus a necessary condition for the occurrence of group selection is that there be differential reproduction (propagation) among groups. But this necessary condition is not sufficient. For the differential reproduction of groups to be group selection—that is, selection at the group level[5]—there must be some group property (which, abstractly characterized, is the group adaptedness) that screens off all other properties from group reproductive success.

It is by no means necessary that such a property exist. For instance, if the fitness of a group is simply a linear function of the sum of the fitness values of its members, then group "adaptedness" does not screen off all nongroup properties from group reproductive success.[6] In particular it does not screen off the aggregate of the individuals' adaptedness values. The probability of such a group producing n propagule groups, given the "adaptedness" value of the group and the adaptedness values of each of the members of the group, does equal the probability of the group producing n propagules given just the adaptedness value of the group. In symbols, $P(n, A_G \cdot [a_1 \cdot a_2 \cdot \ldots \cdot a_k]) = P(n, A_G)$ (where A_G is the adaptedness value of the group and a_i is the adaptedness value of the ith member of the group). However, it is not the case that

$P(n, A_G) \neq P(n, a_1 \cdot a_2 \cdot \ldots \cdot a_k)$. Thus the group adaptedness does not screen off the aggregate of the group members' adaptedness values.

Notice that the aggregate doesn't screen off the group adaptedness value either; the relation between the two is symmetric. That symmetry relative to group reproductive success gives sense to the claim that the group "adaptedness" value is "nothing more than" the aggregate of the individual adaptedness values.[7]

In summary, group selection occurs if and only if: (1) There is differential reproduction of groups; and (2) Group adaptedness values screen off all other properties (of entities at any level) from group reproductive success (see note 8 for qualification). One way to restate clause (2) is this: Differential group reproduction is *best* explained in terms of group-level properties (in terms of differential group adaptedness to a common environment). Still another way to restate (2), a way that would have appeared question-begging prior to what has been said concerning screening off, is this: The causal process of selection acts directly on groups.

What has been said about group selection is easily generalizable into the following definition:

Selection occurs at a given level if and only if:

(1) There is differential reproduction among the entities at that level; and

(2) The adaptedness values of these entities screen off the adaptedness values of entities at every other level from reproductive values at the given level.[8]

Let us return to the case mentioned above where there was differential group reproduction but no group selection. Recall that the group "adaptedness" values did not screen off the aggregate of the individual adaptedness values from group reproductive success. Thus, according to our definition, the case was not a case of group selection. But also recall that the individual adaptedness values did not screen off the group adaptedness values from group reproductive success. Should one conclude from this that selection is not occurring at the individual (organismic) level either? No. That individual adaptedness values do not screen off group adaptedness values from *group* reproductive success does not entail that individual values do not screen off group values from *individual* (organismic) reproductive success. The latter is what is required by our definition if selection is to be at the level of the individual organism.

I should also point out that our definition allows, as it should, selection to act simultaneously at various levels. For example, in the well known case of the *t*-allele in the house mouse *Mus musculus* (see Lewontin and Dunn, 1960) selection acts at three levels. I will not discuss this case in detail because

Sober (1981) has recently done so. But briefly, in this case there is differential reproduction at three levels: the chromosomal, the organismic, and the group. In the formation of sex cells, chromosomes containing the *t*-allele are disproportionately produced relative to their homologous competitors lacking the *t*-allele. At this level a chromosomal property screens off all others from the differential reproduction of this pair of chromosomes. At the organismic level males homozygous for the *t*-allele are sterile. This organismic property, sterility (organismic adaptedness of 0), screens off all others from this lack of organismic reproductive success. Finally, at the group level, groups whose males are all homozygous for the *t*-allele become extinct. This is not analogous to the case of differential group reproduction that was not group selection, since here group reproductive success cannot be satisfactorily explained in terms of the aggregate of the group members' adaptedness values. That would be the case if we were dealing with groups all of whose members were sterile. But here only the males are sterile. That fact explains the group extinction only when conjoined with other facts about the group structure, such as females mating only with males from their own group. In sum, according to the screening-off criterion the above example is indeed one where selection occurs at three distinct levels. (I should at least mention that cases of simultaneous multilevel selection raise complications for the notion of adaptedness. But dealing with these complications will have to await another paper.)

I have shown that my definition of levels of selection is not equivalent to Wimsatt's definition of units of selection. In cases of organismic selection— that is, selection at the level of the organismic phenotype—the units are genomes, gene-complexes, or even genes, depending on the amount of epistasis and gene linkage. Yet it is curious that at many other levels of selection, e.g., chromosomal, kin-group, and group, the units and levels analyses agree.[9] (I must leave it to the reader to confirm this assertion for himself.)

Why is this? Some units, e.g., groups, interact directly with their environment. Differential reproduction of these entities is best explained in terms of differences in their (direct) interactions with the environment. Other units, e.g., genes or even whole genomes, interact with their environment mediately through their phenotypes. The screening-off argument shows that their differential reproduction is best explained in terms of properties of their mediating phenotypes. For directly interacting units, the units and levels analyses agree. For mediately interacting units the two analyses disagree, with the level of selection being the level of the mediator.[10] I am not convinced that this answer is wholly satisfactory. I am convinced it is headed in the right direction.

At the beginning of this paper I said that there are at least two important questions that have heretofore been conflated by people working on what has been called the units of selection problem. I have offered a bipartite defense of this claim: (1) I have given a definition of levels of selection and have shown that it is not equivalent to what is the best extant definition of units of selection; and (2) I have tried to motivate the levels of selection question.

Basically I have argued that if one is concerned with explaining the causal process of natural selection, then one is interested in the levels of selection question. Put differently, if one is concerned with the question "At what level(s) does the causal machinery of natural selection really act?", one is concerned with levels of selection. The above question is fairly described as an ontological question. We reify the things that we decide are *really* acted on by selection. For example, genes have been, mistakenly I believe, reified so that selfishness is attributed to them. The question is of obvious philosophical as well as biological interest.

My argument that there are two important questions in this area has an obvious gap. I have not explained why the units of selection question is important. I have pointed out that some of the considerations that have previously been used to motivate that question properly apply only to the analysis of levels of selection. It remains for others to motivate the units of selection question.

Notes

1 This point is also made by Mills and Beatty (1979), but they stick with the term "fitness."

2 The terminology used here is potentially misleading. To say that variance in fitness is context-independent is not to say that the actual fitness values are not dependent on the actual context—i.e., environment. Obviously fitness values are context-dependent in that sense. But the actual *variance* in fitness may or may not be attributable to differences between entities in a given environment. That part of the variance that can be so accounted for is context-independent variance. Sober (1981, expecially note 7) fell victim to this confusion. The reason context-independent variance is important is that only the context-independent variance is heritable. For a discussion of the same point in different terms, see Brandon (1981).

3 Although the first two claims are debatable, I know of no plausible counterexample to the claim that more immediate causes screen off more remote causes from their effects.

4 The latter claim is controversial. One might argue, as David Hull and an anonymous referee have suggested, that it is possible to tamper with the sex cells, e.g., by irradiation, and affect reproductive success without changing the phenotype. I view this as a conceptual question and would take my claim as a fixed point in drawing the phenotype-genotype and levels of selection distinctions.

5 Henceforth, when I speak of group selection I will mean only selection at the group level; likewise for chromosomal selection, organismic selection, kin-group selection, etc.

6 Here adaptedness values are attributed to groups only tentatively, while the hypothesis of group selection is still alive. See Sober (1981) for discussion of an example of differential group reproduction that is not group selection.

7 Salmon's notion of screening off has been used before in the literature on the units of selection. In discussing a case relevantly similar to the above, Wimsatt (1980, 1981) claimed that the group-adaptedness value is screened off by the individual values. This, as we have seen, is not the case, since the relevant inequality does not hold.

8 A stronger, I think unnecessarily stronger, version of (2) reads as follows: (2) The adaptedness values of these entities screen off all other properties of entities at any level from the reproduction values at the given level. I have eschewed this stronger clause because in this paper I cannot demarcate legitimate properties from the potentially problematic crazy pseudo-properties philosophers are fond of dreaming up.

9 I will not discuss Sober's (1981) definition of group selection. Wimsatt (1981) argues that when suitably generalized, Sober's definition is equivalent to his definition of units of selection. I think that Wimsatt is wrong and that Sober's aim is closer to mine, but I am not sure of this.

10 In Hull's (1980) terminology, the units and levels analyses agree if and only if the units are *interactors*.

References

Asquith, P. D. and Giere, R. N., eds. (1981). *PSA 1980*, Vol. 2, East Lansing Michigan, Philosophy of Science Association.

Brandon, R. N. (1978). "Adaptation and evolutionary theory," *Studies in History and Philosophy of Science*, 9:181–206.

———. (1981). "A structural description of evolutionary theory," in Asquith and Giere (1981), pp. 427–439.

Hull, D. (1980). "Individuality and selection," *Annual Review of Ecology and Systematics*, 11:311–332.

Lewontin, R. C. (1974). *The Genetic Basis of Evolutionary Change*, New York, Columbia University Press.

——— and Dunn, R. (1960). "The evolutionary dynamics of a polymorphism in the House Mouse," *Genetics*, 45:705–722.

Mayr, E. (1954). "Change of genetic environment and evolution," in *Evolution as a Process*, ed. J. Huxley, et al., London, Allen and Unwin, pp. 157–180.

———. (1963). *Animal Species and Evolution*, Cambridge (Mass.), Harvard University Press.

Mills, S. and Beatty, J. (1979). "The propensity interpretation of fitness," *Philosophy of Science*, 46:263–286.

Salmon, W. C. (1971). *Statistical Explanation and Statistical Relevance*, Pittsburgh, University of Pittsburgh Press.

Sober, E. (1981). "Holism, individualism and the units of selection," in Asquith and Giere (1981), pp. 93–121.

Wimsatt, W. C. (1980). "Reductionistic research strategies and their biases in the units of selection controversy," in *Scientific Discovery, Volume II, Historical and Scientific Case Studies,* ed. Thomas Nickles, Dordrecht, Reidel, pp. 213–259. Reprinted in part in this volume.

———. (1981). "The units of selection and the structure of the multi-level genome," in Asquith and Giere (1981), pp. 122–183.

10

Units of Evolution: A Metaphysical Essay

David Hull

One of the most persistent and frustrating controversies in biology concerns the level (or levels) at which selection can take place. Richard Dawkins (1976, 1978) has presented the most parsimonious view. According to him, genes are the primary focus of selection. In asexual reproduction, the entire genome might be the unit of selection. In cases in which no crossover occurs between homologous chromosomes, entire chromosomes might function as units of selection. But sexually reproducing organisms and anything that might be considered a group can never function as units of selection. In the vast majority of cases, genes are selected and everything else goes along for the ride.

The current majority view is that genes mutate, organisms are selected, and species evolve (Ayala, 1978; Mayr, 1963, 1978). Any changes in higher taxa are merely consequences of changes occurring at the species level or lower. Because genes are parts of organisms, they are selected but only indirectly by means of the selection of entire organisms. Finally, some authors argue that under special circumstances entities more inclusive than organisms can be selected, entities such as kinship groups, populations, and species. Because these higher-level entities have been thought of traditionally as groups, the advocates of this position have been termed "group selectionists," in one sense of this term (Eldredge and Gould, 1972; Gould and Eldredge, 1977; Stanley, 1975; Van Valen, 1975; see Sepkoski, 1978, p. 224, for additional references).[1]

The empirical issues involved in this controversy, as complex and indecisive as they may be, have at least been dealt with at some length (Lewontin, 1970; Sepkoski, 1978; Wade, 1978). However, another sort of problem has plagued

From U. L. Jensen and R. Harré, eds., *The Philosophy of Evolution*, Brighton: Harvester Press (1981), pp. 23–44. Numerous people have read early versions of this and related papers. I wish to express special thanks to J. Cracraft, R. Dawkins, S. Gould, S. Kimbrough, E. Reed, M. Ridley, S. Salthe, E. Sober, E. Wiley, and W. Wimsatt. The research was supported in part by N.S.F. grant Soc 75-035-35.

the group-selection controversy and has been addressed, if at all, only indirectly. It is so fundamental that it deserves to be called "metaphysical." The close connection between metaphysics and the controversy over levels of selection can be seen in the arguments provided by advocates of the two extreme positions. Given our relative size and perceptual acuity, organisms and species appear to be very different sorts of things. Organisms seem to be paradigm individuals, so much so that biologists tend to use the terms "organism" and "individual" interchangeably. Populations and species, to the contrary, give every appearance of being groups. Advocates of organism selection argue that our perceptions are veridical. The first thing that gene and species selectionists contend is that regardless of how they might seem, organisms and species are really the same sort of thing. However, they disagree about the sort. For example, Dawkins (1976, p. 36) is forced to argue that, regardless of how they might appear from the human perspective, from the evolutionary point of view organisms are not stable, coherent individuals. Instead they are actually as amorphous and ephemeral as populations and species:

In sexually reproducing species, the individual is too large and too temporary a genetic unit to qualify as a significant unit of natural selection. The group of individuals is an even larger unit. Genetically speaking, individuals and groups are like clouds in the sky or duststorms in the desert. They are temporary aggregations or federations.

Eldredge and Gould agree that appearances are deceiving, but the illusion is just the opposite to that claimed by Dawkins. Regardless of how they might appear from the human perspective, from the evolutionary point of view, populations and species are not groups. Instead they are as much unified and cohesive wholes as are organisms. For example, in response to a variety of questions about the nature of biological species, Eldredge and Gould (1972, p. 114) conclude:

The answer probably lies in a view of species and individuals as homeostatic systems—as amazingly well-buffered to resist change and maintain stability in the face of disturbing influences. ... If we view a species as a set of subpopulations, all ready and able to differentiate but held in check only by the rein of gene flow, then the stability of species is a tenuous thing indeed. But if that stability is an inherent property both of individual development and the genetic structure of populations, then its power is immeasurably enhanced, for the basic property of homeostatic systems, or steady states, is that they resist change of self-regulation.

The initial reaction to being told that organisms are temporary federations or that species are homeostatic systems is likely to be, "But that doesn't sound right." Many of the things that scientists say when they are reworking the foundations of their discipline sound peculiar, as peculiar as subatomic particles being able to move from one place to another without traversing the distance between, or space being curved, but that cannot be helped. Inherent in the scientific enterprise is the need to go beyond ordinary usage and common conceptions. Given our relative size and duration, we can see the distance between organisms, their diversity and gradual replacement. However, the cells that comprise an organism are just as diverse and even more rapidly replaced. If we were the size of atoms, organisms would look like clouds of atoms, comprised mainly of empty space. If we were the size of planets, species would take on the appearance of giant amoebae, expanding and contracting over the face of the earth (Williams, 1980). Questions such as these cannot be decided by common conceptions. Instead, whether organisms and species are the same or different sorts of things must be decided in the context of the interplay between current scientific theories and empirical phenomena.

One reason that the controversy over the levels at which selection takes place has remained so intractable is that some of the issues are basically metaphysical: what sorts of things are organisms in contrast to groups, what general characteristics must an entity have to be selected, can entities which have what it takes to be selected also evolve or are the requisite characteristics mutually exclusive, etc.? Biologists discuss these issues but only indirectly and sporadically. In this paper I attempt to set out explicitly and in detail a metaphysics that is adequate to handle evolutionary phenomena. Secondly, the phrase "unit of selection" is inherently ambiguous. Sometimes it means those entities which differentially replicate themselves, sometimes those which interact with their environments in ways that are responsible for this replication being differential. Both processes are *necessary* for evolution by natural selection to occur. In most cases, entities at *different* levels of organization perform these two functions. In this paper I consistently differentiate between these two functions and the entities that perform them, set out the general characteristics these entities have, and show which problems can be dissolved by making the necessary distinctions. I also distinguish between these two processes—replication and interaction—and a third process they produce—evolution. I argue that the entities that function in all three processes are the best sort of thing—individuals. Groups play no role whatsoever in the evolutionary process. However, many things commonly treated as groups or even classes are actually "individuals" in the generic sense of this term.

Individuals, Classes, and Lineages

The metaphysical categories I use in this paper to discuss the evolutionary process are *individual, class,* and *lineage.* I place no special weight on these particular terms. Dozens of others would do as well. I have settled on "individual" and "class" because these terms are used by Ghiselin (1966, 1969, 1974) in his initial discussion of these issues, and "lineage" seems to be standard usage in this connection. Terminology to one side, the conceptual distinctions are important. By "individual" I mean any spatiotemporally localized entity that develops continuously through time, exhibits internal cohesiveness at any one time, and is reasonably discrete in both space and time. Individuals are historical entities, individuated in terms of their insertion into history (Hull, 1975). Although they can be in principle absolutely simple, in most cases they themselves are composed of other individuals. Thus most individuals are "complex particulars" (Suppe, 1974).

The term "class" is used by philosophers, scientists, and the general public in a wide variety of ways. When I use it in this paper, I intend to refer to things that can have members, regardless of how this membership is determined, just so long as it is *not* determined in ways that limit it in advance to a finite number of entities or to a particular spatiotemporal location. As I am using these terms, Mars is an individual while planet is a class. Mars is a spatiotemporally localized individual. Planets are the class of all relatively large, nonluminous bodies revolving around stars. At any one time there may be no planets or a finite number of planets. If the universe exists for a finite duration, the total number of planets *sub specie aeternitatis* is also finite. However, "planets" still refers to a class because any entity, anywhere and at any time, that has the requisite characteristics would count as a planet.

All sorts of ways exist for defining classes, fixing referents, etc. I couch my exposition in terms of spatiotemporally unrestricted classes because of the role traditionally played by classes in laws of nature. Classes are a dime a dozen, but the only classes that concern scientists are those which function in scientific laws, that is, natural kinds. On the traditional definition, scientific laws are generalizations (preferably universal in form) that are spatiotemporally unrestricted. The claim that the earth is the third planet out from the sun is true and important, but it cannot count as a law of nature because it refers to particular individuals. The law of universal gravitation is at least a candidate for a genuine law of nature because it refers to any entities that happen to have the appropriate characteristics. Generalizations are also a dime a dozen, but the only generalizations of interest to scientists are those that hold some claim to being laws of nature. Hence, as I am using these terms, "natural kind" and "law" are interdefined.

Because the connections between individuals, classes, and laws are so central to my exposition, they must be spelled out in greater detail and possible misunderstandings avoided. The distinction between genuine laws of nature and other generalizations that just happen to be true is as central to our understanding of science as it is problematic. Although numerous marks of genuine laws of nature have been proposed, no analysis has as yet proved to be totally satisfying (see, for example, Smart, 1963, 1968). But the intuition remains strong that not all generalizations that turn out to be true are equally important in our understanding of the empirical world. A similar felt difference exists for classes in general and genuine natural kinds. Difficulties in presenting a completely adequate analysis of this felt difference are equally infamous. I happen to think that the source of our intuitions about laws and natural kinds is the same source. The fact that (nearly) all organisms here on earth use the same genetic code is important, but it is not a law of nature. It results from the fact that life most likely had a single origin here on earth. To put the point in just the opposite way, since all organisms here on earth use the same genetic code and we know of no lawful reason for the universality of the genetic code, we conclude that all organisms are descended from common ancestors who first developed the code.

The crucial factor is the relative primacy of similarity and descent. If similarity takes priority over descent, then the entity is a class and at least a candidate for inclusion in a scientific law. For example, all particular samples of gold may have developed originally from hydrogen, but that genesis is irrelevant on current physical theory to something being gold. Gold is a genuine class, a natural kind. If descent takes priority to similarity, then the entity is not a class and hence reference to it must be excluded from any genuine laws of nature. For example, there may be a star somewhere else in the universe with exactly the same characteristics as the sun, save spatiotemporal location. Yet, on no account would this star count as the sun. Hence, "Sol" refers not to a class but to an individual, an historical entity. Statements about Sol may well be true, important in science, etc. They are not, however, laws of nature.[2]

The final metaphysical category that I need to introduce is a *lineage*. Certain individuals come into existence, persist for a while, and then cease to exist. They may consist of other individuals as parts, but these individuals do not "give rise" to one another. For example, a fleet of ships might be considered an individual. Ships enter the fleet and leave it, but ships typically do not give rise to other ships. However, some individuals form *lineages,* spatiotemporal sequences of entities that causally produce one another. Entities in the sequence are in some sense "descended" from those earlier in the sequence. Terms like "descent," "ancestor," and "successor" are used in a variety of ways in a variety of contexts. For example, in mathematics 6 is the successor of 5. That does not mean that cardinal numbers form a "lineage" or that 6 is "descended" from 5 in the sense relevant to the operation of selection processes.

That we conceptualize lineages as individuals and not classes can be seen by the decisions we make when similarity and descent do not universally covary. Usually entities related by descent are similar to one another. A is similar to B because A gave rise to B. However, they need not be similar, and even when they are not, they remain part of the same lineage. Human family trees are paradigm examples of lineages. Any baby produced by the union of two parents belongs to their lineage regardless of how peculiar, abnormal, or dissimilar this baby might be. Conversely, no matter how similar a person might be to the people in a particular lineage, that person cannot belong to that lineage in the absence of the appropriate descent relations.

Lineages differ from other individuals in a second way. Not only are they made up of individuals that tend to be similar to one another because they are related by descent, but also they are capable of indefinite amounts of change. Most individuals have relatively discrete beginnings and endings in time and are capable of only a finite amount of change in the interim. As much as an organism can change during the course of its ontogenetic development, that development is circumscribed and to some extent programmed by its genetic makeup. However, organisms form lineages that are capable of indefinite change. Whether these lineages are coextensive with species is another matter.

In sum, individuals are spatiotemporally localized, internally cohesive entities that develop continuously through time. Usually an individual exists for a finite time and has an upper limit to how much it can change without becoming numerically a new individual. Lineages are those individuals composed of entities that serially give rise to one another in ancestor-descendant sequences. As such, lineages can continue to change indefinitely through time. Classes are the sorts of things that have members, not parts. Classes can be defined in a wide variety of ways. However, classes that function in spatiotemporally unrestricted laws must themselves be spatiotemporally unrestricted. From a purely philosophical point of view, the distinction between classes that function in genuine scientific laws and those that do not might seem extraneous. From the point of view of philosophy of science, it is not. Scientists are not interested in all classes or all individuals. One of their chief goals is to discover ways to divide up the world into classes that function in natural regularities. Similarly, the only individuals that are scientifically important are those that are acted upon by natural processes. (For further discussion, see Wiley, 1980.)

Replicators, Interactors, and Lineages

Dawkins' work on evolutionary theory has elicited comment primarily because of his heavy emphasis on selection at the level of particular genes. He has taken the arguments which organism selectionists have used against group selection and turned them on the organism selectionists themselves. Although

I find a certain poetic justice in this maneuver, I think Dawkins' work is worth commenting on for quite a different reason. Although he is likely to be shocked, if not offended, at being told so, Dawkins (1976, 1978) has made an important contribution to the metaphysics of evolution in his explication of "replicators." Like Monsieur Jourdain, who was astonished to discover that he had been speaking prose all his life, Dawkins may well be surprised to discover that he has committed an act of metaphysics. Dawkins' discussion has two important virtues: in it he provides a general analysis of replicators and leaves as a separate issue the question which entities in the empirical world happen to have the requisite characteristics. He happens to think that in most instances only single genes possess these characteristics, but nothing in his general analysis precludes other, more inclusive entities from also functioning as replicators. However, Dawkins' analysis has one vice. In it he tends to run two quite distinct functions together into one: replication and the interaction of entities with their environments. In this section, I set out Dawkins' general analysis of replicators, distinguish between replication and interaction, and introduce a term of my own, "interactor."

Dawkins interrupts his analysis of replicators to ask:

Why "replicator selection" rather than "gene selection"? One reason for preferring replicator selection is that the phrase automatically preadapts our language to cope with non-DNA-based forms of evolution such as may be encountered on other planets, and perhaps also cultural analogues of evolution. ... The term replicator should be understood to *include* genetic replicators, but not to exclude any entity in the universe which qualifies under the criteria listed (Dawkins, 1978, p. 68).

By using the flexible word *replicator,* we can safely say that adaptation is for the good of the replicator, and leave it open exactly how large a chunk of genetic material we are talking about. One thing we can be sure of is that, except in special circumstances like asexual reproduction, the *individual organism* is not a replicator (Dawkins, 1978, p. 69).

According to Dawkins (1978, p. 68), the qualities of a good replicator may be summed up in a slogan reminiscent of the French Revolution: Longevity, Fecundity, Fidelity. As striking as this slogan is, it can easily be misunderstood. The fidelity which Dawkins is talking about is copying-fidelity, and the relevant longevity is longevity-in-the-form-of-copies (Dawkins, 1976, pp. 19, 30). Neither material identity nor extensive material overlap is necessary for copying-fidelity. The genetic material is reduced by half at each replication until a descendant gene may contain little if any of the matter that had been part of the physical makeup of a distant ancestor. What counts in replication is the retention of *structure.* When we are told that an organism receives half its genes from each of its parents, on an average a quarter from each of its grandparents, etc., genes are being individuated on the basis of substance, not structure. In most formulations of the problems posed by the cost of meiosis, once again genes are treated as material bodies. But what really matters in selection processes is, as Dawkins points out, *retention of structure through descent* (see also Cassidy, 1978). Two atoms of gold can be structurally identical to each other without one being a replicate of the other or both being replicates of some other atom. Descent is missing. Conversely, a complex organic molecule can be broken down into smaller molecules by rupturing its quarternary bonds, and these molecules broken into even smaller molecules, etc., but the resulting molecules would not form replicates because retention of structure is missing.

For selection to take place, spatiotemporal sequences of replicates are necessary. Similar entities alone won't do; neither will spatiotemporal sequences of entities alone. Dawkins' exposition is couched, however, not in terms of *similarity* of structure, but in terms of *identity* of structure. Although nothing much rides on the decision, I find requiring structural identity too strong. For example, physicists consider two atoms to be atoms of the same element even if they are not structurally identical. Isotopes are allowed. Similarly, biochemists consider cytochrome *c* to be a single protein even though extensive variation in its composition is common. Such examples could be multiplied indefinitely.

Even though Dawkins requires structural identity for replicators, he allows for considerable variation in the amount of genetic material which can count as a single replicator. Following G. C. Williams (1966, 1975), Dawkins (1976, p. 30) defines a gene as "any portion of the chromosomal material which potentially lasts for enough generations to serve as a unit of natural selection." The structure of the genetic material can be altered chiefly in two ways—mutation and crossover. "Now comes the important point. The shorter the genetic unit is, the longer—in generations—it is likely to live. In particular, the less likely it is to be split by any one crossover." Thus Dawkins' definition of a gene as a replicator is "not a rigid all-or-nothing definition, but a kind of fading-out definition, like the definition of 'big' or 'old'" (Dawkins, 1976, p. 34).[3]

One might be tempted to suggest to Dawkins that he make his notion of a replicator more widely applicable by adding a second dimension of fading out—degree of structural similarity. In general, the modification of a single amino acid rarely makes a molecule a new molecule, any more than the few corrections that Darwin made in the second edition of his *Origin of Species* made it a new book. Ideally, on Dawkins' view, the ultimate replicator is the single nucleotide. It is so small that it is never subdivided by crossover. It is also so small that it lacks an equally important characteristic of replicators—

a pattern worth preserving. A replicator must be small enough to retain its structural pattern through numerous replications, yet large enough to have a structural pattern worth preserving. Dawkins' analysis of genes as replicators already includes one gradually changing variable. A second wouldn't hurt. In line with Williams' definition of the gene, one might say that two genes are similar enough to count as the same replicator if they react similarly to similar selection pressures.

Replication by itself is sufficient for evolution of sorts, but not evolution through natural selection. In addition, certain entities must interact causally with their environment in such a way as to bias their distribution in later generations. Originally, as life evolved on this planet, the same entities may have performed both of these functions simultaneously, but the characteristics of a good replicator are sufficiently different from those of a good interactor that eventually these functions began to be performed by different entities at different levels of organization. However, in one place Dawkins (1978, p. 67) attributes both functions to one and the same entity—the replicator:

We may define a *replicator* as any entity in the universe which interacts with its world, including other replicators, in such a way that copies of itself are made. A corollary of the definition is that at least some of these copies, in their turn, serve as replicators, so that a replicator is, at least potentially, an ancestor of an indefinitely long line of identical descendant replicators. In practice no replication process is infallible, and defects in a replicator will tend to be passed on to descendants. If a replicator exerts some power over the world, such that its nature influences the survival of itself and its copies, natural selection, and hence progressive evolution, may occur through differential survival.

In this quotation, Dawkins is running two powers together—the power to reproduce one's structure and the power to do so differentially. These powers are sufficiently different to be distinguished terminologically. As Mayr (1978, p. 52) emphasizes, evolution through natural selection is a two-step process, "(I repeat!), a two-step process." Thus I think Dawkins' general analysis of replicators needs supplementing with a general analysis of the entities that function in this second step. For want of a better term, I suggest "interactor":

replicators—entities that pass on their structure directly in replication;

interactors—entities that produce differential replication by means of directly interacting as cohesive wholes with their environments.

A pervasive ambiguity in the literature on levels of selection can be eliminated by consistently distinguishing between replication and interaction. When gene selectionists like Dawkins argue that genes are *the* unit of selection, they mean to claim at very least that genes are the only entities capable of replication. When organism selectionists like Mayr argue that organisms are *the* unit of selection, they mean to claim at very least that organisms are an important focus of interaction with the environment. Genes, of course, can also function as interactors. They interact directly with their cellular environment, but they interact only indirectly with more inclusive environments via the interactors of which they are part. The point at issue is whether entities more inclusive than single genes or possibly entire genomes can function as replicators.

Both replicators and interactors exhibit structure; the difference between them concerns the directness of transmission. Genes pass on their structure in about as direct a fashion as can occur in the material world. But entities more inclusive than genes possess structure and can pass it on largely intact. For example, one paramecium can divide into two, each new individual possessing the same structure as the original. In such cases, Dawkins would say that the entire genome is functioning as a replicator because its structure remains intact in the process. The justification I am suggesting concerns the structure of the organism itself. But a quite similar situation can occur in sexual reproduction. When two organisms mate which are genetically homozygous and quite similar to each other, the resulting offspring are likely to be equally similar, regardless of how much recombination occurs. Once again, Dawkins would say the genomes are functioning as replicators, while I would argue that the organisms themselves might be viewed as replicators, the only difference being in how direct the mechanism of replication happens to be. We part company most noticeably in cases of sexual reproduction between genetically heterogeneous organisms. Dawkins would argue that only those segments of the genetic material that remained undisturbed can count as replicators, while I see no reason not to consider the organisms themselves replicators if the parents and offspring are sufficiently similar to each other.

Genes tend to be the entities that pass on their structure most directly, while they interact with ever more global environments with decreasing directness. Other, more inclusive entities interact directly with their environments but tend to pass on their structure, if at all, more and more indirectly. *Both* processes must be performed successfully if evolution by natural selection is to take place. Reasons for choosing one necessary element over the other as *the* unit of selection are hard to come by. The best I can do is the following. Everyone agrees that both genes and organisms are individuals, and that genes form lineages by replication. Any change in a gene is reflected immediately and directly in successive replicates of that gene. Because the sort of inheritance attributed (inappropriately) to Lamarck does not occur, changes in the phenotype cannot be transmitted directly to the genetic material to be passed on to future generations. Instead, the only influence that changes in the phenotype exert is on which organisms succeed in reproducing themselves and which not. Genes causally produce other genes. They also enter into causal production of organisms. But the only thing that organisms can do is influence quite indirectly the statistical distribution of genes in future gene pools. In passing from the action of genes to the action of organisms, we proceed from definite gene lineages to amorphous gene pools, from causal connections to relative frequencies. As persuasive as these considerations may (or may not) be, they depend on viewing species as classes rather than as lineages, an interpretation which biologists are beginning to question in increasing numbers.[4] However, before discussing this highly controversial issue, two minor points need mentioning.

Dawkins hopes to reason analogically from selection of genes in biological evolution to the selection of memes in cultural evolution. If both genes and memes are to function as replicators, then Dawkins is going to have to make his notion of a replicator a good deal more general. The structure of memes, like the structure of genes, is what counts, but memetic structure is hardly transmitted directly the way that genetic structure is. Dawkins (1976, p. 206) says that "memes propagate themselves in the meme pool by leaping from brain to brain via a process which, in the broad sense, can be called imitation." Maybe so, if mind-reading were a prevalent mode of human communication, but as things stand, we must resort to some sort of system of symbols. I express my thoughts in words which, if I am lucky, may lead you to have similar, possibly identical, thoughts. However, the causal transmission of memes in culture is easily as indirect as the causal transmission of the structure of organisms in biological evolution. Either memes cannot function as replicators, or else the notion of a replicator must be expanded somewhat. I prefer the second alternative (Hull, 1981).

Finally, even if Dawkins' general analysis of replicators is accepted, his blanket rejection of sexually reproducing organisms as replicators does not apply as totally as he thinks. If biologists like Mayr (1963), Carson (1970), and Eldredge and Gould (1972, 1977) are right, speciation among sexually reproducing organisms usually occurs when a very few organisms become isolated from the main body of their species. The effects of such a rapid reduction in population size are numerous and fundamental. For example, in most populations several different alleles exist at most loci. One pregnant female, to mention the most extreme case, is unlikely to express much of the genetic heterogeneity of her population in her offspring. The ensuing inbreeding characteristic of such small populations is likely to increase homozygosity even further. It may well be true that the genomes of sexually reproducing organisms are "torn to smithereens" at meiosis in large, genetically heterogeneous populations, but according to the model of speciation by "genetic revolutions" currently so popular, all that is going on in such large populations is the haphazard fluctuation of allele frequencies. When it really matters, when new species are arising, sexually reproducing organisms converge on functioning as replicators.

Groups as Individuals

Another instance of the relevance of metaphysical considerations in the controversy over levels of selection is the claim made by advocates of group selection that species are not "groups" but individuals, possibly homeostatic systems. In the preceding section I distinguished between replicators and interactors. Although they differ in several important respects, replicators and interactors are both individuals. Hence, anyone who wishes to argue that species can function as units of selection, in either of these two senses, must first argue that they are individuals. Although homeostatic systems are not the only sort of individual that can function as replicators or as interactors, they are paradigm examples of such systems and as such warrant some discussion. In particular, the similarities and differences between homeostatic systems and selection processes need to be pointed out.

Homeostatic systems consist in a larger system and smaller included subsystem, usually thought of as a regulating device. The two systems differ both with respect to relative size and with respect to rapidity and magnitude of action. Relative to the total system, the changes that occur in the subsystem are minor and rapid and require only a minimal expenditure of energy. They, in turn, produce more massive, ponderous changes in the system at large. One of the minor effect of these latter changes is to alter the smaller included system, and so on. The causal feedback loop between the two systems involves minimal energy flow. Most of the energy expended in the system is used in the functioning of the larger system.

In homeostatic systems, the feedback loops are so organized that one or more parameters of the larger system are kept within certain limits in the face of considerable (though not unlimited) changes in its environment. One variation on this theme is a system that undergoes progressive, programmed change. Instead of the system being maintained in roughly the same state, it is changed with each action of the feedback loop to a partially predetermined new state, a type of system termed "homeorhetic" by Waddington (1957). Organisms as they function at any one time are good examples of homeostatic systems. As the temperature external to poikilothermal organisms varies, the temperature of the organism as a whole begins to vary, activating processes that counteract the effects of the environment. Organisms as they undergo ontogenetic development are just as good examples of the progressive variant. The interplay between an organism's environment, its genetic constitution, and the developing organism produces a series of changes in the state of the organism. Although the genetic constitution of an organism does not rigidly program its development, it constrains it somewhat, sometimes quite narrowly.

This same cybernetic model has been used to characterize selection process. For example, C. J. Bajema (1971, p. 2) says:

Natural selection, when viewed from the perspective of cybernetics (see diagram), is the feedback mechanism which favors the production of DNA codes —"programs"—which enables the species to adapt to the environment. It is via natural selection that information about the environment is transmitted to the gene pool of a population. This is accomplished by differential reproduction of different genotypes changing the frequency of genes in populations.

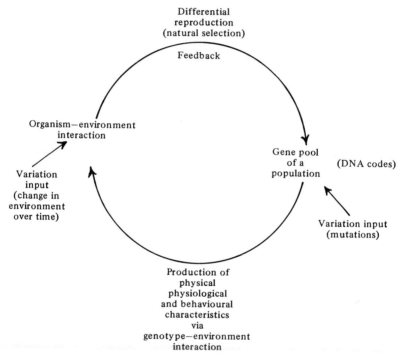

Figure 1. A cybernetic model of selection, after Bajema (1971).

In the diagram referred to by Bajema (see Figure 1), changes in both the genetic makeup of the organisms involved and in the environment affect the organism-environment interaction, resulting in differential reproduction, which in turn changes the gene pool in the next generation. These changes, along with additional mutations and environmental variation, further modify the organism-environment interaction, and so on around the circular diagram. As described, the operation of natural selection does appear to be quite similar to the functioning of a homeostatic (or homeorhetic) system. However, if the highest-level system recognized in biological evolution is the organism, then appearances are deceiving, because no feedback loops are actually becoming established. In both homeostatic and homeorhetic systems, changes in the smaller subsystem produce changes in the larger system, which in turn produce changes in the *original* subsystem, which feed back into the *original* total system, and so on. The states of these systems may change, but as systems they remain numerically the same. In selection processes, they do not.

In Bajema's diagram, genes help produce the organism of which they are part as well as new genes. In the production of new genes, mistakes can be made. If these mistakes occur in somatic cells, the organism itself is affected and feedback loops can become established. However, if they occur in the germ cells, the organism itself is not affected, only its progeny, and its progeny are numerically different systems. Hence, no feedback loops can be established. Wimsatt (1972) has argued that functionally organized systems arise only through selection processes. As I have argued elsewhere (Hull 1980), selection processes give rise to functional systems by themselves *becoming* functional systems. The chief difference between the organization of the two sorts of systems is that, in functional systems, the effects of a single interaction between the larger and smaller included systems feed back into numerically the same systems, while in selection processes they do not. They affect new, distinct systems.

According to gene selectionists, genes are individuals that form lineages. Only genes, or possibly entire genomes, can function as replicators, because only genes can pass on their structure directly in replication. Gene selectionists admit that more inclusive individuals exist, that interactions between these individuals and their environments play a role in the evolutionary process, but for some reason this role need not be mentioned in evolutionary theory itself. Evolutionary theory can be couched entirely in terms of replicators and replication. Gene lineages, not species, are the things that evolve. According to organism selectionists, both genes and organisms are individuals and both form lineages. Genes certainly function as replicators. Organisms also might function as replicators in certain circumstances, but at the very least they function as interactors, and both replication and interaction must be mentioned in any adequate theory of evolution. On their view, both gene lineages and organism lineages can be said to evolve.

Advocates of species selection go one step further. Not only are genes and organisms significant individuals in the evolutionary process, but also species themselves are properly construed as individuals. If species are monophyletic units, then they have the continuity in space and time required of historical entities. Whether they are also sufficiently well-integrated, cohesive wholes is more problematic. Biologists can be found on both sides of this issue. However, one thing is certain: if species are to function as either replicators or interactors, they *must* be individuals. In order to function as replicators, species must exhibit structural characteristics and be able to pass on these characteristics. Species must somehow "reproduce" themselves as distinct individuals. One of the major reservations which biologists have to species selection is that they do not see how species can make the necessary copies of themselves to permit selection at the level of species. But even if species cannot function as replicators, they still might be sufficiently cohesive to function as interactors. If so, then a species would survive or become extinct because of characteristics which the species as a whole has, not because of the aggregative effects of the success or failure of individual organisms. In either case, according to the species selectionists, species do not and cannot evolve. A species, once formed, is not capable of extensive change. Instead, species form lineages, and it is these lineages which evolve (Hull, 1981).

Conclusion

The main purpose of this paper has been to set out the general characteristics that replicators and interactors exhibit and the roles that they play in the evolutionary process. A process is a selection process because of the interplay between replication and interaction. The structure of replicators is differentially perpetuated because of the relative success of the interactors of which the replicators are part. In order to perform the functions they do, both replicators and interactors must be discrete individuals that come into existence and cease to exist. In this process they produce lineages that change indefinitely through time. Because lineages are integrated on the basis of descent, they are spatiotemporally localized and not classes of the sort that can function in laws of nature.

This general description is straightforward enough. It gets complicated only when one tries to pin it down to particular levels of biological organization. For example, Dawkins argues that variable amounts of the genetic material can function as replicators, possibly entire chromosomes, on occasion entire genomes, but nothing more inclusive. Species selectionists do not argue that everything taxonomists call a species can actually function as a replicator or an interactor but that *some* do. For example, they argue that nothing more inclusive than the single organism in cases of asexual reproduction functions in the evolutionary process. Asexual species really are not "species" or, to put it differently, if asexual species count as species, then not all species are individuals.

The main conceptual problem in the dispute over levels of selection is that selection, in both senses of this term, seems to wander over traditional levels of organization. In certain groups, nothing more inclusive than single genes may function as replicators, in others entire genomes, in others possibly organisms. In certain groups, one and the same entity may function as a replicator and as an interactor. For example, Dawkins agrees with Eldredge and Gould about asexual organisms, Dawkins admitting that the entire genome functions as a replicator in strictly asexual reproduction, while Eldredge and Gould argue that the organism in such cases is the most inclusive entity that functions in the evolutionary process. If one wants to formulate widely applicable generalizations about evolution, a good strategy might be to abandon the usual ontology of genes, organisms, kinship groups, populations, and the like, and adopt an ontology designed specifically for this purpose—the ontology of replicators, interactors, and lineages.

Notes

1 Several different but related issues are commonly discussed under the heading of "group selection." The one that has received the greatest attention concerns how "altruistic" genes can become established in a population. How can a gene that decreases the fitness of the organism that possesses it become established in a population even if it benefits the group to which the organism belongs? One answer leaves the status of groups untouched: by helping organisms that also possess this gene. Another is to argue that certain common-sense groups are really not "groups" at all but well-organized wholes. For early discussion of these issues, see Wynne-Edwards (1962) and Williams (1966).

2 The knee-jerk response to the claim that genuine laws of nature cannot make uneliminable reference to spatiotemporally localized individuals is to cite Kepler's laws, which mention the sun. However, if Kepler's laws had turned out to be true only for the sun and not generalizable to other star systems, they would have gone the way of Bode's law. A scientist calling something a law does not automatically make it one.

3 Dawkins' "perverse" definition of genes in terms of selection pressures irritates Gunter Stent (1977) because it "denatures the meaningful and well-established central concept of genetics into a fuzzy and heuristically useless notion." Memory is short. Mendelian geneticists raised exactly the same objections to the perverse redefinitions of the gene being urged on them a generation ago by such molecular biologists as Stent (Carlson, 1966). Mary Midgley (1979) is even more irate over "altruism" being turned into a technical term in science. The dangers of equivocation are too great. Such protests over changes in language are almost as effective in redirecting the evolution of language as prayers are in stopping the flow of molten lava.

4 L. J. Cohen (1974) responds to the claims made by Ghiselin (1966, 1969, 1974) and Hull (1974) that species are not classes by defining species in terms of spatiotemporal relations to spatiotemporal foci. However, if this sort of definition were acceptable, then particular organisms could also be viewed as classes, by defining them in terms of cellular descent from the zygote which gave rise to them. On this view, nearly everything becomes a class. The

maneuver also accomplishes nothing because the need remains to distinguish spatiotemporally unrestricted classes (like planets and gold) from spatiotemporally restricted "classes" (like Richard Nixon and *Homo sapiens*). Of course, the relevant distinctions can be made in terms other than those I have used (e.g., Reed, 1979; Sober, 1980, 1981). Conversely, certain philosophers have argued that laws need not refer to natural kinds (Dretske, 1977), or be spatiotemporally unrestricted (Earman, 1978).

References

Ayala, F. J., Sept., 1978. "The mechanisms of evolution," *Scientific American*, 239(3):56-69.

Bajema, C. J., 1971. *Natural Selection in Human Populations*, New York, John Wiley and Sons.

Carlson, E. A., 1966. *The Gene: A Critical History*, Philadelphia, Saunders.

Carson, H. L., 1970. "Chromosome tracers of the origin of species," *Science*, 168:1414-18.

Cassidy, J., 1978. "Philosophical aspect of the group selection controversy," *Philosophy of Science*, 45:575-594.

Cohen, L. J., 1974. "Professor Hull and the evolution of science," *British Journal for the Philosophy of Science*, 25:334-336.

Dawkins, R., 1976. *The Selfish Gene*, New York and Oxford, Oxford University Press.

Dawkins, R., 1978. "Replicator selection and the extended phenotype," *Zeitschrift für Tierpsychologie*, 47:61-76.

Dretske, F., 1977. "Laws of nature," *Philosophy of Science*, 44:248-268.

Earman, J., 1978. "The universality of laws," *Philosophy of Science*, 45:173-181.

Eldredge, N., and S. J. Gould, 1972. "Punctuated equilibria: An alternative to phyletic gradualism," in *Models of Paleobiology*, ed. T. J. M. Schopf, San Francisco, Freeman, Cooper.

Ghiselin, M. T., 1966. "On psychologism in the logic of taxonomic principles," *Systematic Zoology*, 15:207-215.

Ghiselin, M. T., 1969. *The Triumph of the Darwinian Method*, Berkeley, University of California Press.

Ghiselin, M. T., 1974. "A radical solution to the species problem," *Systematic Zoology*, 23:536-544.

Gould, S. J., and N. Eldredge, 1977. "Punctuated equilibria: The tempo and mode of evolution reconsidered," *Paleobiology*, 3:115-151.

Hull, D. L., 1974. "Are the 'members' of biological species 'similar' to each other?" *British Journal for the Philosophy of Science*, 25:332-334.

Hull, D. L., 1975. "Central subjects and historical narratives," *History and Theory*, 14:253-274.

Hull, D. L., 1976. "Are species really individuals?", *Systematic Zoology*, 25: 174-91.

Hull, D. L., 1978. "A matter of individuality," *Philosophy of Science*, 45: 335-360.

Hull, D. L., 1980a. "Biology and philosophy," in *Contemporary Philosophy: A New Survey*, Vol. 2, *Philosophy of Science*, ed. G. Fløistad, The Hague, Martinus Nijhoff.

Hull, D. L., 1980b. "Individuality and selection," *Annual Review of Ecology and Systematics*, 11:311-332.

Lewontin, R. C., 1970. "The units of selection," *Annual Review of Ecology and Systematics*, 1:1-18.

Mayr, E., 1963. *Animal Species and Evolution*, Cambridge, Mass., Harvard University Press.

Mayr, E., Sept., 1978. "Evolution," *Scientific American*, 239(3):46-55.

Midgley, M., 1979. "Gene-Juggling," *Philosophy*, 54:439-458.

Reed, E., 1979. "The role of symmetry in Ghiselin's 'radical solution to the species problem,'" *Systematic Zoology*, 28:71-78.

Sepkoski, J. J., Jr., 1978. "A kinetic model of phanerozoic taxonomic diversity, I," *Paleobiology*, 4:223-251.

Smart, J. J. C., 1963. *Philosophy and Scientific Realism*, London, Routledge and Kegan Paul.

Smart, J. J. C., 1968. *Between Science and Philosophy*, New York, Random House.

Sober, E., 1980. "Evolution, population thinking, essentialism," *Philosophy of Science*, 47:350-383.

Sober, E., 1981. "Significant units and the group selection controversy," in *PSA 1980*, Vol. 2, ed. P. Asquith and R. Giere, East Lansing, Michigan, Philosophy of Science Association.

Stanley, S. M., 1975. "A theory of evolution above the species level," *Proceedings of the National Academy of Science*, 72:646-650.

Stent, G., 1977. "You can take ethics out of altruism but you can't take the altruism out of ethics," *Hastings Center Report*, 7:33-36.

Suppe, F., 1974. "Some philosophical problems in biological speciation and taxonomy," in *Conceptual Basis of the Classification of Knowledge*, ed. J. A. Wojciechowski, Pullach and Munich, Verlag Dokumentation.

Van Valen, L., 1975. "Group selection, sex, and fossils," *Evolution*, 29:87-94.

Waddington, C. H., 1957. *The Strategy of the Gene*, New York, Macmillan.

Wade, M. J., 1978. "A critical review of the models of group selection," *Quarterly Review of Biology*, 53:101-114. Reprinted in this volume.

Wiley, E. O., 1980. *Phylogenetics: The Theory and Practice of Phylogenetic Systematics*, New York, John Wiley and Sons.

Williams, G. C., 1966. *Adaptation and Natural Selection,* Princeton, N.J., Princeton University Press. Chapter 4 is reprinted in part in this volume.

Williams, G. C., 1975. *Sex and Evolution,* Princeton, Princeton University Press.

Williams, M. B., 1980. "Is biology a different kind of science?" in *Pragmatism and Purpose,* ed. J. G. Slater, F. Wilson, and L. W. Sumner, Toronto, University of Toronto Press.

Wimsatt, W. C., 1972. "Teleology and the logical structure of function statements," *Studies in History and Philosophy of Science,* 3:1–80.

Wynne-Edwards, V. C., 1962. *Animal Dispersion in Relation to Social Behavior,* Edinburgh, Oliver & Boyd.

11

Replicators and Vehicles

Richard Dawkins

The theory of natural selection provides a mechanistic, causal account of how living things came to look as if they had been designed for a purpose. So overwhelming is the appearance of purposeful design that, even in this Darwinian era when we know "better," we still find it difficult, indeed boringly pedantic, to refrain from teleological language when discussing adaptation. Birds' wings are obviously "for" flying, spider webs are for catching insects, chlorophyll molecules are for photosynthesis, DNA molecules are for . . . What *are* DNA molecules for? The question takes us aback. In my case it touches off an almost audible alarm siren in the mind. If we accept the view of life that I wish to espouse, it is the forbidden question. DNA is not "for" anything. If we wish to speak teleologically, all adaptations are for the preservation of DNA; DNA itself just *is*. Following Williams (1966), I have advocated this view at length (Dawkins 1976, 1978), and I do not want to repeat myself here. Instead I shall try to clear up an important misunderstanding of the view, a misunderstanding that has constituted an unnecessary barrier to its acceptance.

The identity of the "unit of selection" has been controversial in the literature both of biology (Williams, 1966; Lewontin, 1970; Leigh, 1977; Dawkins, 1978; Alexander and Borgia, 1978; Alexander, 1980) and philosophy (Hull, 1981). In this paper I shall show that only part of the controversy is real. Part is due to semantic confusion. If we overlook the semantic element, we arrive at a simplistic hierarchical account of the views that have been expressed in the literature. Living matter is nested in a hierarchy of levels, from ecosystem through species, deme, family, individual, cell, gene, and even nucleotide base pair. According to this analysis, each one of the protagonists in the debate on units of selection is perched on a higher or a lower rung of a ladder, sniping at those above and below him. Thus Gould (1977) remarks that in the last fifteen years

From King's College Sociobiology Group, eds., *Current Problems in Sociobiology*, Cambridge, Cambridge University Press (1982), pp. 45–64.

challenges to Darwin's focus on individuals have sparked some lively debates among evolutionists. These challenges have come from above and from below. From above, Scottish biologist V. C. Wynne-Edwards raised orthodox hackles fifteen years ago by arguing that groups, not individuals, are units of selection, at least for the evolution of social behavior. From below, English biologist Richard Dawkins has recently raised my hackles with his claim that genes themselves are units of selection, and individuals merely their temporary receptacles.

At first blush, Gould's hierarchical analysis has a neatly symmetrical plausibility. Much as my sense of mischief is tickled by the idea of being allied with Professor Wynne-Edwards in a pincer-attack on Darwin's individual, however, I reluctantly have to point out that the dispute between individual and group is different in kind from the dispute between individual and gene. Wynne-Edwards's attack from above is best seen as a factual dispute about the level at which selection is most effective in nature. My attack from below is a dispute about what we ought to *mean* when we talk about a unit of selection. Much the same point has been realized by Hull (1981), but I prefer to persist in expressing it in my way rather than to adopt his terminology of "interactors" and "evolvors."

To make my point I shall develop a distinction between *replicator survival* and *vehicle selection.* To anticipate the conclusion: there are two ways in which we can characterize natural selection. Both are correct; they simply focus on different aspects of the same process. Evolution results from the differential survival of *replicators.* Genes are replicators; organisms and groups of organisms are not replicators, they are vehicles in which replicators travel about. Vehicle selection is the process by which some vehicles are more successful than other vehicles in ensuring the survival of their replicators. The controversy about group selection versus individual selection is a controversy about whether, when we talk about a unit of selection, we ought to mean a vehicle *at all,* or a replicator. In any case, as I shall later argue, there may be little usefulness in talking about discrete vehicles at all.

Replicators

A replicator may be defined as any entity in the universe of which copies are made. Replicators may be subclassified in two overlapping ways (Dawkins, 1982, chapter 5). A germ-line replicator, as distinct from a dead-end replicator, is the potential ancestor of an indefinitely long line of descendant replicators. Thus DNA in a zygote is a germ-line replicator, while DNA in a liver cell is a dead-end replicator. Cutting across this classification: an active, as distinct from a passive, replicator is a replicator that has some causal influence on its own probability of being propagated. Thus a gene that has phenotypic expression is an active replicator. A length of DNA that is never transcribed and has no phenotypic expression whatever is a passive replicator. "Selfish DNA" (Dawkins, 1976, p. 47; Doolittle and Sapienza, 1980; Orgel and Crick, 1980), even if it is not transcribed, should be considered passive only if its nature has absolutely no influence on its probability of being replicated. It might be quite hard to find a genuine example of a passive replicator. Special interest attaches to *active germ-line replicators,* since adaptations "for" their preservation are expected to fill the world and to characterize living organisms. Automatically, those active germ-line replicators whose phenotypic effects happen to enhance their own survival and propagation will be the ones that survive. Their phenotypic consequences will be the attributes of living things that we see, and seek to explain.

Active, germ-line replicators, then, are units of selection in the following sense. When we say that an adaptation is "for the good of" something, what is that something? Is it the species, the group, the individual, or what? I am suggesting that the appropriate "something," the "unit of selection" in that sense, is the active germ-line replicator. The active germ-line replicator might, therefore, be called the "optimon," by extension of Benzer's (1957) classification of genetic units (recon, muton, and cistron).

This does not mean, of course, that genes or other replicators literally face the cutting edge of natural selection. It is their phenotypic effects that are the proximal subjects of selection. I have been sorry to learn that the phrase "replicator selection" can be misunderstood along those lines. One could, perhaps, avoid this confusion by referring to replicator survival rather than replicator selection. (In passing I cannot help being reminded of Wallace's (1866) passionate plea to Darwin to abandon "natural selection" in favor of "survival of the fittest," on the grounds that many people thought "natural selection" implied a conscious selecting "agent" (see also Young, 1971). My own prejudice is that anybody who misunderstands "replicator selection" is likely to have even more trouble with "individual selection").

Natural selection does not inevitably follow whenever there exist active germ-line replicators. Certain additional assumptions are necessary, but these, in turn, are almost inevitable consequences of the basic definition. First, no copying process is perfect, and we can expect that replicators will sometimes make inexact copies of themselves, the mistakes or mutations being preserved in future descendants. Natural selection, of course, depends on the variation so created. Second, the resources needed to make copies, and to make vehicles for propagating copies, may be presumed to be in limited supply, and replicators may therefore be regarded as in competition with other replicators. In the complicatedly organized environments of eukaryotic cells, each replicator is a competitor specifically of its alleles at its own locus on the chromosomes of the population.

There is a problem over how large or how small a fragment of genome we choose to regard as a replicator. Is it one cistron (recon, muton), one chromosome, one genome, or some intermediate? The answer I have given before, and still stick by, is that we do not need to give a straight answer to the question. Nobody is going to be hanged as a result of our decision. Williams (1966) recognized this when he defined a gene as "that which segregates and recombines with appreciable frequency" (p. 24), and as "any hereditary information for which there is a favorable or unfavorable selection bias equal to several or many times its rate of endogenous change" (p. 25). It is clear that we are never going to sell this kind of definition to a generation brought up on the "one gene–one protein" doctrine, which is one reason why I (Dawkins, 1978) have advocated using the word "replicator" itself, instead of "gene" in the sense of the Williams definition. Another reason is that "replicator" is general enough to accommodate the theoretical possibility, which one day may become observed reality, of nongenetic natural selection. For example, it is at least worth discussing the possibility of evolution by differential survival of cultural replicators or "memes" (Dawkins, 1976; Bonner, 1980), brain structures whose "phenotypic" manifestation as behavior or artifact is the basis of their selection.

I have lavished much rhetoric, or irresponsibly purple prose if you prefer, on expounding the view that "the unit of selection" (I meant it in the sense of replicator, not vehicle) must be a unit that is potentially immortal (Dawkins, 1976, chapter 3), a point I learned from Williams (1966). Briefly, the rationale is that an entity must have a low rate of spontaneous, endogenous change, if the selective advantage of its phenotypic effects over those of rival ("allelic") entities is to have any significant evolutionary effect. For a replicator such as a small length of chromosome, mutation and crossing over within itself are hazards to its continued replication, in exactly the same sense as are predators and reluctant females. Any arbitrary length of DNA has an expected half-life measured in generations. The world tends to become full of replicators with a long half-life, and therefore full of their phenotypic products. These products are the characteristics of the animals and plants we see around us. It is these that we wish to explain. Of those phenotypic products, the ones that we, as whole animal biologists, are particularly interested in are those that we see at the whole animal level, adaptations to avoid predators, to attract females, to secure food economically, and so on. Replicators that tend to make the successive bodies they inhabit good at avoiding predators, attracting females, etc., tend to have long half-lives as a consequence. But if such a replicator has a high probability of internal self-destruction, through mutation in its broad sense, all its virtues at the level of whole animal phenotypes come to naught.

It follows that although any arbitrary length of chromosome can in theory be regarded as a replicator, too long a piece of chromosome will quantitatively disqualify itself as a potential unit of selection, since it will run too high a risk of being split by crossing over in any generation. A replicator worthy of the name, then, is not necessarily as small as one recon, one muton, or one cistron. It is not a discrete, all or none, unit at all, but a segment of chromosome whose length is determined by the strength of the "whole animal level" selection pressure of interest. As Francis Crick (1979) has written, "The theory of the 'selfish gene' will have to be extended to any stretch of DNA."

It further follows that critics of the view advocated here cannot score debating points by drawing attention to the existence of within-gene (cistron) crossing over. I am grateful to Mark Ridley for reminding me that most within-gene crossovers are, in any case, indistinguishable in their effects from between-gene crossovers. Obviously, if the gene concerned happens to be homozygous, paired at meiosis with an identical allele, all the material exchanged will be identical, and the effect will be indistinguishable from a crossover at either end of the gene. If the gene is heterozygous, but differs from its allele by only one nucleotide, a within-gene crossover will be indistinguishable in effect from a crossover at one of the two ends of the gene. Only on the rare occasions when the gene differs from its allele in two places, and the crossover occurs between the two places, will a within-gene crossover be distinguishable from a between-gene crossover. The general point is that it does not particularly matter where crossovers occur in relation to cistron boundaries. What matters is where crossovers occur in relation to heterozygous nucleotides. If, for instance, a sequence of six adjacent cistrons happens to be homozygous throughout an entire species, a crossover anywhere within the six will be exactly equivalent to a crossover at either end of the six.

The possibility of widespread linkage disequilibrium, too, does not weaken the case (Clegg, 1978). It simply increases the length of chromosomal segment that we expect to behave as a replicator. *If* (as seems doubtful) linkage disequilibrium is so strong that populations contain "only a few gametic types" (Lewontin, 1974, p. 312), the effective replicator will be a very large chunk of DNA. When what Lewontin calls l_c, the "characteristic length" (the distance over which coupling is effective), is only "a fraction of the chromosome length, each gene is out of linkage equilibrium only with its neighbours but is assorted essentially independently of other genes farther away. The characteristic length is, in some sense, the unit of evolution since genes within it are highly correlated. The concept is a subtle one, however. It does not mean that the genome is broken up into discrete adjacent chunks of length l_c. Every locus is the center of such a correlated segment and evolves in linkage with the genes near it" (Lewontin, 1974, p. 312). In the same spirit, I played with the idea of entitling an earlier work "The slightly selfish big bit of chromosome and the even more selfish little bit of chromosome" (Dawkins, 1976, p. 35).

I used to think that, in species with asexual reproduction, the whole organism could be thought of as a replicator, but further reflection shows this to be equivalent to the Lamarckian heresy. The asexual organism's *genome* may be considered a replicator, since any alteration in it tends to be preserved. But an alteration in the organism itself is quite likely to have been imprinted from the environment and will not be preserved. It is not replicated. Asexual organisms do not make copies of themselves, they work to make copies of their genomes.

An adaptation is a tool by which the genes that made it have levered themselves through the past into the present, where it demands our explanation. But the tools and levers do not rattle around loose in the world; they come neatly packaged in tool kits: individual organisms or other vehicles. It is to vehicles that we now turn.

Vehicles

Replicators are not naked genes, though they may have been when life began. Nowadays, most of them are strung along chromosomes, chromosomes are wrapped up in nuclear membrances, and nuclei are enveloped in cytoplasm and enclosed in cell membranes. Cells, in turn, are cloned to form huge assemblages which we know as organisms. Organisms are vehicles for replicators, survival machines as I have called them. But just as we had a nested hierarchy of would-be replicators—small and large fragments of genome—so there is a hierarchy of nested vehicles. Chromosomes and cells are gene vehicles within organisms. In many species organisms are not dispersed randomly but go around in groups. Multispecies groups form communities or ecosystems. At any of these levels the concept of vehicle is potentially applicable. Vehicle selection is the differential success of vehicles in propagating the replicators that ride inside them. In theory selection may occur at any level of the hierarchy.

One of the clearest discussions of the levels of selection is that of Lewontin (1970), although his paper, like my own first discussion of the matter (Dawkins, 1976), suffers from its failure to make a clear distinction between replicators and vehicles. Lewontin does not mention the gene as one of the levels in his hierarchy, presumably because he rightly regards it as obvious that it is changes in gene frequency that ultimately matter, whatever level selection may proximally act on. Thus it is easy, and probably largely correct, to interpret his paper as being about levels of *vehicle*. On the other hand, at one point he says the following:

The rate of evolution is limited by the variation in fitness of the units being selected. This has two consequences from the point of view of comparison between levels of selection. First, the rapidity of response to selection depends upon the heritability of differences in fitness between units. The heritability is highest in units where no internal adjustment or reassortment is possible since such units will pass on to their descendent units an unchanged set of information. Thus, cell organelles, haploid organisms, and gametes are levels of selection with a higher heritability than diploid sexual genotypes, since the latter do not perfectly reproduce themselves, but undergo segregation and recombination in the course of their reproduction. In the same way, individuals have a greater heritability than populations and assemblages of species. (Lewontin, 1970, p. 8)

This point makes sense only if the units being referred to are would-be replicators; indeed it is the same point I made a few pages back. This suggests that Lewontin was not entirely clear over whether he was talking about units of selection in the sense of replicators (entities that become more or less numerous as a consequence of selection) or vehicles (units of phenotypic power of replicators). The same is suggested by the fact that he cites M. B. Williams's (1970) axiomatization of Darwin's theory as indicating that "the principles can be applied equally to genes, organisms, populations, species, and at opposite ends of the scale, prebiotic molecules and ecosystems." I would maintain that genes and prebiotic molecules do not belong in the hierarchical list. They are replicators; the rest are vehicles.

An organism is not a replicator, not even a very inefficient replicator with a high probability of endogenous change. An organism's *genome* can be regarded as a replicator (a very poor one if reproduction is sexual), but to treat an organism as a replicator in the same sense as a gene is tantamount to Lamarckism. If you change a replicator, the change will be passed on to its descendants. This is clearly true of genes and genomes. It is not true of organisms, since acquired characteristics are not inherited.

The reason we like to think in terms of vehicle selection is that replicators are not directly visible to natural selection. Gould (1977, p. 24) put it well, albeit he mistakenly thought he was scoring a point against the whole replicator concept: "I find a fatal flaw in Dawkins's attack from below. No matter how much power Dawkins wishes to assign to genes, there is one thing he cannot give them—direct visibility to natural selection. Selection simply cannot see genes and pick among them directly. It must use bodies as an intermediary." The valid point being made is that replicators do not expose themselves naked to the world; they work via their phenotypic effects, and it is often convenient to see those phenotypic effects as bundled together in vehicles such as bodies.

It is another matter whether the individual body is the only level of vehicle worth considering. That is what the whole group selection versus individual selection debate is about. Gould comes down heavily in favor of the individual organism, and this is the main one of the would-be units that I shall consider.

Of all the levels in the hierarchy of vehicles, the biologist's eye is drawn most strongly to the individual organism. Unlike the cell and the population, the organism is often of a convenient size for the naked eye to see. It is usually a discrete machine with an internally coherent organization, displaying to a high degree the quality that Huxley (1912) labeled "individuality" (literally indivisibility—being sufficiently heterogeneous in form to be rendered non-functional if cut in half). Genetically speaking, too, the individual organism is usually a clearly definable unit, each of whose cells has the same genes as the others but different genes from the cells of other individuals. To an immunologist, the organism has a special kind of "uniqueness" (Medawar, 1957), in that it will easily accept grafts from other parts of its own body but not from other bodies. To the ethologist—and this is really an aspect of Huxley's "individuality"—the organism is a unit of behavioral action in a much stronger sense than, say, half an organism, or two organisms. The organism has one central nervous system. It takes "decisions" (Dawkins and Dawkins, 1973) as a unit. All its limbs conspire harmoniously together to achieve one end at a time. On occasions when two or more organisms try to coordinate their efforts, say when a pride of lions cooperatively stalks prey, the feats of coordination among individuals are feeble compared with the intricate orchestration, with high spatial and temporal precision, of the hundreds of muscles within each individual. Even a starfish, each of whose tube-feet enjoys a measure of autonomy and may tear the animal in two if the circum-oral nerve ring has been surgically cut, looks like a single entity, and in nature behaves as if it had a single purpose.

For these and other reasons we automatically prefer to ask functional questions at the level of the individual organism rather than at any other level. We ask, "Of what use is that behavior pattern to the animal?" We do not ask, "Of what use is the behavior of the animal's left hind leg to the left hind leg?" Nor yet do we usually ask "Of what use is the behavior of that pair of animals to the pair?" We see the single organism as a suitable unit about which to speak of adaptation. No doubt this is why Hamilton (1964a, b), in his epoch-making demonstration that individual altruism was best explained as the result of gene selfishness, sugared the pill of his scientific revolution by inventing "inclusive fitness" as a sop to the individual organism. Inclusive fitness, in effect, amounts to "that property of an individual organism which will appear to be maximized when what is really being maximized is gene survival" (Dawkins, 1978). Every consequence that Hamilton deduced from this theory could, I suggest, be derived by posing the question: "What would a selfish gene do to maximize its survival?" In effect, Hamilton was accepting the logic of gene (replicator) selection while affirming his faith in the individual organism as the most salient gene vehicle.

Presumably it would, in principle, be possible to imagine a group-level equivalent of individual inclusive fitness: that property of a group of organisms which will appear to be maximized when what is really being maximized is the survival of the genes controlling the phenotypic characters of the group. The difficulty with this is that, while we can conceive of ways in which genes can exert phenotypic power over the limbs and nervous systems of the bodies in which they sit, it is rather harder to conceive of their exerting phenotypic power over the "limbs" and "nervous systems"of whole groups of organisms. The group of organisms is too diffuse, not coherent enough to be seen as a unit of phenotypic power.

And yet to some extent the individual organism, too, may be not quite such a coherent unit of phenotypic power as we have grown to think. It is certainly much less obviously so to a botanist than to a zoologist:

The individual fruit fly, flour beetle, rabbit, flatworm or elephant is a population at the cellular but not at any higher level. Starvation does not change the number of legs, hearts or livers of an animal but the effect of stress on a plant is to alter both the rate of formation of new leaves and the rate of death of old ones: a plant may react to stress by varying the number of its parts. (Harper, 1977)

Harper feels obliged to coin two new terms for different kinds of "individual." "The 'ramet' is the unit of clonal growth, the module that may often follow an independent existence if severed from the parent plant" (Harper, 1977, p. 24). The "genet," on the other hand, is the unit that springs from one single-celled zygote, the "individual" in the normal zoologists' sense. Janzen (1977) faces up to something like the same difficulty, suggesting that a clone of dandelions should be regarded as equivalent to a single tree, although spread out along the ground rather than raised in the air, and divided up into separate physical "plants" (Harper's ramets). Janzen sees a clone of aphids in the same way, although Harper presumably would not: each aphid in a clone develops from a single cell, albeit the cell is produced asexually. Harper would therefore say that a new aphid is produced by an act of *reproduction,* whereas Janzen would regard it as having *grown* like a new limb of its parent.

It might seem that we are now playing with words, but I think Harper's (1977, p. 27) distinction between reproduction by means of a single-celled (asexual or sexual) propagule, and growth by means of a multicellular propagule or runner, is an important one. What is more, it can be made the basis of a sensible criterion for defining a single vehicle. Each new vehicle comes into being through an act of reproduction. New parts of vehicles come into being through growth. The distinction has nothing to do with that between sexual and asexual reproduction, nor with that between ramet and genet.

One Act of Reproduction, One Vehicle

I do not know whether Harper had the same thing in mind, but for me the evolutionary significance of his distinction between growth and reproduction is best seen as arising out of a view of development that I learned from the works of J. T. Bonner (e.g., 1974). In order to make complex adaptations at the level of multicellular organs—eyes, ears, hearts, etc.—a complex developmental process is necessary. An amoeba may give rise to two daughters by splitting down the middle, but an eye, or a heart, cannot give rise to two daughter eyes, or two daughter hearts, by binary fission. Eyes and hearts are so complex that they have to be developed from small beginnings, built by orderly cell division and differentiation. This is why insects whose life cycle takes them through two radically different bodies, like caterpillar and butterfly, do not attempt to transform larval organs into corresponding adult organs. Instead, development restarts from undifferentiated imaginal discs, the larval tissues being broken down and used as the equivalent of food. Complexity can develop from simplicity, but not from a wholly different kind of complexity. The evolution of one complex organ into another can take place only because in each generation the development of individuals restarts at a simple, single-celled beginning (Dawkins, 1982, chapter 14).

Complex organisms all have a life cycle which begins with a single cell, passes through a phase of mitotic cell division in which great complexity of structure may be built up, and culminates in reproduction of new single-celled propagules of the next generation. Evolutionary change consists in genetic changes which alter the developmental process at some crucial stage in the life cycle, in such a way that the complex structure of the organism of the next generation is different. If organisms simply grew indefinitely, without returning cyclically to a single-celled zygote in a sequence of generations, the evolution of complexity at the multicellular organ level would be impossible. For lineages to evolve, individuals must develop from small beginnings in each generation. They cannot just grow from the multicellular bodies of the previous generation.

We must beware of falling into the trap of "biotic adaptationism" here (Williams, 1966). We cannot argue that a tendency to reproduce rather than grow will evolve in order to allow evolution to happen! Rather, when we look at complex living things we are looking at the end products of an evolutionary process which could only occur because the lineages concerned showed

repeated reproduction rather than just growth. A related point is that repeated cycles of reproduction are only possible if there is also death of individual vehicles, but this is not, in itself, a reason that explains why death
occurs. We cannot say that the biological function of death is "to" allow repeated reproduction, hence evolution (Medawar, 1957). But given that death
and reproduction do occur in a lineage, evolution in that lineage becomes possible (Maynard Smith, 1969).

Is the distinction between growth and reproduction a rigid one? As so far
defined it seems so. A life cycle that restarts with a single cell represents a
new reproductive unit, a new discrete vehicle. All other apparent reproduction should be called growth. But couldn't there be a new life cycle that was
initiated not by a single-celled propagule but by a small multicellular propagule? When a new plant grows from a runner sent out by an old plant, is this
reproduction or growth? If Harper's definition is rigidly applied, everything
depends on an embryological detail. Are all the cells of the new "plant" the
clonal descendants of one cell at the growing tip of the runner? In this case
we are dealing with reproduction. Or is the runner a broad-fronted meristem,
so that some cells in the new plant are descended from one cell in the old
plant, while other cells in the new plant are descended from another cell in
the old plant? In this case the Harper definition forces us to classify the phenomenon as growth, not reproduction. It is, in principle, not different from
the growth of a new leaf on a tree.

That is what follows from the Harper definition, but is it a sensible definition? I can think of one good reason for saying yes. It makes sense if we are
regarding reproduction as the process by which a new vehicle comes into
existence, and growth as the process by which an existing vehicle develops.
Imagine a plant that sends out vegetative suckers that are broad-fronted
meristems, and suppose that this species never reproduces sexually. How
might evolutionary change occur? By mutation and selection in the usual
way, but *not* by selection among multicellular organisms. A mutation would
affect the cell in which it occurred, and all clonal descendants of that cell.
But because the runner is broad-fronted, new "plants" (ramets) would be
heterogeneous mosaics with respect to the mutation. Some of the cells of a
new plant would be mutant, others would not. As the vegetation creeps over
the land, mutant cells are peppered in haphazard bunches around the "individual" plants. The apparent individual plants, in fact, are not genetic individuals at all. Since they are genetic mosaics, the largest gene vehicle that can be
discerned as having a regular life cycle is the cell. Population genetics would
have to be done at the cellular level, not at the "individual" level. And vehicle
selection would give rise to adaptive modification at the cellular level, but not
at the level of the whole "plant." The whole "plant" would not function as a

vehicle propagating the genes inside it, because different cells inside it would contain different genes. Cells would function as vehicles, and adaptations would not be for the good of the whole plant but for the good of smaller units within the plant. To qualify as a "vehicle," an entity must come into being by reproduction, not by growth.

That is my justification for the importance of the Harper definition. But now suppose that the runner is a narrow bottleneck of mitotic cell descent, so that the life cycle consists of an alternation between a growth phase and a small, if multicellular, restarting phase. "Individual plants" would now be statistically unlikely to be genetic mosaics. In this case vehicle selection at the level of whole plants could go on, in a statistical sense, since most, though not all, plants would be genetically uniform. Genetic variation within the cells of individual plants would be less than that between cells of different plants. A kind of "group selection" (J. Hartung, personal communication) at the cellular level could therefore go on, leading to adaptation at the level of the multicellular vehicle, the level of the "individual plant." We might therefore tolerate a slight relaxation of Harper's criterion, using "reproduction" whenever a life cycle is constricted into a narrow bottleneck of cells, even if that bottleneck is not always quite as narrow as a single cell.

We are now, incidentally, in a position to see a reason, additional to those normally given, why the individual organism is so much more persuasive a unit of natural selection (vehicle) than the group of organisms. Groups do not go through a regular cycle of growth (development), alternating with "reproduction" (sending off a small "propagule" which eventually grows into a new group). Groups grow in a vague and diffuse manner, occasionally fragmenting like pack ice. It is significant that models of group selection that come closest to succeeding tend to incorporate some reproduction-like process. Thus Levins, and Boorman and Levitt (reviewed by Wilson, 1973) postulate a metapopulation of groups, in which populations "reproduce" by sending out "propagules" consisting of migrant individuals or small bands of individuals. Moreover, "group selection" in the sense of D. S. Wilson (1980) can only work if there is some mechanism by which genetic variation between groups is kept higher than genetic variation within groups (Maynard Smith, 1976; Grafen, 1980, and in preparation). This point is analogous to the one I made in my discussion of "cellular selection" in plants with narrow runners. In practice the most likely way for intergroup variation to be higher than intragroup variation is through genetic relatives tending to associate together. In this case we are dealing with what has been called kin-group selection. Is "kin selection," then, an authentic case where we have a vehicle larger than the individual body, in the same way group selection would be if it existed?

Kin Selection and Kin Group Selection

There are those who see kin selection as a special case of group selection (E. O. Wilson, 1973; D. S. Wilson, 1980; Wade, 1978). Maynard Smith (1976) disagrees, and emphatically so do I (Dawkins, 1976, 1978, 1979). Maynard Smith is too polite in suggesting that the disagreement is merely one between lumpers and splitters. Hamilton (1975) at first reading might be thought to be endorsing the lumping of kin and group selection. To avoid confusion I quote him in full:

> If we insist that group selection is different from kin selection the term should be restricted to situations of assortation definitely not involving kin. But it seems on the whole preferable to retain a more flexible use of terms; to use group selection where groups are clearly in evidence and to qualify with mention of "kin" (as in the "kin-group" selection referred to by Brown, 1974). (Hamilton, 1975, p. 141, citation of Brown corrected)

Hamilton is here making the distinction between kin selection and kin-group selection. Kin-group selection is the special case of group selection in which individuals tend to be closely related to other members of their own group. It is also the special case of kin selection in which the related individuals happen to go about in discrete family groups. The important point is that the theory of kin selection does not *need* to assume discrete family groups. All that is needed is that close relatives encounter one another with higher than random frequency, or have some method of recognizing each other (Maynard Smith, 1982). As Hamilton says, the term "kin selection" (rather than "kin-group selection") "appeals most where pedigrees are unbounded and interwoven."

I have previously quoted Hull (1976) on mammary glands: "mammary glands contribute to individual fitness, the individual in this case being the kinship group." Hull is here using "individual" in a special, philosopher's sense, as "any spatio-temporally localized, cohesive and continuous entity." In this sense "organism" is not synonymous with "individual" but is only one of the class of things that can be called individuals. Thus Ghiselin (1974) has argued that species are "individuals." The point I wish to make here is that the "kinship group" is an "individual" only if families go about in tightly concentrated bands, rigidly discriminating family members from nonmembers, with no half measures. There is no particular reason for expecting this kind of rigid family structure in nature, and certainly Hamilton's theory of kin selection does not demand it. As I suggested when I originally quoted Hull (Dawkins, 1978), we are not dealing with a discrete family group but with

> an animal plus 1/2 of each of its children plus 1/2 of each sibling plus 1/4 of each niece and grandchild plus 1/8 of each first cousin plus 1/32 of each second cousin ... Far from being a tidy, discrete group, it is more like a sort

of genetical octopus, a probabilistic amoeboid whose pseudopodia ramify and dissolve away into the common gene pool.

Where they exist, tightly knit family bands, or "kin groups," may be regarded as vehicles. But the general theory of kin selection does not depend on the existence of discrete family groups. No vehicle above the organism level need be postulated.

Doing Without Discrete Vehicles

It will have been noted that my "vehicles" are "individuals" in the sense of Ghiselin and Hull. They are spatiotemporally localized, cohesive, and continuous entities. Much of my section on organisms was devoted to illustrating the sense in which bodies, unlike groups of bodies, are "individuals." My sections on vegetatively propagating plants and on kin groups suggested that while they sometimes *may* be discrete and cohesive entities, there is no reason, either in fact or in theory, for expecting that they usually will be so. Kin selection, as a logical deduction from fundamental replicator theory, still leads to interesting and intelligible adaptation, even if there are not discrete kin-group vehicles.

I now want to generalize this lesson: although selection sometimes chooses replicators by virtue of their effects on discrete vehicles, it does not have to. Let me repeat part of my quotation from Gould (1977): "Selection simply cannot see genes and pick among them directly. It must use bodies as an intermediary." Well, it must use *phenotypic effects* as intermediaries, but do these have to be bodies? Do they have to be discrete vehicles at all? I have suggested (Dawkins, 1982) that we should no longer think of the phenotypic expression of a gene as being limited to the particular body in which the gene sits. We are already accustomed to the idea of a snail shell as phenotypic expression of genes, even though the shell does not consist of living cells. The form and color of the shell vary under genetic control. In principle the same is true of a caddis larva's house, though in this case building behavior intervenes in the causal chain from genes to house. There is no reason why we should not perform a genetic study of caddis houses, and a question such as "Are round stones dominant to angular stones?" could be a perfectly sensible research question. A bird's nest and a beaver dam are also extended phenotypes. We could do a genetic study of bower bird bowers in exactly the same sense as a genetic study of bird of paradise tails. I continue this conceptual progression further in the book referred to, concluding that genes in one body may have phenotypic expression in another body. For instance, I argue that genes in cuckoos have phenotypic expression in host behavior. When we look at an animal behaving, we may have to learn to say, not "How is it benefiting its inclusive fitness?" but rather "Whose inclusive fitness is it benefiting?"

Gould is right that genes are not naked to the world. They are chosen by virtue of their phenotypic consequences. But these phenotypic consequences should not be regarded as limited to the particular individual body in which the gene sits, any more than traditionally they have been seen as limited to the particular cell in which the gene sits (red blood corpuscles and sperm cells develop under the influence of genes that are not inside them). Not only is it unnecessary for us to regard the phenotypic expression of a gene as limited to the body in which it sits. It does not have to be limited to any of the discrete vehicles it can be described as inhabiting—cell, organism, group, community, etc. The concept of the discrete vehicle may turn out to be superfluous. In this respect, if I understand him aright, I am very encouraged by Bateson (1982, p. 136) when he says, "Insistence on character selection and nothing else does not commit anyone to considering just the attributes of individual organisms. The characters could be properties of symbionts such as competing lichens or mutualistic groups such as competing bands of wolves." However, I think Bateson could have gone further. The use of the word "competing" in the last sentence quoted suggests that he remains somewhat wedded to the idea of discrete vehicles. An entity such as a band of wolves must be a relatively discrete vehicle if it is to be said to compete with other bands of wolves.

I see the world as populated by competing replicators in germ lines. Each replicator, when compared with its alleles, can be thought of as being attached to a suite of characters, outward and visible tokens of itself. These tokens are its phenotypic consequences, in comparison with its alleles, upon the world. They determine its success or failure in continuing to exist. To a large extent the part of the world a gene can influence may happen to be limited to a local area that is sufficiently clearly bounded to be called a body, or some other discrete vehicle—perhaps a wolf pack. But this is not necessarily so. Some of the phenotypic consequences of a replicator, when compared with its alleles, may reach across vehicle boundaries. We may have to face the complexity of regarding the biosphere as an intricate network of overlapping fields of phenotypic power. Any particular phenotypic characteristic will have to be seen as the joint product of replicators whose influence converges from many different sources, many different bodies belonging to different species, phyla, and kingdoms. This is the doctrine of the "extended phenotype."

Conclusion

In the present paper I have mainly tried to clear up a misunderstanding. I have tried to show that the theory of replicators, which I have previously advocated, is not incompatible with orthodox "individual selectionism." The confusion over "units of selection" has arisen because we have failed to distinguish between two distinct meanings of the phrase. In one sense of the term "unit," the unit that actually survives or fails to survive, nobody could seriously claim that either an individual organism or a group of organisms was a unit of selection; in this sense the unit has to be a replicator, which will normally be a small fragment of genome. In the other sense of unit, the "vehicle," either an individual organism or a group could be a serious contender for the title "unit of selection." There are reasons for coming down on the side of the individual organism rather than larger units, but it has not been a main purpose of this paper to advocate this view. My main concern has been to emphasize that, whatever the outcome of the debate about organism versus group as *vehicle,* neither the organism nor the group is a *replicator.* Controversy may exist about rival candidates for replicators and about rival candidates for vehicles, but there should be no controversy over replicators *versus* vehicles. Replicator survival and vehicle selection are two aspects of the same process. The first essential is to distinguish clearly between them. Having done so, we may argue the merits of the rival candidates for each, and we may go on to ask, as I briefly did at the end, whether we really need the concept of discrete vehicles at all. If the answer to this turns out to be *no,* the phrase "individual selection" may be misleading. Whatever the upshot of the latter debate about the extended phenotype, I hope here to have removed an unnecessary source of semantic confusion by exposing the difference between replicators and vehicles.

Summary

(1) The question of "units of selection" is not trivial. If we are to talk about adaptations, we need to know which entity in the hierarchy of life they are "good" for. Adaptations for the good of the group would look quite different from adaptations for the good of the individual or the good of the gene.

(2) At first sight, it appears that "the individual" is intermediate in some nested hierarchy between the group and the gene. This paper shows, however, that the argument over "group selection" versus "individual selection" is a different kind of argument from that between "individual selection" and "gene selection." The latter is really an argument about what we ought to *mean* by a unit of selection, a "replicator" or a "vehicle."

(3) A replicator is defined as any entity in the universe of which copies are made. A DNA molecule is a good example. Replicators are classified into active (having some "phenotypic" effect on the world which influences the replicator's chance of being copied) and passive. Cutting across this they are classified into germ-line (potential ancestor of an indefinitely long line of descendant replicators) and dead-end (e.g., a gene in a liver cell).

(4) Active, germ-line replicators are important. Wherever they arise in the

universe, we may expect some form of natural selection and hence evolution to follow.

(5) The title of "replicator" should not be limited to any particular chunk of DNA such as a cistron. Any length of DNA can be treated as a replicator, but with quantitative reservations depending on its length, on recombination rates, linkage disequilibrium, selection pressures, etc.

(6) An individual organism is not a replicator, because alterations in it are not passed on to subsequent generations. Where reproduction is asexual, it is possible to regard an individual's whole genome as a replicator, but not the individual itself.

(7) Genetic replicators are selected not directly but by proxy, via their phenotypic effects. In practice, most of these phenotypic effects are bundled together with those of other genes in discrete "vehicles"–individual bodies. An individual body is not a replicator; it is a vehicle containing replicators, and it tends to work for the replicators inside it.

(8) Because of its discreteness and unitariness of structure and function, we commonly phrase our discussions of adaptation at the level of the individual vehicle. We treat adaptations as though they were "for the good of" the individual, rather than for the good of some smaller unit like a single limb, or some more inclusive vehicle such as a group or species.

(9) But even the individual organism may be less unitary and discrete than is sometimes supposed. This is especially true of plants, where it seems to be necessary to define two different kinds of "individuals"–"ramets" and "genets."

(10) An individual may be defined as a unit of *reproduction,* as distinct from *growth.* The distinction between reproduction and growth is not an easy one, and it should not be confused with the distinction between sexual and asexual reproduction. Reproduction involves starting anew from a single-celled propagule, while growth (including vegetative "reproduction") involves "broad-fronted" multicellular propagation.

(11) Kin selection is quite different from group selection, since it does not need to assume the existence of kin groups as discrete vehicles. More generally, we can question the usefulness of talking about discrete vehicles at all. In some ways a more powerful way of thinking is in terms of replicators with *extended phenotypes* in the outside world, effects which may be confined within the borders of discrete vehicles but do not have to be.

(12) The concept of the discrete vehicle is useful, however, in clarifying past discussions. The debate between "individual selection" and "group selection" is a debate over rival vehicles. There really should be no debate over "gene selection" versus "individual (or group) selection," since in the one case we are talking about replicators, in the other about vehicles. Replicator

survival and vehicle selection are two views of the same process. They are not rival theories.

I have benefited from discussion with Mark Ridley, Alan Grafen, Marian Dawkins, and Pat Bateson and other members of the conference at King's College. Some of the arguments given here are incorporated, in expanded form, in chapters 5, 6 and 14 of *The Extended Phenotype* (Dawkins, 1982).

References

Alexander, R. D., 1980. *Darwinism and Human Affairs,* London, Pitman.

Alexander, R. D., and Borgia, G., 1978. "Group selection, altruism, and the levels of organization of life," *Annual Review of Ecology and Systematics,* 9: 449–474.

Bateson, P. P. G., 1982. "Behavioural development and evolutionary processes," in *Current Problems in Sociobiology,* ed. King's College Sociobiology Group, Cambridge (Eng.), Cambridge University Press.

Benzer, S., 1957. "The elementary units of heredity," in *The Chemical Basis of Heredity,* ed. W. D. McElroy and B. Glass, Baltimore, Johns Hopkins Press, pp. 70–93.

Bonner, J. T., 1974. *On Development,* Cambridge (Mass.), Harvard University Press.

Bonner, J. T., 1980. *The Evolution of Culture in Animals,* Princeton, Princeton University Press.

Brown, J. L., 1974. "Alternate routes to sociality in jays–with a theory for the evolution of altruism and communal breeding," *American Zoologist,* 14: 63–80.

Clegg, M. T., 1978. "Dynamics of correlated genetic systems, II. Simulation studies of chromosomal segments under selection," *Theoretical Population Biology,* 13:1–23.

Crick, F. H. C., 1979. "Split genes and RNA splicing," *Science,* 204:264–271.

Dawkins, R., 1976. *The Selfish Gene,* Oxford, Oxford University Press.

Dawkins, R., 1978. "Replicator selection and the extended phenotype," *Zeitschrift für Tierpsychologie,* 47:61–76.

Dawkins, R., 1979. "Twelve misunderstandings of kin selection," *Zeitschrift für Tierpsychologie,* 51:184–200.

Dawkins, R., 1982. *The Extended Phenotype,* Oxford, Freeman.

Dawkins, R., and Dawkins, M., 1973. "Decisions and the uncertainty of behaviour," *Behaviour,* 45:83–103.

Doolittle, W. F., and Sapienza, C., 1980. "Selfish genes, the phenotype paradigm and genome evolution," *Nature,* 284:601–603.

Ghiselin, M. T., 1974. "A radical solution to the species problem," *Systematic Zoology,* 23:536–544.

Gould, S. J., December, 1977. "Caring groups and selfish genes," *Natural History*, 86(12):20–24.

Grafen, A., 1980. "Models of *r* and *d*," *Nature*, 284:494–495.

Hamilton, W. D., 1964a. "The genetical evolution of social behaviour, I," *Journal of Theoretical Biology*, 7:1–16.

Hamilton, W. D., 1964b. "The genetical evolution of social behaviour, II," *Journal of Theoretical Biology*, 7:17–54.

Hamilton, W. D., 1975. "Innate social aptitudes of man: An approach from evolutionary genetics," in *Biosocial Anthropology*, ed. R. Fox, London, Malaby Press. Reprinted in part in this volume.

Harper, J. L., 1977. *Population Biology of Plants*, London, Academic Press.

Hull, D. L., 1976. "Are species really individuals?" *Systematic Zoology*, 25: 174–191.

Hull, D. L., 1981. "The units of evolution: A metaphysical essay," in *Studies in the Concept of Evolution*, ed. U. J. Jensen and R. Harré, Hassocks, The Harvester Press. Reprinted in this volume.

Huxley, J. S., 1912. *The Individual in the Animal Kingdom*, Cambridge (Eng.), Cambridge University Press.

Janzen, D. H., 1977. "What are dandelions and aphids?" *American Naturalist*, 111:586–589.

Leigh E., 1977. "How does selection reconcile individual advantage with the good of the group?" *Proceedings of the National Academy of Sciences of the U.S.A.*, 74:4542–46.

Lewontin, R. C., 1970. "The units of selection," *Annual Review of Ecology and Systematics*, 1:1–18.

Lewontin, R. C., 1974. *The Genetic Basis of Evolutionary Change*, New York and London, Columbia University Press.

Maynard Smith, J., 1969. "The status of neo-Darwinism," in *Towards a Theoretical Biology*, 2, *Sketches*, Edinburgh, Edinburgh University Press.

Maynard Smith, J., 1976. "Group selection," *Quarterly Review of Biology*, 51:277–283. Reprinted in this volume.

Maynard Smith, J., 1982. "The evolution of social behaviour—a classification of models," in *Current Problems in Sociobiology*, ed. King's College Sociobiology Group, Cambridge (Eng.), Cambridge University Press.

Medwar, P. B., 1957. *The Uniqueness of the Individual*, London, Methuen.

Orgel, L. E., and Crick, F. H. C., 1980. "Selfish DNA, the ultimate parasite," *Nature*, 284:604–607.

Wade, J. J., 1978. "A critical review of the models of group selection," *Quarterly Review of Biology*, 53:101–114. Reprinted in this volume.

Wallace, A. R., 1866. "Letter to Charles Darwin dated July 2nd," in *More Letters of Charles Darwin*, Vol. 2, ed. F. Darwin, London, Murray, 1903.

Williams, G. C., 1966. *Adaptation and Natural Selection*, Princeton, Princeton University Press. Chapter 4 is reprinted in part in this volume.

Williams, M. B., 1970. "Deducing the consequences of evolution: A mathematical model," *Journal of Theoretical Biology*, 29:343–385.

Wilson, D. S., 1980. *The Natural Selection of Populations and Communities*, Menlo Park, California, Benjamin Cummings. Chapter 2 is reprinted in part in this volume.

Wilson, E. O., 1973. "Group selection and its significance for ecology," *Bioscience*, 23:631–638.

Young, R. M., 1971. "Darwin's metaphor: Does nature select?" *The Monist*, 55:442–503.

III

Models of Selection: Kin, Group, and Hierarchical

Introduction to Part III

One of the central problem areas in population biology during the last twenty years has concerned selection acting at levels other than that of the individual organism. Social or altruistic behavior seemed to exist in nature, and its evolution seemed to demand higher levels of selection. How could such behavior evolve? As discussed in Part I, Wynne-Edwards (1962 and this volume) suggested the differential reproduction of semi-isolated groups. This is (a type of) *group selection.* Hamilton (1963, 1964a, b) suggested that sociality evolved by altruistic benefits being distributed nonrandomly—usually (though not necessarily) nonrandomly with respect to kinship. Thus altruistic genes could increase in frequency by coding for behavior that benefits other carriers of those genes. Maynard Smith (1964) called this form of selection *kin selection.*

Kin and group selection were conceived of as competing models of higher-level selection. Among the important questions asked was: Which is the dominant force in the evolution of sociality? Although posed as an empirical question, it could not be approached until considerable theoretical work had been done. It would be premature to claim that a theoretical consensus has developed, but many of the key theoretical questions have been clarified by the mathematical models that have been developed over the last few years. This part of the book presents some of those models, with discussions of their ramifications.

W. D. Hamilton is considered the founder of modern kin-selection theory. In the article reprinted here he presents a general model of selection based on Price's (1970 and 1972) covariance formula, which separates levels of selection. One of the virtues of his model is that it makes very clear that selection at any given level depends on the variance at that level. Any form of assortive grouping would create the variance necessary for selection to occur at a level above that of the individual organism.

As stated earlier, higher-level selection seems to be necessary for the evolution of altruism. Hamilton derives the following formula (often called Hamilton's rule) describing the criterion for the positive selection of altruism:

$$\frac{K}{k} > \frac{1}{F}$$

where k represents the fitness effect on the actor (the "cost" of altruism), K the total fitness effect on all those affected by the action ("benefit" to the recipient), and F the correlation between two randomly selected members of the group. One population structure that would yield a positive correlation between group members is one where the total population is broken down into groups based on kinship. This is the sort of structure Hamilton originally considered and is why the term "kin selection" has been applied to his models. The idea, of course, was that an altruistic allele can spread in a population if the altruist mainly benefits his close kin who also are likely to carry the altruistic allele. But all that matters here is that the beneficiary of the altruistic act be likely to carry the altruistic allele, not that he be likely to carry that allele *because* he is closely related to the altruist. In the article reprinted here Hamilton makes this clear by using F, a correlation coefficient, rather than some coefficient of relationship.

Hamilton defines his notion of *inclusive fitness* as follows: The inclusive fitness of A equals A's nonsocial (or noninteractive) fitness plus all of the fitness effects of A's actions when each has been devalued by a regression coefficient between A and the affected party. Hamilton argues that the concept of inclusive fitness is more general than that of kin selection, since kinship is just one way of getting a positive altruist-recipient regression. Based on these considerations, Hamilton sees kin selection as one type of a more general process, not as something that could be dichotomously opposed to group selection.

Michod reviews the major models of kin selection, putting them in a common population-genetics framework—that is, a framework of models of gene frequency change. He categorizes the models into two types: *inclusive fitness models* and *family structured models*. The inclusive-fitness models are based on Hamilton's notion of inclusive fitness. As such they depend on some coefficient of genetic correlation. From these models one can derive Hamilton's rule (see above) for a wide variety of conditions. The models also allow one to determine the conditions under which Hamilton's rule is not satisfied. The family-structured models do not explicitly use the notion of inclusive fitness. Rather, in these models the total population is divided into family groups, and the fitness of a genotype is dependent on the frequencies of the relevant genotypes within its group. Using these within-group frequency-dependent fitness values the models then predict gene frequency changes in the total population.

These two types of models seem quite different. In particular, they lend themselves to two radically different verbal descriptions of kin selection. The inclusive-fitness models seem to support a "gene's eye view" of evolution. We can describe those models in terms of what a gene has to do in order to increase in frequency. It can increase either the fitness of its carrier or the fitness of other carriers of that allele. Thus the inclusive-fitness models seem to support a reductionist theory of evolution. On the other hand, the family-structured models seem to support an antireductionist theory. We can describe those models in terms of what a family has to do in order to increase its productivity. Here we seem to be talking about a level of organization higher than that of the individual organism.

Interestingly, Michod points out that in their common range of application the two classes of models are equivalent—that is, they make the same predictions about gene-frequency changes (see also Abugov and Michod, 1981). Furthermore, it should be noted that the two sorts of models can be generalized along the same lines. As Hamilton points out, the concept of inclusive fitness applies whenever there is genetic correlation between interactants, no matter what the origins of the correlation. Likewise, the family-structured models could be extended to apply to all cases of assortative grouping, not just those where the grouping is based on kinship. Thus the applicability of either of these two types of models to a given case or range of cases does not suffice to resolve questions about the causes of the relevant changes in gene frequency. A further account of the dynamics of the situation is required to support either a reductionist or an antireductionist account of the matter.

What do these models have to say about the relationship between kin and group selection? Michod defines kin selection as follows:

To evolve by kin selection a genetic trait expressed by one individual (termed the actor) must affect the genetic fitness of one or more other individuals who are genetically related to the actor in a nonrandom way at the loci determining the trait. (chapter 13, this volume)

Michod adopts Uyenoyama and Feldman's definition of a group:

A group is the smallest collection of individuals within a population defined such that genotypic fitness calculated within each group is not a (frequency-dependent) function of the composition of any other group. (Uyenoyama and Feldman 1980, p. 395)

(It should be noted that this is essentially equivalent to Wimsatt's definition of a group as a unit of selection.) Group selection, then, is the differential extinction and/or productivity of groups. Michod stresses that this definition does not require the spatial, temporal, or reproductive isolation of the groups. Furthermore, neither this definition nor that of kin selection require altruism. Altruism is just one of many possible fitness interactions. Michod suggests that most cases of kin selection are cases of group selection. That is, in most cases evolution by kin selection will proceed via the differential reproduction of kin groups. However, the relationship between kin and group selection is not one of logical inclusion. Michod argues that even if the per-family output to the general mating pool is fixed so that there could be no (family-)group selection, there could still be kin selection operating within the families. Such a situation would, however, severely constrain the behavioral traits that could evolve; in particular, altruism could not evolve (see also Boyd, 1982).

Maynard Smith, who introduced the term "kin selection" (Maynard Smith, 1964), did so in order to distinguish sharply the process that Hamilton was describing from the process of group selection. In the article reprinted here, Maynard Smith again argues for a sharp distinction between the two. Although we disagree with his view, it has been very influential and is worth considering.

Maynard Smith suggests that we draw the distinction between kin and group selection in terms of population structure. According to him, group selection requires the partial reproductive isolation of groups, whereas kin selection does not. In population biology the term "deme" is defined as the population unit within which breeding is random. As the distribution of a species approaches continuity, separation of the population into distinctive demes or well-defined groups becomes implausible. Demes are also called local populations, as opposed to global populations. If there is partial reproductive isolation between two groups of organisms, they cannot be parts of the same deme. Maynard Smith, then, is saying, first, that kin selection does not require interdemic selection (that is, the differential reproduction and/or extinction of demes) and, second, that the term "group selection" should be reserved for cases of interdemic selection.[1]

On the first point, Maynard Smith is quite right. The second point raises a nontrivial semantic issue. If we use the definition of groups given above, then *intrademic* group selection is quite possible. Many of the authors in this volume either explicitly or implicitly support such a definition (see, especially, the articles by Wimsatt, Michod, Wade, and Wilson), so we shall not argue its merits here. Rather, we wish to explore the reasons why someone might want to support Maynard Smith's view (as of 1976) and whether that can be done consistently.

Consider the following two population structures: (1) Individuals group together during some part of their life cycle, interact in ways that affect fitness, and then disperse to mate randomly in the global population; (2) individuals form groups that have complete reproductive isolation. In both cases the fitness of an individual is a frequency-dependent function of the composition of its group and is not a frequency-dependent function of the composition of any other group (that is, in both cases we have groups in the sense defined above). These two population structures form the end points of a continuum. Following Wade and Breden (1981), we can describe this continuum as follows: a proportion of the global population, f, mates within groups and the remainder of the population, $1 - f$, mates at random (within the global population). Structure (1) results when $f = 0$, and structure (2) when $f = 1$. Clearly f can range between 0 and 1, and we therefore have a continuum based on degree of breeding discontinuity.

Wade and Breden (1981) show that inbreeding facilitates the evolution of altruism. (See also Michod, 1979 and 1980. When altruism is extreme, there are exceptions to this rule, but they are not important to the purposes at hand.) That is, higher values of f increase both the range of conditions under which an altruistic allele will increase in frequency and the rate of increase. We would suggest that this result is fairly intuitive and that this intuition partially explains Maynard Smith's influential view.

Maynard Smith stresses the importance of reproductive isolation or discontinuities in the population breeding structure. In light of the above-mentioned result, this makes perfect sense. Such isolation does increase the between-group variance and so facilitates group selection. This also explains, we think, why so many people have thought that spatial and temporal isolation of groups are required for group selection. Spatial and temporal isolation are a way, and a very good one, of achieving reproductive isolation. But reproductive isolation is a matter of degree. How, then, can one draw a line through this continuum in a nonarbitrary way to make a sharp distinction between kin and group selection? We suggest that one cannot, and would cite the above considerations as well as our discussions of Hamilton and Michod to support our view. To put the point briefly, no matter where the line is drawn, there will be cases of kin selection on either side of it, and, if one accepts the definition of groups given above, the same is true of group selection. This point should become clearer in our discussions of Wade and D. S. Wilson, which follow.

Maynard Smith objected to lumping group and kin selection together, partly because group selection has had such a sullied past. In the last seven years Michael Wade has done as much as anyone to free group selection from its past associations and make it respectable. He has attempted that, both through experimental studies (Wade 1976, 1977, 1979b) and theoretical analyses (Slatkin and Wade 1978, Wade 1979a, Wade and Breden 1981). The backdrop for this work has been the general conclusion, drawn from the major models of group selection, that group selection is possible but is unlikely to be a significant force in nature, because it is unlikely that it will ever override the force of organismic selection. Wade's experimental work did not support this conclusion, and in the article reprinted here he argues that this conclusion is an artifact of certain assumptions made by the models.

Wade reviews the major models of group selection and divides them into two groups. The first he labels the *traditional group,* because of their affinity to Wright's shifting-balance theory of evolution (Wright 1929, 1931, 1945, and this volume). These models assume that the global population is divided into a number of demes between which there is some genetic interchange (migration). Group selection occurs by the differential extinction and recolonization of these demes. A more descriptive label for this group of models would be *interdemic selection models*. Recall that Maynard Smith would restrict the term "group selection" to just such models.

Wade labels the second category of models the *intrademic group*. In these models, individuals within a single panmictic population (a single deme) group together during some part of their life cycle and interact in a way that affects fitness. As a result of differences in these interactions, groups contribute differentially to the next generation, and so an individual's fitness is a frequency-dependent function of the genotypic composition of its group. (Recall the discussion of population structure (1) above. D. S. Wilson's models are in the intrademic group and will be discussed more fully below.)

By reviewing twelve models, Wade uncovers five common assumptions. All of the models make at least three of the five assumptions, and five models make all five assumptions. All of the five assumptions are simplifying assumptions, made to increase the analytical tractability of the models. But Wade found that all five are inherently unfavorable to group selection and, furthermore, he argues, there is no good biological reason for assuming them. Thus, Wade concludes, what was apparently a robust conclusion concerning the significance of group selection is in fact nothing but an artifact of certain biologically implausible assumptions.

D. S. Wilson has been one of the leading proponents of intrademic group selection. In the chapter excerpt presented here he argues that his model structure describes many, if not most, species in nature. Wilson points out that when fitnesses are frequency dependent, the standard population genetic models make an assumption concerning spatial homogeneity. That is, they assume that the frequency one organism experiences is the same for all others. Wilson argues that such spatial homogeneity is unrealistic for most species and that relaxing the assumption has important consequences. When it is relaxed, one gets population structure relevant to evolutionary dynamics.

Consider a trait, *A*, which affects fitness in a frequency-dependent manner. In a large deme the spatial-homogeneity assumption is not likely to be true. Thus two individuals with trait *A* may well experience significantly different frequencies of traits relevant to the fitness effect of *A*. Wilson suggests that every trait has a "sphere of influence" within with the homogeneity assumption is roughly satisfied. He labels this a *trait group*. He argues that, in general, trait goups are much smaller than demes.

The latter point is crucial to Wilson's project. In the above example two individuals with trait *A* have their fitnesses affected differently by *A*. This is because the fitness of A is frequency dependent and the two individuals experience relevantly different frequencies. Thus, from the point of view of determining fitness, they seem to be in different ecological settings. Within trait groups, however, A affects the fitness of its bearers equally. Thus we might describe trait groups as the unit of ecological homogeneity. Wilson's point is that the unit of ecological homogeneity will not always be the same as, and usually will be smaller than, the unit of genetic homogeneity—that is, the deme. When that is so, group selection can be a signficiant force—that is, traits can evolve that would be counterpredicted by models of pure individual selection.

Like all models of group selection, Wilson's model of intrademic group selection requires some between-group variance. With no variance the trait group would just be the deme. This represents a point of pure individual selection (at least within the deme). But as mentioned earlier, Wilson argues that this absence of intrademic structure is generally implausible. If it *is* implausible, what produces the between-group variance? As a conservative hypothesis, Wilson suggests the random distribution of individuals into trait groups. This would yield a roughly binomial distribution of types in the trait groups. Wilson shows that just this much variance will significantly affect the sorts of traits that can evolve.

Wilson is concerned with traits that influence not only the fitness of the individuals possessing them, but also the fitnesses of others. Such traits have an effect d on the fitness of self and r on the fitness of others. (It is plausible that all traits affecting fitness in a frequencey-dependent manner can be so described.) For a trait to increase in frequency by individual selection $d > r$ —that is, the trait must increase the *relative fitness* of its possessors. Wilson shows that with just random variance between trait groups, the criterion for the positive selection of a trait is $d > 0$—that is, the trait must increase the *absolute fitness* of its possessors.[2] Among such traits are those where $r > d > 0$. These "weakly altruistic" traits increase the fitness of others more than that of self and so would be selected against by individual selection.

With variance greater than the binomial distribution there can be selection for "strong altruism"—that is, traits where $r > 0 > d$. Although strong altruism has received much more attention than weak altruism in the literature on the evolution of sociality, Wilson thinks it is likely to be less prevalent in nature, since it is evolutionarily unstable. That is, for a given value of r, a trait with $r > d > 0$ will, if available, be favored over one where $r > 0 > d$ as long as individual selection is operating. In other words, although group selection will select for group benefit (traits increasing group productivity), the least costly way of achieving that benefit will always be selected for by individual selection. In any case strong altruism can evolve if there is sufficient between-trait-group variance. One way, perhaps the commonest way, of getting this variance is by grouping according to kinship (for example, where the trait group is a single sibship).

A final possibility is that all of the variance within a deme is between-group variance, so that there is no within-group variance. In such a population there could be no individual selection, and the criterion for the positive selection of a trait would be simply $r > 0$. This represents pure group selection. Wilson thinks that this possibility is as implausible as that of no intrademic structure.

Part III ends as it began, with an analysis of evolution by natural selection based on Price's (1970 and 1972) covariance selection equations. But Arnold and Fristrup go much further than Hamilton in extending the Pricean analysis into what they hope is a truly general, hierarchical model of evolution by natural selection. The aim for a general hierarchy is in accord with much of the work in this volume (see especially the articles by Wimsatt and Brandon), but the model developed by Arnold and Fristrup is, in one respect, importantly different from most of the major models of kin and group selection (for example, those reviewed by Michod and Wade).

According to Michod, the "hard core" of population genetics is "the view that gene frequency changes *are* evolution" (Michod, 1981, p. 30, but see Mayr, this volume, or Brandon, 1978). Most of the major models of kin and group selection are population-genetics models—that is, they represent evolution as change in gene frequency. The model developed by Arnold and Fristrup is not such a model, nor can it be transformed into one. Their model decouples higher-level selection from lower-level effects. Let us explain.

Sober and Lewontin assent to a view they attribute to Williams (this volume) and Dawkins (1976)—namely, that all selection processes "can be 'represented' in terms of selection coefficients attaching to single genes" (Sober and Lewontin, this volume). (They are quick to point out that it does not follow from this that all selection processes are *explainable* in terms of genic selection coefficients.) But is it true that all selection processes are so describable? It is true that in standard population genetics models higher-level selection can be so expressed. But that is just what makes them population genetics models. Arnold and Fristrup clearly show that it is at least conceptually possible for higher-level selection to fail to be expressible in terms of lower-level effects.

To illustrate their point, Arnold and Fristrup ask us to consider two hypothetical grasshopper species living in two separate resource-limited environments in such a way that the total number of individuals in each environment does not change through time. Suppose that the species of type A remains intact through a given time period while the species of type B speciates into numerous (smaller) species still of type B. This species-level trend, the increase of species of type B over species of type A, cannot be expressed—let alone explained—in terms of individual fitnesses, since by hypothesis the relative frequency of individuals in *A*-type species to individuals in *B*-type species has not changed. This is a powerful argument against any single-level (for example, genic) reductionistic theory of evolution.

(We should note that an analogous argument could be given for groups within a species. That is, what is true of species selection vis-à-vis individual (or genic) fitnesses is also true of interdemic group selection vis-à-vis individual (or genic) fitnesses. We do not think, however, that this means that population genetic models of interdemic group selection are fundamentally wrong-headed. But we cannot pursue that issue here.)

Arnold and Fristrup are particularly interested in species selection. In their model, species selection proceeds, like selection at other levels, via the Darwinian principle of the differential reproduction of heritable variation. As we have discussed earlier, many have argued against the effectiveness of group selection on the grounds that there would rarely be sufficient between-group variation in nature. Arnold and Fristrup point out that the analogous argument cannot be made against the effectiveness of species selection—there seems to be plenty of between-species variation.

In their multilevel model, a given level can be influenced from both above and below. For example, if the focal level is individual selection, then lower-level selection—for example, meiotic drive—may appear as an inheritance bias at the focal level, and higher-level selection—for example, group selection—may affect the focal level by affecting the covariance between focal-level fitness and character values. The general conclusion they draw from their model is that lower levels *constrain* but do not *direct* higher-level selection. If this is true, one must take higher-level selection seriously.

In closing we should note that the hierarchical picture developed by Arnold and Fristrup is in some ways similar to that of Wimsatt. In particular their hierarchy contains both replicators and interactors (see the introduction to Part II). It is not clear that this is a weakness of their model, given its use, but one should be wary of the confusion this ambiguity can cause.

Notes

1 In the preface to his article, written for this anthology, Maynard Smith suggests that we drop the term "group selection" altogether. He suggests that, instead, we use such terms as "interdemic selection" and "species selection" in order to fit the case at hand. He would reject the suggestion put forward in the next paragraph of our text on the grounds, first, that the term "group selection" should not be employed for both intrademic and interdemic phenomena and, second, that all (or virtually all) of the phenomena encompassed by "intrademic group selection" are properly described as frequency-dependent selection. This latter claim is surely controversial, among other reasons because

the term "frequency-dependent selection" itself already encompasses a number of disparate phenomena.

2 The similarity of this formulation to Hamilton's should be noted. Taking Wilson's "*d*" and "*r*" to correspond to Hamilton's "*k*" and "*K*" respectively, the same prediction follows from Hamilton's theory.

References

Abugov, R. and Michod, R. E., 1981. "On the relation of family structured models and inclusive fitness models for kin selection," *J. Theor. Biol.*, 88:743–754.

Boyd, R., 1982. "Density-dependent mortality and the evolution of social interactions," *Anim. Behav.*, 30:972–982.

Brandon, R. N., 1978. "Evolution," *Phil. Sci.*, 45:96–109.

Dawkins, R., 1976. *The Selfish Gene*, Oxford, Oxford University Press.

Hamilton, W. D., 1963. "The evolution of altruistic behavior," *Am. Nat.*, 97:354–356.

Hamilton, W. D., 1964a. "The genetical evolution of social behavior, I," *J. Theor. Biol.*, 7:1–16.

Hamilton, W. D., 1964b. "The genetical evolution of social behavior, II," *J. Theor. Biol.*, 7:17–52.

Maynard Smith, J., 1964. "Group selection and kin selection," *Nature*, 201:1145–47.

Michod, R. E., 1979. "Genetical aspects of kin selection: Effects of inbreeding," *J. Theor. Biol.*, 81:223–233.

Michod, R. E., 1980. "Evolution of interactions in family structured populations: Mixed mating models," *Genetics*, 96:275–296.

Michod, R. E., 1981. "Positive heuristics in evolutionary biology," *Brit. J. Philos. Sci.*, 32:1–36.

Price, G. R., 1970. "Selection and covariance," *Nature*, 227:520–521.

Price, G. R., 1972. "Extension of covariance selection mathematics," *Ann. Hum. Genet.*, 35:485–490.

Slatkin, M. and Wade, M. J., 1978. "Group selection on a quantitative character," *Proc. Natl. Acad. Sci. U.S.A.*, 75:3531–34.

Uyenoyama, M., and Feldman, M. W., 1980. "Theories of kin and group selection: A population genetics perspective," *Theor. Pop. Biol.*, 19:87–123.

Wade, M. J., 1976. "Group selection among laboratory populations of *Tribolium*," *Proc. Natl. Acad. Sci. U.S.A.*, 73:4604–07.

Wade, M. J., 1977. "An experimental study of group selection," *Evolution*, 31:134–153.

Wade, M. J., 1979a. "The evolution of social interactions by family selection," *Am. Nat.*, 113:399–417.

Wade, M. J., 1979b. "The primary characteristics of *Tribolium* populations group selected for increased and decreased population size," *Evolution,* 33: 749–764.

Wade, M. J. and Breden, F., 1981. "The effect of inbreeding on the evolution of altruistic behavior by kin selection," *Evolution,* 35:844–858.

Wright, S., 1929. "Evolution in a Mendelian population," *Anat. Record.,* 44: 287.

Wright, S., 1931. "Evolution in Mendelian populations," *Genetics,* 16:93–159.

Wright, S., 1945. "*Tempo and Mode in Evolution:* A Critical Review," *Ecology,* 26:415–419.

Wynne-Edwards. V. C., 1962. *Animal Dispersion in Relation to Social Behavior,* New York, Hafner.

12

Innate Social Aptitudes of Man: An Approach from Evolutionary Genetics

W. D. Hamilton

It has become clear that, although learning has great importance in the normal development of nearly all phases of primate behaviour, it is not a generalized ability; animals are able to learn some things with great ease and other things only with the greatest difficulty. Learning is part of the adaptive pattern of a species and can be understood only when it is seen as a process of acquiring skills and attitudes that are of evolutionary significance to a species when living in the environment to which it is adapted.

Washburn, Jay, and Lancaster (1965)

Survival of the Fittest

The phrase directs attention to differential survival. Darwin accepted it from Herbert Spencer as adequately expressing the idea of natural selection. While accusations of tautology seem hardly fair on this small phrase itself, it must be admitted that some descendent ideas in the theory of natural selection are open to attack. For example, the idea of measuring ability to survive and re-produce—biological "fitness"—has undoubtedly been useful, but a slight haziness still lingers, a lack of precise and general definition: we do not know exactly what qualities natural selection is after. I think it is doubt like this rather than doubt about the reality and effectiveness of natural selection that inspires a present spirit of caution in evolutionary biology, including caution and distrust towards Spencer's ideogram whenever it renews aspirations to become a slogan.

A part of the difficulty, and the part I am mainly concerned with now, is that of saying exactly what are the things that natural selection is supposed to select. The fittest what? Is it a trait, an individual, a set of individuals bearing a trait, or bearing its determinants expressed or latent? Can it be a population, a whole species, perhaps even an ecosystem? In such a confusion of possibil-ities (and of fervent opinions either way) the individual organism stands out

From pp. 133–141 and 154–155 of *Biosocial Anthropology*, ed. R. Fox, London: Malaby Press, 1975. Original article, pp. 133–155.

as one clear and obvious choice, with the number of its offspring as the measure of its fitness. But, beyond the problem of when to count and how to weight offspring for their ages, there is the problem that in sexual species the individual is really a physical composite of contributions from two parents, and it may be composite in slightly different ways for different parts. Moreover, Mendel's principles concerning the fair distribution of genes to gametes and fair competition of these in fertilization do not always hold, so that the set of offspring of a given individual may carry a biased sample from the composite. Does this matter? For safe conclusions, do we have to descend to the level of the individual gene, perhaps ultimately to that of changed or added parts of the replicating molecule? Or can we, on the contrary, confidently follow the consensus of biologists to a higher level, in believing that the generally significant selection is at the level of competing groups and species? I shall argue that lower levels of selection are inherently more powerful than higher levels, and that careful thought and factual checks are always needed before lower levels are neglected. In this I follow a recent critical trend in evolutionary thought (Williams, 1966; Lewontin, 1970; Hamilton, 1972; and references in these works). Incidentally, to a biologist, a rather similar critique seems to be invited by the supposition that cultural evolution is independent of evolution in its biological substratum: to come to our notice, cultures too have to survive and will hardly do so when by their nature they undermine the viability of their bearers.[1] Thus we would expect the genetic system to have various inbuilt safeguards and to provide not a blank sheet for individual cultural development but a sheet at least lightly scrawled with certain tentative outlines. The problem facing a humane civilization may be how to complete a sketch suggesting some massive and brutal edifice—say the outlines of an Aztec pyramid—so that it reappears as a Parthenon or a Taj Mahal. These ideas concerning cultural evolution will not be expanded in what follows, but I hope to produce evidence that some things which are often treated as purely cultural in man—say racial discrimination—have deep roots in our animal past and thus are quite likely to rest on direct genetic foundations. To be more specific, it is suggested that the ease and accuracy with which an idea like xenophobia strikes the next replica of itself on the template of human memory may depend on the preparation made for it there by selection—selection acting, ultimately, at the level of replicating molecules.

Returning to the problem of units of selection, Darwin himself, vague about the process of heredity, based most of his arguments on considerations of the fitness of individuals. He made occasional exceptions—as for the social insects, where he treated the "family group" as the unit of selection. I believe even these limited concessions were incautious (Hamilton, 1972), and value his judgment more where, discussing the evolution of courage and self-sacrifice in man, he left a difficulty apparent and unsolved. He saw that such traits would naturally be counterselected *within* a social group whereas in competition *between* groups, the groups with the most of such qualities would be the ones best fitted to survive and increase. This open problem which Darwin left is really the starting-point of my own argument, but it is historically interesting to note that after some initial wavering between the calls of Spencer, Kropotkin, and others, almost the whole field of biology stampeded in the direction where Darwin had gone circumspectly or not at all.

Until the advent of Mendelism, uncritical acceptance of group selection could be understood partly on grounds of vagueness about the hereditary process. For example, courage and self-sacrifice could spread by cultural contagion and, in so spreading, modify heredity as well. But in the event neither the rediscovery of Mendel's work nor the fairly brisk incorporation of Mendelism into evolutionary theory had much effect. From about 1920 to about 1960 a curious situation developed where the models of "Neo-Darwinism" were all concerned with selection at levels no higher than that of competing individuals, whereas the biological literature as a whole increasingly proclaimed faith in Neo-Darwinism, and at the same time stated almost all its interpretations of adaptation in terms of "benefit to the species." The leading theorists did occasionally point out the weakness of this position, but on the whole concerned themselves with it surprisingly little (references in Hamilton 1964, 1971, 1972).

With facts mostly neutral and theory silent, it seems that we must look to the events and the "isms" of recent human history to understand how such a situation arose. Marxism, trade unionism, fears of "social darwinism," and vicissitudes of thought during two world wars seem likely influences. Confronted with common social exhortations, natural selection is easily accused of divisive and reactionary implications unless "fittest" means the fittest species (man) and "struggle" means struggle against nature (anything but man). "Benefit-of-the-species" arguments, so freely used during the period in question, are seen in this light as euphemisms for natural selection. They provide for the reader (and evidently often for the writer as well) an escape from inner conflict, exacting nothing emotionally beyond what most of us learn to accept in childhood, that most forms of life exploit and prey on one another.

Levels of Selection

Often the problem is not acute. There are many traits like resistance to disease, good eyesight, dexterity which are clearly beneficial to individual, group, and species. But with most traits that can be called social in a general sense there is some question. For example, as language becomes more sophisticated, there is more opportunity to pervert its use for selfish ends: fluency is an aid to persuasive lying as well as to conveying complex truths that are socially useful. Consider also the selective value of having a conscience. The more consciences are lacking in a group as a whole, the more energy the group will need to divert to enforcing otherwise tacit rules or else face dissolution. Thus considering one step (individual vs. group) in a hierarchical population structure, having a conscience is an "altruistic" character. But for the next step—group vs. supergroup—it might be selfish, in the sense that the groups with high levels of conscience and orderly behavior may grow too fast and threaten to overexploit the resources on which the whole supergroup depends. As a more biological instance, similar considerations apply to sex ratio, and here a considerable amount of data has accumulated for arthropods (Hamilton, 1967).

A recent reformulation of natural selection can be adapted to show how two successive levels of the subdivision of a population contribute separately to the overall natural selection (Price, 1972). The approach is not limited to Mendelian inheritance but its usefulness in other directions (for example, cultural evolution) has not yet been explored.

Consider a population consisting of a mixture of particles, and suppose we are interested in the frequency of a certain kind of particle G. Suppose the particles are grouped: let the subscript s denote the sth subpopulation. For subpopulation and for the whole we define parameters relevant to natural selection as follows:

	Subpopulation	Whole population
Number of particles:	n_s	$N = \Sigma n_s$
Frequency of G:	q_s	$q = \Sigma n_s q_s / N$
Mean fitness:	w_s	$w = \Sigma n_s w_s / N$

Fitness measures the amount of successful replication of particles in one 'generation'. Thus the total population of the next generation will be $N' = \Sigma n_s w_s$. The symbol $'$, denoting "next generation," is used again in the same sense in the following further addition to notation:

	Subpopulation	Whole population
Change in frequency of G in one generation:	$\Delta q_s = q_s' - q_s$	$\Delta q = q' - q$

With such notation it is easy to derive:

$$w \, \Delta q = \Sigma n_s w_s (q_s - q)/N + \Sigma n_s w_s \, \Delta q_s / N$$
$$= Covariance \, (w_s, q_s) + Expectation \, (w_s \, \Delta q_s) \tag{1}$$

where *Covariance* and *Expectation* are understood to involve weighting by the n_s as indicated. This is Price's form.[2] The covariance term represents the contribution of *intergroup* selection, so quantifying the intuitive notion that high q_s must cause high w_s for selective change to occur. The expectation term represents the contribution of *intragroup selection*. It is possible to apply the formula within itself, to expand $w_s \Delta q_s$. For example, if the next level is that of diploid individuals and si indexes the ith individual of the sth group, we have $n_s = \Sigma 2 n_{si}$, $q_s = \Sigma 2 q_{si}/n_s$ and $w_s = \Sigma 2 w_{si}/n_s$ where these summations are understood to cover all i instead of all s as previously. Then $w_s \Delta q_s$ decomposes into two terms, one of which represents ordinary diploid selection with strictly Mendelian inheritance, while the second represents the effects of genetic "drift" (random sampling effects), and "drive" (non-Mendelian ratios). Even this latter term can be reformulated using (1), but then our "groups" are the fundamental particles themselves which, neglecting mutation, must give $\Delta q_{particle} = 0$, so that here finally the second term goes out.

An often useful rearrangement of (1), which shows the dependence of selection on the variability in its units, introduces the regression coefficient of w_s on q_s. If β_1 is this coefficient:

$$w \Delta q = \beta_1 \ Variance \ (q_s) + Expectation \ (w_s \Delta q_s) \qquad (2)$$

Conceptual simplicity, recursiveness, and formal separation of levels of selection are attractive features of these equations. But, of course, being able to point to a relevant and generally non-zero part of selective change is far from showing that group selection can override individual selection when the two are in conflict. Moreover, even the possibility of devising model circumstances in which a positive group-selection term (first term) outweighs a negative individual selection one (second term, assuming no further levels), gives no guarantee that "altruism" can evolve by group selection: we have to consider whether the population can get into the specified state, and, if it can, whether its present trend will continue. For example, if we suppose persistent groups with no extinction and no intergroup migration, it is easy to arrange that the group-beneficial effect (β_1), of frequent altruism in a certain group is so large that the rapid expansion of the group with the highest frequency of G (q_m say) draws the population q rapidly upwards. But q will never reach or pass q_m, and must eventually fall, remaining below the ever-falling value of q_m. Admittedly, all this is reasonably obvious without the equation, but the equation does emphasize that natural selection depends on a certain variance which in this model must at last die away as the best group increasingly predominates. This is the essential objection to an algebraic model of Haldane (1932) for selection of altruism, which other writers have wrongly treated as the first successful analytical model for altruism. In verbal discussion Haldane himself admitted the necessity of a device to maintain diversity. He suggested that if groups split on reaching a certain size, random assortment of altruists and egotists would raise the frequency of altruists in some daughter moieties, and if the critical size was low enough and the group advantage of altruism high enough, a process having endless overall enrichment in altruism might be devised. Increasing the intergoup variance by random (or, better, associative) division of existing tribes leaves less variance within groups, which, as a development of the equation will shortly make plain, weakens the power of individual selection, and this further improves the case. But Price's equation does not seem to lend itself to a detailed analysis of Haldane's suggestion— indeed the lack of analysis by Haldane himself suggests that it is not easy. The value of the covariance approach lies not so much in analytical penetration as in clarifying the approach to a problem.

Therefore, noting hopeful auguries in Haldane's tribe-splitting no-migration idea, let us now turn to a model at the opposite extreme in which groups break up completely and re-form in each generation. Suppose that on reaching maturity the young animals take off to form a migrant pool, from which groups of n are randomly selected to be the group of the next generation. Assume completely asexual reproduction (or perfect matriclinal or patriclinal inheritance of a cultural trait in an ordinary population), and assume that an altruist gives up k units of his own fitness in order to add K units to the joint fitness of his $(n-1)$ companions. These companions are a random selection from the gene pool and therefore, in a supposed infinite population, have the expected gene frequency of the gene pool. Thus compared to a non-altruist, the altruist is putting into the next gene pool fewer of his own genes plus a random handful from the pool of the last generation. Obviously his trait is not enriching the population with genes that cause the trait. The specification of grouping has been a mere gesture. Nevertheless it is instructive to see how equation (2) handles the matter.

With asexuality, individuals are basic particles; so, as already explained, the recursive use of (2) to expand its second term gives simply:

$$w \Delta q = \beta_1 \ Var(q_s) + E \{ \beta_0 \ Var_s (q_{si}) \}$$

All units are now of the same size, so $Var(iance)$ and $E(xpectation)$ can have their conventional meanings. Since β_0 does not vary with group constitution,

$$w \Delta q = \beta_1 \ Var(q_s) + \beta_0 \ E \{ Var_s (q_{si}) \} \tag{3}$$

and the expectation is what is commonly called the within-group variance.

With random grouping, the distribution of the different compositions of groups will be binomial with parameters (q, n). The variance of q_s is $\frac{1}{n} pq$. Likewise it is easily shown that $E \{ Var_s (q_{si}) \} = \frac{n-1}{n} pq$, so that

$$w \Delta q = \frac{1}{n} pq \{ \beta_1 + (n-1) \beta_0 \} \tag{4}$$

This already shows the characteristically greater power of the lower level of selection as dictated by a ratio of variances that is bound to hold when grouping is random or nearly so.

In a group with v of its n members altruistic fitnesses are as follows:

Group mean	Selfish member	Altruistic member
$1 + \dfrac{v}{n}(K - k)$	$1 + v\,\dfrac{K}{n-1}$	$1 - k + (v - 1)\,\dfrac{K}{n-1}$

Thus by inspection and by subtraction respectively

$$\beta_1 = K - k \text{ and } \beta_0 = -k - \frac{K}{n-1} \tag{5}$$

Substituting in (4) we find:

$$w\,\Delta q = -k\,p\,q \tag{6}$$

This confirms the earlier argument that altruism cannot progress in such a model. It seems at first glance that the benefits dispensed by altruists have been entirely null in the working of the model, but they affect it through their involvement in mean fitness:

$$w = p + q(K - k)$$

This being the only involvement of K, we see that the most that altruism can achieve in the model is a slowing of the rate at which natural selection reduces its frequency—an effect which I explained earlier as altruism diluting each new gene mixture by adding, as it were, handfuls taken randomly from the previous one. Apart from this minor effect, the model, like Haldane's algebraic one, is a failure, in spite of having shifted to the opposite extreme in respect of migration. It reveals a group-selection component that is not zero but is bound in an unchanging subordination to the individual selection component. However, the relation between the two variances in this case suggests how we must change the model to make altruism succeed: $Var(q_s)$ must be increased relative to $E\{Var_s(q_{si})\}$. As already mentioned, this can be done by making G assort positively with its own type in settling from the migrant cloud. Suppose it assorts to such a degree that the correlation of two separate randomly selected members of a group is F. If this correlation is achieved by having a fraction F of groups made pure for each type and then the remainder again formed randomly, then it is easily shown that the between and within group variances are respectively:

$$\frac{1}{n}pq\,(1 - F + nF) \text{ and } \frac{1}{n}pq\,(n - 1)(1 - F)$$

Putting these results and those of (5) into equation (3) we find as the generalization of (6):

$$w\,\Delta q = p\,q\,(FK - k) \tag{7}$$

so that the criterion for positive selection of altruism is

$$\frac{K}{k} > \frac{1}{F}$$

Now the model can be made to work. Moreover, the simple form and the independence of group size suggest that the criterion may hold beyond the limits of the rather artificial model discussed here. Careful thought confirms that this is indeed the case: the criterion is completely general for asexual models with non-overlapping generations, and also holds for sexual diploid models when the coefficient F is suitably redefined (Hamilton, 1964, 1970). The easiest way to see the basis of generality is to notice that the benefits of altruism do not now fall on a random section of the population and therefore do not simply enlarge the existing gene pool; instead they fall on individuals *more likely to be altruists* than are random members of the population. Indeed, the existence of the positive correlation F could be interpreted as implying in this case that there is a chance F that the K units of fitness are definitely given to a fellow altruist, while with chance $(1 - F)$ they are given (as they always were in the previous version) to a random member of the population.

The redefinition necessary for diploid organism involves specifying a regression coefficient, b_{AB}, representing the regression of the genotype of recipient B on genotype of donor A. Often this is the same as the correlation coefficient of such genotypes (it always is so in the haploid case); but where they differ, it is the regression coefficient that gives the prediction of gene content that we need. To get the form like (7), which applies to diploid selection, other changes are obviously necessary, notably dividing pq by two to get the variance of gene frequency between pairs instead of that between individuals and other more complex changes connected with dominance and details of the assortative process. However, it is striking that a criterion like $(FK - k) > 0$ can be shown to determine positive selection of each genotype, and can be generalized to cover cases where A distributes various effects, positive or negative, to numerous individuals B, C, D, . . . all having different regressions on A. Including A himself in the list of recipients, we arrive at the idea of A's "inclusive fitness"; his basic nonsocial fitness, plus all the effects caused by his action when each has been devalued by a regression coefficient.

The usefulness of the "inclusive fitness" approach to social behavior (i.e. an approach using criteria like $(b_{AB} K - k) > 0$) is that it is more general than the "group selection," "kin selection," or "reciprocal altruism" approaches and so provides an overview even where regression coefficients and fitness effects are not easy to estimate or specify. As against "group selection" it provides a useful conceptual tool where no grouping is apparent—for example, it can deal with an ungrouped viscous population where, owing to restricted migration, an individual's normal neighbors and interactants tend to be his genetical kindred.

Because of the way it was first explained, the approach using inclusive fitness has often been identified with "kin selection" and presented strictly as an alternative to "group selection" as a way of establishing altruistic social behavior by natural selection (for example, Maynard Smith, 1964; Lewontin, 1970). But the foregoing discussion shows that kinship should be considered just one way of getting positive regression of genotype in the recipient, and that it is this positive regression that is vitally necessary for altruism. Thus the inclusive-fitness concept is more general than "kin selection." Haldane's suggestion about tribe-splitting can be seen in one light as a way of increasing intergroup variance and in another as a way of getting positive regression in the population as a whole by having the groups that happen to have most altruists divide most frequently. In this case the altruists are helping true relatives. But in the assortative-settling model it obviously makes no difference if altruists settle with altruists because they are related (perhaps never having parted from them) or because they recognize fellow altruists as such, or settle together because of some pleiotropic effect of the gene on habitat preference. If we insist that group selection is different from kin selection, the term should be restricted to situations of assortation definitely not involving kin. But it seems on the whole preferable to retain a more flexible use of terms; to use group selection where groups are clearly in evidence and to qualify with mention of "kin" (as in the "kin-group" selection referred to by Brown, 1974), "relatedness" or "low migration" (which is often the cause of relatedness in groups), or else "assortation," as appropriate. The term "kin selection" appeals most where pedigrees tend to be unbounded and interwoven, as is so often the case with man.

Although correlation between interactants is necessary if altruism is to receive positive selection, it may well be that trying to find regression coefficients is not the best analytical approach to a particular model. Indeed, the problem of formulating them *exactly* for sexual models proves difficult (Hamilton, 1964). One recent model that makes more frequent group extinction the penalty for selfishness (or lack of altruism) has achieved rigorous and striking conclusions without reference to regression or relatedness (Eshel, 1972). But reassuringly the conclusions of both this and another similar model (more general but less thorough and much less well explained; Levins, 1970) are of the general kind that consideration of regression leads us to expect. The regression is due to relatedness in these cases, but, classified by approach, these were the first working models of group selection.

Notes

1 Fox (1967) has also emphasized this in discussing human kinship systems and why some that are easily conceivable never actually occur. His discussion of the incest taboo is also very pertinent to the idea that follows.

2 Price (1970) first pointed out the generality and usefulness of this relation, but earlier partial recognition of it seems to be due to Robertson (1966).

References

Brown, J. L., 1974. "Alternative routes to sociality in jays," *American Zoologist*, 14:63–80.

Eshel, I., 1972. "On the neighbor effect and the evolution of altruistic traits," *Theoretical Population Biology*, 3:258–277.

Fox, R., 1967. *Kinship and Marriage*, London, Penguin.

Haldane, J. B. S., 1932. *The Causes of Evolution*, Ithaca, N.Y., Cornell Universtiy Press, 1966.

Hamilton, W. D., 1964. "The genetical evolution of social behavior, I and II," *Journal of Theoretical Biology*, 7:1–52.

Hamilton, W. D., 1967. "Extraordinary sex ratios," *Science*, 156:477–488.

Hamilton, W. D., 1970. "Selfish and spiteful behavior in an evolutionary model," *Nature*, 228:1218–1220.

Hamilton, W. D., 1971. "Selection of selfish and altruistic behavior in some extreme models," in *Man and Beast: Comparative Social Behavior*, ed. J. F. Eisenberg and W. S. Dillon, Washington, D.C., Smithsonian Institution Press, pp. 57–91.

Hamilton, W. D., 1972. "Altruism and related phenomena, mainly in social insects," *Annual Review of Ecology and Systematics*, 3:193–232.

Levins, R., 1970. "Extinction," in *Some Mathematical Questions in Biology*, ed. M. Gerstenhaber, Providence, R.I., American Mathematical Society, pp. 77–107.

Lewontin, R. C., 1970. "The units of selection," *Annual Review of Ecology and Systematics*, 1:1–18.

Maynard Smith, J., 1964. "Group selection and kin selection," *Nature*, 201: 1145–1147.

Price, G. R., 1970. "Selection and covariance," *Nature*, 227:520–521.

Price, G. R., 1972. "Extension of covariance selection mathematics," *Annals of Human Genetics*, 35:485–490.

Robertson, A., 1966. "A mathematical model of the culling process in dairy cattle," *Animal Production*, 8:95–108.

Washburn, S. L., Jay, P. C., and Lancaster, B., 1965. "Field studies of Old World monkeys and apes," *Science*, 150:1541–1547.

Williams, G. C., 1966. *Adaptation and Natural Selection: A Critique of some Current Evolutionary Thought*, Princeton, N. J., Princeton University Press.

13

The Theory of Kin Selection

Richard E. Michod

Introduction

Apart from some comments by Fisher (32) and Haldane (34, 35) and the practice of artificial selection based on relatives—for example, (56) and (117); see (6), p. 20, for Darwin's views on this—the evolutionary implications of genetic correlations between interactants remained unexplored until 1963, when W. D. Hamilton published the first of his seminal papers. In these papers, Hamilton (37-39) developed the central tools of what is termed (59) the theory of kin selection: the concept of inclusive fitness and the cost-benefit rule. These two theoretical tools have revolutionized the way biologists (and some social scientists) view the evolution of social behavior. In addition, these tools provide the formal framework for most empirical studies in this area and have given rise to a new subdiscipline of evolutionary biology: sociobiology (109), whose empirical growth and progress they continue, in large part, to direct.

In this paper, I review the apparently diverse theoretical studies of kin selection in a common population-genetic framework. Thus the first part of the review is devoted to constructing a theoretical framework within which the various models can be put in perspective. The definitions of all terms and symbols used are given in Table 1. At the expense of blurring the different utilities of the many models, I emphasize their similarities in the hope of clarifying the logical and conceptual correlates of kin selection. In the second part of the review, I discuss the implications of this theory for many of the terms and concepts used in sociobiology. I have been careful in these sections to concentrate on what the theory says about the terms and concepts discussed. I have noted when this is at odds with other uses in the literature; however, my purpose here is not to discuss and compare all of the various uses of such terms as individual selection, group selection, or even kin selection. Rather I

From *Annual Review of Ecology and Systematics* (1982), 13:23-55.

Table 1
Definitions of terms used in text

Fitness

---

w_{ij}	fitness of genotype i when interacting with genotype j (Eqs. 9)
W_i	fitness of genotype i (Eqs. 1, 22)
W_{im}	fitness of genotype i in family m (Eq. 23)
$\overline{W}_m$	average fitness of family m (Table 3)
$\overline{W}$	average or population fitness (Eqs. 3, 30)
$F(p)$	Wright's (120) fitness function (Eqs. 4, 11, 13)
b_i	fitness effect of genotype i's behavior on others
c_i	fitness effect of genotype i's behavior on self
e_i	inclusive fitness effect (Eq. 12)
$\overline{e}$	average inclusive fitness effect (Eq. 13)

Probability Distributions

P_{ij}	joint distribution of genotypes
$P_{i|j}$	conditional distribution of genotypes
P_i	marginal distribution of genotypes
$P_{j|F_m}$	probability of genotype j in family m
$P_{F_m|i}$	probability of family m given genotype i
$P_{ij|I_k}$	joint distribution of genotypes given identity event k
Δ_k	probability of identity event k
$M_{j|F_m}$	expected Mendelian frequency of genotype j in family m

Variables

---

p	frequency of A allele
q	frequency of a allele ($= 1 - p$)
g_i	frequency of genotype i after selection
f_m	frequency of diploid family m

Coefficients

ψ_X, ψ_Y	inbreeding (Eq. 6)
ψ_{XY}	consanguinity (Eq. 7)
ρ	rho (71, 72)
r	$= \dfrac{Cov\,(sib_g, sib_g)}{Var(sib_g)}$, where sib_g represents the additive genotypic values of sibs (see 90–92 for calculations).

Events and Miscellaneous Terms

I_k	identity state k (see Figure 1)
F_m	family m (see Table 3)

Table 1 (continued)

Events and Miscellaneous Terms

i, j	genotypes i and j ($i, j = 0, 1, 2$ for AA, Aa, aa)
X, Y	interacting individuals
d	propensity of heterozygote to behave socially
A, a	alleles at a hypothetical locus causing a difference in social behavior
α	fraction of offspring manipulated into being altruists by parents

---

hope to state, as clearly as the theory allows, the distinctions the theory suggests between these and other terms.

I pay no attention in this review to the growing body of empirical work dealing with kin selection. Specifically, I do not consider whether the theory is an empirically verified theory or whether the theoretical growth described in what follows has led to empirical growth. Rather, I focus on the logical structure of the theory itself and to what extent its heuristics are rooted in evolution's hard core—the theory of gene frequency change (67). Is the theory a cohesive, logically structured theory or is it simply a collection of more or less disconnected, disjointed models separate from the main body of population genetics theory? Answers to these questions are a necessary prerequisite to sound empirical work. However, both aspects of theory—its logical development from first principles and its empirical import and utility—are crucial to a healthy research program (49, 50).

Because of space limitations, I do not explicitly cover the subfield dealing with kin selection and sex-ratio evolution (20, 41, 57, 74, 87, 88). Nor do I include the various theoretical applications of "inclusive fitness thinking" in a game-theoretic or optimization context (for example, 45, 74).

Theoretical Framework
Genotypic Distribution of Social Interactions
To study the evolution of social behavior in a traditional population-genetic context, the effects of the various social interactions on genotypic fitness must be specified. In the genetic approach, differences in social behavior are assumed to result, in part, from differences in genotype. Once genotypes are assigned their behavioral phenotypes defined in terms of their effects on fitness, genotypic fitness can be calculated from the frequency distribution of interactions between genotypes.

Fisher (32), Haldane (34, 35), and Hamilton (37, 38) all realized that if the genotypic distribution of interactions were random, then many social behaviors

such as altruism could not evolve. Nonrandom associations between genotypes can occur because of a number of factors: kinship recognition, geographical structure, dispersal systems, and mating systems, to name a few.
These factors that give rise to nonrandom associations between genotypes
are the essence of the theory of kin selection. I use the term "population
structure" to refer to these nonrandom associations between genotypes that
affect fitness. Traditionally, in population genetics, population structure refers
to any deviation from panmixia resulting in nonrandom association between
genotypes during mating. It is natural to extend the term to nonrandom associations during other portions of the life cycle.

Consider the simplest possible case of pairwise interaction between genotypes. Denote the various genotypes by a single subscript, i or j, and let w_{ij} be
the *association-specific fitness*, the fitness of genotype i when interacting with
genotype j (23). In those cases in which genotypic fitness includes only the
survivorship component, w_{ij} is the probability of survival to adulthood of
genotype i if it associated only with genotype j. The association-specific fitnesses, w_{ij}, can be further decomposed into specific models of behavior—for
example, the additive and multiplicative models to be considered later (equation 9). Let P_{ij} be the *joint distribution of interactions* or the probability that
an individual of genotype i interacts with an individual of genotype j. Similar-
ly, define $P_{j|i} = P_{ij}/P_i$, where P_i is the *frequency of genotype* i in the total pop-
ulation. The distributions, P_i, P_{ij}, and $P_{j|i}$, obtain in a generation before
selection occurs. The conditional distribution $P_{j|i}$ measures the population
structure, since in the case of random interactions $P_{j|i} = P_j$. Charnov (18) was
the first to use this conditional distribution explicitly in a population-genetic
model of kin selection, although Hamilton (38) called attention to it. D. S.
Wilson's (105–107) model of "trait-group selection" is also based on this dis-
tribution (his "experienced frequencies" are equivalent to the $P_{j|i}$'s). Various
ways exist for calculating the genotypic distribution of interactions depending on the model used, and I take this up shortly. Once the distribution is obtained, genotypic fitness, W_i, can be calculated in a natural way as the average
of the w_{ij}'s over the distribution of interactions (3, 14, 18, 66, 68, 89–92, 94–
97):

$$W_i = \sum_j w_{ij} P_{j|i}. \qquad 1.$$

Although most models given in the literature utilize the average given in
equation 1, in some population-genetic models averages besides the arithmetic are often more appropriate for predicting the evolutionary dynamics and
outcome of selection. For example, if fitness varies spatially, the most appropriate overall measure of fitness is the harmonic average of the fitnesses in
different niches (51). However, if fitness varies temporally, the geometric

average is more appropriate (36). The same is likely to be true in models of social behavior if the social interactions are separated in space or in time. However, most work to date assumes, either explicitly or implicitly, an arithmetic average as in equation 1. Exceptions include those family-structured models discussed below that use general family-specific fitnesses W_{im} without assuming an explicit decomposition as in equation 1 (8, 52, 58, 83).

Basic Gene Frequency Equation

It is usual to consider two alleles, A and a, at a single hypothetical locus controlling social behavior in a randomly mating population with discrete generations. Exceptions include work assuming several loci (73, 95), multiple alleles at a single locus (91), quantitative inheritance (9, 122), nonrandom mating (10, 66, 99), and overlapping generations (17).

Let p be the frequency of A and $q = 1 - p$ the frequency of a, with genotypic notation i or $j = 0, 1, 2$ for, respectively, AA, Aa, aa. One form of the standard recurrence equation for gene frequency is (120):

$$\Delta p = \frac{pq}{2\overline{W}} \frac{dF}{dp}, \qquad\qquad 2.$$

where the average fitness, $\overline{W}$, is

$$\overline{W}(p) = \sum_i P_i W_i, \qquad\qquad 3.$$

and the *fitness function, F,* is defined as

$$F(p) = \int dp \sum_i W_i \frac{dP_i}{dp}. \qquad\qquad 4.$$

For randomly mating populations, the genotypic frequencies before selection, P_i, are in their Hardy-Weinberg proportions,

$$P_0 = p^2 ; P_1 = 2pq ; P_2 = q^2. \qquad\qquad 5.$$

Equation 2 can be used to study social evolution in a randomly mating population so long as the genotype fitnesses depend only upon p, the present gene frequency. This, in turn, requires that selection be weak (1, 16, 85). The graph of F, given as the indefinite integral in equation 4, corresponds to Wright's (116) concept of *adaptive topography* since it controls the gene frequency changes (via equation 2) leading to adaptation. The fitness function F can have great heuristic value in suggesting what overall variable or quantity summarizes the qualitative outcome of selection at this locus. In those cases where fitness is constant, it is well known that $F(p) = \overline{W}(p)$, where $\overline{W}$ is the average or population fitness (equation 3). In the case considered below of frequency-dependent selection in which the fitness effects of interactions are additive, the fitness function in equation 4 equals what Hamilton (38, 39) termed the average "inclusive fitness effect" [see equation 13 below; (1, 16, 43, 68)].

Models Based on Genetic Identity Coefficients

Hamilton's original model of kin selection was based on genetic identity coefficients (38). He realized that the use of such coefficients to study selection was an approximation, valid only if selection is weak or nonexistent at internal points of the pedigree relating the interactants. In spite of these shortcomings, the identity coefficient approach has been useful in modeling kin selection. It can be used to study kin selection between interactants of arbitrary genetic relationship, while the family-structured approach discussed in the next section is restricted to the study of close kin, such as sibs. Although I present here only the single-locus model, identity coefficients (when interpreted as genetic correlation coefficients) have been used in quantitative genetic models of kin selection (9, 122). The results of the quantitative genetic models parallel in several important respects the single locus results discussed shortly in that conditions analogous to Hamilton's rule can be shown to apply to the increase of altruism—especially if selection is weak (9).

Identity by Descent

Relatives are more likely to share identical genes than are randomly selected individuals from the population. Alleles may be considered identical for a number of reasons. They may have an identical DNA sequence or they may simply have an identical expression on the phenotype. There is always a probability that two alleles are identical in this sense even if they are selected from unrelated individuals. However, if the alleles are selected from two related individuals, the alleles may be identical for another reason—they may be copies of the same DNA sequence in a common ancestor. This "extra" identity is termed *identity by descent* and the two alleles are said to be identical by descent. A pedigree diagram of the two kin can be used to trace out the various pathways by which the alleles are identical by descent (for example, see 46).

For ease of discussion, the two interactants are labeled individual X and individual Y. If X and Y are diploid, there are four alleles that must be considered at any locus and there are nine possible *identity states*, if no distinction is made concerning the parental origin (♀ or ♂) of the alleles (Figure 1). Identity state k is denoted Ik and occurs with probability Δ_k ($k = 1, 2, \ldots, 9$), which can be calculated from any pedigree diagram by a variety of methods (22, 27, 44).

The probabilities of being inbred, or inbreeding coefficients ψ_X and ψ_Y, are calculated by summing up the appropriate Δ_k's (Figure 1):

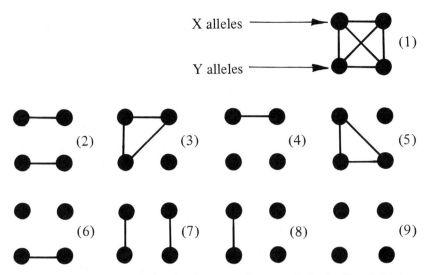

Figure 1. Nine states of identity between the two alleles in X and the two alleles in Y. These states, designated I_1–I_9, have probabilities Δ_1–Δ_9, respectively, which can be calculated from any pedigree or mating system by a variety of means. It is important to note that these coefficients consider identity states among four alleles at a time. The more common two-allele coefficients can be obtained as shown in the text (equations 6 and 7).

$$\psi_X = \Delta_1 + \Delta_2 + \Delta_3 + \Delta_4 \qquad \psi_Y = \Delta_1 + \Delta_2 + \Delta_5 + \Delta_6. \qquad 6.$$

Define ψ_{XY} as the probability that a randomly chosen gamete from X be identical by descent at this locus with a randomly chosen gamete from Y. It can be calculated from the Δ_i's in a straightforward manner as:

$$\psi_{XY} = \Delta_1 + \tfrac{1}{2}(\Delta_3 + \Delta_5 + \Delta_7) + \tfrac{1}{4}\Delta_8. \qquad 7.$$

Initially, Hamilton (38, p. 3) assumed outbreeding ($\Delta_1 - \Delta_6 = 0$ so, $\psi_X = \psi_Y = 0$ and $\psi_{XY} = \tfrac{1}{2}\Delta_7 + \tfrac{1}{4}\Delta_8$), which is discussed in more detail below (1, 16, 43). Most of the analysis here is in terms of all nine states of identity and is based on references (65, 69, 70), which are themselves based on references [(28); (46), Ch. 6.2)]. In this approach it is assumed that the locus under consideration codes for a social behavior that is only expressed in the context of a certain genetic relationship—the relationship being summarized by the Δ_k's. No explicit consideration is given to the proximate mechanisms which assure this. The genotypes are assumed to be alike with regard to other behaviors or characteristics. Similar assumptions are made in all models based on identity coefficients (3, 16, 33, 37–39, 43, 65, 69, 70, 80).

Calculation of P_{ij}

As a convention, let the first subscript of a pair of genotypic subscripts denote the genotype of X and the second subscript the genotype of Y, so that P_{ij} is the probability that X is i and Y is j. Since the nine identity states are mutually exclusive events covering the sample space,

$$P_{ij} = \sum_k \Delta_k \, P_{ij|Ik},\qquad\qquad 8.$$

where $P_{ij|Ik}$ is the conditional probability of X being i and Y being j given Ik. It can be calculated from the current gene frequency in a straightforward manner by taking into account the various constraints which Ik imposes on the joint genotypes of X and Y (28, 46, 65, 70). When this is done, genotypic fitness (equation 1) is a function of gene frequency and the constants $w_{ij}(j = 0, 1, 2)$ and Δ_k $(k = 1, 2 \ldots 9)$.

It should be stressed that this procedure by which the genotypic distribution of interactions is calculated from the pedigree constraints and the current gene frequency assumes no evolutionary forces are acting to change gene frequencies at this hypothetical locus. For example, if the common ancestor connecting X and Y were seven generations back, the calculations would be strictly correct only if the gene frequencies had remained constant over the past seven generations. The alleles connected by lines (and hence identical by descent) enter the pedigree seven generations ago, while the unconstrained alleles are picked at random in the present generation. Obviously the use of the same gene frequenceis for both kinds of alleles assumes that the gene frequencies have not changed. It is generally assumed that if selection is weak so that gene frequencies change slowly, this assumption of constant gene frequencies is approximately satisfied for short intervals of time (16, 85). However the more removed the common ancestor and more complicated the pedigree, the more dubious this procedure becomes. Of course, the more distant the relationship, the less likely kin selection is an important force.

Analysis

The genotypic distribution of interactions calculated in the last section can be substituted into the definition of genotypic fitness given by equation 1, which in turn yields the evolutionary dynamics given by equation 2. For the case of inbreeding, the fitness function (equation 4) is, in general, too complicated to interpret (although it can be calculated).

Following Hamilton (38), assume that the effect of social interactions on fitness are independent and additive so that

$$w_{ij} = 1 + c_i + b_j.\qquad\qquad 9a.$$

Another common formulation is the multiplicative model (14, 15, 66, 92), which also assumes that the effects are independent:

$$w_{ij} = (1 + c_i)(1 + b_j).\qquad\qquad 9b.$$

In the formulation of fitness in equations 9, genotype i is assumed to behave in such a way that it directly affects its own fitness by increment c_i and the fitness of its associate by b_i. In the additive model (equation 9a), the association-specific fitness, w_{ij}, is the sum of the effects of i on itself, c_i, plus the effects of j on i, b_j; while in the multiplicative model (equation 9b), the product of the two effects is taken. Several kinds of behavioral interactions that lead to the additive or multiplicative models have been discussed by Maynard Smith (62). The fitness increments c_i and b_i may each be positive or negative depending on the kind of social behavior of interest. It should be stressed that since the model is one of discrete generations, the fitness effects are the net effects of i's behavior on itself, c_i, and on others, b_i.

With the additive model in equation 9a, the fitness function (equation 4) is still too complicated to interpret biologically, if all nine identity states are nonzero. However, in the case of outbreeding ($\Delta_1 - \Delta_6 = 0$), it is possible to interpret the fitness function. First calculate the P_{ij}'s in the manner described in the last section [see also (28, 46, 65, 70)] and use the definition of conditional probability to obtain

$$P_{0|0} = \Delta_7 + p\Delta_8 + p^2\Delta_9 \quad P_{1|0} = q\Delta_8 + 2pq\Delta_9 \qquad P_{2|0} = q^2\Delta_9 \qquad 10.$$
$$P_{0|1} = \tfrac{1}{2}p\Delta_8 + p^2\Delta_9 \quad P_{1|1} = \Delta_7 + \tfrac{1}{2}\Delta_8 + 2pq\Delta_9 \quad P_{2|1} = \tfrac{1}{2}q\Delta_8 + q^2\Delta_9$$
$$P_{0|2} = p^2\Delta_9 \qquad P_{1|2} = p\Delta_8 + 2pq\Delta_9 \qquad P_{2|2} = \Delta_7 + q\Delta_8 + q^2\Delta_9.$$

Using equations 10, 1, 9a, and 4, one obtains

$$F(p) = \int \sum_i e_i \frac{dP_i}{dp} \, dp, \qquad 11.$$

where

$$e_i = c_i + 2\psi_{XY} b_i \qquad 12.$$

is termed the *inclusive fitness effect* of genotype i. In the outbred case, ψ_{XY} can be interpreted as the fraction of Y's gametes that are identical by descent at this locus to alleles in X. Consequently, the inclusive fitness effect of i's behavior (equation 12) includes the behavior's "direct effect" on i's individual fitness, c_i, plus the "indirect effect," $2\psi_{XY} b_i$, on copies of i's genes carried by its relative whom is related to i by $2\psi_{XY}$ (13).

Since the e_i's are independent of gene frequencies, equation 11 becomes

$$F(p) = \sum_i e_i P_i = \bar{e}, \qquad 13.$$

where $\bar{e}$ is the average inclusive fitness effect in the population. Consequently, in outbreeding populations with an additive model of fitness and weak selection, evolution proceeds along adaptive topographies determined by the mean inclusive fitness effect. This generalizes the approach and results of reference (68) to interactants of arbitrary genetic relationship. It should be pointed out that it is the inclusive fitness *effect* that controls the outcome of selection in these simple genetical models and not the average fitness of relatives (self included) weighted by genetic relatedness, which is often used in optimization models of kin selection (for example, 74).

Internal equilibria, $\hat{p}$, are found by setting the derivative of equation 13 equal to zero and solving for p:

$$\hat{p} = \frac{e_2 - e_1}{e_0 + e_2 - 2e_1}.$$ 14.

Consequently, the standard equilibrium equation of population genetics can be used to determine the equilibrium, so long as the genotypic inclusive fitness effects are substituted for genotypic fitnesses. From equation 14, there must be heterozygote superiority or inferiority in the inclusive fitness effects for this equilibrium to exist. By differentiating equation 13 twice, it is found that $\hat{p}$ will be stable whenever there is heterozygote superiority in the e_i's.

A special case of the additive model is often considered in which the A allele is assumed to code for a social behavior and the a allele is nonsocial. Consequently, aa homozygotes behave nonsocially, AA homozygotes behave socially, and Aa heterozygotes behave socially with propensity d, where d measures dominance. In this case, the fitness increments in equation 9 become

$$b_0 = b \qquad\qquad b_1 = db \qquad\qquad b_2 = 0$$
$$c_0 = c \qquad\qquad c_1 = dc \qquad\qquad c_2 = 0.$$ 15.

The condition for increase of such a gene can be obtained by setting $d\bar{e}/d\,p > 0$. Using equations 15 and 13, one obtains the following condition for increase of the A allele:

$$(c + 2\psi_{XY}b)(p + d - 2pd) > 0.$$ 16.

Often d is interpreted as the probability of behaving socially and so $0 \leqslant d \leqslant 1$. In this case, the expression $(p + d - 2pd)$ is always positive so

$$c + 2\psi_{XY}b > 0$$ 17.

is the condition for increase of the A allele. Consequently, the allele must have a positive effect on inclusive fitness to increase in frequency. If the hypothetical allele is altruistic, then $c < 0$ and $b > 0$, and equation 17 can be rewritten as

$$\frac{-c}{b} < 2\psi_{XY}.$$ 18.

Condition 18 is often termed *Hamilton's rule* for increase of an altruistic trait in an outbreeding population. If there are age-structure and sex-specific effects, then Hamilton's rule is modified by including the sex-ratio of the population, if the behavior only affects fucundity, and the sex-ratio and reproductive values of donor and recipient, if the behavior affects only survivorship (17). If Hamilton's rule is satisfied, the model predicts that the altruistic allele will increase to fixation and no internal equilibria are possible ($0 \leqslant d \leqslant 1$). This is no longer necessarily true if selection is strong (85, 90, 91). In addition, if over-dominance is allowed for, $d > 1$, an internal equilibrium is possible even if selection is weak, since there is now heterozygote superiority or inferiority in the e_i's. Setting the derivative of equation 13 to zero and using equation 14 yields ($d > 1$)

$$\hat{p} = \frac{d}{2d-1} . \qquad\qquad 19.$$

Equilibrium 19 is of the same form as the "viability-analogous" equilibria studied by Uyenoyama and co-workers (90, 91) for the special case of sibling interactions. Other equilibria, termed the "structural equilibria," have been discovered (90, 91) in the case of sibling interactions by using the family-structured approach to be discussed shortly. Interestingly, equilibrium 19 is independent of the parameters of selection, c and b, or even the degree of genetic relationship, $2\psi_{XY}$. However, its stability properties do depend upon these factors. As already noted, $\hat{p}$ is globally stable only if there is hetero-zygote superiority in the e_i's. In the case of equation 15, this requires inequality 17 to hold.

I now consider the conditions for increase of an altruistic allele when the interactants are inbred. A rule for increase analogous to condition 17 can be derived in this case. However, as we will see, the rule for inbreeding differs in several important respects from the outbred case. First the $P_{j|i}$'s must be obtained as outlined in the last section (see 70). These conditional probabilities are substituted into equation 1, which in turn can be used in equation 2 to obtain the condition for the allele to increase in frequency, $\Delta p > 0$. The resulting condition can be expressed in a variety of ways depending on the specific model used (33, 40, 41, 65, 71, 72). These various conditions can be shown to be equal to one another and in addition equal (70; see also 80 for a further refinement):

$$\frac{-c}{b} < \frac{Cov(Y_g, X_p)}{Cov(X_g, X_p)} , \qquad\qquad 20.$$

where X_g, X_p and Y_g, Y_p are the genotypes (either $1, \frac{1}{2}, 0$) and phenotypes (either $1, d, 0$) of individuals X and Y, respectively. This form of Hamilton's rule makes intuitive sense. X is the altruist and the right-hand side of equation 20 is the ratio of two covariances involving X's phenotype, X_p. In the numerator is the covariance of the recipient's genotype Y_g with X's phenotype, while in the denominator is the covariance of X's genotype with X's pheno-type. In essence, the right-hand side of equation 20 asks the question: "How well do Y's genes covary with X's behavior compared with X's own genes?" The right-hand side of equation 20 equals Orlove's $(71, 72)$ ρ if there is no inbreeding (see 80 for more discussion). If gene effects are additive $(d = .5)$, then equation 20 becomes

$$\frac{-c}{b} < \frac{2\psi_{XY}}{1 + \psi_X} \; , \qquad\qquad 21.$$

as suggested by Hamilton (40).

Family-Structured Model

An alternate approach to modeling kin selection assumes the total population is structured into groups, usually single families, within which social interactions occur (1-3, 8, 10, 14, 15, 18, 19, 24, 52, 60, 66, 68, 71, 83, 89-92, 94-99, 104). One advantage to the family-structured approach is that there is no need to use genetic identity coefficients to study selection, since the genetic relationships between interactants are provided implicitly by the family structure. The presentation of the family-structured approach here parallels reference (66), which is based on references (23) and (52). The relation of other family-structured models to the present approach is given in Table 2. In addition, Abugov and Michod (3) discuss the relation to Hamilton's (38) original model.

As with the first approach, a single-locus is usually considered with two alleles that affect social behavior in a specified manner. The various families possible are detemined by the genotypes of the parents. In the two-allele single-locus case, there are six families possible for both diploidy and haplodiploidy (Table 3).

Model Life History

The model life history is as follows. After birth, organisms associate with their sibs and engage in social interactions that affect fitness. It is not necessarily assumed that these associations last throughout the life cycle. However, it is assumed that the genotypes are alike with respect to all other interactions that occur outside the context of the family. There has been some work concerning multi-family groups, in which the offspring from two or more families associate together (94, 97); however, most work to date has concentrated on the evolution of interactions in single family groups. It is usually assumed that the social interactions affect only the survivorship component of fitness and that all matings have the same fecundity, although the model is especially suited for the study of fecundity effects (V. A. Delesalle and R. E. Michod, in preparation). After surviving to the adult stage, organisms mate. The usual assumption is random mating over the total population; however, certain mixed-mating models have been considered (10, 66, 99). An advantage of the

Table 2
Relation of other family-structured models to the model used in the present paper

Formulation in terms of present framework	Reference
W_{im}	83
$A(1) = W_{01}, A(\frac{1}{2} + \frac{1}{2}d) = W_{02}, S(1) = W_{26}$, etc.	8[a], 52
W_i, using equations 1 and 9a or 9b	14, 31, 89–92
W_i, using equations 9a, 15, 22 and 23. See (3) for more discussion.	18
W_{im} with $w_{ij} = 1 + c_i + b_j(N-1)$ using equations 23, 15 and	10, 94–98 105–108[b]

$$P_{j|F_m} = \begin{cases} \dfrac{M_{j|F_m} \, N-1}{N-1} & i = j \\[2ex] \dfrac{M_{j|F_m} \, N}{N-1} & i \neq j \end{cases}$$

	Model 1	Model 2	
W_{14}	$d(1-c) + (1-d)[1 + b(\frac{1}{2}d-1)]$	$d(1-c)(1+\frac{1}{2}bd) + (1-d)[1+\frac{1}{2}bd]$	15[c]
W_{15}	$d(1-c) + (1-d)[1 + b(d-1)]$	$d(1-c)(1+bd) + (1-d)(1+bd)$	

$W_{01} = (1-c)(1-b), W_{12} = 1 - \dfrac{b}{2}(1+d) - dc(1-b)$ 123[d]

$W_{26} = 1, W_{15} = 1 - \dfrac{db}{2} - cd + \dfrac{dbc}{2}$

$\bar{\phi}_A(1) = W_{01} = W_{13}, \bar{\phi}_A(3/4) = W_{04} = W_{14}, \bar{\phi}_B(3/4) = W_{24}$, etc.   58[e], appendix

W_i, using equations 1, 9b and 15.   104[a]

[a] Formulation restricted to dominant or recessive genes ($d = 1$ or 0).

[b] N is sibship size. There are assumed to be $N-1$ interactions per generation. Reference is made to (105–108) in the case of family trait groups.

[c] Rare or common genes considered. Only haplodiploid case given here, see Table 2b for notation. Charlesworth's (15) $p/(1+p) = d$. Model 1 and 2 refer to Charlesworth's designation.

[d] Only rare or common gene frequencies considered. Family-specific fitness obtained by calculating the conditional probability of having zero, one or two affected parents, multiplying these probabilities by the fitness assumed in each case ($1, 1-b/2, 1-b$), and then summing over the various possibilities.

[e] Formulation restricted to dominant genes.

family-structured approach is the explicit specification of the group structure so that nonrandom mating can be formulated explicitly and its effect on sociality explored.

The basic model is given in Table 3, where the offspring arrays, offspring fitnesses, and family fitnesses are presented for diploidy and haplodiploidy. I concentrate on the diploid case in what follows. Let F_m denote diploid family m and let f_m be the frequency of family m at the start of the generation, after mating but before selection. The m subscript will always denote a family variable. An important aspect of the model is that fitness interactions vary among families. Thus, define W_{im} as the fitness of genotype i in family m. The overall fitness, W_i, of a genotype can be obtained as

$$W_i = \sum_m W_{im} P_{F_m|i}, \qquad\qquad 22.$$

where $P_{F_m|i}$ is the conditional probability of being in family m given you are of genotype i. For example:

$$P_{F_1|0} = f_1/P_0, P_{F_2|0} = \tfrac{1}{2}f_2/P_0, P_{F_4|0} = \tfrac{1}{4}f_4/P_0 \text{ and } P_{F_3|0} = P_{F_5|0} = P_{F_6|0} = 0,$$
where $P_0 = f_1 + \tfrac{1}{2}f_2 + \tfrac{1}{4}f_4$.

If fitness interactions are pairwise, then W_{im} can be expressed in terms of the association-specific fitnesses. Define $P_{j|F_m}$ as the probability of interacting with genotype j in family m. For example, in family 4, assuming the expected Mendelian ratios obtain,

$$P_{0|F_4} = \tfrac{1}{4}, P_{1|F_4} = \tfrac{1}{2}, \text{ and } P_{2|F_4} = \tfrac{1}{4}.$$

Keeping in mind the limitations mentioned above concerning the arithmetic average, we have

$$W_{im} = \sum_j w_{ij} P_{j|F_m}. \qquad\qquad 23.$$

Using equation 23 in 22,

$$W_i = \sum_m \sum_j w_{ij} P_{j|F_m} P_{F_m|i},$$

which equals equation 1. It is important to note that, in general, the genotypic fitness depends upon the family frequencies, since $P_{F_m|i}$ does.

It should be stressed that equation 23 assumes that the overall effect of a given type of interaction, say j on i, is linearly related to the frequency of j in the sibship. Of course, this is unrealistic, and in nature there may often be thresholds below or above which the frequency of a certain type has little effect. An advantage of the family-structured model is that the family-specific fitnesses, W_{im}, can be easily modified to incorporate these and other nonlinearities (2, 8, 52). In addition, analyses in terms of W_{im} are general in this respect and do not depend upon any specific formulation (8, 52, 58, 83, and equations 29–34).

Table 3
Model of selection in a family-structured population

(a) Diploidy

Mating	Frequency	Offspring array	Offspring fitness	Family fitness
$AA \times AA$	f_1	AA	W_{01}	$\bar{W}_1 = W_{01}$
$AA \times Aa$	f_2	$\frac{1}{2}AA, \frac{1}{2}Aa$	W_{02}, W_{12}	$\bar{W}_2 = \frac{1}{2}W_{02} + \frac{1}{2}W_{12}$
$AA \times aa$	f_3	Aa	W_{13}	$\bar{W}_3 = W_{13}$
$Aa \times Aa$	f_4	$\frac{1}{4}AA, \frac{1}{2}Aa, \frac{1}{4}aa$	W_{04}, W_{14}, W_{24}	$\bar{W}_4 = \frac{1}{4}W_{04} + \frac{1}{2}W_{14} + \frac{1}{4}W_{24}$
$Aa \times aa$	f_5	$\frac{1}{2}Aa, \frac{1}{2}aa$	W_{15}, W_{25}	$\bar{W}_5 = \frac{1}{2}W_{15} + \frac{1}{2}W_{25}$
$aa \times aa$	f_6	aa	W_{26}	$\bar{W}_6 = W_{26}$

(b) Haplodiploidy

Mating	Female offspring array	Male offspring array	Female offspring fitness	Male offspring fitness
$AA \times A$	AA	A	W_{01}	W_{31}
$AA \times a$	Aa	A	W_{12}	W_{32}
$Aa \times A$	$\frac{1}{2}AA, \frac{1}{2}Aa$	$\frac{1}{2}A, \frac{1}{2}a$	W_{03}, W_{13}	W_{33}, W_{43}
$Aa \times a$	$\frac{1}{2}Aa, \frac{1}{2}aa$	$\frac{1}{2}A, \frac{1}{2}a$	W_{14}, W_{24}	W_{34}, W_{44}
$aa \times A$	Aa	a	W_{15}	W_{45}
$aa \times a$	aa	a	W_{26}	W_{46}

Note: In haplodiploid families (b), A and a are notated as $i = 3$, 4, respectively. The haplodiploid families are numbered 1–6, beginning with $AA \times A$ and ending with $aa \times a$.

Use of Mendelian Ratios

In the examples given above concerning the calculations of $P_{j|F_m}$ for use in equation 23, it is assumed that the expected Mendelian ratios obtain in the sibships. This, in effect, assumes infinite sibship size. Of course, sibship size is finite and perhaps even small in many social species. Unfortunately, most theoretical work does not address this problem. Wade and Breden (98) provide some justification for the use of the expected Mendelian ratios in the calculation of equation 23. The following discussion represents a generalization of their approach. Let $P_{j|F_m}$ be a random variable with

$$E\left[P_{j|F_m}\right] = M_{j|F_m},\qquad\qquad 24.$$

where $M_{j|F_m}$ is the expected Mendelian frequency of genotype j in family m (e.g., $M_{0|F_4} = \frac{1}{4}$, $M_{1|F_4} = \frac{1}{2}$, $M_{2|F_4} = \frac{1}{4}$), and $E[X]$ denotes the expected value of X. Using equation 23 we have

$$E[W_{im}] = E\left[\sum_j w_{ij} P_{j|F_m}\right].\qquad\qquad 25.$$

It is then obvious from equation 25 that

$$E[W_{im}] = \sum_j w_{ij} E[P_{j|F_m}] = \sum_j w_{ij} M_{j|F_m}.\qquad\qquad 26.$$

Consequently, the average fitness of genotype i in family m is that obtained by using the expected Mendelian ratios in equation 23. The average value given in equation 26 can only be used in conditions 32 below for increase of the A allele, so long as the number of families is infinite and the recurrence equations remain deterministic. The distribution of $P_{j|F_m}$ need not be multinomial within family m as Wade & Breden (98) assume, so long as equations 23 and 24 hold. It is the arithmetic average in equation 23 that is critical and allows for the reversal of function and expectation to get equation 26. As already mentioned, if the social interactions are separated in time or space, then this arithmetic average is inappropriate. In these cases, it is unlikely that equation 26 would hold.

Analysis

The genotypic fitnesses, W_i, given in equations 1 or 22 can be used to study the dynamics of social genes in family-structured populations. As already noted, these individual fitnesses depend upon the six family frequencies before selection, f_m. Consequently the f_m's are the dynamically sufficient state variables for the study of family-specific social behaviors. However, it is possible to reduce the dimensionality of the problem to genotypic space by the assumption of random mating, and to gene frequency space by the assumption of weak selection. Let g_i be the frequency of genotype i after selection; then by the assumption of random mating:

$$f_1 = g_0^2; f_2 = 2g_0g_1; f_3 = 2g_0g_2,$$
$$f_4 = g_1^2; f_5 = 2g_1g_2; f_6 = g_2^2. \tag{27}$$

If it is further assumed that selection is weak, the adult genotypic frequencies can be approximated by their Hardy-Weinberg frequencies (1-3, 18, 60, 68, 83, 94-98, 104, 119; see 1, 85 for justification):

$$g_0 = p^2; g_1 = 2pq; g_2 = q^2. \tag{28}$$

Equation 28 can then be substituted in equations 27 and 23 to give equation 1. Consequently if selection is weak, the genotypic fitnesses depend only on the gene frequencies and so equation 2 can be used to study the dynamics.

However if selection is not weak, equation 28 will not hold. In this case, equation 27 must be used in equation 23 to calculate the genotypic fitnesses in equation 1. Consequently, to study kin selection of arbitrary intensity in randomly mating populations the dynamically sufficient state variables are the three (two are independent) adult genotypic frequencies, g_i. The genotypic recurrence equations are then (for example, 8, 52, 58, 66; where the prime superscript $'$ denotes the next generation):

$$g_0' \bar{W} = W_0(g_0^2 + g_0g_1 + \tfrac{1}{4}g_1^2)$$
$$g_2' \bar{W} = W_2(g_2^2 + g_2g_1 + \tfrac{1}{4}g_1^2), \tag{29}$$

$$\bar{W} = \sum_m f_m \bar{W}_m, \tag{30}$$

with the f_m's obtained from equation 27. In equations 29, the $\bar{W}_m$'s are given in Table 3 and the W_i's in equation 22. For the purpose of further analysis, equation 29 can be reexpressed in terms of the family-specific fitnesses,

$$\bar{W}g_0' = g_0^2 W_{01} + g_0g_1 W_{02} + \tfrac{1}{4}g_1^2 W_{04}$$
$$\bar{W}g_2' = g_2^2 W_{26} + g_2g_1 W_{25} + \tfrac{1}{4}g_1^2 W_{24}, \tag{31}$$

with equation 30 still holding. Similar genotypic equations in terms of general fitnesses can be developed for haplodiploidy (8, 52).

With the exception of genes for total altruism (66) analyses of equations 31, or their haplodiploid counterparts, have been restricted to the conditions for increase of the A allele when it is rare or common. In terms of the general family-specific fitnesses, the A allele will increase when rare if (8, 52, 58, 66)

$$W_{15} > W_{26}, \tag{32a}$$

and when common if

$$W_{12} < W_{01}. \tag{32b}$$

Using the arithmetic average given in equation 23 and the additive model of altruism (equation 9a) with equation 15, conditions 32 require $-c/b < \tfrac{1}{2}$ (cf. equation 18) for increase of the gene. Assuming single insemination of females, the haplodiploid analogs of equations 32 are (R. E. Michod, unpublished manuscript; using the notation of Table 3b):

$$\frac{W_{14}}{W_{26}} + \frac{W_{15}}{W_{26}} \frac{W_{34}}{W_{46}} > 2 \tag{33a.}$$

$$\frac{W_{13}}{W_{01}} + \frac{W_{12}}{W_{01}} \frac{W_{43}}{W_{31}} < 2. \tag{33b.}$$

Conditions 32 and 33 reduce to those obtained elsewhere (e.g. 14) when equations 9a or 9b are substituted in to the various fitness interactions considered (e.g. sister-brother, sister-sister, etc). Under certain situations of resource limitation it may be that all families produce the same number of adults. In this case, the family-specific fitnesses are set equal and, in the case of diploidy, equations 32 become

$$W_{15} > \overline{W}_5 \tag{34a.}$$

$$W_{12} < \overline{W}_2 . \tag{34b.}$$

Equations 34 imply that in such extreme situations of density regulation, altruism cannot evolve but "spite" ($b < c < 0$ in equations 9) may. The implications of density dependence for social evolution are modeled and discussed in more detail by Boyd (8a).

Discussion and Conclusions
What is Kin Selection?
Definition
To evolve by kin selection a genetic trait expressed by one individual (termed the actor) must affect the genotypic fitness of one or more other individuals who are genetically related to the actor in a nonrandom way at the loci determining the trait. These conditions are necessary and sufficient for kin selection to occur and embody the essential characteristics of the models presented above as well as preserving the original intent of Maynard Smith (59) when he coined the term kin selection.

Comments on Proposed Definition
This definition indicates the testability of kin selection as an evolutionary hypothesis. If either there is no fitness interaction or the interactants are randomly related, then kin selection cannot be an explanation of the observed behavior. The definition does not specify the relation of kin selection to other evolutionary processes, such as individual, group, or frequency-dependent selection, and I discuss these relations below.

Altruism. The definition does not require altruism, in which the actor has a net beneficial effect on the genotypic fitness of others, while suffering a net decrease in fitness relative to the recipients of the altruism (that is, $b > 0$, $c <$ 0 in equation 15). Alternative definitions have been proposed that unfortunately do not relate in a meaningful way to the theory presented here (for example, 75). Altruism is a special kind of fitness interaction embraced by the theory of kin selection. Nevertheless many models of kin selection have specifically focused on altruism. Unfortunately, this has led several workers to suggest incorrectly that altruism is necessary for kin selection (48, 55, 124). Theorists have focused on altruism because altruism can increase under kin selection but cannot be selected for under traditional models of individual selection in a homogeneous population. It is natural to apply a theory to those phenomena that it uniquely explains. This does not mean, however, that kin selection is irrelevant to other classes of fitness interaction. On the contrary, there are no constraints on the signs and magnitudes of the fitness effects (c_i and b_i) imposed by the above theory. Of particular interest is the case in which both effects are positive so that the behavior increases both the actor's and a relative's fitness. It appears that just this situation arises in the case of helping behavior in cooperatively breeding birds (11-13, 29, 30, 54, 112, 113).

The utility of the concept of altruism has recently been questioned by Williams (101), who, among others (82), points out that a genotype cannot increase in frequency unless its overall genotypic fitness (i.e. equations 1 or 22) is higher than that of other genotypes. Williams concludes from this that there cannot be genetic altruism and suggests further that this brings into question the usefulness of the theory of kin selection. While Williams is usually correct (overdominance creates exceptions) that for any trait to increase, genotypes with the trait must have a higher overall fitness than genotypes without the trait—this does not bear on the definition of altruism used here or in most formal discussions of kin selection (for example, 89). If the context of altruism is the family, then the definition of altruism requires altruists to have a lower fitness than nonaltruist sibs. Consequently altruism always decreases in frequency within the sibship, as was first pointed out by Williams and Williams (104). As will be discussed in the section on group selection, families with altruists may contribute more to the mating pool than families with nonaltruists. The fact that this can cause the overall genotypic fitness of altruists to be higher than nonaltruists (again as was pointed out in 104) does not compromise the notion of altruism in any way.

Parental care. According to this definition, parental care evolves by kin selection, since offspring are just a special case of kin. Hamilton (38, p. 1) realized that no additional concepts were needed to explain many aspects of parental care beyond traditional notions of Darwinian fitness. While this is true, it is equally true that the genetic contexts of offspring care and sibling care can be identical (for discussion see 25, p. 101; 38, p. 2; 26; 47). In this regard, I think it is of some value to understand the more general context of a phenomenon, even if the general principles provide no additional explanatory power in the specific case of interest. However, in the specific case of parental care, the concept of inclusive fitness does provide additional explanatory power in terms of parent-offspring conflict (19, 86). Let $-C$ be the effect of the care on the parent's future reproductive success and B the effect on present offspring fitness ($-C < 0$, $B > 0$). Then by using equation 17, parents will be selected to provide care so long as $C/B < \frac{1}{2}$; however, offspring will be selected to "demand" care so long as $C/B < 2$. Thus there is a conflict of "interest" in the region $\frac{1}{2} < C/B < 2$ (19, 86).

"Green beard effect." The evolution of the "green beard effect" (25, p. 96; 26) or "signal genes" (69), in which an altruistic gene confers some noticeable effect on the phenotype and the benefits are dispensed only to those with the effect, qualifies as kin selection according to the proposed definition. The purpose of emphasizing only the genetic correlations at the loci controlling the trait in the above definition is not specifically to include signal genes. Instead, I hope to emphasize (*a*) the irrelevance of loci that do not determine the trait and hence the incidental nature of genome-wide considerations, such as the fraction of genes shared by two individuals, which have been emphasized by several authors (7; this fallacy is also discussed in 25, p. 197) and (*b*) the possibility that other mechanisms besides kinship may produce genetic correlations at some loci (see, for example, 25, p. 187; 61; 106; 107). In regard to point (*a*), I should insert as a caveat a point made by Templeton (84) that shows the limitations of the single-locus approach. Yokoyama and Felsenstein (122) consider a quantitative genetic model of kin selection and show that the evolution of altruism is affected by the degrees of additive and nonadditive genetic covariance between relatives. It is known that linkage between loci determining a trait will increase the nonadditive covariance between sibs for these loci (21), and hence factors that affect linkage (such as chromosome number, if the loci are spread throughout the genome) may have some effect on the evolution of a polygenic social trait. In this sense, then, genome-wide considerations would be relevant.

Social selection. There is an interesting social effect of severe genetic disorders such as Huntington's chorea, in which the relatives of afflicted individuals suffer a loss in fitness because they are less likely to find a mate for social reasons (77, 100). This social component of selection on genetic disorders has been termed "social selection" (100), and recently Yokoyama (123) has argued that social selection is "fundamentally different" from kin selection. However, according to the above definition, social selection is kin selection, since the genetic disorder affects the fitness of relatives. The formal relations are given in Table 2 above.

Relation to Frequency-Dependent Selection

As already stressed, in both modeling approaches the evolution of social behavior is a form of frequency-dependent selection (14, 18, 66, 89, 90). The use of the association-specific genotypic fitnesses above makes the correspondence of social evolution and traditional frequency-dependent selection (23) explicit.

Relation to Individual Selection

The fitness effects of the interactions, which are so central to kin selection, are defined here in terms of traditional genotypic fitness (proposed definition; equations 1, 9, 22, 23). This is necessary in order to base kin selection on the axioms of traditional population genetics. Thus genotypic fitness is a sufficient parameter to study kin selection in these models.

Lewontin (53, pp. 7–8) defines individual selection as the gene frequency changes that result from the absolute reproductive and survival rates of genotypes—i.e., from absolute genotypic fitness. Such a definition is appropriate for selection in a nonstructured population. However, it is inappropriate for structured populations, since it obscures the effects of population structure on the selection process. Indeed, the many explicit models of group selection (for example, 58, 89) would be classified as individual selection according to Lewontin's definition, since they too are based on absolute genotypic fitness.

The context and relevance of individual selection can be made more explicit by reference to the family-structured model. As already mentioned in the case of altruism, the altruist genotype has by definition a lower genotypic fitness when compared with nonaltruists in its sibship (see also 89, p. 395; 96; 104). Consequently, the altruist genotype decreases in frequency within the family group. Consider, for example, the case of a rare allele, A, at a diploid locus. In this case, only families 5 ($Aa \times aa$) and 6 ($aa \times aa$) exist in appreciable frequencies. If A is an altruist allele and nonrecessive, then the definition of altruism requires the genotypic fitness of a heterozygote altruist to be less than that of the nonaltruist homozygote when both are in family 5:

$$W_{15} < W_{25}. \qquad\qquad 35.$$

Note that both the additive and the multiplicative models of altruism (equation 9) satisfy condition 35. Consequently, after selection within a family group but before mating, heterozygote altruists will have decreased in frequency within family 5 from their initial frequency of .5. Obviously, to increase in frequency the genotypic fitness of an altruist in family 5 must be greater than that of nonaltruists *from family 6,* as required by condition 32a. Consequently, when considering evolution in a structured population it is best to restrict the term individual selection to those changes in gene frequency that occur within a group (96; 108; 121, p. 455). According to this definition, individual selection is a necessary component of kin selection.

Some authors have suggested that all individual selection is kin selection (47, 81), since offspring are kin. However, according to the proposed definition (see also 59), kin selection is restricted to traits that affect the fitness of *other* individuals. Producing offspring is the *expression* of individual fitness but does not in itself qualify as a fitness interaction. According to the (rather narrow) definition used in the simple models studied here, genotypic fitness includes only the probability of survival to reproduction of a genotype and the number of gametes produced by that genotype and *not* the probability of survival of the resulting offspring (cf. 15, p. 318; see 78, pp. 26–29 for a discussion of a genotypic fitness). It is for this reason that parental care qualifies as a fitness interaction.

Relation to Group Selection

The term "group selection" has had a controversial history in population biology, and since many reviews are available (61, 63, 89, 93, 107, 108), I will not review its various uses here.

I use Uyenoyama and Feldman's (89, p. 395) definition of a group, which has been used in other studies of group selection (105-107) and is a special case of "context independence" (110, 111) applied to groups: "A group is the smallest collection of individuals within a population defined such that the genotypic fitness calculated within each group is not a (frequency-dependent) function of the composition of any other group."

It should be stressed that this definition of a group does not require spatial, temporal, or reproductive isolation of the group (cf. 59; 61; 63; 102, p. 93). For example, if individuals sought out other individuals with a certain trait (such as sibs, or individuals with a green beard) and then affected their genotypic fitnesses in some manner, the class of individuals with the designated trait (that is, sibs or "green beards") qualify as a group according to the above definition. In other words, groups may exist because of active discrimination by individuals, or "passively" because geographic factors structure the population into groups, within which individuals are indiscriminant. This distinction corresponds to Alexander's (6, pp. 106-107) distinction between discriminant and indiscriminant nepotism. In any event, the mechanism by which groups exist is not restricted by the definition of group used here. In the special case of family groups, Uyenoyama and Feldman's definition requires W_{im} to be independent of the offspring arrays of other families, which it is.

I define group selection in the usual way as the changes in gene frequency resulting from the differential extinction or productivity of groups. In the family-structured model and other "assortment" models (89), groups are short-lived (usually one generation or less), and so extinction is not nearly so relevant to selection as is the differential productivity of groups, which is often taken to be the contribution of a group to the mating pool. However, most verbal discussions of group selection and its relation to kin selection concentrate only on differential extinction of groups as the main component of group selection (6, p. 48; 26; 59). I now show why, as was first pointed out by Williams and Williams (104), the differential *productivity* of family groups is so essential to kin selection among sibs.

Consider, again, the case of altruism. As discussed in the last section, altruists have a lower fitness relative to nonaltruists in their family group (equation 35). To increase in frequency, altruists must do better than nonaltruists from family 6 (equation 32a). If there is no differential productivity of families, then each family would have the same $\bar{W}_m$ and alleles could increase on a population-wide basis only if they increase within families (that is, equations 34). Of course, this would prohibit the evolution of altruism (cf. equation 35, which implies $W_{15} < \bar{W}_5$ with equation 34a). Thus we see that selection among family groups is absolutely necessary for the evolution of altruism in a family-structured population (see also 96 for a more detailed analysis in the case of the additive model with weak selection). In the words of G. C. Williams (102, p. 198; see also 104), "There is an unfavorable selection within family groups that must be balanced by a favorable selection between groups." The generality of the importance of group selection beyond sib-sib interactions has been explored for a haploid model (42, pp. 136–140), where it is possible to partition the within- and between-group components of gene frequency change and to show, by using Price's (76) covariance form of equation 2, that the rate of change of social genes depends upon the between-group variance in fitness.

In discussing group selection, Alexander and Borgia (5, p. 450, following 102, 103) state that "differential extinction of groups can account for the direction of evolutionary change in a trait only when groups differ in the trait and when this difference accounts for the difference in extinction rate. We regard this as the criterion for group selection." So long as reproduction is substituted for extinction in this quotation, kin selection for altruism among sibs clearly satisfies these criteria for group selection. The frequency of altruism in the total population is the trait to be explained. Different family groups differ with respect to the frequency of altruists. This difference in frequency directly causes (through $\bar{W}_m$) different families to contribute different numbers of adults to the mating pool. This family effect is the only cause by which altruism can increase, since altruism is always selected against within families.

The role of group selection in kin selection is even more perspicuous when conditions 32 are compared to those for increase of altruism when rare in general group-structured models (58, p. 367; 89, equations 17). The fitness of an altruist in a group with a single altruist (similar to W_{15}) must be greater than the fitness of a nonaltruist in a group with no altruists (W_{26}). In family groups, because of identity by descent, there are usually no groups with only a single altruist. Instead, altruists exist in a frequency of .5d in family 5, which is the only family with altruists when the gene is rare. As in the general group-structured models, equation 32a requires altruists from groups with the least possible altruists when the gene is rare to have a higher fitness than non-altruistis from groups with no altruists. A similar parallel exists for common altruistic genes.

Although group selection is necessary for the evolution of altruism, it is not necessary for kin selection in general. If, for some environmental reason, there could be no differential output of families to the mating pool, there would still be kin selection operating on interactions between sibs within families. However, the lack of group selection would severely constrain the behavioral traits possible (see 8a for more discussion).

Formal Relations of Family-Structured Model to Identity Coefficient Model

As shown above in the case of weak selection, both of these approaches use equation 2. Therefore the two approaches are directly comparable in the case of weak selection and sibling interactions. If the two models yield identical genotypic distributions of interactions, they are in fact equivalent, since then the genotypic fitnesses in equation 1 will be the same (3). It is a simple matter to calculate $P_{j|i}$ in the family-structured model using equation 27 and equation 28 (for example, see 3, 18, 68). It is then possible to verify that $P_{j|i}$ obtained in this manner for weak selection (that is, using equation 28) is identical to that obtained using identity coefficients (equation 10) if the identity coefficients between outbred diploid sibs ($\Delta_7 = \frac{1}{4}\Delta_8 = \frac{1}{2}$ and $\Delta_9 = \frac{1}{4}$) are substituted into equation 10 (see 3 for more discussion). Consequently, the two approaches are equivalent under these assumptions. The conclusions obtained above for the identity coefficient model concerning the relation between the mean inclusive fitness effect and Wright's (120) fitness function (equation 13), along with its derivative results (equations 14, 16–19), also hold for the family-structured model so long as selection is weak (68).

Parental Manipulation

Kin selection and parental manipulation are often seen as two competing hypotheses for the evolution of sociality (for example, 4, 64). The family-structured model provides a convenient setting to explore the logical and conceptual relations between these two apparently different routes to sociality. As discussed elsewhere (15, 19, 24), the social interactions that take place within a family and give rise to the family-specific fitnesses may be thought of as arising in two different ways. First, the social allele may be assumed to be expressed at the offspring stage and to code for social behavior among siblings. In this case of "offspring control," differences in sibling behavior are directly caused by differences in their genotypes. This is the interpretation made in most discussions of kin selection. Second, the allele may be assumed to be expressed in the parents and to cause the parent to manipulate a portion of its offspring into behaving socially. In this case, there is no one-to-one relation between differences in phenotype and genotype among siblings. This is the interpretation made in most discussions of parental manipulation.

Consider, for example, family 5 (Table 3) and assume that the parents manipulate a fraction a of their offspring into being altruists. We then have $W_{15} = W_{25} = 1 - ac + ab$. Consequently (using $W_{26} = 1$), condition 32a requires $c/b < 1$ for parental manipulation to increase when rare as compared to $c/b < \frac{1}{2}$ for offspring control (15, 19, 24). It is easier for altruism to increase via parental manipulation since the costs of altruism are distributed over both alleles (15).

An additional effect is observed if generations overlap so that an individual can increase its parents' fecundity by directly rearing sibs in place of offspring (19, 24). In this case, the conditions for increase of the altruistic trait are less restrictive by a factor of two, since the gain in fitness through the recipient is expressed directly as offspring: $c/b < 2$ for parental manipulation and $c/b < 1$ for offspring control (19, 24). This result has implications for the origin of eusocial behavior in the Hymenoptera (19, 24).

Kin selection and parental manipulation share certain logical correlates, since the same family-structured model can be used to study either process. Both processes are a form of frequency-dependent selection and both require family-level selection to select for altruism among siblings (there is no differential survivorship of genotypes within a family in the case of parental manipulation). In addition, they both require the presence of kinship (the family structure) to operate. The only modeling difference is the life stage at which the hypothetical allele is assumed to be expressed, and this gives rise to different conditions for the spread of altruism. Due to these logical correlates, it is more accurate to view kin selection and parental manipulation as two aspects of one phenomenon, population structure into families, rather than as two competing and mutually exclusive hypotheses.

Effects of Inbreeding

As already discussed a rule for increase of altruism can be derived from the identity coefficient model if the interactants are inbred. The inbred rule for nonadditive genes (equation 20) differs in several important respects from either the outbred rule (equation 18) or the inbred rule for additive genes (equation 21). The right-hand side of equation 20 depends upon gene frequency and dominance in addition to the degree of genetic relationship. These complications do not enter into the outbred rule (equation 18) or the inbred rule for additive genes (equation 21), so long as selection is weak as is assumed in the derivation of equations 18, 20, or 21. Consequently, if the altruistic allele increases in frequency, the condition for further increase can itself change. This gene frequency dependence of the rule may give rise to stable polymorphisms (65, 80). It is also interesting to note that there is no general effect of inbreeding per se on the conditions for increase of the altruistic allele. It is often thought that inbreeding will always facilitate sociality. However, as I have discussed elsewhere (65), it is not the case that as ψ_X increases, the right-hand side of equation 20 decreases, as one would expect if inbreeding always facilitated sociality. The numerator is also a function of the inbred identity states and so the effect of inbreeding depends upon the exact effect of the inbreeding of the Δ_k's. Consequently, it is necessary to study specific consanguineous mating systems to understand the effects of inbreeding in more detail.

Various mixed mating systems have been studied, including mixed-selfing and random mating and mixed-sib and random mating (10, 66, 99). If the fitness effects combine additively (equation 9a), then inbreeding tends to facilitate the evolution of altruism by decreasing the cost-benefit threshold (66) and increasing the rate of gene frequency change (10, 99). If the fitness effects combine multiplicatively (equation 9b), this is usually the case, so long as the costs of altruism are not too great (66). In the case of total altruism, in which altruists have zero individual fitness, inbreeding usually retards the evolution of altruism (66). It appears from these results that inbreeding facilitates most forms of altruism but retards extreme altruism. These results can be understood by noting that inbreeding increases the within-family relatedness by increasing the between-family variance in allele frequency (10, 66, 99). In most cases, this facilitates altruism. However, in the case of total altruism, only heterozygotes can pass on the trait and inbreeding tends to decrease the frequency of heterozygotes (66). The important effect of inbreeding on kin selection lies in its altering the genotypic distribution of interactions (66).

Hamilton's Rule and Inclusive Fitness

Hamilton's $-c/b < R$ rule for spread of an altruistic trait (here R simply means "relatedness" and is left ambiguous for the present discussion) and the attendant concept of inclusive fitness are the most useful results of the theory of kin selection. Indeed, these heuristics rank alongside Fisher's (32) "fundamental theorem" as evolutionary insights of great generality and heuristic utility. In addition, Hamilton's rule is quantitative and predictive. However, like Fisher's theorem, Hamilton's rule and inclusive fitness rigorously apply to gene or genotype frequency models only under certain special conditions. Recent work utilizing the family-structured model has clarified the domain of rigorous application and successful approximation of these results, as well as indicating conditions that are not adequately described by them. The purpose of this section is briefly to review this work. Inbred populations have already been discussed and so I focus here on the outbred, random mating model presented above. More extensive discussions may be found in the literature (14, 69, 70, 89-92).

All analyses to date of the family-structured model with random mating have confirmed Hamilton's rule (as given in Table 2 of 41) for increase of an altruist allele, so long as selection is weak and there is no overdominance (see discussion of equation 19; 3, 8, 14, 15, 18, 68, 89, 90, 94, 95). The most complete catalog of the conditions for increase of rare or common altruist alleles is given by Cavalli-Sforza and Feldman (14, Tables I and II) for a variety of fitness interactions in diploid and haplodiploid populations. These authors consider the additive (equation 9a) and multiplicative (equation 9b) models of fitness (with equation 15) for selection of arbitrary intensity. The conditions they present may be obtained from the present model by substituting equations 9a or 9b into equations 32 and 33 for the various cases they considered. For the multiplicative model, Cavalli-Sforza and Feldman (14) found departures from Hamilton's rule (41) to be common. However, if selection is weak, the multiplicative model converges to the additive, since the product terms involving the parameters of selection in equation 9b are negligible. Counterexamples to Hamilton's rule were also reported in the additive case for intersex altruism in haplodiploid populations (14). However, these conditions also converge to those proposed by Hamilton (41) as the parameters of selection get small. Thus if selection is weak, Hamilton's rule with the *frequency-independent* regression coefficient of relatedness (equation 18) proposed by Hamilton (41) accurately gives the conditions for increase of altruist alleles in explicit population genetic models (for more discussion see 85).

If selection is not weak, so that the products of the parameters of selection can no longer be safely ignored, then departures from the rule as given by Hamilton (41) or by equation 18 occur. As already noted in the additive case, departures from equation 18 occur in models of intersex altruism in haplodiploid populations (14). However, these departures can be removed if the *genotype-frequency-dependent* regression coefficient of the additive genotypic values of recipient on those of the altruist, r (Table 1), is used as the right-hand side of equation 18 (90-92). The genotype-frequency-dependent measure, r, has the added advantage of predicting much of interest concerning the internal equilibrium structure of these models, as I discuss below (90-92).

In addition, the departures in the case of the multiplicative model observed with the frequency-independent measure of relatedness (equation 18) can be removed by using r (92). In calculating the regression, r, in this case, a new benefit parameter must be defined that depends upon b_i and the genotype of the recipient (92).

The existence and stability of internal equilibria are two aspects of the genetic dynamics not predicted by Hamilton's rule as originally proposed using the pedigree-derived measure of relatedness. For example, in the case of sib-sib interactions in diploid populations using the additive model (equation 9a) with equation 15, if $c = 1.0$, $b = 2.1$, and $d = .2$, then two internal equilibria exist, one ($\hat{p} = .22$) stable and the other ($\hat{p} = .63$) unstable. It should be noted that Hamilton's rule, $c/b < \frac{1}{2}$, is satisfied in this case.

There are two classes of internal equilibria in kin-selection models (90–92). The first is analogous to the standard equilibrium equation of constant viability selection and is termed the viability analogous equilibrium. As already discussed, this equilibrium may exist if selection is weak and requires overdominance in the propensity to behave as an altruist. The second class of internal equilibria are termed "structural" and are obtained from the relation $c/b = r$, where r is the genotype-frequency-dependent regression coefficient given in Table 1 (91, 92). As selection gets weak, the domain of parameter values (c, b, and d) that beget these structural equilibria gets vanishingly small (85), which is why the models that assume weak selection (equation 28) do not predict this class of equilibria.

The concept of inclusive fitness has received little explicit attention in this theoretical work. Indeed, several authors have noted that the concept is not needed to describe the genetic dynamics (14, 31, 89). Since there has been discussion about the vagueness of the concept of inclusive fitness, I would like to point out that the concept is well-defined (see, for example, equation 12), and that it is not equal to genotypic fitness (cf. equations 12 and 1) as has been suggested (89, 101). As originally discussed by Hamilton (38), the concept of inclusive fitness had two roles in his theory. First, he suggested that the population mean inclusive fitness was maximized and that social evolution proceeded along adaptive topographies determined by mean inclusive fitness. As already discussed, the accuracy of this use in explicit genetic models depends upon selection being weak (3, 16, 38, 43, 68). Second, Hamilton proposed that alleles with a positive effect on inclusive fitness ($c + Rb > 0$) should increase in frequency (see equation 17). This condition when rearranged for altruistic traits becomes Hamilton's $-c/b < R$ rule. Thus the concept of inclusive fitness and Hamilton's rule are intimately related. Consequently, the research just discussed, which adequately justifies Hamilton's rule (or refinements of it), implicitly supports the concept of inclusive fitness at least in one of its original uses.

In conclusion, the central heuristics of kinship theory receive adequate justification from explicit population genetic models. They apply most appropriately when selection is weak, requiring, in addition, a host of other assumptions, most of which are "usual" in population-genetics theory.

Acknowledgments

I would like to thank the following people whose criticisms of previous versions of this reivew helped improve it: Bob Abugov, Felix Breden, Bob Boyd, Jerry Brown, Brian Charlesworth, Bill Hamilton, Jon Seger, Paul Sherman, Joan Silk, Marcy Uyenoyama, Michael Wade, Dave Wilson, Bill Wimsatt. This work was supported in part by NSF grant DE B-8118248.

References

1 Abugov, R., 1981. "The population genetics of social behavior," Ph.D. thesis. University of Arizona, Tucson, 71 pp.

2 Abugov, R., 1981. "Non-linear benefits and the evolution of eusociality in the Hymenoptera," *J. Theor. Bio.*, 88:733–742.

3 Abugov, R., Michod, R.E., 1981. "On the relation of family structured models and inclusive fitness models for kin selection," *J. Theor. Biol.*, 88: 743–754.

4 Alexander, R.D., 1974. "The evolution of social behavior," *Ann. Rev. Ecol. Syst.*, 5:325–383.

5 Alexander, R.D., Borgia, G., 1978. "Group selection, altruism, and the levels of organization of life," *Ann. Rev. Ecol. Syst.*, 9:449–474.

6 Alexander, R.D., 1979. *Darwinism and Human Affairs*, Seattle, University of Washington Press, 317 pp.

7 Barash, D.P., Greene, P.J., 1978. "Exact versus probabilistic coefficients of relationship: Some implications for sociobiology," *Am. Nat.*, 112:355–363.

8 Boorman, S.A., Levitt, P.R., 1980. *The Genetics of Altruism*, New York, Academic Press, 459 pp.

8a Boyd, R., 1982. "Density-dependent mortality and the evolution of social interactions," *Anim. Behav.*, forthcoming.

9 Boyd, R., Richerson, P.J., 1980. "Effect of phenotypic variation on kin selection," *Proc. Natl. Acad. Sci.* (USA), 77:7506–7509.

10 Breden, F., Wade, M.J., 1981. "Inbreeding and evolution by kin selection," *Ethol. Sociobiol.*, 2:3–16.

11 Brown, J.L., 1978. "Avian communal breeding systems," *Ann. Rev. Ecol. Syst.*, 9:123–155.

12 Brown, J.L., 1982. "Cooperation—a biologist's dilemma," in *Advances in*

the Study of Behavior, ed. J. S. Rosenblatt, R. A. Hinde, C. Beer, M. C. Busnel, New York, Academic Press.

13 Brown, J. L., Brown, E. R., 1981. "Kin selection and individual selection in babblers," in *Natural Selection and Social Behavior: Recent Research and New Theory,* ed. R. D. Alexander, D. W. Tinkle, New York, Chiron Press, pp. 244–256.

14 Cavalli-Sforza, L. L., Feldman, M. W., 1978. "Darwinian selection and 'altruism,'" *Theor. Popul. Biol.* 14:263–281.

15 Charlesworth, B., 1978. "Some models of the evolution of altruistic behavior between siblings," *J. Theor. Biol.,* 72:297–319.

16 Charlesworth, B., 1980. "Models of kin selection," in *Evolution of Social Behavior: Hypotheses and Empirical Tests,* ed. H. Markl, Berlin, Dahlem Konferenzen, pp. 11–16.

17 Charlesworth, B., Charnov, E. L., 1981. "Kin selection in age-structured populations," *J. Theor. Biol.,* 88:103–119.

18 Charnov, E. L., 1977. "An elementary treatment of the genetical theory of kin selection," *J. Theor. Biol.,* 66:541–550.

19 Charnov, E. L., 1978. "Evolution of eusocial behavior: Offspring choice or parental parasitism," *J. Theor. Biol.* 75:451–465.

20 Charnov, E. L., 1978. "Sex ratio selection in eusocial Hymenoptera," *Am. Nat.,* 112:317–326.

21 Cockerham, C. C., 1956. "Effects of linkage on the covariances between relatives," *Genetics,* 41:138–141.

22 Cockerham, C. C., 1971. "Higher order probability functions of identity of alleles by descent," *Genetics,* 69:235–246.

23 Cockerham, C. C., Burrows, P. M., Young, S. S., Prout, T., 1972. "Frequency dependent selection in randomly mating populations," *Am. Nat.,* 106:493–515.

24 Craig, R., 1979. "Parental manipulation, kin selection, and the evolution of altruism," *Evolution,* 33:319–334.

25 Dawkins, R., 1976. *The Selfish Gene,* Oxford, Oxford University Press, 224 pp.

26 Dawkins, R., 1979. "Twelve misunderstandings of kin selection," *Z. Tierpsychol.,* 51:184–200.

27 Denniston, C., 1974. "An extension of the probability approach to genetic relationships: One locus," *Theor. Popul. Biol.,* 6:58–75.

28 Elston, R. C., Lange, K., 1976. "The genotypic distribution of relatives of homozygotes when consanguinity is present," *Ann. Hum. Genet.* 39:493–496.

29 Emlen, S. T., 1978. "The evolution of cooperative breeding in birds," in *Behavioural Ecology: An Evolutionary Approach,* ed. J. Krebs, N. Davies, pp. 245–281.

30 Emlen, S. T., 1981. "Altruism, kinship and reciprocity in the white-fronted bee-eater," Reference 13, pp. 217–230.

31 Feldman, M. W., Cavalli-Sforza, L. L., 1981. "Further remarks on Darwinian selection and 'altruism,'" *Theor. Popul. Biol.,* 19:251–260.

32 Fisher, R. A., 1930. *The Genetical Theory of Natural Selection,* Oxford, Clarendon Press, 2nd rev. ed., 1958, New York, Dover, 291 pp.

33 Flesness, N. R., Holtzman, R. C., 1982. "Inbreeding and the kin selection threshold," *Am. Nat.,* forthcoming.

34 Haldane, J. B. S., 1932. *The Causes of Evolution,* New York, Longmans, Green. Paperback ed. 1966, Ithaca, Cornell University Press, 235 pp.

35 Haldane, J. B. S., 1955. "Population genetics," *New Biol.,* 18:34–51.

36 Haldane, J. B. S., Jayakar, S. D., 1963. "Polymorphism due to selection of varying direction," *J. Genet.* 58:237–242.

37 Hamilton, W. D., 1963. "The evolution of altruistic behavior," *Am. Nat.,* 97:354–356.

38 Hamilton, W. D., 1964. "The genetical evolution of social behavior, I," *J. Theor. Biol.,* 7:1–16.

39 Hamilton, W. D., 1964. "The genetical evolution of social behavior, II," *J. Theor. Biol.,* 7:17–52.

40 Hamilton, W. D., 1971. "Selection of selfish and altruistic behavior in some extreme models," in *Man and Beast: Comparative Social Behavior,* ed. J. F. Eisenberg, W. S. Dillon, Washington, D.C., Smithsonian Institution Press, pp. 59–91.

41 Hamilton, W. D., 1972. "Altruism and related phenomena, mainly in social insects," *Ann. Rev. Ecol. Syst.,* 3:192–232.

42 Hamilton, W. D., 1975. "Innate social aptitudes of man: An approach from evolutionary genetics," in *Biosocial Anthropology,* ed. R. Fox, New York, Wiley, pp. 133–155. Reprinted in part in this volume.

43 Harpending, H. C., 1979. "The population genetics of interactions," *Am. Nat.,* 113:622–630.

44 Harris, D. L., 1964. "Genotypic covariances between inbred relatives," *Genetics,* 50:1319–1348.

45 Hines, G., Maynard Smith, J., 1979. "Games between relatives," *J. Theor. Biol.,* 79:19–30.

46 Jacquard, A., 1974. *The Genetic Structure of Populations,* New York, Springer, 569 pp.

47 Krebs, J. R., 1980. "Measuring fitness in social systems," Reference 13, pp. 205–219.

48 Krebs, J. R., Davies, N. B., 1981. *An Introduction to Behavioral Ecology,* Sutherland, Mass., Sinauer, 292 pp.

49 Lakatos, I., 1970. "Falsification and methodology of scientific research programmes," in *Criticism and the Growth of Knowledge,* ed. I. Lakatos, A. Musgrave, Cambridge, England, Cambridge University Press, pp. 91–195.

50 Lakatos, I. 1971. "History of science and its rational reconstruction," *Boston Stud. Philos. Sci.,* 8:91–136.

51 Levene, H., 1953. "Genetic equilibrium when more than one ecological niche is available," *Am. Nat.*, 87:311-313.

52 Levitt, P. R., 1975. "General k in selection models for genetic evolution of sib altruism in diploid and haplodiploid species," *Proc. Natl. Acad. Sci.* (USA), 72:4531-35.

53 Lewontin, R. C., 1970. "The units of selection," *Ann. Rev. Ecol. Syst.*, 1: 1-18.

54 Ligon, J. D., 1981. "Demographic patterns and communal breeding in the green woodhoopoe, *Phoeniculus purpureus*," Reference 13, pp. 231-243.

55 Ligon, J. D., 1981. "Sociobiology is for the birds," *Auk*, 98:409-412.

56 Lush, J. L., 1947. "Family merit and individual merit as bases for selection," *Am. Nat.*, 81:241-61, 362-379.

57 MacNair, N. R., 1978. "An ESS for the sex ratio in animals, with particular reference to the social Hymenoptera," *J. Theor. Biol.*, 70:449-459.

58 Matessi, C., Jayakar, S. D., 1976. "Conditions for the evolution of altruism under Darwinian selection," *Theor. Popul. Biol.*, 9:360-387.

59 Maynard Smith, J., 1964. "Group selection and kin selection," *Nature*, 201:1145-1147.

60 Maynard Smith, J., 1965. "The evolution of alarm calls," *Am. Nat.*, 94: 59-63.

61 Maynard Smith, J., 1976. "Group selection," *Q. Rev. Biol.*, 51:277-283. Reprinted in this volume.

62 Maynard Smith, J., 1980. "Models of the evolution of altruism," *Theor. Popul. Biol.*, 18:151-159.

63 Maynard Smith, J., 1981. "The evolution of social behavior—a classification of models," in *Current Problems in Sociobiology*, ed. King's College Sociobiology Group, Cambridge, Cambridge University Press, pp. 29-44.

64 Michener, C. D., Brothers, D. J., 1974. "Were workers of eusocial Hymenoptera initially altruistic or oppressed?" *Proc. Natl. Acad. Sci.* (USA), 71: 671-674.

65 Michod, R. E., 1979. "Genetical aspects of kin selection: Effects of inbreeding," *J. Theor. Biol.*, 81:223-233.

66 Michod, R. E., 1980. "Evolution of interactions in family structured populations: Mixed mating models," *Genetics*, 96:275-296.

67 Michod, R. E., 1981. "Positive heuristics in evolutionary biology," *Brit. J. Philos. Sci.*, 32:1-36.

68 Michod, R. E., Abugov, R., 1980. "Adaptive topographies in family structured models of kin selection," *Science*, 210:667-669.

69 Michod, R. E., Anderson, W. W., 1979. "Measures of genetic relationship and the concept of inclusive fitness," *Am. Nat.*, 114:637-647.

70 Michod, R. E., Hamilton, W. D., 1980. "Coefficients of relatedness in sociobiology," *Nature*, 288:694-697.

71 Orlove, M. J., 1975. "A model of kin selection not involving coefficients of relationship," *J. Theor. Biol.*, 49:289–310.

72 Orlove, M. J., Wood, C. L., 1978. "Coefficients of relationship and coefficients of relatedness in kin selection: A covariance form for the rho formula," *J. Theor. Biol.*, 73:679–686.

73 Orlove, M. J., 1981. "The elevator effect or a lift in a lift: How a locus in neutral equilibrium can provide a free ride for a neutral allele at another locus," *J. Theor. Biol.*, 90:81–99.

74 Oster, G. F., Wilson, E. O., 1978. *Caste and Ecology in the Social Insects,* Princeton, Princeton University Press, 352 pp.

75 Power, H. W., 1981. "Searching for altruism in birds," *Auk,* 98:512–515.

76 Price, G. R., 1970. "Selection and covariance," *Nature,* 227:529–531.

77 Reed, T. E., Neel, J. V., 1959. "Huntington's chorea in Michigan, 2: Selection and mutation," *Am. J. Hum. Genet.,* 11:107–136.

78 Roughgarden, J., 1979. *Theory of Population Genetics and Evolutionary Ecology: An Introduction.* New York, Macmillan, 634 pp.

79 Scudo, F. M., Ghiselin, M. T., 1975. "Familial selection and the evolution of social behavior," *J. Genet.,* 62:1–31.

80 Seger, J., 1981. "Kinship and covariance," *J. Theor. Biol.*, 91:191–213.

81 Sherman, P. W., 1980. "The meaning of nepotism," *Am. Nat.,* 116:604–606.

82 Stern, J. T., 1970. "The meaning of 'adaptation' and its relation to the phenomenon of natural selection," in *Evolutionary Biology,* ed. Th. Dobzhansky, M. K. Hecht, W. C. Steere, New York, Appleton-Century-Crofts, 4: 38–66.

83 Templeton, A. R., 1979. "A frequency dependent model of brood-selection," *Am. Nat.,* 114:515–524.

84 Templeton, A., 1979. "Chromosome number, quantitative genetics and eusociality," *Am. Nat.,* 113:937–941.

85 Toro, M., Abugov, R., Charlesworth, B., Michod, R. E., 1982. "Exact versus heuristic models of kin selection," *J. Theor. Biol.*, forthcoming.

86 Trivers, R. L., 1974. "Parent-offspring conflict," *Am. Zool.,* 14:249–264.

87 Trivers, R. L., Hare, H., 1976. "Haplodiploidy and the evolution of the social insects," *Science,* 191:249–263.

88 Uyenoyama, M. K., Bengtsson, B. O., 1981. "Towards a genetic theory for the evolution of the sex ratio, II: Haplodiploid and diploid models with sibling and parental control of the brood sex ratio and brood size," *Theor. Popul. Biol.,* 20:57–79.

89 Uyenoyama, M., Feldman, M. W., 1980. "Theories of kin and group selection: A population genetics perspective," *Theor. Popul. Biol.,* 17:380–414.

90 Uyenoyama, M. K., Feldman, M. W., 1981. "On relatedness and adaptive topography in kin selection," *Theor. Popul. Biol.,* 19:87–123.

91 Uyenoyama, M. K., Feldman, M. W., Mueller, L. D., 1981. "Population genetic theory of kin selection, I: Multiple alleles at one locus," *Proc. Natl. Acad. Sci.* (USA), 78:5036–5040.

92 Uyenoyama, M. K., Feldman, M. W., 1982. "Population genetic theory of kin selection, II: The multiplicative model," *Am. Nat.,* forthcoming.

93 Wade, M. J., 1978. "A critical review of models of group selection," *Q. Rev. Biol.,* 53:101–114. Reprinted in this volume.

94 Wade, M. J., 1978. "Kin selection: A classical approach and a general solution," *Proc. Natl. Acad. Sci.* (USA), 75:6154–6158.

95 Wade, M. J., 1979. "The evolution of social interactions by family selection," *Am. Nat.,* 113:399–417.

96 Wade, M. J., 1980. "Kin selection: Its components," *Science,* 210:665–667.

97 Wade, M. J., 1982. "The evolution of interference competition by individual, family, and group selection," *Proc. Natl. Acad. Sci.* (USA), forthcoming.

98 Wade, M. J., Breden, F., 1980. "The evolution of cheating and selfish behavior," *Behav. Ecol. Sociobiol.,* 7:167–172.

99 Wade, M. J., Breden, F., 1981. "The effect of inbreeding on the evolution of altruistic behavior by kin selection," *Evolution,* 35:844–858.

100 Wallace, D. C., 1976. "The social effect of Huntington's chorea on reproductive effectiveness," *Ann. Hum. Genet.,* 39:375–379.

101 Williams, B. J., 1981. "A critical review of models in sociobiology," *Ann. Rev. Anthropol.,* 10:163–192.

102 Williams, G. C., 1966. *Adaptation and Natural Selection,* Princeton, Princeton University Press, 307 pp. Chapter 4 is reprinted in part in this volume.

103 Williams, G. C., 1975. *Sex and Evolution,* Princeton, Princeton University Press, 200 pp.

104 Williams, G. C., Williams, D. C., 1957. "Natural selection of individually harmful social adaptions among sibs with special reference to social insects," *Evolution,* 11:32–39.

105 Wilson, D. S., 1975. "A theory of group selection," *Proc. Natl. Acad. Sci.* (USA), 72:143–146.

106 Wilson, D. S., 1977. "Structured demes and the evolution of group advantageous traits," *Am. Nat.,* 111:157–185.

107 Wilson, D. S., 1980. *The Natural Selection of Populations and Communities.* Menlo Park, Cal., Benjamin/Cummings. Chapter 2 is reprinted in part in this volume.

108 Wilson, D. S., 1983. "Individual and group selection: A historical and conceptual review," *Ann. Rev. Ecol. Syst.,* forthcoming.

109 Wilson, E. O., 1975. *Sociobiology: The New Synthesis,* Cambridge, Mass. Harvard University Press, 697 pp.

110 Wimsatt, W., 1980. "Reductionistic research strategies and their biases in

the units of selection controversy," in *Scientific Discovery*, Vol. II: *Case Studies*, ed. T. Nickles, Dordrecht, Reidel, pp. 213–259. Reprinted in part in this volume.

111 Wimsatt, W., 1981. "Units of selection and the structure of the multilevel genome," *PSA 1980*. Vol. 2, ed. R. N. Giere, P. D. Asquith. East Lansing, Mich., Philos. Sci. Assoc.

112 Woolfenden, G. E., Fitzpatrick, J. W., 1980. "The selfish behavior of avian altruists," *Proc. 17th Int. Ornithol. Congr.*, pp. 886–889.

113 Woolfenden, G. E., 1981. "Selfish behavior by Florida Scrub Jay helpers," Reference 13, pp. 257–260.

114 Wright, S. 1922. "Coefficients of inbreeding and relationship," *Am. Nat.*, 56:330–338.

115 Wright, S., 1931. "Evolution in Mendelian populations," *Genetics*, 16: 97–159.

116 Wright, S., 1932. "The roles of mutation, inbreeding, crossbreeding and selection in evolution," *Proc. 6th Int. Congr. Genet.*, 1:356–66. Reprinted in this volume.

117 Wright, S., 1932. "On the evaluation of dairy sires," *Proc. Am. Soc. Anim. Prod.*, 1931:71–78.

118 Wright, S., 1951. "The genetical structure of populations," *Ann. Eugen.*, 15:323–354.

119 Wright, S., 1955. "Classification of the factors of evolution," *Cold Spring Harbor Symp. Quant. Biol.*, 20:16–24.

120 Wright, S., 1969. *Evolution and the Genetics of Populations, Vol. 2: The Theory of Gene Frequencies*, Chicago, University of Chicago Press, 511 pp.

121 Wright, S., 1977. *Evolution and the Genetics of Populations, Vol. 3: Experimental Results and Evolutionary Deductions*. Chicago, University of Chicago Press, 613 pp.

122 Yokoyama, S., Felsenstein, J., 1978. "A model of kin selection for an altruistic trait considered as a quantitative character," *Proc. Natl. Acad. Sci. (USA)*, 75:420–422.

123 Yokoyama, S., 1981. "Social selection in human populations, I: Modification of the fitness of offspring by an affected parent," *Am. J. Hum. Genet.*, 33:407–417.

124 Zahavi, A., 1981. "Some comments on sociobiology," *Auk*, 98:412–415.

14

Group Selection

J. Maynard Smith

Preface, August 1983

Recent disagreements over "group selection" are largely semantic. The phrase has been used in two different senses:

1) Evolution by natural selection requires that there be entities with the properties of multiplication, variation, and heredity. Given these properties, entities will evolve characteristics ensuring their survival and reproduction ("adaptations"). Individual organisms have these properties. Wynne-Edwards proposed that groups of organisms might also have them, and hence might acquire adaptations ensuring group survival (for example, epideictic displays). It was this meaning of group selection—a phrase describing a whole evolutionary mechanism, not just a selective process—which was criticized, I think rightly, by G. C. Williams and myself, among others. My own objection was quantitative: there is usually too much intrademic selection for the process to be effective.

2) The fitness of individuals is determined in the course of interactions with others. Sometimes the interacting individuals form groups ("trait groups"), and therefore D. S. Wilson called the process group selection. This was unfortunate, partly because the term was already in use with a different meaning, and partly because group structure is largely irrelevant to it. Thus the processes discussed by Wilson operate equally well in a continuously distributed population, provided that individuals interact with neighbors. Even if groups exist, there is no reproductive isolation between them, as there is in the process envisaged by Wynne-Edwards.

The result of this dual usage is that confusion is now widespread. I suggest we drop the term "group selection" altogether, and use "interdemic selection" and "species selection" (depending on the nature of the "group") for the process discussed by Wynne-Edwards. But if so, we must remember that interdemic selection was proposed by Wright, in his "shifting balance" theory, as a means whereby *individually* advantageous genotypes could spread, the group structure being needed only to enable those genotypes to arise in the first place, whereas Wynne-Edwards proposed it as a means whereby individually disadvantageous traits could spread if they were good for the group. If a group of interacting individuals has "emergent" properties (for example, a group of spiders can build a web across a stream), the term "trait-group selection" is appropriate. For the more general case in which individual fitnesses are determined in interactions with others, the old term "frequency-dependent selection" is entirely adequate. Finally, if interactions are between relatives, the term "kin selection" is still (I hope) unambiguous.

Text of 1976 Article*

The purpose of this short review is to look a some recent discussions of group selection, in particular those by E. O. Wilson (1975), D. S. Wilson (1975) and M. E. Gilpin (1975). Earlier work will be referred to only briefly; the need for a review arises because the three references given either propose a blurring of the distinction between "group" and "kin" selection, or suggest an importance for group selection greater than it has usually been given, or both.

The first point to establish is that the argument is quantitative, not qualitative. Group selection will have evolutionary consequences; the only question is how important these consequences have been. If there are genes which, although decreasing individual fitness, make it less likely that a group (deme or species) will go extinct, then group extinction will influence evolution. It does not follow that the influence is important enough to play the role suggested for it by some biologists.

The present phase of the debate about group selection was opened by the publication of Wynne-Edwards' *Animal Dispersion* (1962), which applied to animals a concept first proposed by Carr-Saunders (1922) to explain human population dynamics; it ascribed to group selection a major role in the evolution of population regulation. Although his thesis has had its adherents, the orthodox response from ecologists has been to argue that the patterns of behavior he described can be explained by individual selection, and from population geneticists that the mechanism he proposes is insufficient to account for the results. It is in the nature of science that once a position becomes orthodox it should be subjected to criticism; hence the papers by D. S. Wilson (1975), Gilpin (1975), Levin and Kilmer (1974), Gadgil (1975), and others. It does not follow that, because a position is orthodox, it is wrong; hence this review.

Is the argument important? In a recent review of E. O. Wilson's *Sociobiology,* C. H. Waddington referred to group selection as "a fashionable topic

*From *The Quarterly Review of Biology,* 51 (1976), 277–283.

for a rather foolish controversy." Doubtless some foolish things have been said, but there is an important issue at stake. If group selection has played the role suggested by Wynne-Edwards, no one can doubt its importance. But why should it be important to argue that it has not? The reason for the vehemence with which Williams (1966, 1975), Ghiselin (1974), Lack (1966) and other opponents of group selection have argued their case is, I think, their conviction that group selection assumptions, often tacit or unconscious, have been responsible for the failure to tackle important problems. So long as we fail to distinguish group and individual selection, or assume that an explanation in terms of advantage to the species is adequate to account for the evolution of some behavior pattern or genetic process, without asking what is its effect on individual fitness, we shall make little progress.

The extent of unconscious group selectionism, particularly among ecologists, has recently been documented by Ghiselin (1974). Similar views are still widespread among ethologists. It is, however, in the study of the evolution of genetic mechanisms that group selection assumptions are most pervasive. Fisher (1930) argued that sexual reproduction owed its existence to the fact that sexually reproducing populations can evolve more rapidly than asexual ones. Darlington (1939) attempted to explain a wide range of adaptations in chromosome structure and recombination frequency in terms of inter-population selection. Since that time, the interpretation of genetic mechanisms in terms of species advantage has become almost commonplace.

Of course, group advantage cannot be ruled out a priori as an explanation of the evolution of ecological adaptations, of behavior, or of genetic mechanisms. But the quantitative difficulties must be faced. It is plausible, for example, to suppose that, whatever its origin, sexual reproduction is maintained in higher organisms because populations which abandon sex go extinct in competition with more rapidly evolving sexual species. This plausibility depends on the assumption that the origin of new ameiotically parthenogenetic strains is a sufficiently rare event for each such origin to be balanced by the extinction of such a strain. It is less plausible to suppose that the chiasma frequency or recombination frequency within a species is determined by group selection, because there is widespread within-species genetic variation of recombination rate, and we would therefore expect individual selection acting on this variation to outweigh any long-term effects of interspecies selection.

It is not the purpose of this review to discuss the evolution of sex or recombination. The problem has been mentioned because it illustrates particularly clearly the quantitative difficulties faced by group selection explanations. In view of these difficulties, an explanation in terms of group advantage should always be explicit, and always calls for some justification in terms of the frequency of group extinction. Wynne-Edwards' great merit is that he made the assumption explicit, and in so doing forced population geneticists to make the argument quantitative.

The Distinction Between Group and Kin Selection

The frequency of a gene in a population will be influenced not only by the effects that gene has on the survival and fertility of individuals carrying it, but also by its effects on the survival and fertility of relatives of that individual. The second kind of effect has been called "kin selection" (Maynard Smith, 1964). The effect is obvious when the "relatives" are the children or other direct descendants of the individual; it has always been appreciated that genes improving parental care will be selected. Fisher (1930) and Haldane (1932) saw clearly that the effect would work for other relatives (e.g., sibs or cousins). In the vaguer forms of "inter-family selection" the idea goes back to Darwin's *Origin of Species.*

Wright (1945) discussed the evolution of altruistic traits in terms of "interpopulation selection." Despite his use of this phrase, his model, which is sketched rather than fully worked out, would fall under the heading of kin selection rather than group selection if the distinction suggested below is accepted.

Attempts to apply the idea of kin selection in detail to the evolution, first of social insects and later of other animal societies, originated with Hamilton (1963, 1964), and are the central theme of E. O. Wilson (1975).

With the almost simultaneous publication of Hamilton's papers and Wynne-Edwards' book, it seemed desirable to draw a clear distinction between the two processes of kin and group selection, and to coin a term for the former (Maynard Smith, 1964). It is always difficult to draw unambiguous distinctions in biology, but it is often valuable to try. I still think that the attempt was on the right lines, although in retrospect I can see that there is one essential feature of group selection, namely group extinction, which I failed to emphasize, although it was present in my mathematical model. The basic distinction made concerned the population structure required for the two processes. For kin selection (as described by the first sentence in this section) it is necessary that relatives live close to one another, but it is not necessary (although it may be favorable) that the population be divided into reproductively isolated groups. All that is essential for kin selection is that relatives live close to one another, so that an animal's behavior can influence the survival or fecundity of its relatives.

For group selection, the division into groups which are partially isolated from one another is an essential feature. If group selection is to be responsible for the establishment of an "altruistic" gene, the groups must be small, or must from time to time be re-established by a few founders. This is because in a large group there is no way in which a new "altruistic" gene can be established. If a new mutant is to be established in a large group, then it must increase the fitness of individuals carrying it, or more precisely, it must increase their "inclusive fitness" relative to other members of the group (Hamilton, 1964); if this is so, group selection is not needed to explain its spread. Small group size is not needed for the maintenance of an altruistic gene, only for its establishment. The involvement of genetic drift as an essential feature of group selection has been queried by D. S. Wilson (1975); I will return to this point later.

What I should have said in my 1964 paper, but did not, is that the extinction of some groups and the "reproduction" of others are essential features of evolution by group selection. If groups are the units of selection, then they must have the properties of variation, multiplication, and heredity required if natural selection is to operate on them. In a finite universe, multiplication implies death. Group selection could operate for a short time on differences in group reproduction, without group extinction, but in the long run evolution by group selection requires group extinction just as evolution by individual selection requires individual death.

The relevance of group reproduction and extinction can best be illustrated by a partly imaginary example. Anubis baboons live in troops; females remain in their natal troop whereas males must move to another troop before breeding (Packer, 1975). Suppose that a gene were to arise which caused females to help other females in their troop to raise their offspring (in fact, females do help one another to defend their young against males). This gene would increase in frequency in the whole population—more males would be produced by a troop whose females carried the gene, and these males would transmit the gene to other troops. Despite the existence of troops, I would regard this as an example of kin selection. The gene would not increase in frequency unless the females in a troop were related to one another. But the increase does not depend on small group size and hence on genetic drift, nor does it depend on group reproduction or extinction; indeed, it would work in much the same way if there were no groups, provided that females bred close to where they were born, and that males dispersed before breeding.

There will doubtless be cases in which the distinction is difficult to draw. E. O. Wilson (1975) has argued that "pure kin and pure interdemic selection are the two poles at the end of a gradient of selection on ever enlarging nested sets of related individuals." In similar vein, D. S. Wilson (1975) writes "the traditional concepts of group and individual selection are seen as two extremes of a continuum." The disagreement between us, if there is one, is one of semantics and the strategy of research rather than of fact. In the history of ideas as in taxonomy, there are lumpers and splitters; I am a splitter. I think we would do best to draw as clear a distinction as we can between different processes. I welcome E. O. Wilson's distinction between inter-demic and inter-species selection, although both are forms of group selection.

Why do I think it desirable to sharpen rather than to blur the distinction between different modes of selection? Ultimately, the importance or otherwise of these different modes can only be decided by comparing different species, and asking whether particular traits, such as altruistic, prudent, or selfish behavior, are associated with particular population structures. For this to be a meaningful enterprise, we must be clear about what are the relevant features of population structure. In particular, we must be clear whether our theory asserts that the evolution of a trait requires the existence of groups, or merely that relatives should be neighbors.

To sum up, "group" selection should be confined to processes that require the existence of partially isolated groups which can reproduce and which go extinct; the origin of new altruistic traits requires that the groups be small or be founded by a few individuals. Kin selection can operate whenever relatives live close to one another, and hence can influence one another's chances of survival and reproduction; they may or may not live in groups.

Models of Group Selection

Maynard Smith (1964) proposed a model, the "Haystack" model, whereby an "altruistic" gene, which is eliminated by its "selfish" allele from mixed groups, can increase in frequency by group selection. In this model all groups necessarily became extinct since they depend on a transitory resource (a "haystack"), but groups containing only the altruistic gene produce more potential founders of new groups. In most other models of group selection, extinction has been made stochastic rather than necessary, with the probability of extinction being lower in groups with a higher frequency of the altruistic allele. Thus, in my model, groups differed in "fecundity," whereas in most subsequent models they differ in "viability."

More general models for the spread of altruistic alleles brought about by differential group extinction were proposed by Levins (1970) and by Boorman and Levitt (1973). Although different in detail, these models have in common that they confirm the logical possibility of group selection, but show that the population structure in time and space required for its operation is of a kind which may be rather infrequent in practice. Levin and Kilmer (1974) reach similar conclusions on the basis of a computer-simulated model. Genetically effective deme sizes of less than 25 and usually closer to 10 were required, and the rate of gene flow by migration could not be greater than 5 per cent per generation.

Gilpin (1975) presents a very thoroughly worked out model. His proposed mechanism is clearly a case of group selection as defined above. It is of particular interest because the altruistic trait he considers, "prudence" on the part of predators leading them not to overexploit their food supply, is precisely the one for which Wynne-Edwards proposed group selection. The new features which Gilpin has introduced into the argument relate to the dynamics of predator-prey systems. For a wide class of models describing the interaction between a predator and prey (the model of Rosenzweig and MacArthur, 1963, is a familiar example), a small change in the properties of the predator can cause a large change in system behavior. Suppose we start from a state of stable coexistence of predator and prey, and suppose individual selection to be acting to improve the hunting ability of the predators. The equilibrium will change gradually, with the predator numbers increasing and the prey decreasing, until a critical point is reached. If hunting ability continues to increase beyond this point, the equilibrium becomes unstable and the system passes into a stable oscillation (a limit cycle). With further improvement in hunting ability, the amplitude of the oscillation rises until, with finite populations, chance extinction of one or both species would ensue.

Gilpin imagines an environment composed of patches. A predator population may contain only genotypes *aa*, in which case stable coexistence is possible, or only *AA*, which leads to rapid extinction, or some mixture of *aa, Aa* and *AA*. A mixed population evolves by individual selection to the fixation of allele *A*, and hence to extinction. In his model, Gilpin allows for migration between patches, and genetic drift within them. He shows that for a reasonably wide range of parameter values the altruistic allele *a* can maintain itself against *A*.

The problem remains whether the range of parameter values includes cases likely to correspond to natural predator-prey systems. The very complexity of Gilpin's model makes this difficult to decide. Fortunately, however, I believe it possible to replace Gilpin's model of group selection (and many other models) by a much simpler model, and to identify a single parameter which will determine the fate of an altruistic gene. In Gilpin's model, there are at any moment three kinds of patch: "empty" patches, E, containing no predators (although they may contain prey); "altruistic" patches, A, containing only *aa* predators; and "selfish" patches, S, containing at least some *AA* or *Aa* predators. The types of patch, and the possible transitions between them, are shown in Fig. 1. The transition from E to S is shown by a broken arrow because, although it is permitted in Gilpin's model, it would not be in some other models of group selection.

The model is formally similar to one analyzed by Maynard Smith (1974), but with a different biological interpretation. In that model, E represented empty patches; A, patches with prey individuals only; and S, patches contain-

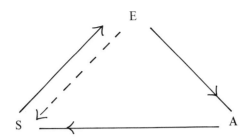

Figure 1. A Model of Group Selection. For explanation see text.

ing both predator and prey and destined to become empty. The model is also formally similar to an unpublished model by Ivar Heuch of the University of Bergen for the evolution of the sex ratio in the butterfly *Acraea encedon*. In this species there is a "driving" Y* chromosome, such that XY* females have only daughters. In a panmictic population this should lead to species extinction. Heuch suggests that the species survives because of its patchy distribution. Again, E represents empty patches; A represents patches with only normal XY females; S represents "infected" patches containing at least one XY* female and destined for extinction. In effect, Heuch's model is one of balance between gametic selection for Y* and group selection for Y.

In such models, it is easy to see that the fate of the system depends on the single parameter M, which is the expected number of successful "selfish" emigrants from an S patch during the lifetime of the patch, from the moment it becomes "infected" to the time it becomes extinct. By a "selfish" emigrant is meant an *AA* or *Aa* predator in Gilpin's model, a predator in my model, or an XY* female in Heuch's model. By "successful" is meant that the migrant established itself and leaves descendants in a new patch (either E or A). If $M > 1$ the frequency of S patches will increase. The continued existence of the system requires $M < 1$.

In Gilpin's model, this means that during the history of a patch, from the moment when it is "infected" by an *Aa* or *AA* immigrant to the time of its extinction, there must on the average be less than one successful *Aa* or *AA* migrant to another patch. It is thus fairly easy to understand the features of his model which make for the maintenance of prudent *aa* genotypes. They are small population size per patch, little migration, and rapid extinction of a patch once infected. Rapid extinction arises from the nature of the predator-prey dynamics (a plausible assumption which is Gilpin's main innovation), and from the assumption that a single gene substitution in a small population is sufficient to tip the balance from stability to extinction.

It is hard to say how often the condition $M < 1$ will hold in nature. But it may be easier to decide whether group selection is a plausible mechanism in particular cases by concentrating on this inequality than by considering all the details and parameter values of the full model.

Finally, before leaving this topic, it is helpful to note the analogy between the equilibrium condition, $M = 1$, and the well-known principle of individual selection, that the mutational load equals the mutation rate. The latter principle states that each individually harmful mutation must be balanced by a death; the former that each socially harmful infection must be balanced by an extinction.

A quite different approach to the problem of group selection is taken by D. S. Wilson (1975). He considers a population which, although breeding at random, is divided for some part of the life cycle into "trait groups," within which altruistic or selfish interactions can take place. For a pair of alleles A and a, such that a determines an altruistic behavior which decreases the individual's chance of survival but increases the survival chances of all other members of the group, he shows that a can increase in frequency, but only if the between-trait-group genetic variance is greater than random—i.e., than would be expected if the members of trait groups were a random sample of the whole population.

This is an interesting result, but seems to me to refer to kin selection and not to group selection. Indeed, there is no reason other than mathematical convenience why he should consider trait "groups." His argument would work equally well if there were no discontinuities in spatial distribution provided that there was a genetic similarity between neighbors. The obvious reason why the members of a trait group might resemble one another genetically is that they are relatives. Wilson's result is then fully in accord with Hamilton's (1964) assertion that an altruistic gene will increase in frequency only if $k > 1/r$, where r is the coefficient of relationship between donor and recipient, and k the ratio of the gain of fitness of the recipient to the loss of fitness of the donor. Clearly, if $r = 0$ altruism will not increase in frequency.

Wilson argues from his model that genetic drift is not needed for group selection; since I do not think he is discussing group selection, I do not find his argument convincing. In fact, it is not clear why Wilson does not regard his model as one of kin selection. For example, he writes "consider a situation in which larval insects are deposited into the trait-groups by adult females. The larvae upon hatching intermix within the trait-group, and so do not fall under the traditional concept of kin selection." This is precisely the type of situation I intended to fall under the term kin selection. If, for example, animals behave with an equal degree of altruism to all their "neighbors," or to all fellow members of their "trait-group," and if *on average* animals are related to their neighbors, then I would regard this as an example of kin selection. It is not a necessary feature of kin selection that an animal should distinguish different degrees of relationship among its neighbors, and behave with greater altruism to the more closely related.

Apart from relatedness, there are other possible reasons why members of a trait-group might resemble one another genetically. If individuals of like genotype tend to associate together, either because they are attracted to one another, or because they are attracted by common features of the environment, or because they are the survivors of a common selective force, then altruism can be selected for. Before invoking this mechanism, however, it is important to remember that if an altruistic allele *a* is to replace a selfish allele *A*, then the members of a trait-group must resemble one another *at that locus*. If they are not related in the normal sense, this would require that the altruistic locus have pleiotropic effects determining association. Thus, these other reasons for genetic similarity between neighbors seem likely to be unimportant compared with identity by descent.

Conclusions

It is useful to distinguish as sharply as possible the processes of "kin" and "group" selection. The terms group selection should be confined to cases in which the group (deme or species) is the unit of selection. This requires that groups be able to "reproduce," by splitting or by sending out propagules, and that groups should go extinct. The origin of an altruistic trait (but not its maintenance) requires that the groups be small, or that new groups be established by one or a few founders. Kin selection requires only that relatives should live close to one another. The division of the population into groups, either permanently or for part of the life cycle, may favor the operation of kin selection but is not a necessary feature.

Group selection can maintain "altruistic" alleles—that is, alleles which reduce individual fitness but increase the fitness of groups carrying them. The conditions under which this can happen are stringent, so that the main debate concerns whether the process has had evolutionarily important consequences. The main function of models is to indicate the circumstances in which group selection can be important. For one large class of models, it can easily be seen that the condition for the maintenance of an altruistic allele by group selection is $M < 1$, where M is the expected number of successful migrants carrying the selfish allele produced by a group during the whole period from the moment when it was first "infected" by a selfish immigrant to the times of its extinction.

It follows that the features favoring group selection are small group size, low migration rates, and rapid extinction of groups infected with the selfish allele. The ultimate test of the group selection hypothesis will be whether populations having these characteristics tend to show "self-sacrificing" or "prudent" behavior more commonly than those which do not.

References

Boorman, S. A., and Levitt, P. R., 1973. "Group selection at the boundary of a stable population," *Theoret. Pop. Biol.*, 4:85–128.

Carr-Saunders, A. M., 1922. *The Population Problem: A Study in Human Evolution*, Oxford, Clarendon Press.

Darlington, C. D., 1939. *The Evolution of Genetic Systems*, Cambridge (Eng.), Cambridge University Press.

Fisher, R. A., 1930. *The Genetical Theory of Natural Selection*, Oxford, Clarendon Press.

Gadgil, M., 1975. "Evolution of social behavior through interpopulation selection," *Proc. Nat. Acad. Sci. U.S.A.*, 72:1199–1201.

Ghiselin, M. T., 1974. *The Economy of Nature and the Evolution of Sex*, Berkeley, University of California Press.

Gilpin, M. E., 1975. *Group Selection in Predator-Prey Communities*, Princeton, Princeton University Press.

Haldane, J. B. S., 1932. *The Causes of Evolution*, London, Longmans, Green.

Hamilton, W. D., 1963. "The evolution of altruistic behavior," *Am. Natur.*, 97:354–356.

Hamilton, W. D., 1964. "The genetical theory of social behavior, I, II," *J. Theoret. Biol.*, 7:1–52.

Lack, D., 1966. *Population Studies of Birds*, Oxford, Oxford University Press.

Levin, B. R., and Kilmer, W. L., 1974. "Interdemic selection and the evolution of altruism: A computer simulation study," *Evolution*, 28:527–545.

Levins, R., 1970. "Extinction," in *Some Mathematical Problems in Biology*, ed. M. Gerstenhaber, Providence, American Mathematical Society, pp. 77–107.

Maynard Smith, J., 1964. "Group Selection and kin selection," *Nature*, 201:1145–1147.

Maynard Smith, J., 1974. *Models in Ecology*, Cambridge (Eng.), Cambridge University Press.

Packer, C., 1975. "Male transfer in olive baboons," *Nature*, 255:219–220.

Rosenzweig, M. L., and MacArthur, R. H., 1963. "Graphical representation and stability conditions of predator-prey interactions," *Am. Natur.*, 97:209–223.

Williams, G. C., 1966. *Adaption and Natural Selection: A Critique of Some Current Evolutionary Thought*, Princeton, Princeton University Press. Chapter 4 is reprinted in part in this volume.

Williams, G. C., 1975. *Sex and Evolution*, Princeton, Princeton University Press.

Wilson, D. S., 1975. "A theory of group selection," *Proc. Nat. Acad. Sci. U.S.A.*, 72:143–146.

Wilson, E. O., 1975. *Sociobiology*, Harvard University Press, Cambridge.

Wright, S., 1945. *"Tempo and Mode in Evolution:* A critical review," *Ecology,* 26:415–419.

Wynne-Edwards, V.C., 1962. *Animal Dispersion in Relation to Social Behavior.* Edinburgh, Oliver and Boyd.

15

A Critical Review of the Models of Group Selection

Michael J. Wade

Introduction

Group selection is defined as that process of genetic change which is caused by the differential extinction or proliferation of groups of organisms (Wright, 1945; Wynne-Edwards, 1962; Maynard Smith, 1964; Williams, 1966; Lewontin, 1970; Wade, 1976). These groups may be any unit of population structure ranging from families (kin selection) to whole populations (interdeme or interpopulation selection). [In keeping with this genetical definition, I will not directly consider selection between species (Van Valen, 1975) or between ecosystems (Dunbar, 1960), both of which have been called group selection. Although the general principles of genetical variation and heritable fitness differences would apply to selection at these levels of organization, many of the other concepts discussed, such as non-additive components of variance and gene flow, clearly would not.] The gene-frequency changes caused by group selection (as is also true for individual selection) consist of changes in the genetic composition of individuals within populations. Individual selection requires genetic differences between individuals; group selection requires, in addition, that there be genetic differences between the units of population structure. Besides this between-group variation, the ecological processes of extinction, dispersion, and colonization are of primary importance in evaluating the role of population structure in evolution.

It is important to emphasize that both group selection and individual selection are *processes* that can change gene frequencies. They differ in the mechanism whereby gene-frequency changes are produced. As processes, group and individual selection may operate in the same direction or in opposite directions to change gene frequencies. Alternatively, one process can occur without the action of the other.

A very large proportion of the literature concerned with group selection

From *The Quarterly Review of Biology*, 53 (1978), 101–114.

consists of theoretical papers. Several authors, among them Maynard Smith (1964), Levins (1970), Eshel (1972), Boorman and Levitt (1973), Levin and Kilmer (1974), D.S. Wilson (1975, 1977), Gadgil (1975), Charnov and Krebs (1975), Gilpin (1975), Matessi and Jayakar (1973, 1976), and Cohen and Eshel (1976), have addressed the genetic problems of group selection from various, and sometimes divergent, mathematical viewpoints. Although all of the models have shown that group selection is possible, the general conclusion has been that selection *between* groups cannot override the effects of individual selection *within* groups except for a highly restricted set of parameter values. Since it is unlikely that conditions in natural populations would fall within the bounds imposed by the models, group selection, by and large, has been considered an insignificant force for evolutionary change (Williams, 1966; Slobodkin, 1974; Alexander, 1974; Ghiselin, 1974; Maynard Smith, 1976; Weins, 1976). Indeed, the general rule of thumb used by most ecologists and theorists at the present time is the "principle of parsimony" suggested by Williams (1966): if the evolution of an adaptation can be explained by individual selection there is no need to invoke group selection. Those authors taking exception to this general view (Levin and Kilmer, 1974; D.S. Wilson, 1975, 1977) have argued primarily that the theoretical conditions favorable to group selection occur more frequently in nature than has previously been believed.

However, these theoretical conclusions and the assumptions from which they have been derived can be re-evaluated in the light of recent empirical studies of group selection with laboratory populations of the flour beetle, *Tribolium* (Wade, 1976, 1977). This review will examine the major theoretical contributions to the discussion of group selection, and certain of the underlying assumptions of each model will be considered in some detail. It will be shown that, in addition to the many assumptions which are unique to any specific model, the models in general have a number of assumptions in common which are inherently unfavorable to the operation of group selection. Alternative assumptions derived from the empirical studies are suggested.

It is not my intention in this review to advocate group selection as a major force for evolutionary change, but rather to stimulate further theoretical and empirical inquiry into this controversial subject. For this reason, the discussion will be concerned with group selection as a *process,* and it will not focus on group selection as an *explanatory principle* for the evolution of particular traits in natural populations. Just as the utility of a model lies in its potential ability to suggest new avenues of experimentation, empirical observations can provide grounds for modifying prevailing theoretical opinion (cf. Mertz, Cawthon, and Park, 1976, for a recent example). Because of the recent expansion of theory in ecology and population biology, a close interaction between theory and experiment is not only desirable but necessary for understanding the genetical and ecological processes governing evolution in natural populations.

General Assumptions of the Models of Group Selection

Extinction, dispersion, and colonization are essential features of any model of group selection. The extent to which group selection can influence gene frequencies is determined by the interaction of these three processes. In particular, several different modes of extinction and dispersion are possible; each has different effects on the distribution of selective forces within groups, the amount of genetic variation between groups, and the "heritability" of genetic traits at the group level. All of the theoretical attempts to describe group selection mathematically have made assumptions concerning extinction, dispersion, and colonization which were considered biologically realistic by the authors and which served to reduce a formidable problem to more tractable proportions.

On the basis of those assumptions, the models of group selection can be classified into two broad categories depending upon the paradigm of population structure employed. One set of models can be called the *traditional group*, since they are essentially analytic approximations of Sewall Wright's shifting balance theory of evolution (Wright, 1929, 1931, 1932, 1945, and, more recently 1977). The traditional models assume that the species consists of many randomly mating local populations that are genetically interconnected by some small number of dispersing individuals at each generation. In these models gene frequencies can be altered by the differential extinction and recolonization of these partially isolated local populations. The models by Wright (1945), Maynard Smith (1964), Levins (1970), Eshel (1972), Boorman and Levitt (1973), Levin and Kilmer (1974), and Gilpin (1975) fall into this category of traditional models.

The second category of group selection models can be labeled the *intrademic group*. These models postulate a single panmictic population whose members are distributed into isolated neighborhoods or "trait groups" (*sensu* D.S. Wilson, 1975, 1977) during some stage of development. The interactions between individuals within the trait groups result in viability differences between the members of the different groups. Differently put, the genotypic composition of a trait group determines the viability of its members. Owing to these viability differences, some trait groups make a larger contribution of individuals to the mating pool than do others. Thus, group selection in these models occurs by the differential dispersion of the trait groups. The models in this category are those of D. S. Wilson (1975, 1977), Gadgil (1975), Charnov and Krebs (1975), Cohen and Eshel (1976), and Matessi and Jayakar (1973, 1976). The models of kin selection (Hamilton,

1964a, b) represent a special case of the intrademic models in which the trait groups or neighborhoods consist of related individuals (see D. S. Wilson, 1977, or Charnov, 1977, for mathematical proof of this equivalence).

The models in both groups share some or all of the following five assumptions, which will be discussed seriatim:

(1) It is assumed that the frequency of a single allele within a population can produce a significant change in the probability of survival of that population, or in the genetic contribution which the population makes to the next generation.

(2) All populations contribute migrants to a common pool, called the "migrant pool" (Levins, 1970), from which colonists are drawn at random to fill vacant habitats.

(3) The number of migrants contributed to the migrant pool by a population is often assumed to be independent of the size of the population. Thus, the frequency of an allele in the migrant pool can be represented by the mean allele frequency of all contributing populations.

(4) It is assumed, often implicitly, that the variance between populations (which is a prerequisite for the operation of group selection) is created primarily by genetic drift within the populations and, to a lesser extent, by sampling from the migrant pool.

(5) Group and individual selection are assumed to be operating in opposite directions with respect to the allele in question. In short, the allele is favored by selection between groups but disfavored by selection within groups.

A theoretical framework is specified by these postulates and group selection is constrained a priori to operate within the given limits of the models. The models to be discussed and their attendant assumptions are presented in Table 1, which will be referred to from time to time in the text. In the sections to follow, the effects of each of these five assumptions upon the process of group selection are discussed, and alternative assumptions that can be derived from the empirical results (Wade, 1976, 1977) are suggested.

Assumption 1: Selection on a Single Locus

Theoretical inquiry into group selection has been mainly concerned with clarifying the conditions under which a single allele can increase in frequency by means of group selection when that allele is disfavored by individual selection (cf. Table 1, column 1). Deterministic models of selection on a single locus are standard practice in population genetics theory and are a direct and reasonable approach to many genetic problems. Several genetical aspects of natural populations important to the process of group selection, however, cannot adequately be discussed in the simplified context of such models.

Table 1
The Models of Group Selection and Their Assumptions

Author	Single Locus (1) or Alternative Phenotypes (2)	Mechanism of Group Selection: Extinction (E) or Migration (M)	Migrant Pool	Origin of Between-Group Variation	Group vs. Individual Selection*
Tradition Models					
Wright (1945)	1	E	+	genetic drift	+
Maynard Smith (1964)	1	M	+	genetic drift	+
Levins (1970)	1	E	+	genetic drift, sampling error	+
Eshel (1972)	2	E	Intermediate[a]	genetic drift	+
Boorman and Levitt (1973)	1[b]	E	+[c]	genetic drift	+
Levin and Kilmer (1974)	1	E	+	genetic drift	+
Gilpin (1975)	1	E	+	genetic drift	+, (−)[d]
Intrademic Models					
Wilson (1975, 1977)	1	M	+	sampling error[e]	+, (−)[d]
Gadgil (1975)	1	M	+	(unclear)	−
Charnov and Krebs (1975)	2	M	+	sampling error	+
Matessi and Jayakar (1973, 1976)	2	M	+	sampling error[e]	+
Cohen and Eshel (1976)	1	M	+	sampling error	+

*+ indicates that the assumption is a part of the structure of the model; − indicates that the assumption is not a part of the model.

[a] The model can consider the effects of a migrant pool, a propagule pool, or an intermediate form of colonization by adjusting parameter values.

[b] A two-locus model is outlined but not developed.

[c] Instead of a migrant pool, the model assumes that a larger stable source of migrants exists independent of the local demes. This structure is mathematically equivalent to the migrant pool.

[d] Group selection and individual selection acting in the same direction are discussed, although not analytically considered.

[e] The sampling error can be enhanced by nonrandom assortment into trait groups on the basis of phenotype or kinship.

These are, namely, genotype-genotype interactions, epistatic effects between loci, and local variation in the direction and intensity of individual selection.

The strong effect of the biotic environment on fitness by means of genotype-genotype interactions has been abundantly demonstrated empirically (Wright and Dobzhansky, 1946; Lewontin, 1955; Levene, Pavlovsky, and Dobzhansky, 1954; Lewontin and Matsuo, 1963; Sokal and Huber, 1963; Sokal and Karten, 1964; Ehrmann, 1966, 1967, 1968; Spiess, 1968; Bryant, 1969, 1970; Bryant and Turner, 1972; Taylor and Sokal, 1973), and epistatic effects are demonstrated by most alleles which have been investigated in different genetic backgrounds (e.g., Wright and Dobzhansky, 1946; Wright, 1949; Wallace, 1968; Sokal et al., 1974; McCauley, 1977). Spatial variation in selection pressures has also been reported frequently in both laboratory and field studies, and it can often be related to environmental variation in microhabitats (e.g., Gordon, 1935; Dobzhansky, 1948; Selander, Hunt, and Yang, 1969; Koehn and Mitton, 1972; Koehn, Milkman, Mitton, 1976).

These multivarious effects of the same allele when in different genetic backgrounds or different local habitats can result in continual change in both the direction and the intensity of individual selection. Depending upon the initial genotypic composition of the population, individual selection could result in the attainment of any of a number of different gene frequencies corresponding to local "adaptive peaks" (Wright, 1956). Although the particular gene frequency attained may not be the optimum when all possible genotypes are considered, individual selection within the population would prevent a shift from the local peak to the optimum. The net result is a "multiplicity of adaptive peaks on a selection surface" (Wright, 1931, 1956, 1959), with no single gene or gene frequency conferring more than a temporary or local advantage. Individual selection itself would contribute to the genetic variation between populations.

That is, to the extent that individual selection pressures vary in sign or magnitude among local populations—owing to frequency dependence, density dependence, epistatic effects, or combinations of these—individual selection will act to generate and maintain genetic differences among the local populations. This could occur, as indeed it has been shown in many of the experiments cited above, even in the absence of conspicuous environmental variation among the local habitats. Thus, even in those cases where the net effect of individual selection is opposite to that of group selection, temporal and spatial variation in the components of selection at the individual level can assist the opposing process of group selection by contributing to the amount of variation between populations.

In contrast, the group selection models examine populations which are genetically subdivided but experience a uniform selective environment. In such populations individual selection upon alleles at a single locus (in the absence of heterosis, which is not treated by the models) can operate only to increase or decrease gene frequencies in a deterministic way. The models postulating alternative phenotypes (cf. Table 1) without specifying the underlying genetic system are no more realistic in this respect. Because of this, Wright's concept of a multiplicity of adaptive peaks on a selection surface is not applicable in the context of the group selection models, and several of the potentially important forces for creating genetic variation between populations have been omitted from previous theoretical work. Multiple loci were considered briefly in outline by Boorman and Levitt (1973) in their model of group selection among small populations at the border of a larger stable population. They assumed, however, that the individual genetic processes within the boundary populations were negligible relative to the time scale of extinctions, and thus they excluded an important feature of the two-locus case from their analysis.

In addition to the above-mentioned genetical phenomena, models of group selection on a single locus are lacking in a second respect. Many such models postulate that the frequency of a single allele could affect the probability of extinction or proliferation of an entire population, whereas group selection is more likely to be involved in the evolution of polygenic characters and characters which are emergent properties of populations, such as population density (Wright, 1931; Wynne-Edwards, 1962; Boorman and Levitt, 1973; Gilpin, 1975).

Data which are available tend to support this polygenic hypothesis. Group selection for increased or decreased population size at 37-day intervals in *Tribolium* (Wade, 1976) resulted in significant and simultaneous changes in several of the primary characteristics known to affect population size (for recent reviews see King and Dawson, 1972; Mertz, 1972; Sokoloff, 1974), namely, fecundity, fertility, body size, developmental time, and various cannibalistic pathways. Furthermore, measurement of the between-populations variance for each of these characters indicated that different populations within the same group-selection treatment had responded in different ways (Wade, 1976). Theoretical studies of selection on a single locus are not likely to contribute insights into such genetically complex processes!

Models of selection on quantitative characters which assume an underlying polygenic mode of inheritance, such as the models of Bossert (1963), Slatkin (1970), Slatkin and Lande (1976), and Lande (1976), may be more appropriate to the theoretical study of group selection. This type of model permits a more realistic description of the effects of selection on quantitative traits with respect to the genetic variance between and within populations. Specifically, the mean values of a trait among local populations can be varied independently of the within-populations variance of that trait. This is different from the single-locus case, where the variance is a function of the gene frequency. Laboratory selection experiments have shown that directional selection among individuals can bring about large changes in the mean value of a quantitative character without substantially altering the variance (Robertson and Reeve, 1952; Tantawy and Tayel, 1970). Although the additive components of the variance generally decline under selection, the epistatic components which can contribute to the variance between populations are often increased. This is important because selection *within* populations depends upon the additive components of the genetic variance, whereas selection *between* populations depends upon the total genetic variance.

Assumption 2: The Migrant Pool

The term "migrant pool" was introduced into the discussion of group selection by Levins (1970), and all of the earlier and later models employ mathematically equivalent structures (cf. Table 1). This concept is useful from a mathematical point of view, since it permits a simple and straightforward analytical treatment of the process of colonization. The expected value of the gene frequency in habitats newly colonized by dispersing individuals is equal to the frequency in the migrant pool. Also, the frequency in the migrant pool is the average frequency of the surviving populations.

The migration of individuals between populations and the colonization of new or vacant habitats have not been systematically studied in natural populations, but certain general and relevant features of the dispersion process may be inferred. From a biological point of view, a migrant pool implies a population structure in which migrants from any one population are as likely to colonize a vacant habitat as migrants from any other population. Differently put, whatever population structure exists, that structure in no way constrains migrating individuals. This assumption, although biologically realistic for the intrademic models, is quite unrealistic for the traditional models. With the possible exception of benthic fauna with pelagic larvae or, perhaps, those plant species with wind-dispersed seeds, it is not likely that natural populations of most other organisms have the population structure specified by the traditional models. Indeed, geographical barriers to migration as well as behaviorally restricted movement patterns are believed to interact with and give rise to population structure.

Besides restricting the biological scope of the traditional models, the assumption of a migrant pool is extremely unfavorable to the operation of group selection in both types of models in certain additional respects. These are discussed separately in the next two sections.

Assumption 3: Migration and Population Size

If all populations are assumed to contribute equal numbers of migrants to the migrant pool—as is often done in the traditional models (cf. Table 1)—then the gene frequency in the pool is the average frequency of all the contributing populations. With such an assumption, however, there is no possibility of group selection by means of the differential proliferation of populations.

For example, let population N_1 contain 20 haploid individuals, of whom 4 carry the gene A and 16 the gene B. The frequencies of A and B in N_1 are, respectively, 0.20 and 0.80. Let a second population, N_2, consist of 100 individuals and let the frequency of A in N_2 equal 0.90 and B equal 0.10. If N_1 and N_2 contribute equally to the common pool of migrants, the frequencies of A and B in the migrant pool are simply:

$$[A] = (0.20 + 0.90)/2 = 0.55 \qquad (1)$$

and

$$[B] = (0.80 + 0.10)/2 = 0.45. \qquad (2)$$

However, if the populations each contribute some equal proportion, p, of their numbers to the migrant pool, then the frequencies in the pool are the weighted average frequencies:

$$[A] = \frac{(20)(p)(0.20) + (200)(p)(0.90)}{(20 + 200)(p)} = 0.84 \qquad (3)$$

and

$$[B] = \frac{(20)(p)(0.80) + (200)(p)(0.10)}{(20 + 200)(p)} = 0.16. \qquad (4)$$

Thus, the differential contribution of populations on the basis of size can have a significant effect upon the composition of the migrant pool. This is the mechanism responsible for the genetic changes observed in the intrademic models, but it has been ignored in the traditional models.

On the other hand, the intrademic models generally assume that the initial sizes of the trait groups are equal and constant (but see Matessi and Jayakar, 1976; and Cohen and Eshel, 1976). Differential viability within the trait groups owing to the genotypic composition then results in some groups being larger than others at the time of mating. It is possible to increase the intensity of group selection in the intrademic models by making a somewhat different assumption. It can be shown that, if initial group size and gene frequency are correlated, equation (3) of D. S. Wilson (1975),

$$f_d > f_r(1 - N) \qquad (5)$$

becomes

$$f_d > f_r(1 - \bar{N} - \text{Cov}(N_{Ai}, N_i)/\bar{N}_A) \qquad (6)$$

where f_d is the fitness change of an individual performing a certain behavior; f_r, the fitness change to the individual receiving the behavior; N_{Ai}, the number of A individuals in population N_i; $\bar{N}$, the average population size; and $\bar{N}_A$, the average number of A individuals per population.

The ratio f_d/f_r must exceed the quantity $(1 - N)$ in Wilson's model in order for group selection to override successfully the effects of individual selection within groups. However, it is clear from expression (6) that, when population size is positively correlated with gene frequency, this condition is relaxed by an amount proportional to the covariance (*Cov*) between the number of A individuals, N_{Ai}, and the size of the groups, N_i.

It can reasonably be argued that in many cases group size should be positively correlated with other traits also undergoing group selection. Consider two groups of identical genotypic composition which differ in initial size. If the viability within the trait groups is a function only of gene frequency, then the larger group will make a larger contribution to the randomly mating pool. To the extent that the difference in size is genetically determined, group selection will favor large initial trait-group size. In addition, since the viability differences are the result of interactions between individuals, it must often be the case that the effects of these interactions increase with increasing density.

These effects of variable group size were considered by Matessi and Jayakar (1976), who found that group size was a "critical factor" only when the within-group fitnesses were a function of the frequency of altruists, and not when they were a function of the numbers of altruists. However, in examining the effects of numbers they considered a case in which the number of altruists was uncorrelated with group size, a situation which is different from the kind of density dependence suggested.

My own experimental studies of group selection (Wade, 1976, 1977) have empirically demonstrated that group selection can occur by the differential proliferation of populations in the absence of differential extinctions. The "random extinctions" treatment ("*D*") of Wade (1976, 1977) consisted of 48 populations, each population having been founded with a propagule of 16 adult beetles chosen at random from a laboratory stock culture. At each 37-day interval or generation thereafter, a table of random numbers was used to determine which populations would become extinct and which ones would survive. Thus, group selection by the differential extinction of populations was by design not possible in this treatment.

Extinct populations were subsequently recolonized by selecting propagules at random from those populations which, by chance, had survived the extinction process. According to plan, more propagules were taken from large populations than were taken from small populations. This differential proliferation of populations on the basis of size was continued for 233 days, or nine generations. The results demonstrated a significant increase in the average density of populations so treated, relative to the average density in a control population in which group selection could not operate. During the last three generations of the experiment, population size in the populations subjected to random extinctions and differential proliferation exceeded that of the control populations by an average of 23 adult beetles per population (range of population size for the control was from 49 to 106 adults per population). This represents an average difference in population size of 30 percent (P < 0.001).

This discussion has focused for the most part on the group-selective effect of differential proliferation on the basis of population size. Although population density is known to affect the emigratory rate of several species (Strecker, 1954; Sakai et al., 1958; Ziegler, 1976), it should be noted that any other factor that differentially influences migration could also result in group selection.

Assumption 4: The Origin of Variation Between Populations

The traditional models discussed above assume that the variation between populations necessary for group selection is created primarily by genetic drift within the semi-isolated sub-groups. The intrademic models assume that the necessary variation arises in the sampling of colonists from the migrant pool. It is useful to separate these two types of sampling error because they represent two different biological processes, which usually occur at two very different stages in the life history. These theoretical assumptions regarding the origins of between-populations variance are responsible in large part for the conclusion that group selection is not likely to be a significant force for evolutionary change in natural populations.

The traditional models specify several necessary conditions for the operation of group selection, namely, small group size, low levels of intergroup migration, and weak individual selection within groups. These limitations are identical to those for which genetic drift is important to the differentiation of local populations. The intrademic models also require small initial group size in order to create a large between-group variance when sampling from the migrant pool. It is clear that the results of both models are strongly dependent upon the mechanisms which give rise to genetic variation between populations. Moreover, the potential amount of variance between populations is limited by the migrant pool per se for reasons which are explained hereafter. Natural populations are not likely to lie at either of the extremes represented in Fig. 1, but discussion of the effects of these possibilities serves two purposes. First, all of the group selection models but two (cf. Table 1) employ either a migrant pool or a "propagule pool"; and, second, an understanding of these

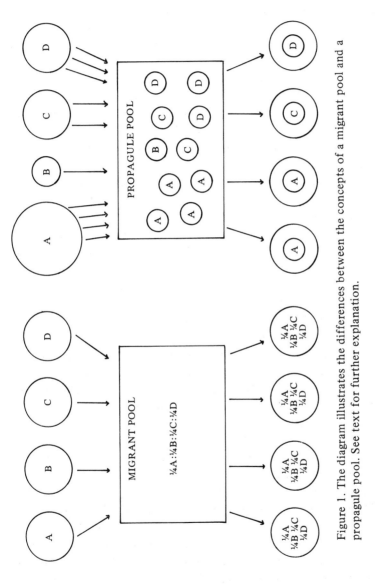

Figure 1. The diagram illustrates the differences between the concepts of a migrant pool and a propagule pool. See text for further explanation.

two extreme cases can provide insight into the more intermediate processes of colonization.

If colonists are chosen at random from the migrant pool, the gene frequencies of the newly colonized populations will be normally distributed about the mean of the migrant pool. Specifically, these populations will have an expected gene frequency equal to that of the migrant pool; the genetic variance among them will be equal to the variance of the migrant pool divided by the size of the sample or colonizing propagule. (It will be recalled from section 3 that the mean of the migrant pool is simply the average frequency of populations contributing migrants for many of the models.) A portion of the genetic variance between populations is lost because of migration at each generation. The genetic variance must therefore be regenerated by the sampling process at each colonizing episode if group selection is to be effective. If the genetic variance between populations is not renewed, the process of group selection will come to a halt. Uniform and directional individual selection operating within each local population or trait group will also tend to decrease the sampling variance from the migrant pool. In addition, owing to the extensive mixing of individuals from different populations, the migrant pool greatly reduces the correlation or "heritability" of traits between group and propagule. (This aspect of the migrant pool will be discussed in greater detail below.)

The effects of the migrant pool are most extreme in the intrademic models of group selection. In this case the migrant pool is a single panmictic population from which individuals disperse at random into isolated groups at some other stage in the life history. Thus, extensive mixing occurs at every generation.

An alternative mode of recolonization was employed in my experimental studies of group selection (Wade, 1976, 1977). Groups of colonists were chosen at random directly from *each* population, and one new population was established with each such propagule. Therefore, according to the experimental design, migrants were chosen from a "propagule pool" instead of a migrant pool, and no mixing of colonizing individuals from different populations was permitted to occur.

In the absence of selection, it can be shown that this mode of colonization has an effect on the between-populations variance which is very different from the effect of the migrant pool. The equilibrium variance between populations is greater for the case of the propagule pool by an amount proportional to the ratio of the extinction rate to the sum of the migration and individual selection rates (Slatkin and Wade, in press). In my own empirical studies (Wade, 1976, 1977), this process of random extinctions with recolonization from a propagule pool was observed to convert a large proportion of the total variance in population size into the between-populations component of the variance. It was pointed out that this process ". . . will establish the ideal and favorable conditions for group selection to occur. In this way group selection need only be a sporadic event in nature and still accomplish large genetic change."

The differences between the concepts of the migrant pool and the propagule pool are illustrated schematically in Fig. 1. The letters *A* through *D* in this figure represent population phenotypes. The differences to be noted are the following:

(1) the differential contribution of populations to the propagule pool on the basis of population size;

(2) the propagules' persistence as distinct units in the propagule pool, unlike the mixing that takes place in the migrant pool;

(3) propagules drawn from the migrant pool result in populations with identical genetic composition, whereas new populations founded from the propagule pool are genetically heterogeneous; and

(4) the founding of populations by propagules from the propagule pool is followed by a period of population growth, whereas populations colonized from the migrant pool of the models are established at the carrying capacity of the habitats.

The different effects of the migrant and propagule pools on the process of group selection are analogous to the different effects of blending and particulate inheritance on individual selection. To explain: in a randomly mating population with blending inheritance, the average value of a quantitative trait among the offspring of a given mating is equal to the parental average of that trait. It can be shown that the variance of the population is thus reduced by a factor of one half at each generation (Fisher, 1930). For this reason, a large amount of new variation must be generated in each generation if individual selection is to be effective in producing evolutionary change under blending inheritance. Darwin, unaware of Mendel's results that illustrated the particulate nature of inheritance, discussed at length many hypothetical and biologically unfounded solutions of this problem of evolution by natural selection with blending inheritance.

The complete mixing of individuals from several populations in a migrant pool can be considered a form of blending inheritance at the population level. Just as blending inheritance reduces the variance within a population, the migrant pool reduces the variance between populations. This loss of variation between populations is the result of the tendency of new colonies to regress to the mean of the populations contributing to the migrant pool, as analogously, under blending inheritance, the offspring regress to the mean of the parental generation. Thus, group selection with a migrant pool cannot be very effective unless a significant amount of between-populations variance can be generated at each colonizing episode.

In order for colonization to create variation between populations, the size of the founding group drawn at random from the migrant pool must be small. This follows directly from the well-known statistical fact that the variance among sample means increases as the sample size decreases. A somewhat different situation obtains in the case of the propagule pool, where propagules of intermediate size are more favorable to group selection than either large or small propagules. (It will be recalled from Fig. 1 that in the propagule pool colonists are selected at random directly from *each* population.) On the one hand, small propagule size increases the variance between propagules as it does with the migrant pool. A large propagule, on the other hand, will be a more representative sample of the population from which it was chosen, and, for this reason, the heritability of traits at the populational level (i.e., the correlation between "parent" population and "offspring" propagule) increases with increasing propagule size. Because of this trade-off between populational variation and populational heritability, a propagule pool with an intermediate propagule size is expected to be most favorable to group selection.

Another method of increasing the variation between trait groups, despite the homogenizing influence of the migrant pool, is to invoke some degree of non-random assortment of individuals into the trait groups. Clearly, this assortment must be of the positive type where "like" associates with "like," for negative assortment would make the trait groups more similar to one another and would reduce the variation below that expected on a random basis. In many of the intrademic models, most notably those of D. S. Wilson (1977) and Matessi and Jayakar (1976), various ways of achieving a positive assortment of genotypes into the trait groups are discussed.

Natural populations are not likely to lie at either of the extremes represented by Fig. 1, but, depending on the nature and the extent of migration, will lie somewhere between a migrant pool and a propagule pool. Group selection is expected to be more important wherever migration and colonization occur with little or no mixing of individuals from different populations or groups than wherever they occur with extensive and random mixing. It is generally believed, however, that even a small amount of migration is antithetical to the maintenance of genetic variation between populations which must be present for the operation of group selection (Maynard Smith, 1964; Williams, 1966).

Maynard Smith's "haystack" model arrives at this conclusion partly as a result of the extreme nature of individual selection within groups in his model. In that model, despite the original pattern of variation among the local groups after colonization, only two alternative types of groups remain after individual selection against the altruists, namely, groups composed entirely of altruists, or groups composed entirely of non-altruists. Differently put, any group which contains even a single non-altruist will be converted by individual selection within the group to a completely non-altruistic group. Any migration between the altruistic and non-altruistic groups or any mixing of their propagules has disastrous consequences for the evolution of altruism.

Wright (1931) and Maruyama (1970) have shown, on theoretical grounds, that populations that exchange on the average one migrant every other generation will be genetically identical at equilibrium. Although this result is correct, the argument as it applies to group selection has been somewhat misconceived (Wright, pers. commun.). It is not the expected value of the gene frequency, but rather the variance about that expectation which is important for group selection. Wright (1931) has emphasized that the equilibrium variance between populations is not negligible even for moderate amounts of migration.

Furthermore, to the extent that populations are isolated by distance, migrants from populations close to one another are more likely to disperse to the same area than are migrants from distant populations. Just as assortative mating can retard the rate at which individual variation is lost under blending inheritance (Fisher, 1930), migration "assortative by distance" will modify the effects of mixing in the migrant pool.

Assumption 5: Group and Individual Selection in Opposite Directions

Wynne-Edwards (1962) has suggested that individual selection within populations generally tends to increase population size and that this tendency is opposed by the extinction of large populations because of an overexploitation of resources. It is also likely, however, that propagule number is often proportional to population size in many cases of biological interest, and group selection could thus favor increased productivity. Although it is clear that group and individual selection could operate in the same direction with respect to a particular trait, this possibility has rarely been considered (cf. D. S. Wilson, 1975; Gadgil, 1975). Indeed, Williams' advocacy of parsimony states that if the evolution of a trait can be explained by individual selection there is no need to invoke group selection. The use of this widely adopted principle clearly restricts the discussion of group selection to those cases in which it operates in a direction opposite to individual selection. Most of the models in Table 1 explicitly or implicitly assume that group and individual selection are opposing forces, and the theoretical discussion has focused mainly on the evolution of those traits for which the levels of selection are in conflict.

Any trait which directly or indirectly decreases the likelihood of extinction or increases the likelihood of the successful proliferation of populations will be favored by group selection. If that same trait enhances the survivorship or reproductive success of individuals within populations, then individual selection will also favor that trait. In such a case, the rate of gene frequency change is expected to be greater than the rate of change when either group or individual selection is acting alone.

In the "Control Treatment" (C) of Wade (1976, 1977), individual selection was observed to change the mean population size at day 37 from greater than 200 adults per population in generation one to less than 50 adults per population in generation nine. Group selection for decreased population size was also studied in a second treatment (B). A comparison of the two treatments permits an evaluation of the effect of group and individual selection acting *together* relative to the effect of individual selection acting alone. Population size at day 37 changed much more rapidly in the B Treatment; the mean population size in this treatment was less than *half* of the Control mean during the last four generations of the experiment (P < 0.0001).

When further experiments were conducted to determine the cause of the decline in population size in both treatments, another significant and surprising difference was discovered. Individual selection in the populations of the Control Treatment had caused an increase in the cannibalism rate of adults feeding on pupae and a small but significant increase in the developmental time of males and females relative to the group-selected populations (Wade, 1976). In contrast, populations from that treatment (B) where both group and individual selection had favored small population size responded in a more heterogeneous fashion. In some of those populations cannibalism rates had increased significantly while fecundity remained unchanged, and in other populations developmental time had been lengthened while fecundity had increased. Many other traits exhibited this same between-populations heterogeneity in the B Treatment (Wade, 1976). Thus, not only was the rate of change accelerated when group and individual selection were operating in the same direction, but also the genetical nature of the outcome was fundamentally different.

This new aspect of group selection has not been studied theoretically or considered seriously.

Conclusion

In the preceding discussion the assumptions underlying the models of group selection have been presented and evaluated. My own empirical studies of group selection on laboratoy populations of *Tribolium* have indicated several biologically realistic ways in which these assumptions can be modified and made more favorable to the process of group selection. Additional laboratory studies of the group selection process are currently underway and examine the effects of migration, propagule size, and extinction rates, separately and in combination, along the lines suggested. It remains for these ecological processes and their effects to be systematically studied in field populations.

I believe that when the *process* of group selection is more clearly understood, a more realistic evaluation of its utility as an *explanatory principle* for evolution in natural populations will be possible.

Acknowledgments

It gives me great pleasure to acknowledge the encouragement and cogent discussion of Thomas Park of the University of Chicago throughout the preparation of this manuscript. Some of the ideas presented herein were strengthened and clarified in conversation with Sewall Wright, to whom I am most grateful. I am also indebted to A. Ross Kiester for his comments on a draft of this manuscript and to William Wimsatt for his observation that Fig. 1 looks remarkably similar to the contrast between blending and particular inheritance. M. Hallihan, D. McCauley, P. McElroy, and S. Teleky provided further critical comments, much to the improvement of the paper. And, I thank an unnamed reviewer for calling additional references to my attention and for suggesting grouping the models into the "traditional" and "intrademic" categories, which greatly facilitated discussion.

This work was supported by NIH grant, 1 R01 GM22523-01, and by a University of Chicago Block Fund Grant to the author.

Ms. Ora Lee Mathews McCoy Watts has provided technical assistance.

References

Alexander, R. D., 1974. "The evolution of social behavior," *Annu. Rev. Ecol. Syst.*, 5:325–383.

Boorman, S. A., and Levitt, P. R., 1973. "Group selection on the boundary of a stable population," *Theor. Popul. Biol.*, 4:85–128.

Bossert, W. H., 1963. "Simulation of character displacement," Unpub. Ph.D. thesis, Cambridge (Mass.), Harvard University.

Bryant, E., 1969. "The fates of immatures in mixtures of two housefly strains," *Ecology*, 50:1049–1069.

Bryant, E., 1970. "The effect of egg density on hatchability in two strains of the housefly," *Physiol. Zool.*, 43:288–295.

Bryant, E., and Turner, C. R., 1972. "Rapid evolution of competitive ability in larval mixtures of the housefly," *Evolution*, 26:161–170.

Charnov, E. L., 1977. "An elementary treatment of the genetical theory of kin-selection," *J. Theor. Biol.*, 66:541–550.

Charnov, E. L., and Krebs, J. R., 1975. "The evolution of alarm calls: Altruism or manipulation?" *Am. Nat.* 109:107–112.

Cohen, D. and Eshel, I., 1976. "On the founder effect and the evolution of altruistic traits," *Theor. Popul. Biol.*, 10:276–302.

Dobzhansky, Th., 1948. "Genetics of natural populations, XVI: Altitudinal and seasonal changes produced by natural selection in certain populations of *Drosophila pseudoobscura* and *Drosophila persimilis*," *Genetics*, 33:158–176.

Dunbar, M. S., 1960. "The evolution of stability in marine environments: Natural selection at the level of the ecosystem," *Am. Nat.*, 94:129–136.

Ehrmann, L., 1966. "Mating success and genotypic frequency in *Drosophila*," *Anim. Behav.*, 14:332–339.

Ehrmann, L., 1967. "Further studies on genotypic frequency and mating success in *Drosophila*," *Am. Nat.*, 101:415–424.

Ehrmann, L., 1968. "Frequency dependent mating success in *Drosophila psuedoobscura*," *Genet. Res.*, 11:135–140.

Eshel, I., 1972. "On the neighbor effect and the evolution of altruistic traits," *Theor. Popul. Biol.*, 3:258–277.

Fisher, R. A., 1930. *The Genetical Theory of Natural Selection.* Oxford, Oxford University Press.

Gadgil, M., 1975. "Evolution of social behaviors through interpopulation selection," *Proc. Natl. Acad. Sci. U.S.A.*, 72:1199–1201.

Ghiselin, M. T., 1974. *The Economy of Nature and the Evolution of Sex,* Berkeley, University of California Press.

Gilpin, M. E., 1975. *Group Selection in Predator-Prey Communities,* Princeton, Princeton University Press.

Gordon, E., 1935. "An experiment on a released population of *D. melanogaster*," *Am. Nat.*, 69:381.

Hamilton, W. D., 1964a. "The genetical evolution of social behavior, I," *J. Theor. Biol.*, 7:1–16.

Hamilton, W. D., 1964b. "The genetical evolution of social behavior, II," *J. Theor. Biol.*, 7:17–52.

Herbert, P. D. N., 1974. "Enzyme variability in natural populations of *Daphnia magna*, I: Population structure in East Anglia," *Evolution*, 28:546–556.

King, C. E., and Dawson, P. S., 1972. "Population biology and the *Tribolium* model," *Evol. Biol.*, 5:133–227.

Koehn, R. K. and Mitton, J. B., 1972. "Population genetics of marine pelecypods, I: Ecological heterogeneity and adaptive strategy at an enzyme locus," *Am. Nat.*, 106:47–56.

Koehn, R. K., Milkman, R., and Mitton, J. B., 1976. "Population genetics of marine pelecypods, IV: Selection, migration, and genetic differentiation in the Blue Mussel, *Mytilus edulis*," *Evolution*, 30:2–32.

Lande, R., 1976. "The maintenance of genetic variability by mutation in a polygenic character with linked loci," *Genet. Res.*, 26:221–235.

Levene, H., Pavlovsky, O., and Dobzhansky, Th., 1954. "Interaction of the adaptive values in polymorphic experimental populations of *Drosophila pseudoobscura*," *Evolution*, 8:335–349.

Levin, B. R., and Kilmer, W. L., 1974. "Interdemic selection and the evolution of altruism," *Evolution*, 28:527–545.

Levins, R., 1970. "Extinction," in *Some Mathematical Questions in Biology*, ed. M. Gerstenhaber, Providence, R.I., American Mathematical Society, pp. 77–107.

Lewontin, R. C., 1955. "The effects of population density and composition on viability in *Drosophila melanogaster*," *Evolution*, 9:27–41.

Lewontin, R. C., 1970. "The units of selection," *Annu. Rev. Ecol. Syst.*, 1: 1–18.

Lewontin, R. C., and Matsuo, Y., 1963. "Interaction of genotypes determining viability in *Drosophila busckii*," *Proc. Natl. Acad. Sci. U.S.A.*, 49:270–278.

Maruyama, T., 1970. "Effective number of alleles in a subdivided population," *Theor. Popul. Biol.*, 1:273–306.

Matessi, C., and Jayakar, S. D., 1973. "A model for the evolution of altruistic behavior," *Genetics*, 74:S174.

Matessi, C., and Jayakar, S. D., 1976. "Conditions for the evolution of altruism under Darwinian selection," *Theor. Popul. Biol.*, 9:360–387.

Maynard Smith, J., 1964. "Group selection and kin selection," *Nature*, 201: 1145–1147.

Maynard Smith, J., 1976. "Group selection," *Q. Rev. Biol.*, 51:277–283. Reprinted in this volume.

Mayr, E., 1975. *Populations, Species, and Evolution*, Cambridge (Mass.), Harvard University Press.

McCauley, D. E., 1977. "Co-adaptation and loss of variation in *Tribolium*," *Heredity*, 39:145–148.

Mertz, D. B., 1972. "The *Tribolium* model and the mathematics of population growth," *Annu. Rev. Ecol. Syst.*, 3:51–78.

Mertz, D. B., Cawthon, A., and Park, T., 1976. "An experimental analysis of competitive indeterminancy in *Tribolium*," *Proc. Natl. Acad. Sci. U.S.A.*, 73: 1368–1372.

Robertson, F. W., and Reeve, E. C. R., 1952. "Studies in quantitative inheritance, I: The effects of selection on wing and thorax length in *Drosophila melanogaster*," *J. Genet.*, 50:414–448.

Sakai, K., Narise, T., Hiraizumi, Y., and Iyama, S., 1958. "Studies on competition in plants and animals, IX: Experimental studies on migration in *Drosophila melanogaster*," *Evolution*, 12:93–101.

Selander, R. K., Hunt, W. G., and Yang, S., 1969. "Protein polymorphism and genic heterozygosity in two European subspecies of the house mouse," *Evolution*, 23:379–390.

Slatkin, M., 1970. "Selection and polygenic characters," *Proc. Natl. Acad. Sci. U.S.A.*, 66:87–93.

Slatkin, M., and Lande, R., 1976. "Niche width in a fluctuating environment-density independent model," *Am. Nat.*, 110:31–55.

Slatkin, M., and Wade, M. J. In press. "Group selection on a quantitative character," *Proc. Natl. Acad. Sci. U.S.A.*

Slobodkin, L. B., 1974. "Prudent predation does not require group selection," *Am. Nat.,* 108:665–678.

Sokal, R. R., and Fujii, K., 1972. "The effects of genetic background on the ecology of selection in *Tribolium* populations." *Evolution,* 26:489–512.

Sokal, R. R., and Huber, I., 1963. "Competition among genotypes in *Tribolium castaneum* at varying densities and gene frequencies (the Sooty locus)," *Am. Nat.,* 97:169–184.

Sokal, R. R., and Karten, I., 1964. "Competition among genotypes in *Tribolium castaneum* at varying densities and gene frequencies (the Black locus)," *Genetics,* 49:195–211.

Sokal, R. R., Kence, A., and McCauley, D. E., 1974. "The survival of mutants at very low frequencies in *Tribolium* populations," *Genetics,* 77:805–818.

Sokoloff, A., 1974. *The Biology of Tribolium, Volume 2,* Oxford, Clarendon Press.

Spiess, E. B., 1968. "Low frequency advantage in mating of *Drosophila pseudoobscura* karyotypes," *Am. Nat.,* 102:363–379.

Strecker, R. L., 1954. "Regulatory mechanisms in house-mouse populations: The effect of limited food supply on an unconfined population," *Ecology,* 35:249–253.

Tantawy, A. O., and Tayel, A. A., 1970. "Studies on natural populations of *Drosophila,* X: Effects of disruptive and stabilizing selection on wing length and the correlated response in *Drosophila melanogaster,*" *Genetics,* 65:121–132.

Taylor, C. E., and Sokal, R. R., 1973. "Some new experiments on competition between housefly strains," *Egypt. J. Genet. Cytol.,* 2:102–120.

Van Valen, L., 1975. "Group selection, sex, and fossils," *Evolution,* 29:87–94.

Wade, M. J., 1976. "Group selection among laboratory populations of *Tribolium,*" *Proc. Natl. Acad. Sci. U.S.A.,* 73:4604–4607.

Wade, M. J., 1977. "An experimental study of group selection," *Evolution,* 31:134–153.

Wallace, B., 1968. *Topics in Population Genetics,* New York, W. W. Norton.

Weins, J. A., 1976. "Population responses to patchy environments," *Annu. Rev. Ecol. Syst.,* 7:81–120.

Williams, G. C., 1966. *Adaption and Natural Selection,* Princeton, Princeton University Press. Chapter 4 is reprinted in part in this volume.

Wilson, D. S., 1975. "A general theory of group selection," *Proc. Natl. Acad. Sci. U.S.A.,* 72:143–146.

Wilson, D. S., 1977. "Structured demes and the evolution of group advantageous traits," *Am. Nat.,* 111:157–185.

Wright, S., 1929. "Evolution in a Mendelian population," *Anat. Record.,* 44:287.

Wright, S., 1931. "Evolution in Mendelian populations," *Genetics*, 16:93–159.

Wright, S., 1932. "The roles of mutation, inbreeding, crossbreeding, and selection in evolution," *Proc. VI Int. Congr. Genet.*, 1:356–366. Reprinted in this volume.

Wright, S., 1945. "*Tempo and Mode in Evolution:* A Critical review," *Ecology*, 26:415–419.

Wright, S., 1949. "Adaptation and selection," in G. L. Jepson, G. G. Simpson, and E. Mayr, eds., *Genetics, Paleontology, and Evolution*, Princeton, Princeton University Press, pp. 365–389.

Wright, S., 1956. "Modes of selection," *Am. Nat.*, 90:5–24.

Wright, S., 1959. "Physiological genetics, ecology of populations, and natural selection," *Perspect. Biol. Med.*, 3:107–151.

Wright, S., 1977. *Evolution and the Genetics of Populations, Vol. 3*, Chicago, University of Chicago Press.

Wright, S., and Dobzhansky, Th., 1946. "Genetics of natural populations, XII: Experimental reproduction of some of the changes caused by natural selection in certain populations of *Drosphila pseudoobscura*," *Genetics*, 31:125–156.

Wynne-Edwards, V. C., 1962. *Animal Dispersion in Relation to Social Behavior.* New York, Hafner Publishing Co.

Ziegler, J. R., 1976. "Evolution of the migration response: Emigration by *Tribolium* and the influence of age," *Evolution*, 30:579–592.

16

Individual Selection and the Concept of Structured Demes

David Sloan Wilson

Table 2.1
Terms used in Chapter Two

A, B	Two "types" (alleles in a haploid model) that constitute the population
N	Total density of the population
p, q	Frequency of A-types and B-types, respectively ($p + q = 1$)
P_p	Proportion of trait groups containing a frequency of p A-types
σ^2_p	Variance in the frequency of A types among trait groups
p_A, p_B	Average subjective frequencies: the frequency of A experienced by the average A-type and B-type in the global population

(For models assuming constant trait group density)

m, n	Number of A- and B-types, respectively, in a single trait group
$P_{m,n}$	Proportion of trait groups containing m A-types and n B-types
σ^2_m	Variance in the number of A-types among trait groups
m_A, m_B	Average subjective densities: the number of A experienced by the average A- and B-type in the global population

(For models assuming variable trait group density)

f_A, f_B	Absolute individual fitness of A- and B-types within a single local population
F_A, F_B	Average absolute fitness of A- and B-types for global population
T	Number of trait groups in the global population
d	Effect of an A-type on itself
r	Effect of an A-type on every other member of the local population

From Chapter 2 of *The Natural Selection of Populations and Communities*, Menlo Park, Cal., Benjamin/Cummings, 1980, pp. 13–16, 20–24, 43–45.

The Basic Selection Model

Most people are familiar with the basic theory of natural selection. Organisms vary in a heritable fashion. Some variants leave more offspring than others; their characteristics, therefore, are represented at a greater frequency in the next generation.

If one were allowed the luxury of renaming theories, a good name for this one might be the "principle of individual selection." But individual selection as we know it is not equivalent to natural selection. The modern concepts of individual selection, group selection, and all their problems arise at the next link in the chain of reasoning, with the questions, "What are those traits that allow the individuals possessing them to leave more offspring than others? What constitutes fitness in nature?"

To answer these questions, evolutionary biologists built a very simple model, whose properties are well described by Mayr (1963): "Under the impact of modern systematics and population genetics, a usage is spreading in biology that restricts the term 'population' to the *local population,* the community of potentially interbreeding individuals in a given locality. All members of a local population share in a single gene pool, and such a population may be defined also as a 'group of individuals so situated that any two of them have equal probability of mating with each other and producing offspring.'"

In this manner, the bulk of Darwinian theory has been built around the evolutionary forces that operate within local populations, or demes. The mathematical expression of this concept follows an unvarying format. Two types, A and B (these may be alleles, haploid organisms, or genotypes) exist at a combined density of N and in frequencies p and q ($p + q = 1$), respectively. The types are assigned fitnesses (f_A and f_B) which can be constants or functions with any number of variables. By definition, the type with the highest fitness increases its proportionality in the next generation.

Hereafter, the preceding formulation will be referred to as the *basic selection model.* It sounds like an exact mathematical statement of evolution's fundamental rules, and it is—but with at least one additional assumption. By specifying a single frequency of types in the population, the basic selection model expressly forbids the situation in which some individuals experience a frequency of p_1 and others a frequency of $p_2 \neq p_1$. In other words, it assumes a spatial homogeneity in the genetic composition of populations.

A large literature is devoted to relaxing the homogeneity assumption in ecology and population genetics, but the basic selection model still enjoys a special prominence in evolutionary theory, and for good reason. It should be remembered that Darwin and his first followers were devoted to overthrowing a completely different paradigm—special creation. To them, the answer to "what constitutes fitness?" seemed so obvious in so many different ways that they hardly needed to build a model at all. Clearly a bat with wings, a predator with sharper eyes, a plant with a more efficient root system, or a giraffe with a long neck would be more successful in its struggle against nature than others without such endowments. In other words, the first evolutionary biologists were preoccupied with structures and behaviors that are a constant advantage to the individuals who possess them. These traits can be modeled by using constants for f_A and f_B. With constant fitness terms, the expected type is always favored in the basic selection model. A model is only as good as its predictions, and for constant fitness terms, the basic selection model provides a very exact fit to what seemes to happen in nature. Of course, one could build many other models that do not assume spatial homogeneity in genetic composition and that also produce the same conclusions, but the basic selection model is the simplest. Why add complexity when it doesn't increase predictive value?

In other words, the homogeneity assumption is not *necessary* for the selection of traits with constant fitness values; it is simply the easiest way to express their selection. This is a critical point. In fact, the basic selection model can now be resummarized as follows: It consists of evolution's fundamental rules plus an additional assumption of spatial homogeneity. The homogeneity assumption is neither necessary nor realistic. It is simply made because it is convenient and because it doesn't seem to interfere with the selection of traits that can be represented by constant fitness values.

As mentioned previously, the effects of relaxing the homogeneity assumption have been carefully and systematically explored for many areas of evolutionary theory, but not for all of them. Gaps exist in which homogeneity is assumed without the effects of relaxing it being fully known. As I will argue in this book, the concept of individual selection, on which many biologists base their understanding of social behavior and interspecific interactions, represents one such area.

Today the basic fact of evolution is taken for granted, and interest has shifted to more subtle classes of adaptations. One of these classes concerns traits that influence not only the fitness of the individuals possessing them, but other members of the population as well. These traits include overtly social behaviors, such as aggression or cooperation, and also activities that through some modification of the biotic and abiotic environment feed back to affect the population at large (e.g., pollution, resource depletion). If we let d represent an individual A-type's effect on itself and define r as its effect on every other member of the population, then changes in fitness due to the A-type's trait can be calculated in a simple linear haploid basic selection model:

$$f_A = d + (Np - 1)r$$
$$f_B = Npr \tag{2.1}$$

(recall that N is the total density of both types and p is the frequency of the A-type). The term f_A consists of an A-type's effect on its own fitness plus the fitness it receives from $(Np - 1)$ other A-types in the population. The B-type has no effect on itself and serves as a recipient for Np A-types. If the types are equal in other respects, then the A-type is selected only when $f_A > f_B$. That is, when

$$d + (Np - 1)r > Npr \qquad (2.2)$$

$$d > r. \qquad (2.3)$$

To be favored by selection, an individual's effect on itself must be more positive than its effects on others. Although superficially reasonable, this conclusion has some disturbing implications. It predicts that on the most fundamental level there is nothing preventing the following events from routinely occurring in nature:

1. If an individual decreases its own fitness (negative d), it can be selected for, as long as it decreases the fitness of others even more. (This phenomenon has been called "spite"; see Verner 1977 for a recent hypothesis concerning spite in the evolution of territoriality.)

2. If an individual increases its own fitness (positive d), it will be selected against if it increases the fitness of others even more.

In short, this basic selection model predicts that natural selection is insensitive to the fitness of the population as a whole. *Natural selection is sensitive only to the fitness of a genotype relative to other genotypes within that population.* This feature is such a fundamental part of basic selection models in general that the majority actually define fitnesses relative to the most fit type in the population, thereby eliminating a consideration of population productivity from the start.

. . .

The Concept of Structured Demes

It is beyond the scope of this chapter to evaluate the effect of all forms of population structure on the individual-selection model. Instead, my goal is to identify one form of population structure that is fairly general (in other words, applies to many if not most species in nature) and to explore the implications of this structure for the individual-selection model. To do this, it is necessary to examine the deme concept closely. What exactly does it imply?

The deme is defined as a population that is homogeneous with respect to the mixing of genes, but with frequency-dependent fitness values, the basic selection model assumes more than this definition. Actual selection models say nothing about the mixing of genes, but refer instead to the manifestation of traits. In particular, models in the form of equation (2.1) refer to the *ecological effect* of *A*-types on themselves and other members of the population. Therefore, in addition to creating a localized evolutionary arena with equal mating probabilities, basic selection models also specify that the population is homogeneous with respect to the manifestation of traits. They assume that each and every individual in a deme experiences, and thereby has its fitness determined by, exactly the same frequency of genotypes.

Is there any such thing as a population that is homogeneous with respect to the manifestation of traits? Yes, but it is usually rather small. Perhaps this point can be made clear with a series of examples.

1. The pitcher plant mosquito *Wyeomyia smithii* lays its eggs in the water-holding leaves of the pitcher plant. Each pitcher is an isolated habitat unit, usually containing from 1 to 50 mosquito larvae and from 4 to 50 ml of water. Almost certainly the pitcher represents a homogeneous population with respect to the manifestation of larval traits. Each individual feels the effect of every other individual. If any aspect of the social, biotic, or abiotic environment (such as resource depletion, toxin production) is a function of the genotypic composition of the population, all individuals will experience its effects equally. However, there is no reason to expect larval populations in different pitchers to have the same genotypic composition. They will certainly differ, if only at random.

2. A bark insect finds a vulnerable tree and emits a pheromone that attracts conspecifics to the scene. The pheromone can only be detected within a certain radius of its source. All individuals within this radius benefit equally. No one outside the radius benefits. Similarly, once the galleries have been formed, the community within a single gallery may be homogeneous in terms of the effects of genotypes, but will certainly differ from the genotypic composition of other galleries in other trees.

3. A school of fish may be homogeneous for certain traits, yet many schools coalesce to shoal.

4. A female bird has offspring which for a time share a nest. Undoubtedly every sibling interacts with the same individuals in the nest as does every other sibling, but this interaction has no bearing on the interactions within other nests.

5. Many marine invertebrates have pelagic larval stages which later settle to complete development. The deme for such species is very large, sometimes constituting thousands of square miles. However, ecological interactions take place within much smaller populations, consisting of an individual and a few of its neighbors. The boundaries round these smaller populations may not be discrete, as they are for examples 1–4, but lack of boundaries does not appear to be important, as will be demonstrated below.

In sum, every trait has a "sphere of influence" within which the homogeneity assumption is roughly satisfied. It is the area within which every individual feels the effects of every other individual. I have termed the population within this area a *trait group* (Wilson, 1975a, 1977a) to emphasize its dependence on the particular traits being manifested. For instance, the trait group for traits manifested among nestling birds consists of those individuals within a single nest, but the trait group for traits manifested during adulthood consists of a much larger population.

The individual-selection model with its assumption of spatial homogeneity in genetic composition is a viable, realistic concept when applied to single trait groups. But in all the above examples, the trait groups are very small—far smaller than the deme, or population within which genetic mixing occurs. The pitcher plant mosquito larva metamorphoses into an adult and flies throughout the bog. Fish shoal. Marine invertebrate larvae are pelagic. Birds leave their nests. Insects travel long distances on dispersal flights.

A moment's consideration should convince the reader that this fact is true in general. Trait groups are almost always smaller than the deme, and for a very general reason. Most organisms tend to concentrate their movement in a brief dispersal stage—the seeds and pollen of plants, the post-teneral migrating stage of insects (Johnson, 1969), the larvae of benthic marine fauna, the adolescents of many vertebrates. At all other periods of the life cycle, the individuals are relatively sedentary, their movements trivial in scale compared to their dispersal stage. Interactions in the nondispersal stages will be within trait groups smaller than the deme.

The relation between the trait group and the deme also holds for organisms that do not have well-defined dispersal stages. Consider nonmotile microorganisms, such as some soil bacteria that rely on passive dispersal. For a period of generations, single populations will develop on microsites for which the homogeneity assumption is satisfied. However, periodic physical disturbances, such as rain storms, will result in a massive mixing of local populations. Alternatively, consider a population of organisms that mix continuously throughout their life cycle, such as zooplankton. Any trait manifested by an individual that, by the nature of the trait, influences only a small number of surrounding individuals, will necessarily substructure the deme into trait groups, even if the membership of the trait groups is constantly changing.

To summarize, it may be said that while the individual-selection concept is valid, it is valid only for tiny populations (trait groups). Any realistic evolutionary model in which fitness is frequency-dependent must recognize two population units: one that is homogeneous with respect to ecological interactions (the trait group), and another that is homogeneous with respect to genetic mixing (the deme). Even a deme is composed not only of a population of individuals, *but also of a population of trait groups.* The trait groups are isolated with respect to the manifestation of traits, but periodically mix and resegregate due to the dispersal process. While isolated, the trait groups can vary in their genetic composition.

The distinction between the trait group and the deme is probably obvious to most biologists, and has also been recognized in many theoretical models (e.g., Trivers 1971, p. 44), but it has not been sufficiently emphasized as a biological generality. In particular, this distinction is ignored by any mathematical model (and the thinking behind it) that assigns a single frequency to its genotypes, e.g., the basic selection model. In my opinoin, the concept of trait groups represents a biologically realistic form of population structuring that describes many if not most species in nature (Wilson, 1977a, 1979). It is best described by the subdivided population model with hard selection, and to differentiate it from other uses of this model, I have termed it a theory of "structured demes" (Wilson, 1975a, 1977a). Interdemic forms of population structure with low migration, such as the island model, may of course also occur. But in the context of individual selection, each island should be recognized as being further differentiated into trait groups.

Let us explore the effects of deme structure on the predictions of individual selection: first, in terms of the simple linear fitness functions developed on page 274, and then more generally, in equation (2.1), the individual fitness of the A and B types was represented as

$$f_A = d + (Np - 1)r$$
$$f_B = Npr \tag{2.1}$$

where d is the effect of an individual A-type on itself and r is its effect on every other member of the population. These two equations may now be taken to represent the fitnessess within a single trait group.

In structured demes we have a large number of trait groups (T), each of which can be characterized by a single density and frequency. Assume that T is large and let P_{mn} = the proportion of trait groups containing m A-types and n B-types ($m + n = N$). The fitnesses of the two types over the entire deme, designated F_A and F_B, consists of the weighted average of the fitness over all the trait groups:

$$F_A = \frac{T \sum_{m,n=0}^{\infty} P_{mn} m [d + (m - 1)r]}{T \sum_{m,n=0}^{\infty} P_{mn} m} \tag{2.4}$$

$$F_B = \frac{T \sum_{m,n=0}^{\infty} P_{mn} nmr}{T \sum_{m,n=0}^{\infty} P_{mn} n} \;. \tag{2.5}$$

To average over the trait groups is biologically justified because of the physical mixing of the organisms during the dispersal stage. As before, the A-type is selected only when it has a higher relative fitness over the *global* population (the deme) than the B-type, although it need not necessarily have a greater fitness within the local population (the trait group), as we shall see.

$$F_A > F_B$$

$$d + \frac{\sum_{m,n=0}^{\infty} P_{mn} m^2 r}{\sum_{m,n=0}^{\infty} P_{mn} m} - r > \frac{\sum_{m,n=0}^{\infty} P_{mn} nmr}{\sum_{m,n=0}^{\infty} P_{mn} n} \tag{2.6}$$

Rearranging:

$$d > r \left(\frac{\sum_{m,n=0}^{\infty} P_{mn} nm}{\sum_{m,n=0}^{\infty} P_{mn} n} - \frac{\sum_{m,n=0}^{\infty} P_{mn} m^2}{\sum_{m,n=0}^{\infty} P_{mn} m} + 1 \right) \tag{2.7}$$

$$d > r \left[\frac{E(mn)}{E(n)} - \frac{E(m^2)}{E(m)} + 1 \right]. \tag{2.8}$$

Let $\bar{m} = E(m)$, $\bar{n} = E(n)$

$$\sigma_m^2 = E[(m - \bar{m})^2], \quad \sigma_n^2 = E[(n - \bar{n})^2]$$
$$\sigma_{mn}^2 = E[(m - \bar{m})(n - \bar{n})].$$

Then

$$E(mn) = \sigma_{mn}^2 + \bar{m}\bar{n}$$
$$E(m^2) = \sigma_m^2 + \bar{m}^2$$

and (2.8) becomes

$$d > r \left(\frac{\sigma_{mn}^2 + \bar{m}\bar{n}}{\bar{n}} - \frac{\sigma_m^2 + \bar{m}^2}{\bar{m}} + 1 \right) \tag{2.9}$$

$$d > r \left(\frac{\sigma_{mn}^2}{\bar{n}} - \frac{\sigma_m^2}{\bar{m}} + 1 \right). \tag{2.10}$$

Assume that the initial density in each trait group is constant (i.e., $m + n = N$). In that case, $\sigma_{mn}^2 = -\sigma_m^2$ and (2.10) becomes

$$d > r \left[-N \left(\frac{\sigma_p^2}{q} + \frac{\sigma_p^2}{p} \right) + 1 \right] \tag{2.11}$$

where σ_p^2 is now the variance in relative frequency of the A-type. Alternatively, let trait-group density vary, but the covariance between m and n equal zero ($\sigma_{mn}^2 = 0$). Then

$$d > r\left(1 - \frac{\sigma_m^2}{\bar{m}}\right). \tag{2.12}$$

Notice that equations (2.11) and (2.12) resemble the criteria for selection of the A-type in the individual-selection model [equation (2.3)], with the addition of a term that contains the variance in the frequency of the A-type between trait groups. This is the "between trait group" component of natural selection, whose significance will be explored in detail below.

The same result may be achieved through a slightly different pathway, by calculating the frequencies experienced by the average A- and B-type in the deme. These may be termed the "average subjective frequencies" (p_A, p_B: Wilson, 1977a) where

p_A = the frequency of A experienced by the average A-type

p_B = the frequency of A experienced by the average B-type

If we assume a constant starting trait-group density, and let P_p represent the proportion of trait groups with a relative frequency of p, then

$$p_A = \frac{\sum\limits_{p=0}^{1} P_p p^2}{\sum\limits_{p=0}^{1} P_p p} = \bar{p} + \frac{\sigma_p^2}{\bar{p}} \tag{2.13}$$

$$p_B = \frac{\sum\limits_{p=0}^{1} P_p pq}{\sum\limits_{p=0}^{1} P_p q} = \bar{p} - \frac{\sigma_p^2}{\bar{q}}. \tag{2.14}$$

The fitness of average individuals is

$$F_A = d + (Np_A - 1)r = d + [N(\bar{p} + \frac{\sigma_p^2}{\bar{p}}) - 1]r$$

$$F_B = Np_B r = N(\bar{p} - \frac{\sigma_p^2}{\bar{q}})r \tag{2.15}$$

and the A-type is favored by selection when

$$F_A > F_B$$

which can be shown to be equivalent to

$$d > r[-N(\frac{\sigma_p^2}{\bar{q}} + \frac{\sigma_p^2}{\bar{p}}) + 1] \tag{2.16}$$

which is identical to equation (2.11). An "average subjective density" may also be calculated as $\bar{m} + \sigma_m^2/\bar{m}$, which is identical to Lloyd's (1967) concept of "mean crowding."

Average subjective frequencies are useful because they allow one to consider the effects of deme structure in any linear basic selection model simply by re-

Figure 2.1. Four discrete trait groups that vary in their composition of A- and B-types. Ecological interactions occur within trait groups, but individuals from all trait groups mix during a dispersal stage.

placing the average frequency ($\bar{p}$) with the average subjective frequencies (p_A, p_B) without going through calculations (2.6-2.12) in every case. Average subjective frequencies also supply a biologically understandable way to view the effect of structured demes on the natural selection of traits. This is best illustrated by a numerical example. Figure 2.1 shows a deme subdivided into four trait groups, each containing five individuals. The frequency of A varies among trait groups. The average frequency of A over the whole deme may be calculated as

$$\bar{p} = \frac{0.2 + 0.4 + 0.6 + 0.8}{4} = 0.5 .$$

However, the average subjective frequencies of the A- and B-types are

$$p_A = \frac{1(0.2) + 2(0.4) + 3(0.6) + 4(0.8)}{10} = 0.6$$

$$p_B = \frac{4(0.2) + 3(0.4) + 2(0.6) + 1(0.8)}{10} = 0.4 .$$

The subjective frequencies, therefore, are simply the weighted averages over all the trait groups. In other words, only 1 A-type experiences the low frequency of 0.2 A-types (itself), but 4 A-types experience the high frequency of 0.8 A-types, and so on. It may easily be verified from equations (2.13) and (2.14) that any variance in frequency among trait groups causes the average A-type to experience a higher frequency of A-types than actually exists in the deme, while the average B-type experiences a lower frequency (i.e., $p_A > \bar{p} > p_B$ and, conversely, $q_B > \bar{q} > q_A$). Fisher (1958), Hamilton (1963, 1964, 1970, 1971, 1975) and Trivers (1971) realized that altruistic traits which decrease the fitness of the donor to the benefit of the recipients can be favored by selection only if they are directed toward fellow altruists—in other words, toward similar "types." The average subjective frequencies show that to some extent this occurs in all structured demes, and that the strength of the process depends upon the variance in frequency among trait groups (hereafter referred to as trait-group variation).

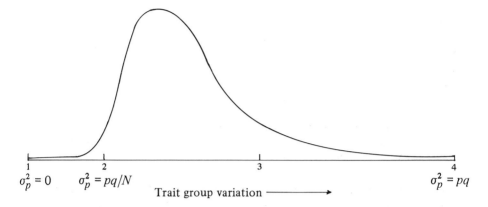

Figure 2.2. A continuum of trait group variation (variance in the frequency of A among trait groups). Points 1 through 4 correspond respectively to individual selection, the binomial distribution, kin selection, and total altruism. The curve gives a hypothetical distribution of populations in nature along this gradient.

More specifically, Figure 2.2 represents a continuum of trait-group variation. Several points on this continuum are of special interest:

Point 1

When no trait-group variation exists, equation (2.16) reduces to $d > r$, the individual-selection model. Mathematically, of course, $\sigma_p^2 = 0$ is nothing more than a return to the homogeneity assumption, but biologically, it is important to recognize that if one accepts the basic concept of structured demes, individual selection represents an absurd extreme of the continuum. Variance within trait groups is zero by definition, but zero variance between trait groups would require a very special mechanism indeed.

Point 2

In the absence of good information, the most conservative assumption that can be made about trait-group variation is that it is random, like tossing red and blue marbles into urns. In this case, the variance can be approximated by the binomial distribution ($\sigma_p^2 = \bar{p}\bar{q}/N$). Substitution of this value into (2.16) becomes

$$d > r\left[-N\left(\frac{\bar{p}\bar{q}}{N\bar{q}} + \frac{\bar{p}\bar{q}}{N\bar{p}}\right) + 1\right] \qquad (2.17)$$

$$d > r[-(\bar{p} + \bar{q}) + 1];$$

but $\bar{p} + \bar{q} = 1$, so

$$d > 0. \hspace{4cm} (2.18)$$

With variable density and $\sigma_m^2 = \bar{m}$, the same result may also be shown using equation (2.12). Stated in words: Given a binomial distribution of types into trait groups, the structured deme model predicts that to be favored by selection, the A-type must increase its own fitness in an absolute sense, not relative to others in the trait group. One could term this process "absolute individual fitness." It cannot be overemphasized how different it is from the "relative individual fitness" of the individual-selection model ($d > r$). In fact, most of the hypotheses developed in the following chapters rest upon equation (2.18), and we shall return to it repeatedly.

For this particular linear model, the difference between absolute and relative individual fitness is the class of traits for which $r > d > 0$, in which the A-type increases its own fitness but lowers it relative to others in the same trait group. Some confusion exists over what to call these traits. Theoreticians (e.g., Matessi and Jayakar, 1976, Cohen and Eshel, 1976, Eshel and Cohen, 1976, Eshel, 1977) tend to lump them with traits for which $d < 0$ and term them both altruistic, because they are selected against by individual-selection models. Nonmathematical treatments often speak of an altruist's "sacrifice" without specifying whether the sacrifice is absolute or is relative to others in the local population. I have been reluctant to term these traits "altruistic" (Wilson, 1975a, 1977a) because in the intuitive sense of the word, traits that fall into this category do not appear altruistic and sometimes appear very selfish (see later chapters for examples). Nevertheless, in order not to deviate too widely from current terminology, the class of traits for which $r > d > 0$ should perhaps be termed "weak altruism" and the class of traits for which $d < 0$ be termed "strong altruism" (Wilson, 1979). This is the usage adopted in this book.

Greater Than Bionomial Distribution

As trait-group variation exceeds the binomial, the bracketed term of equation (2.16) becomes negative and traits that actually decrease the fitness of the individual performing them ($d < 0$, strong altruism) can be selected for, given a sufficiently positive effect on the trait group at large (r). Hence, the structured deme model predicts that the binomial distribution represents a threshold variance for the evolution of strong altruism. As trait-group variation goes from point 2 to point 4 of the continuum, increasingly stronger altruistic traits can be selected for. Natural selection becomes more sensitive to the effect of traits on the population at large.

Point 3, Kin Selection

Kin-selection theory explores the evolutionary effects of individuals on their relatives. In some cases, these effects are behaviorally directed (i.e., an individual recognizes relatives and behaves differently toward them than toward nonrelatives); in other cases, the effects are spatially directed (i.e., an individual cannot distinguish relatives from nonrelatives, but directs most of its behavior toward the former simply because of their spatial proximity). Spatially directed kin selection represents a special case of structured demes in which the kin group equals the trait group. Therefore, one should be able to calculate average subjective frequencies that are characteristic of kin groups and arrive at the same conclusions as classical kin-selection theory (Wilson, 1977a).

Consider a sexual haploid population continaing two alleles, A and B, in proportions p and q (different letters used to preserve terminology). Mating occurs at random, so the frequency of A-A, A-B, and B-B matings are p^2, $2pq$, and q^2 respectively, and

$p^2/(p^2 + pq)$ = the proportion of A-offspring resulting from A-A matings
$pq/(p^2 + pq)$ = the proportion of A-offspring resulting from A-B matings
$q^2/(q^2 + pq)$ = the proportion of B-offspring resulting from B-B matings
$pq/(q^2 + pq)$ = the proportion of B-offspring resulting from A-B matings

Each female has a clutch of offspring (size N) that remains isolated from other clutches. Because interactions are restricted to within a clutch, each clutch constitutes a trait group, and each trait group is composed entirely of siblings.

The subjective frequencies for this situation may be calculated as follows: The clutches from A-A and B-B matings will have frequencies of $p = 1$, $q = 0$ and $p = 0$, $q = 1$, respectively. The clutches from A-B matings will have mean frequencies of $p = q = 0.5$ and a binomially distributed variance of $\sigma^2 = pq/N = 0.25/N$. Thus, the average A offspring from A-B matings will experience a subjective frequency of $p_A = 0.5 + 0.5/N$, while B-offspring from A-B matings will experience a subjective frequency of $p_B = 0.5 - 0.5/N$. The subjective frequencies for all offspring from all matings are then

$$p_A = \frac{p^2(1) + pq(.5 + .5/N)}{p^2 + pq} = p + q(.5 + .5/N) \qquad (2.19)$$

$$p_B = \frac{q^2(0) + pq(.5 - .5/N)}{q^2 + pq} = p(.5 - .5/N). \qquad (2.20)$$

These are the characteristic subjective frequencies when interactions occur exclusively among siblings.

Most kin-selection models deal with the relations between a donor (the A-

type) and a single recipient. In this case, the effect of every A-type is divided among $(N - 1)$ recipients, and inequality (2.16) becomes

$$d + \frac{(Np_A - 1)r}{(N - 1)} > \frac{Np_B r}{(N - 1)}$$

$$d > \frac{r}{(N - 1)} [N(p_B - p_A) + 1]. \tag{2.21}$$

Enter the values for subjective frequencies as follows:

$$d > \frac{r}{(N - 1)} [N(p(.5 - .5/N) - p - q(.5 + .5/N)) + 1] \tag{2.22}$$

$$d > \frac{r}{(N - 1)} [N(-.5(p + q) - .5(p + q)/N) + 1]$$

$$d > \frac{r}{(N - 1)} [-.5(N - 1)]$$

$$d > -.5r. \tag{2.23}$$

This corresponds to the well-known conclusion of kin-selection models: that to be favored by selection, the donor's cost must be less than one-half the recipient's gain, demonstrating the basic equivalence between kin selection and structured demes. (See also Hamilton, 1975, Matessi and Jayakar, 1976, and Eshel and Cohen, 1976). However, this does not mean that no difference exists between the two models (Maynard Smith, 1976). The most fundamental aspect of structured demes is the existence of trait groups. Kin selection pertains only to a certain kind of variation among trait groups, given their existence. See Wilson (1979) for a fuller discussion of the distinction between kin selection, inclusive fitness, and structured demes.

Point 4, Total Altruism

At the opposite end of the continuum from point 1, types are distributed such that any one trait group consists either entirely of A-types or B-types; in other words, total segregation between types exists. This yields a value of $\sigma_p^2 = \bar{p}\bar{q}$; entering into (2.16),

$$d > r \left[-N(\frac{\bar{p}\bar{q}}{\bar{p}} + \frac{\bar{p}\bar{q}}{\bar{q}}) + 1 \right] \tag{2.24}$$

$$d + (N - 1)r > 0. \tag{2.25}$$

Notice that since the left-hand side of inequality (2.25) includes the effect of a single A-type on the entire trait group (the effect on itself plus the effect on the $N - 1$ recipients), satisfying the inequality by definition increases the net fitness of the group. Point 4, therefore, represents a form of pure group selection, in the sense that point 1 represents individual selection.

Point 4 is almost as absurd an extreme on the variation continuum as point 1, but sometimes the former can be found in nature. Pseudo-populations such as coral polyps meet the requirements, as do trait groups composed of single individuals. Less obvious is the fact that trait groups composed of two individuals can be totally altruistic when the individuals are monogamous parents of the same offspring. The sexual haploid model of point 3 yields trait groups composed of AA, AB, and BB parents. In every AB trait group, the fitness of each type is equal (because they literally have the same offspring), so any differences in fitness between the two types must arise from the AA and BB trait groups.

We can summarize the continuum of trait-group variation as follows: Individual selection models predict that to be favored by selection, an organism must have the highest fitness, relative to others in its trait group. In structured demes, natural selection becomes increasingly sensitive to the differential productivity of trait groups as the amount of genetic variation among trait groups increases. The criterion for the selection of the A-type passes from highest relative individual fitness within the trait group ($d > r$) to highest absolute individual fitness ($d > 0$), then through kin selection, and eventually to highest group fitness $[d + r(N - 1)] > 0$.

While the superficial criterion for selection shifts with the degree of trait-group variation in the structured deme model, it is crucial to remember that the same general question is always being asked: Which type has the highest relative fitness in the deme ($F_A > F_B$)? Relative fitness in the global population is one of the fundamental rules of evolution and can never be violated. It simply turns out that on point 2 of the continuum, for instance, the way to maximize relative fitness in the deme is to maximize absolute fitness in the trait group. What occurs in the trait group is not equivalent to what occurs in the deme. That is the difference between individual selection and the theory presented here.

A Graphical Approach

At this point it is desirable to introduce a way to visualize graphically the effect of structured demes on the evolution of traits (Charnov and Krebs, 1975, Wilson, 1977a). Figures 2.3(a)–(f) show various types of functions for f_A (solid line) and f_B (dashed line), with respect to the frequency of A. In Figure 2.3(a) the fitnesses are constants (frequency independent), and the B-type is selected for. This is the kind of obviously adaptive trait that occupied the thinking of early evolutionary biologists.

Figures 2.3 (b) and (c) show the standard concept of frequency-dependent

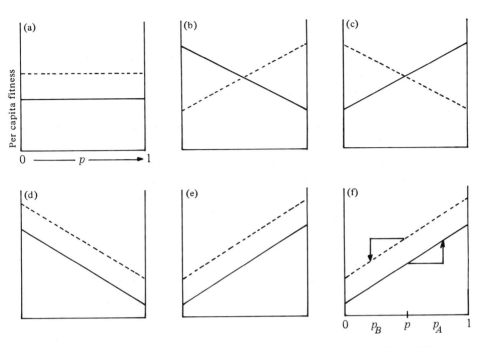

Figure 2.3. Per capita absolute fitness of A (solid line) and B (dashed line) types as a function of frequency. Total density (N) is held constant. Figure 2.3(a) = constant fitness values for each genotype. Figure 2.3(b) = frequency-dependent selection leading to stable, and Figure 2.3 (c) = unstable equilibrium. Figures 2.3(d) and (e) = frequency-dependent selection that does not lead to an equilibrium. Figure 2.3(e) = the concept of an altruistic trait, in which the A-type increases the fitness of the population (positive slopes) but nevertheless is always selected against (solid line always below dashed line). Figure 2.3(f) = the effect of deme structure which under certain circumstances can reverse the outcome of selection, causing the altruist to be favored in evolution.

selection, leading either to a stable equilibrium [2.3(b)] or to selection for the most abundant type [2.3(c)] (Ayala and Campbell, 1974).

Figures 2.3(d) and (e) show a different sort of frequency-dependent selection, seldom mentioned because it does not seem to lead to any interesting conclusions. In both cases the B-type is favored by selection, just as in Figure 2.3(a) (the lines need not be parallel). However, in Figure 2.3(e) selection against the A-type has reduced the absolute fitness of the population. Figure 2.3(e), in fact, corresponds to equation (2.2) where $r > 0$ and $d < r$. It represents the class of traits selected against by individual selection but selected for under certain circumstances in structured demes.

The effect of structured demes is shown in Figure 2.3(f). The subjective frequency and therefore per capita fitness is displaced to the right of the true frequency for the A-type and to the left for the B-type. This fact can reverse the outcome of selection—that is, it can cause the A-type to have a higher per capita fitness than the B-type.

From Figure 2.3(f), it is easily seen that the selection of the A-type can be promoted in three ways: (1) The steeper the slope of the fitness functions, the smaller the displacement necessary to reverse the outcome of selection; (2) the smaller the vertical distance separating the fitness functions, the smaller the displacement necessary to reverse the outcome of selection; and (3) the larger the trait-group variation, the larger the displacement of the subjective from the true frequencies. Also, by applying the same process to the other graphs in Figure 2.3, it may be seen that deme structure has no effect on traits represented by constant fitness functions [2.3(a)] and little effect on frequency-dependent traits represented by Figures 2.3(b) and (c) (if $[f_A(p) + f_B(p)]/2$ is not constant, then the equilibrium point will shift slightly).

Although the use of subjective frequencies is quantitatively inappropriate, the graphical approach may also be used to explore the qualitative effects of nonlinear fitness functions. For instance, concave fitness functions can prevent the evolution of altruism at low frequencies, while convex functions may prevent its evolution at high frequencies, as rigorously demonstrated by Cohen and Eshel (1976).

. . .

Is It Group Selection?

Although Maynard Smith (1976) claimed that the structured deme model is no different from the model of kin selection, I more often encounter the argument that it is no different from the model of individual selection. Because relative fitness within the global population is still the criterion for selection, many people prefer to think of structured demes as a model of individual selection in which the homogeneity assumption is relaxed.

The distinction is largely semantic, but it is worth pointing out that exactly the same criticism applies equally well to traditional models of group selection. For instance, when the appropriate parameter values are chosen in Gilpin's (1975) model, selfish types eliminate altruistic types and then drive themselves to extinction, leaving empty habitats that are differentially colonized by dispersers from populations containing a high frequency of altruistic types —exactly as envisioned by Wynne-Edwards. The frequency of the A-type increases to fixation; i.e., it has the highest relative fitness throughout the global population.

To be consistent, one must either define group selection as that component of natural selection that operates on the differential productivity of local populations within a global system, or abandon the term altogether. There is already a trend toward renaming all forms of altruism that can evolve as "genetic selfishness," which presumably reserves the term "altruism" for anything that can't evolve (Alexander, 1974). This conceptualization is a hollow victory for the individual selectionist.

Obviously, our theories on the evolution of social behavior are becoming rich enough that the relationships between formerly paradoxical elements are beginning to be seen, and a single model can produce the features of individual, kin, and group selection. Just because the relation between them is understood does not mean they need no longer be distinguished by combining them under a single term. To me, there are three strong reasons for retaining the term "group selection."

1. Observations on real organisms are almost always conducted within local populations. The concept of global fitness is fundamental but difficult to observe directly. In a practical sense we look at interactions within trait groups and need a terminology to describe the evolutionary forces that operate within trait groups. The term "individual selection" is appropriate.

2. Thinking of the between trait-group component of natural selection as group selection is profitable, and in many ways it is formally analogous to individual selection, as described in text books and as practiced in the laboratory. For instance, M. J. Wade is currently investigating the concept of group selection in the laboratory (Wade, 1976, 1977). His experiments consist of creating a population of groups of *Tribolium* beetles that vary in their genetic composition, selecting groups on the basis of some criterion (e.g., high population size, low population size—although any measurable parameter would do), and using them to start a new generation of groups. He does with groups exactly what other geneticists do with individuals, and it would be difficult to avoid thinking of the process as group selection.

3. If the between trait-group component of natural selection has a powerful effect on the evolution of traits, then many organisms will be shown to behave in ways that maximize the productivity of the trait group, and, therefore, it is difficult to think of this as individual selection.

The various terms as I define them are summarized in Table 2.2. We may conclude by saying that certain features of the individual selection model, on which many evolutionary biologists base their understanding of intra- and interspecific interactions, are artifacts of a simplifying assumption of spatial homogeneity in the genetic composition of populations. When the homogeneity assumption is relaxed in a way that is biologically realistic for many species, natural selection routinely promotes the evolution of weakly altruistic traits, and also strongly altruistic traits when special mechanisms exist to increase trait-group variation above the binomial distribution. Weakly altruistic

Table 2.2
Definition of terms

Individual selection	The component of natural selection that operates on the differential fitness of individuals within local (homogeneous with respect to genetic composition) populations
Group selection	The component of natural selection that operates on the differential productivity of local populations within a global population
Selfishness	All traits promoted by individual selection ($d > r$ in linear selection model)
Weak altruism	All nonselfish traits selected with a binomial trait-group variation ($0 < d < r$ in linear selection model)
Strong altruism	All nonselfish and nonweakly altruistic traits selected by a greater than binomial trait-group variation ($d < 0$, when r is sufficiently great, in linear selection models)

traits are not spectacularly sacrificial, and at first do not appear to radically alter the conclusions of the individual selection model. Understanding their importance requires an analysis of the relation between group selection and altruism.

References

Alexander, R. D., 1974. "The evolution of social behavior," *Ann. Rev. Ecol. Syst.,* 5:325–383.

Ayala, F. J., and Campbell, C. A., 1974. "Frequency dependent selection," *Ann. Rev. Ecol. Syst.,* 5:115–139.

Charnov, E. L., and Krebs, J. R., 1975. "The evolution of alarm calls: Altruism or manipulation?" *Am. Nat.,* 109:107–112.

Cohen, D. and Eshel, I., 1976. "On the founder effect and the evolution of altruistic traits," *Theor. Pop. Biol.,* 10:276–302.

Eshel, I., 1977. "On the founder effect and the evolution of altruistic traits: An ecogenetical approach," *Theor. Pop. Biol.,* 11:410–424.

Fisher, R. A., 1958. *The genetical theory of natural selection,* 2nd ed. New York, Dover Press.

Gilpin, M. E., 1975. *The Theory of Group Selection in Predator-Prey Communities,* Princeton, Princeton University Press.

Hamilton, W. D., 1963. "The evolution of altruistic behavior," *Am. Nat.,* 97: 354–356.

Hamilton, W. D., 1964. "The genetical evolution of social behavior, I and II," *J. Theor. Biol.,* 7:1–52.

Hamilton, W. D., 1970. "Selfish and spiteful behavior in an evolutionary model," *Nature,* 228(5277):1218–1220.

Hamilton, W. D., 1971. "Selection of selfish and altruistic behavior in some extreme models," in *Man and Beast: Comparative Social Behavior*, ed. J. F. Eisenberg and W. S. Dillon, Washington, D.C., Smithsonian Institution Press, pp. 57–91.

Hamilton, W. D., 1975. "Innate social aptitudes in man: An approach from evolutionary genetics," in *Biosocial Anthropology*, ed. R. Fox, London, Malaby Press, pp. 133–155. Reprinted in part in this volume.

Johnson, C. G., 1969. *Migration and Dispersal of Insects by Flight*. London, Methuen.

Matessi, C., and Jayakar, S. D., 1976. "Conditions for the evolution of altruism under Darwinian selection," *Theor. Popul. Biol.*, 9:360–387.

Maynard Smith, J., 1976. "Group selection," *Quart. Rev. Biol.*, 51:277–283. Reprinted in this volume.

Mayr, E., 1963. *Animal Species and Evolution*. Cambridge, Harvard University Press.

Trivers, R., 1971. "The evolution of reciprocal altruism," *Quart. Rev. Biol.*, 46:35–57.

Verner, J., 1977. "On the adaptive significance of territoriality," *Am. Nat.*, 111:769–775.

Wade, M. J., 1976. "Group selection among laboratory populations of *Tribolium*," *Proc. Nat. Acad. Sci.*, 73:4604–4607.

Wade, M. J., 1977. "Experimental study of group selection," *Evolution*, 31:134–153.

Wilson, D. S., 1975a. "A Theory of group selection," *Proc. Nat. Acad. Sci.*, 72:143–146.

Wilson, D. S., 1977a. "Structured demes and the evolution of group advantageous traits," *Am. Nat.*, 111:157–185.

Wilson, D. S., 1979. "Structured demes and trait-group variation," *Am. Nat.*, 113:606–610.

17

The Theory of Evolution by Natural Selection: A Hierarchical Expansion

Anthony J. Arnold and Kurt Fristrup

Introduction

The tree of life has been a universal and persistent metaphor since the beginning of human culture—for good reasons. Life, whether represented in terms of genealogy or phylogeny, is a branching process, and the unity of living things is best expressed in terms of its hierarchy. This hierarchical view is more than a metaphor.

Hierarchical structure has long been fundamental to our understanding of biology, both in the anatomy of individuals and in the Linnean systematic classification of individuals into higher level aggregates. In particular, species, populations, individuals, and genes are widely recognized as fundamental expressions of the evolutionary process. In this sense the organism represents but a single level of organization, both encompassing and being encompassed by other levels.

It is self-evident that evolutionary theory has acknowledged the utility of hierarchical structure in *describing* biological phenomena. However, this body of evolutionary theory does not incorporate hierarchical structure in its conventional modes of *explanation*. In order to justify a more rigorous statement of the explanatory role of hierarchical structure in evolutionary theory, we shall (1) show that there are hierarchically distributed evolutionary phenomena that are not accounted for by gene- and organism-based selection theories, and (2) demonstrate that existing theory can be modified to account for these problematic observations in a way that mirrors the natural biological hierarchy.

The spectrum of biological entities that we have outlined—from the species to the gene—exhibits two properties that permit a hierarchical application of the principle of natural selection. We will refer to these properties as branching and persistence. At the species level, they are manifested as speciation and species longevity, and they permit the definition of a species-level analog of fitness (see Stanley, 1975) in the same way that organismal reproduction and

From *Paleobiology* (1982) 8:113–129.

survivorship define fitness at the individual level. A similar approach can be taken for any level in the hierarchy. Before expanding this concept into a formal model, we will discuss the motivation for an explicit recognition of the evolutionary hierarchy in our theoretical framework.

Consider two clades of gastropods, one consisting of species with planktotrophic larval development, and the other with nonplanktotrophic species. We might expect that gastropods with planktic larvae would tend to have relatively lower speciation rates because their populations tend to have significant genetic interchange, thus preventing isolation and causing larger effective population sizes. Species with nonplanktic larvae (hence more limited dispersal) might be expected to have higher rates of speciation due to the enhanced probability of isolation. The critical characters—larval strategies—may well have arisen for reasons that can be seen as adaptive in a traditional Darwinian sense. However, regardless of the mechanism by which they became fixed, these strategies behave as properties of species in that they result in distributions of rates of speciation and extinction within this group. [Many readers will recognize that we have extracted this example from Hansen's (1981) work on volutid neogastropods. The inferences made by Hansen and Stanley (1980) regarding this work may not be fully supported by the data, so we use the example as a conceptual illustration rather than an empirical demonstration. We assume for the sake of discussion that the groups of volutids he studied are monophyletic. Documentation of such higher level effects is meager because the recognition of higher levels of selection has only recently pointed the way to this avenue of research.]

It might be tempting to assume that there are fewer planktotrophic species because the individuals in these species were somehow less fit than the individuals in non-planktotrophic species. However, it is obvious that the same result could obtain even if planktotrophic and non-planktotrophic individuals have equal fitnesses, by virtue of the population structures that are concomitants of these larval strategies.

Thus the observed distribution of species types within these gastropods is not predicted from individual level fitness alone, underscoring the necessity of the higher level of analysis.

There is an understandable tendency among evolutionary theorists to account for biological observations without recourse to higher levels of analysis whenever possible (Williams, 1966). Since this reductionistic approach has utility as an avenue to understanding the relationships between levels of analysis, it may be useful to ask how the reductionist would deal with the preceding example. It is true that it is *possible* to express (not explain) many such species level effects solely in terms of individual level fitness, in the following sense. An individual may gain fitness by being a member of a speciose clade, so that it leaves more descendents (by virtue of such speciation) than an individual that is a member of a non-speciose clade. However, it is misleading to imply that this is a simple extension of the established intuitive concept of fitness, since measurement of such fitness would in some cases necessitate extending the time scale of measurement beyond the geological range of the species itself. This does not mean that the reductionistic approach has no merit. We normally think of adaptation within local (temporal and spatial) environments, but the temporal definition of "local" is somewhat more arbitrary than the spatial. There is no logical inconsistency in redefining our estimates of an individual's long-term expectation of success on its evolutionary flexibility—in the same sense that ecological success may often be based on behavioral or ecophenotypic plasticity.

The main point, however, is that the reductionistic approach we have outlined provides only a limited perspective of the evolutionary process, since the only reference to higher level processes is in terms of their influence on the individual's expectation of success—without recognition of speciation and extinction rates and their influence on character distributions among species as units.

There are circumstances in which even this reductionistic mode of description cannot be applied no matter how much one is willing to stretch the intuitive concept of fitness. Consider two species of grasshopper. Let us place them in two separate resource-limited environments so that the total number of individuals does not change through time (that is, let the r's of all individuals in both species be equivalent); further, let the probabilities of group survival and of founding a new group be likewise uniform for all within-species groups. Now specify that the only difference between these two species is that one has a genetic character that enhances the probability of speciation. After a time we return and find differential speciation, the only correlative character being this "speciator gene": we have merely subdivided one species into many without increasing the number of individuals. Thus there is the potential for species level trends that simply cannot be expressed—not to mention explained—in terms of individual fitness. In this sense, the grasshopper example goes further than the gastropod example in asserting the necessity for higher levels of analysis.

The effects of the characters that cause these higher-level trends may be negative, positive, or neutral at the individual level, but their higher-level effects can be studied *without reference to individual level fitness*. Population structure is certainly not a property of individuals, but it has an important effect on speciation (branching) rates by influencing the probability of isolate formation, and an effect on extinction (persistence) rates, since the geographic distribution of populations partly determines how robust a species is to local environmental perturbation. Population structure is influenced by heritable characters such as reproductive strategy and dispersal mechanisms, but the direction of species selection acting on these characters is not necessarily determined by their effects at the individual level.

The preceding examples provide an intuitive demonstration of an obvious—but sometimes overlooked—statement: the characters that increase individual fitness do not necessarily cause speciation or prevent extinction. Thus it is misleading to adopt the convention of expressing all higher-level trends in terms of individual level fitness.

There are well known examples of selection below the level of the organism. An example would be segregation distorters such as that found in *Drosophila* or the t-allele in mice. Both of these types of alleles have strong negative selective impact at the individual level, but they exist at nonzero frequencies in populations by disrupting Mendelian assortment. These alleles can be seen as selfish in the sense that each ensures success at its own level at the expense of a marked reduction in the fitness of the organisms bearing them. Orgel and Crick (1980) discuss the energetic cost of parasitic DNA in a similar context. In these cases, the opposition of lower-level selection and very strong higher-level selection has resulted in intermediate equilibrium frequencies of the characters. A higher-level analogy would be the limited virulence observed in some parasites, which results from the opposition of individual and group selection (Fenner, 1965).

It is becoming increasingly apparent that there is hierarchical structure within the genome. Doolittle and Sapienza (1980) and others have drawn attention to the behavior of modular assemblages of genetic material "whose only function is survival within genomes. When a given DNA, or class of DNAs, of unproven phenotypic function can be shown to have evolved a strategy (such as transposition) which insures its genomic survival, then no other explanation for its existence is necessary." Doolittle and Sapienza (1980) called this "nonphenotypic selection." [Note that even the choice of terminology can be colored by our perception of the individual level as fundamental: when selection is identified as operating at the genic level, it is characterized semantically not by its own level, but by reference to the fact that it is not organismal.] Other such modular genic units have been suggested. If regulatory networks have any reality as functional systems, they may be subject to selection regardless of the particles they subsume.

These examples of suborganismal selection—and, to a certain extent, supraorganismal selection—are often seen as exceptions to "normal" Darwinian selection at the individual level, even though their recognition is a direct outgrowth of the study of organismal selection; in this sense, evolutionary theory has been slow to embrace the consequences of its own development. The acceptance of a hierarchical appraoch to selection will bring these diverse phenomena under the umbrella of a consistent and more tractable theoretical framework.

What Is Fitness?

At the organismal level, Fisher (1930) identified fitness with the Malthusian parameter (intrinsic rate of increase), since this parameter reflects representation in future generations and provides an objective basis for the comparison of evolutionary success between individuals. If neither fecundity nor mortality is age-dependent, then the Malthusian parameter is simply the difference between the birth (branching) rate and the death (persistence) rate: $r = b - d$. Stanley (1975) formalized the species level analog of this equation by defining the intrinsic rate of increase within a clade (R) in terms of speciation rate (S) and extinction rate (E) where $R = S - E$.

With age-dependent schedules of fecundity and mortality, the Malthusian parameter must be extracted from the Euler-Lotka equation:

$$\int_0^\infty l_x m_x e^{-rx} dx = 1$$

or, in discrete form:

$$\sum_{i=0}^\infty l_i m_i e^{-ri} = 1. \tag{1}$$

Both of these formulations (with and without age dependence), can be used to define fitness for any biological entity, and they both reflect the joint dependence of fitness upon branching and persistence.

A simple *post factum* measurement of the Malthusian parameter is an *estimate* of fitness that includes a stochastic component of reproductive success that must be conceptually distinguished from fitness. For example, two organisms that are exactly equivalent in terms of their genotypic and phenotypic character composition may nonetheless exhibit different degrees of reproductive sucess because of fortuitous environmental or hereditary (e.g., mate quality) effects. We would not wish to say that two such organisms have different fitnesses. For this reason we express fitness as an expectation of net reproductive success rather than the realized *post factum* success.

Fitness can be separated into two additional components: that which is correlated with a property of the individual unit of selection under study, and that component, shared by all individuals in a given group, that correlates with a property of the group (conventional group selection). Wimsatt (1980) expressed this distinction by reference to context-independent vs. context-dependent variation in fitness (the group constituting the relevant context). Rather than referring to context independence, we will refer to character-dependent variation in fitness. Fisher's (1930) estimate of this expectation for a given genotype was expressed as a Malthusian parameter averaged over many individuals in different "contexts."

The central theme of our hierarchical approach to evolutionary theory is that branching and persistence are the essential components of fitness and evolutionary success at all levels. We emphasize this point here to counter the common tendency to neglect branching rates in the discussion of selection and adaptation. The concept of natural selection is sometimes clouded by the equation of fitness with survival—a popular misconception that is reinforced by the phrase "survival of the fittest." Some recent formulations of species selection have reflected this confusion: speciation rate was not explicitly included as an essential aspect of species selection (Eldredge and Gould, 1972; Stanley, 1975). This has since been corrected (see Gould and Eldredge, 1977; Stanley, 1980).

What Is Selection?

In the examples we presented in the introduction, we see the hierarchical manifestation of a single principle that can operate regardless of the units involved. Lewontin (1970) stated the conditions necessary for the operation of natural selection:

1. Different individuals in a population have different morphologies, physiologies, and behaviors (phenotypic variation).

2. Different phenotypes have different rates of survival and reproduction in different environments (differential fitness).

3. There is a correlation between parents and offspring in the contribution of each to future generations (fitness is heritable).

[It may be that Lewontin's third statement is better considered as embodying two distinct postulates:

3a. There is a correlation between parents and offspring in various features of their morphology, physiology, and behavior (characters are heritable).

3b. There is consistent character-dependent interaction of organism with environment, and this interaction determines fitness.

We point out that the concepts of "character" and "fitness" are not analogous. Fitness is a summary of the expected performance of a unit of selection, and characters are the inherited determinants of that fitness.]

The central point in this concept is that the "individuals" referred to need not be individual organisms: one can substitute, for example, the species as a unit of selection with a fitness metric based on speciation and extinction rates rather than birth and death rates (see Hull, 1978, 1980).

Careful consideration of the preceding three points will reveal that there is is no statement regarding the causal network(s) that may ultimately determine variation in fitness. Thus variation in individual fitness will sometimes show a dependency on group membership (e.g., presence of an "altruist" or a "selfish strategist" in conventional models of group selection), or that variation in species fitness (speciation and/or extinction rates) will sometimes show a dependency on average (within-species) individual fitness—although our examples have shown that this is not always the case. Any attempt to qualify the concept of selection by reference to the causal networks involved will result in the loss of a general definition of the process—since there is no general causal chain. However, it doesn't follow that the causal networks that influence a particular level of analysis need be ignored or obfuscated by our choice of either a definition of selection or a level of analysis. In fact, the model we present is specifically (but not exclusively) concerned with identifying the influence that various levels of organization have on a chosen level of analysis. It is essential to recognize that we are asking (and answering) different questions when we focus on different levels of analysis. The question "Why are there more species of type A than type B?" simply has a different answer from the question "Why are there more individuals of type A than type B?" The fact that the first question will sometimes (not always) refer to variation in average individual design characteristics does not invalidate the concept of species selection, or reduce the question to one that focuses on the individual level. There is a common intuition that one should not even refer to species selection when our explanation of higher-level trends involves properties attributed to organisms; however, this is but a single (the simplest) example of the multitude of ways in which individual fitness can influence higher-level rates of branching and persistence. For example, fit individuals may tend to make larger populations with larger peripheries and greater likelihood of peripheral isolation—hence greater speciation rates. There is no single agreed-upon mechanism of speciation, and this lack of consensus in the academic community probably reflects an underlying diversity of natural processes by which speciation occurs. Although all of the speciation models may plausibly be argued to be influenced in some way by average individual fitness, it is certainly not the only component involved.

The concept of selection as a process (rather than a force) was applied to individual selection by the early architects of genetic theory (e.g., Fisher, 1930) and is still the most widely accepted usage of the term. Theories of natural selection are descriptions of that process. The multi-leveled causal network involving entities and environment drives the process. This does not require that the level at which we identify selection must also contain the causal network that determines the correlation between fitness and character value.

Any level of analysis is a window on the evolutionary process, with advantages, limitations and biases (cf. Wimsatt, 1980). We believe that explicit awareness of these advantages and limitations will do much to resolve the differences of opinion between those who advocate the primacy of one particular level or another. This approach does not exclude the possibility of simultaneous treatment of several levels of selection; rather, it emphasizes that doing so means stepping out of the selection paradigm to posit specific mechanisms of linkage between fitnesses at various levels of organization. The model we present remains *within* the selection paradigm, *and* it provides a firm platform for analyses of this sort.

The final—and perhaps most important—point we wish to make here is that a terminological confusion has grown out of the historical development of selection theory. An important legacy of Darwin's work (and of our perceptual limitations) is that evolution is still perceived through the "window" of selection between organisms. "Group selection" was initially defined from this perspective in the sense that individual fitness was determined by group membership. In this sense, "group selection" is usually conceptualized as selection between individuals—but based on an individual's group membership rather than on characters attributed to that individual. This is quite distinct from selection between groups as entities, in which different measures of fitness based on group branching and persistence must be used. These concepts must be separated if one is to understand the concept of a unit of selection. For example, species selection involves selection between species as entities and the effect of this process on individual fitness is not addressed. Thus species selection is *not* a higher order form of traditional "group selection." We will therefore refer to a "group (treatment) effect on individual fitness," vs. "selection between groups as units" to preserve this important distinction. [A biological level of organization can have status as a unit of selection only to the extent that it retains its integrity as a unit (Hull, 1978). The specific selection model we present is dependent on an unambiguous definition of fitness, which is only possible when units of selection can be clearly defined. It may often be the case for groups between the level of the species and the individual that character diffusion or non-random migration will result in a blurring of the definition of groups and of group branching. Thus character diffusion between units of selection (as in Wright's shifting balance theory) is an evolutionary phenomenon that is not addressed by pure selection models. Our emphasis is on the hierarchical nature of selection. Wright's concept may have hierarchical application as well.]

What Is Adaptation?
At the organismal level, there is a class of heritable characters that have a positive influence on organismal fitness. These are referred to as adaptations. If this concept is generalized for application at multiple levels of selection,

then non-planktotrophic population structures (in the gastropod example) and the ability to subvert Mendelian mechanisms (in the t-allele) are adaptations—but only with reference to their respective levels of selection: they are species and gametic level adaptations, respectively. Adaptations at any particular level may be adaptive or maladaptive to varying degrees at other levels. For example, planktotrophy has relatively "maladaptive" consequences for rates of speciation at the species level regardless of its adaptive status at the individual level. [Note that this concept of adaptation embraces preadaptation as a subcategory, and that the presence of an adaptation at a particular level of organization does not necessarily imply that it is the product of selection at that level.]

Since selection cannot act to maximize engineering efficiency for each structure independently, it is clear that adaptation cannot be equated with functional design improvement. The presumed benefits of increased survivorship may be more than offset by a drop in fecundity (because of a different allocation of energetic resources) or by a longer developmental schedule, which would delay age at first reproduction. It follows that the "adaptedness" of any isolated structure is a compromise, and a relaxation of the environmental demands upon the function of a given structure may result in selection for increased fecundity or earlier maturation at the expense of perfection of design. Furthermore, when selection acts to increase fecundity, it is proper to refer to that increase as an adaptation. [This means that selection without adaptation (Gould and Lewontin, 1979) is based on a narrow interpretation of adaptation. They make the following argument: if a mutation appears in a population that, say, doubles fecundity, it will sweep through the population (all other things being equal). Since this mutant is no better equipped to deal with its environment in a functional sense, it is not better adapted in the usual sense of adaptation to a local environment. Under our definition, such a character is an adaptation. For this reason we speak of adaptation within (rather than to) a constraining situation, part of which is environment. It may be important to distinguish between "branching oriented" and "persistence oriented" (often functional) adaptations, but they are both integral aspects of the evolutionary process.] If the cost of reproductive advantage must sometimes be a failure to achieve a functional design optimum, then one might say that selection is acting to satisfy the design requirements sufficient to ensure survival to reproduction. This is a sense in which the concept of "satisficing" (Simon, 1957)—as opposed to optimizing—design requirements can be applied to evolutionary theory. ["Satisficing" (Simon, 1957) has been suggested as an alternative response to certain economic conditions. If a corporation wishes to maximize profits, it may be more advantageous to concentrate corporate resources on those subsidiaries that are the greatest impediments to overall corporate success rather than to attempt to optimize each subsidiary's performance.]

Definitions

In order to avoid confusion in the course of our discussion we present here our working definitions of a few key terms.

Success

Measured by the rate of increase in absolute numbers of descendents, or the realized Malthusian parameter. This value is a retrospective measure of the relative increase or decrease in the descendents of a lineage, as a fraction of a specified population over a specified time interval.

Fitness

The expectation of success, or the expected Malthusian parameter, for a given entity.

Selection

The process resulting in the component of variation in success that is caused by variation in biological character states.

Character

Any quantitative or qualitative property of a biological entity. A character value is a metric associated with a character state (e.g., gene frequency, size, shape, presence/absence, averaged measurements of units subsumed by the unit of study).

Adaptation

Any heritable character that increases the fitness of a biological entity within a given set of environments. Also the evolutionary process resulting in the establishment of such a character in a population of biological entities.

Evolutionary entity

Any unit that reproduces and maintains its integrity long enough to permit the action of selection (cf. Williams, 1966). In order for evolution to occur in response to selection, a "parent-offspring" relation in character values is required (heredity). Such entities might be species, populations, demes, individuals, genes, or other intermediate levels of organization. When our analysis focuses on a particular level, we will refer to "focal level entities."

There are two points embodied in these definitions that merit further clarification and emphasis. First, our distinction between success and fitness is intended to highlight the stochastic influences of environmental variability and the mechanisms of inheritance. By this usage, we exclude (from fitness) that variation in success that is independent of the character states attributed to the entity. We do not exclude sources of variation whose effects on success are mediated by the character states attributed to the individual or to the group(s) of which the individual is a member.

The second point is that we do *not* define group- or species-level fitness as an average or sum of the fitnesses of the individuals within groups or species. We make this distinction to point out the two fundamentally different aspects of higher-level selection that we discussed under the final paragraph of "What is selection?"

The Model

These ideas may be clearly illustrated in various forms of the selection equations presented by Price (1970, 1972). In contrast to the classical models of population genetics, these equations are not explicitly linked to genes. They deal with "traits" or "characters," which can be any feature of an entity that can be described by a numeric value. Though this character-oriented approach is in some ways very different from the gene-oriented approach, we note that: (a) it can be applied to genes as characters or as entities, and (b) it shares the same basic approach to selection but allows us to study selection involving complex characters without focusing upon the often cumbersome or intractable details of their genetic derivation.

The model begins by focusing upon the change in the average character value in a population of entities over a single, discrete time interval. We define:

w_i = the fitness of the ith entity (equated with or derived from the Malthusian parameter),

q_i = a character value assigned to the ith entity,

q_i' = the same value average among the descendents of the ith entity (possibly including the surviving ith entity itself),

N = the number of entities in the population,

$\Delta q_i = q_i' - q_i$.

The average values of the character in the population before and after selection are written as:

before:
$$\text{ave}(q_i) = \sum_{i=1}^{N} q_i/N$$

after:
$$\text{ave}_w(q_i') = \sum_{i=1}^{N} w_i(q_i + \Delta q_i)/\sum_{i=1}^{N} w_i. \tag{2}$$

We can rearrange equation (2) in the following form:

$$\text{ave}_w(q_i') = (N/\sum_{i=1}^{N} w_i)(\sum_{i=1}^{N} w_i q_i/N) + \sum_{i=1}^{N} w_i \Delta q_i/\sum_{i=1}^{N} w_i$$

This can be rewritten using some familiar statistical terms:

$$\Delta \text{ave}(q_i) = \text{cov}(w_i, q_i)/\text{ave}(w_i) + \text{ave}_w(\Delta q_i), \tag{3}$$

where

$$\Delta \text{ave}(q_i) = \text{ave}_w (q_i') - \text{ave}(q_i),$$

where $\text{ave}(w_i)$ is the arithmetic mean of the w_i; $\text{cov}(w_i, q_i)$ is the covariance of w_i, q_i, and $\text{ave}_w (\Delta q_i)$ is the weighted arithmetic mean of the Δq_i, with the w_i as the weights. This compact equation can be rewritten in several forms using the following identities:

$$\begin{aligned} \text{cov}(w_i, q_i) &= B(q_i, w_i)\text{var}(q_i) \\ &= \text{corr}(q_i, w_i)\text{s.d.}(q_i)\text{s.d.}(w_i); \end{aligned} \tag{4a}$$

$$\begin{aligned} \text{ave}_w (\Delta q_i) &= \text{ave}(\Delta q_i) + \text{cov}(\Delta q_i, w_i)/\text{ave}(w_i) \\ &= \text{ave}(\Delta q_i w_i)/\text{ave}(w_i) \end{aligned} \tag{4b}$$

where $B(q_i, w_i)$ is the slope of the linear regression; $w = Bq + A$; $\text{corr}(q_i, w_i)$ is the Pearson correlation coefficient; and $\text{s.d.}(q_i)$ is the standard deviation of the q_i.

The first term on the right side of equation (3), the covariance of character and fitness divided by average fitnesses, represents the change in average character value due to selection (the covariance principle—Robertson, 1966, 1968; Crow and Nagylaki, 1976) and it can be called the average excess in fitness associated with the character (cf. the derivation of the Fundamental Theorem of Natural Selection; Fisher, 1930, 1941, 1958). Referring to (4a), we see that the magnitude of this term is dependent upon the intensity of the relationship between character value and fitness (the intensity of selection) and the variation in the character, which provides the raw material for selection to act upon. The second term on the right side of equation (3), which we will refer to as the inheritance term, represents the change in average character value due to the mechanism of inheritance of the character. As written, it is a weighted average of the differences in parent-offspring character values, but from identity (4b), we see that it can be decomposed into two terms. The first is an unweighted average of the parent-offspring differences, representing a biasing process that operates independent of selection. The second is a covariance term that represents the possible correlation between focal fitness and parent-offspring differences.

The inheritance term expresses the effects of a variety of potential influences, including, at the individual level, mutation, mating structure, and differential gametic viability and motility. Although these particular examples are specific to the individual level, the last two typify a general class of phenomena that we might call selection operating below the focal level. If the focal level is taken to be the species, then the effect of within-species transformations on character values among species will appear in the bias term.

In order to modify Price's equation to exhibit the potential influence of lower-level selection upon the mean value of a character in the population of focal entities, we can expand the q in terms of a selection equation that is deemed appropriate for the situation. It is a convenient feature of Price's equation that it can be applied recursively if we assume that the focal character can be represented as a linear combination of the characters possessed by the lower level entities subsumed by the focal entity. This assumption is somewhat restrictive if we wish to represent the genetic determination of a complex character in an individual/gene level model [Crow and Nagylaki (1976) develop a multilocus genetic model at the individual level. They restate Price's covariance principle to account for dominance and multilocus epistasis without assuming random mating or linkage equilibrium. Their model is compatible with the one that we develop, and both approaches result in a covariance term that summarizes the effect of selection.] However, the above assumption is often an appropriate one if we wish to model the impact of individual level selection upon a species level process. Consider a model in which we explore the possibility that the mean individual size or shape in a species affects species level fitness. The focal character—mean size or shape—is basically a simple sum of individual characters, and individual selection acting within these species units could result in a shift in the mean character value that we observe for each species.

Thus, we begin by assuming:

$$q_i = \sum_{j=1}^{n_i} p_j / n_i,$$

$$\Delta q_i = \text{cov}(r_j, p_j)/\text{ave}(r_j) + \text{ave}_r(\Delta p_j).$$

Substitution of this equation for Δq_i results in the following composite equation:

$$\Delta \text{ave}(q_i) = \text{cov}(w_i, q_i)/\text{ave}(w_i)$$
$$\text{focal level}$$
$$\text{selection}$$
$$+ \text{ave}_w [\text{cov}(r_j, p_j)/\text{ave}(r_j)$$
$$\text{lower level}$$
$$\text{selection}$$
$$+ \text{ave}_r(\Delta p_j)] \qquad (5)$$
$$\text{lower level}$$
$$\text{bias in inheritance.}$$

Two features of this expansion must be emphasized. First, the w's and the r's must be defined over the same time interval. In the example of a species/individual selection model, we must use a time interval that is long enough to ensure that speciation will be perceived as an event that never exceeds one time interval in duration. This means that we must adopt a measure of individual fitness that reflects an accounting of how many descendents an individual is likely to have over the number of generations that spans the same time scale over which we measure species selection. Second, lower-level selection makes its appearance in this model only to the extent that it effects a transformation in the character value that is assigned to a focal entity or its descendents. Since we are ignorant of the number of lower-level entities contained within each focal entity, and any changes in these numbers, we cannot translate this limited recognition of lower-level selection into information regarding changes in the distribution of lower-level characters among all lower-level entities contained by our population of focal entitites. Therefore, the average lower-level selection term that is embedded in this equation is not a complete summary of the lower-level selection process. It is solely a summary of how that process affects the focal level, unless the number of lower-level units within each focal-level entity is constant (such as the number of loci per individual in a system without duplication and deletion).

It is possible, without making further assumptions, to modify this expanded form such that we *are* aware of the consequences of the lower level selection at its own level. We simply weight all of the "focal"-level entities according to the number of lower level units that each contains. However, this modification alters the interpretation that we place upon the entire equation. The redefinition of terms that is required to demonstrate this concept is:

n_a = the number of focal entities in group a;

$W_a = \sum_{i=1}^{n_a} w_i/n_a$ = the average focal level fitness of the entities in group a;

$Q_a = \sum_{i=1}^{n_a} q_i/n_a$ = the average focal level character value of the entities in group a.

The final modification is to note that our 'target' variable for this model is now the change in the weighted average of the group means for the focal character:

$$\Delta \text{ave}_n(Q_a) = \text{cov}_n(Q_a, W_a)/\text{ave}_n(W_a) + \text{ave}_{n\,W} \cdot [\text{cov}(q_i, w_i)/\text{ave}(w_i)$$
$$+ \text{ave}_w(\Delta q_i)]. \tag{6}$$

The W's *do not* represent the fitnesses of the groups in the sense of measuring net differences in rates of *group* branching and persistence. These W's are simply averages of the lower-level fitnesses, and this model examines the potential for a common group-level contribution to lower-level fitness, based upon the frequency of some lower level character in the group. For these reasons, we say that the focal level has been shifted downwards by this modification, and the resulting analysis is essentially an analysis of covariance (ANACOVA). In this analysis, the higher-level selection appears as a "treatment effect" upon (the new) focal-level fitness, thus capturing the structure of most "group selection" models (for a review, see Wade, 1978).

We can combine the two expansions of Price's equation to create a somewhat cumbersome form that models both higher- and lower-level influences upon a focal-level evolutionary process. This serves to illustrate one of the asymmetrical aspects of a focal-level perspective. We omit subscripts here for simplicity:

$$\Delta \text{ave}_n(Q) = \text{cov}_n(Q, W)/\text{ave}_n(W)$$
$$\text{higher level}$$
$$\text{selection}$$
$$+ \text{ave}_{nW} \cdot \{\text{cov}(q, w)/\text{ave}(w)$$
$$\text{focal level}$$
$$\text{selection}$$
$$+ \text{ave}_w \cdot [\text{cov}(p, r)/\text{ave}(r)$$
$$\text{lower level}$$
$$\text{selection}$$
$$+ \text{ave}_r(\Delta p)]\} \tag{7}$$
$$\text{lower level}$$
$$\text{bias.}$$

Note that lower-level fitnesses appear directly in this expansion, while at levels above the focal level the "fitness" that we deal with is really an average of focal-level fitness across the appropriate "group." Therefore, if we shift our focus to higher levels, while retaining the same depth of analysis, we increase the number of distinct mechanisms of branching and persistence that we can incorporate directly in our model, but at the cost of measuring evolutionary change in increasingly coarse units.

Since much of this discussion is based upon our expansions of Price's equation, it is legitimate to inquire about the generality of these insights. We point out that the model is founded upon differences in fitness, and it allows for imperfect inheritance/maintenance of characters, without carrying the burden of specific assumptions regarding the mechanism of character determination.

"Group Selection"

One of the recurrent issues in the units of selection literature (Wimsatt, 1980; Sober, 1980) has been that of "causation" or "reducibility." This question usually arises in attempting to determine if differences in mean *individual* fitness among different groups are merely an artifact of individual-level selection and segregation by character value, or if they represent evidence for group-treatment effect on individual fitness. Consider a polymorphic species consisting of red and green individuals, with red individuals less fit than green. If groups tend to consist of either red or green individuals (segregation by character value), then the result will be a high group covariance between color and individual fitness. The treatment effect can thus be misleading in the presence of non-random assortment of individuals by character value.

Thus, the goal is to isolate "irreducible" group-level treatment effects from the effects of individual selection combined with segregation of individuals by character. The extended form of Price's equations offers an intuitive approach that clarifies this source of ambiguity. Equation (6), as an analysis of covariance, tells us how much of the overall change in the average individual character value will be due to (a) covariance between individual fitness and character value within groups, and (b) how much is due to covariance between mean individual fitness and mean character value among groups. Although this has the appearance of yielding information about group-level treatment effects, we are in fact still uninformed, because the artificial group effect discussed above (assortative grouping combined with an advantage that is based solely upon individual performance) may be the cause of the group-level covariance.

In order to remove the "artificial" component from the group term, we must develop a general estimate of the relationship between character value and individual fitness *within* all groups; this yields an appropriate measure of individual selection. We then use this estimator to extract the residual fitness values (observed fitness minus the value predicted from individual performance alone) for all of the individuals in all groups. Now we reapply equation (6) and reexamine the group term, which is now a covariance involving mean individual character value and mean *residual* fitness. If this group term is still significant, when compared in magnitude with the average within-group term or the expected magnitude of genetic drift in the system, then we have found evidence for the existence of an irreducible group treatment effect.

The key to this analysis is our ability to represent properly the relationship between individual character value and fitness, such that when we extract the residuals, we have in effect removed the influence of individual performance.

The likelihood that we can obtain a reasonable estimator of this kind is critically dependent upon the relative magnitudes of the variation in individual character value within groups vs. the variation in mean character value among groups. If the variation within groups is negligible compared to the variation among groups, or, in the extreme case, when individuals are perfectly segregated into groups by character value, then only an a priori knowledge of natural history will allow us to distinguish between true and apparent treatment effect. This is normally not a problem in populations within a species, but may be a common problem between species.

It would be a serious error to attempt to derive our estimator from an analysis that initially ignored the grouping of individuals, as these results would represent a conflation of the individual performance and group-level treatment effects upon individual fitness. The covariance term that is calculated by ignoring group structure represents the effects of the variation in fitness upon the evolution of the character in question at the individual level. Thus it is the proper measure of individual selection even though it does not have explanatory or predictive power in itself, as it fails to recognize the group structure and the role that it plays in determining the fitness values that will be associated with individuals.

The Consequences of Hierarchical Perspective

Having established a formal, hierarchical framework for discussing the evolutionary process, we may find it fruitful to consider some of the consequences of applying established concepts at non-organismal levels of analysis. Since species selection has recently emerged as one of the more controversial aspects of the hierarchical approach, we will devote the first part of our discussion to supraorganismal selection, followed by a brief outline of the role that interaction between levels can play in evolutionary analyses.

Species Selection

The question is sometimes asked: if species selection involves selection between species as units, how can the transformation of species appear in Stanley's formulation? The answer is that it doesn't: the transformation of species—or for that matter the transformation of entities at any level—is brought about through selection between lower-level entities subsumed by the focal unit of study. Species selection is simply answering a different kind of question—about why there are more species of one kind than another. [Note that the covariance equations allow the transformation of species to appear in a species-level selection model, as a bias in the mechanism of inheritance (see discussion of model above).] Our discussion of the gastropod example (above) shows that if we wish to ask these kinds of questions, then we cannot exclude species selection from an evolutionary theory that is based on the selection paradigm. Yet if we restrict our concept of evolution to the transformation of species, then we have excluded species selection by definition—even though it operates on exactly the same basis as Natural Selection among individuals. In this sense it should be clear that our formulation quite explicitly endorses the recognition of species selection as an aspect of evolutionary theory.

Stanley (1975) followed Lewontin (1970) by formally defining species selection as being dependent on variation in R, the relative rate of increase of a kind of species within a population of species. Since it is sometimes assumed that species selection is dependent on individual fitness, species selection is criticized as being a trivial description of selective processes operating at lower levels of organization. The discussion of examples in the introduction shows this criticism to be groundless.

Our initial approach to the evolutionary hierarchy arose from attempts to clarify the concept of species selection. Stanley (1980) outlines the recent history of the idea; we shall apply the reasoning we have developed to address some aspects of species selection that could be seen as inconsistent with our formulation. The first difficulty that we encounter is the persistent notion that speciation is analogous to mutation in that it provides the "raw material" for species selection (Mayr, 1963, p. 600, 1970; Eldredge and Gould, 1972; Stanley, 1975, 1980; Gould and Eldredge, 1977). At the individual level, the idea of reproduction is not burdened with any preconceived notions about the variation that is introduced by the production of offspring. This variation is attributed to the processes of mutation and recombination, which are embodied in the mechanism of inheritance. Mutation holds a unique status in our view, since it is the fundamental source of all biologically heritable variation. Therefore, we feel that speciation should be viewed solely as the analog of reproduction, and the variation introduced by the speciation process should be attributed to mutation/recombination analogs such as founder effects, drift, and the operation of selection in the isolate.

Gould and Eldredge (1977) further stated that the importance of species selection is contingent upon the validity of Wright's rule: that the change in characters that accompanies a speciation event occurs in directions that are random with respect to any directional transformational change taking place within the species. Thus differential speciation rates are properly included in the domain of species selection, but directional speciation is not. We support Gould and Eldredge's statement of contingency, and we add that the rate at which species selection produces change will also be dependent upon the magnitude of the changes associated with speciation. If they are too small, then the rate of species selection will be limited by the variation between species. As the magnitude of these variations increases, the power of directional species selection will increase, but the power of the stabilizing species selection will decrease. It should be noted that the structure of our approach is not dependent on rates of evolution during the speciation event, nor does this approach predict either gradual or punctuational change. We expect that both occur, and both can be accommodated by the model we present.

Species Demography and Constraints Upon Fitness

The formulation of species selection by analogy encourages the application of many of the techniques derived in studying individual selection to the study of species selection. This has prompted unsuccessful attempts to discover "age-structured" speciation and extinction rates within clades through demographic analysis (Van Valen, 1973; Raup, 1978). Their results suggest that, with few exceptions, extinction rates appear to be more or less constant through time. Further, Stanley (1980) maintains that "well established" species will be unlikely to exhibit age specific variation in speciation rate. We would note that since "maturation" time (the earliest age at which reproduction occurs) has the strongest effect upon the Malthusian parameter (Lewontin, 1965), demographic analysis may still be important if the time to become well established is significant and shows some variation between members of a clade.

Another analog that has been suggested is that of "r" and "K" clades (Gould and Eldredge, 1977).

Consider successful clades that are both diverse and long lived. Traditional thought would attribute their abundance and persistence to good morphological design, fashioned and tested in competition against species of other clades. But just as life history parameters of maturation time and reproductive effort have been used to explain "success" in ecological time, so must the macroevolutionary analog of speciation rate be included in our study of successful clades.

They go on to define the macroevolutionary analogs of r and K clades as "increasers" and "survivors" respectively:

We recognize that the "survivors" include species that are both r and K strategists in ecological time. We are not bothered that a macroevolutionary analog of K selection might contain r selected species, for we have emphasized the fallacy of direct extrapolation between levels.

The usefulness of this analogy depends upon the existence of a constraint that determines a trade-off between speciation rate and persistence (Stanley, 1980). Stanley maintains that such a trade-off is unlikely to exist during the early stage of an adaptive radiation (Stanley, 1980, p. 280). However, the larval strategies found in Hansen's volutids carry the suggestion of just such a trade-off. An "easily fragmented" or endemic population structure that leads to high rates of speciation virtually assures that such species will have more restricted ranges and smaller population sizes, thus making them more vulnerable to localized perturbations. The potential existence of constraints of this kind makes it imperative that species selection be viewed as operating jointly upon speciation and extinction rates, rather than as simultaneously maximizing speciation rate and minimizing extinction rate (Stanley, 1980).

This constraint is independent of hypothetical "community saturation" effects associated with the equilibration of the size of a clade. Stanley's

(1975) model was designed to apply to the initial filling of a new adaptive zone through radiation and did not include an analog for carrying capacity. If there is a higher level analog for carrying capacity, then the limiting "resource" at the species level would be adaptive space. This is one way of interpreting the high empirical correlation between S and E found by Stanley (1980): once "K" is reached, speciation events must tend to be accompanied by extinctions if there is no more space to occupy.

Linkage is another established concept that can be applied at the species level. When selection acts on one member of a pair of genetically linked characters, the fate of the other character is at least partially determined by the association. At the end of the Mesozoic, we find tremendous diversity among the Ammonoidea relative to the Nautiloidea. One explanation for this resorts to the traditional adaptive program and looks for design superiority in the peculiar sutures of ammonoids. If we speculate that it happened—for whatever reasons—that ammonoids tended to speciate more than nautiloids, this alone could account for ammonoid diversity. Species selection would tend to favor this tendency toward differential speciation rates, and the ammonoid suture, which may have initially been present as a historical accident, would become widespread by "riding piggyback" on the species level trend. In these cases, the linkage association is established by co-occurrence of two characters in the same species rather than in the same field of the same chromosome. This is a higher level analog of what Gould and Lewontin (1979) called "selection for something else."

Selection Above the Species Level

Organisms are interesting to study as units of selection partly because they are functionally integrated in a way that makes the whole more than the sum of its parts. It is not enough for an organism to have well-designed organ systems, tissues, and genes: the fitness of an organism is dependent upon the way these systems are assembled, how they work together as a functional unit. From the introductory discussion, it is apparent that species fitness shows a similar dependency on characters such as population structure. While it is clear that units in the Linnean "grade" hierarchy or in a cladistic (strictly monophyletic groups) hierarchy can both have coherence as clusters in character space, it is usually assumed that supraspecific taxa lack functional integrity; that they are established on the basis of simple inclusion, rather than part/whole relationships characteristic of lower levels of organization.

The existence of a functional part/whole relationship is not a necessary criterion for a unit of selection (cf. Hull, 1980): if one can define supraspecific units by unambiguously defining reproduction for those units, then selection can operate on variation in fitness between units. Thus, the functional (part/

whole) integration of units lends them explanatory value but is not essential to their status as units of selection. We can therefore address these issues separately while discussing various potential supraspecific units of selection.

1. Consider two sister groups. The group showing more between-species variation may be in a better position to found a new clade by taking advantage of new evolutionary opportunities (adaptive zones) as they appear. Between-clade differences in variability thus give the clade an evolutionary potential that makes it more than the sum of its parts. Particularly flexible *Baupläne* (such as are found in the serially homologous arthropods) lend themselves to the generation of this kind of between-species variability. Any character that causes a tendency toward great morphological divergence during speciation will have a similar effect. Thus, we have the potential for part/whole relationships at the clade level and we can define units clearly (based on monophyly) but we cannot know when a speciation event is a clade founding event or merely an addition to the parental clade. This means that if monophyly is our criterion for establishing supraspecific units of selection, then we cannot use a definition of fitness that is dependent on branching. Fitness measures based solely on persistence are possible—but limited in their explanatory power.

2. If we use a phenetic approach to establish supraspecific units of selection then it becomes possible to define clade founding (branching) in terms of some arbitrary distance (in character space) from the parental taxon. At this point, we must abandon within-clade variation in species morphology as a character if we are to avoid circular reasoning: we cannot establish taxa on the basis of character variation and then use that variation to explain variation in supraspecific fitness (e.g. clade founding and persistence). Thus, by abandoning monophyly in favor of morphologic distance as a criterion for establishing supraspecific units of selection, we have gained an unambiguous definition of fitness but lost the use of an interesting supraspecific character: within-clade variation.

3. Interspecific functional part/whole relationships are also found in communities of species. Communities are subject to selection to the extent that they remain well defined units, but there are obvious problems, both with coalescence of communities and in defining community branching, that may make it more meaningful to concentrate on smaller, better integrated co-evolving communities involving obligate endosymbiont/host and parasite/host relationships.

One might imagine these higher level effects to be rather rare, but there are intriguing examples in the literature. An example would be Hamilton's (1978) inquiry into the effects of certain kinds of mating structure upon the probability of founding new "clades." He examines the peculiar diversity of the insect fauna found under bark in dead trees, which is characterized by unexceptional species diversity, but unparalleled diversity of higher taxa. He postulates that this habitat imposes an inbred mating structure within each log, combined with a fragmented population structure (between trees), such that the species found in this situation have an enhanced potential for rapid evolutionary modification and great divergence in character space. Hamilton makes the intriguing point that when new higher taxa "emerge" from the under bark environment, exploiting the new adaptive zone made accessible by their newly evolved characters, they have higher speciation rates. However, they appear to have lost their potential for evolving the dramatic evolutionary modification necessary to make the transition to other adaptive zones. Thus, the probability of dramatic evolutionary modification is in this case negatively correlated with speciation rate.

The Relationships Between Levels

Thus far we have discussed (1) the necessity for recognizing hierarchical structure in evolution, (2) a formal approach to any chosen level of analysis, and (3) the advantages and limitations inherent in the choice of any single level. There are important consequences of recognizing hierarchical structure that require going beyond pure selection models (within-level analysis) to discuss the relationships between two or more levels. The ways in which levels interact fall under several broad—but related—categories.

The Relative "Importance" of Levels: A Question of Time Scale and Variation

The first of these categories addresses the general question of which level(s) will tend to dominate the evolutionary process, and under what conditions. Much of the group selection literature has been devoted to demonstrating that individual-level selection will be more powerful except under some rather special circumstances, for two reasons. First, the time scales associated with branching and persistence are far shorter for individual selection than for group selection, so the former will proceed more rapidly, everything else being equal (Maynard-Smith, 1964; Williams, 1966; Lewontin, 1970). This argument can be generalized for any two adjacent levels: the time scale for selection at the higher level must be greater than or equal to that of the immediately subordinate level. Second, the variation between groups in mean character value will be far less than the variation about the mean within groups, if assortment is approximately random (Hamilton, 1977). If there is sufficient mixing between different groups such that group composition becomes more or less uniform, then the variation available for a group-level treatment effect to work on is negligible relative to that available to individual selection. This means that group selection will predominate only if intergroup migration is low (to avoid diluting the variation between groups) and the correlation between average group character value and average fitness between groups is very high relative to the correlation at the individual level. These two arguments have led to the widely held perspective of group selection as relatively weak and somewhat peripheral to the "central" issue of Darwinian natural selection at the individual level, a perspective that has been challenged recently by Wade (1978) on both theoretical and empirical grounds. Even if this perspective were justified, it does not follow that selection at the species level must be even less important. Between-species variances are almost always greater than within-species variances. This interspecific variability is maintained by a level of gene flow that is orders of magnitude lower than gene flow between groups, thereby reducing the homogenizing influence of migration and enhancing the power of species selection, although it remains under constraints imposed by lower levels of selection.

Constraint

The influence of selection at other levels acting in opposition to the focal level adaptive process represents a potential form of evolutionary constraint. If one assumes, for the sake of argument, that individuals of planktotrophic and nonplanktotrophic species are equally fit, then species selection is free to act on these two alternative species character states. If individual selection reduces or eliminates the presence of one of these alternative strategies in the evolving system, then the constraints on species selection have been strengthened: there will be less variation to act upon. Thus species selection can proceed in any direction that is not prohibited by lower-level adaptive disadvantage—provided the raw material is available for selection. In this sense, the greater power of lower-level selection acts to constrain—*not to direct*—the path of species selection by setting boundary conditions and influencing the availability of the raw material for higher-level selection.

The study of constraint forms a major part of the biological and paleobiological literature. Seilacher's (1970) elegant treatment of constraint at the organismal level provides a working outline for consideration of constraint at other levels. His ternary system of architectural, historical phylogenetic, and ecological adaptive aspects allows a formal classification of organismal characters in terms of the relative importance of each of these three classes of constraint.

These classes can be generally stated as:

(1) What it is possible to do in an engineering sense, governed by what Simpson (1963) refers to as properties immanent in the material universe (immutable laws of physics, thermodynamics, chemistry).

(2) The subset of what the species (entity) can do with what it has to work with (historical phylogenetic constraint).

(3) The further restricted subset: of the remaining choices, what will increase fitness under the prevailing circumstances. Simpson includes (2) and (3) in his term "configurational universe." Bernal (1951) used the word "contingent" in this context.

Given the ways in which selection in a given level is constrained by other levels (especially lower levels), we can add a fourth constraint that operates, like the above three, at all levels:

(4) Of those changes that will be adaptive at a given level, which will be permitted by processes operating at other levels?

At this point we would like to draw attention to a different perspective of adaptation that emerges from the hierarchical model. It is often assumed that if we wish to explain the prevalence of good—or at least adequate—design in nature, we need look no further than its beneficial effect on organisms. But it is clear from both the t-allele example and from the gastropod example that we cannot expect all characters to be adaptive at all levels in the hierarchy. Nonetheless, our organism-centered viewpoint and our Darwinian heritage have drawn our attention to the harmony of form and function in organisms to the extent that we see them as the rule. We then see segregation distorters and the results of group selection models as exceptional, peripheral to the "central" issue of Darwinian evolution at the organismal level. In fact, these phenomena are only rare at the organismal level because they tend to entail a cost at that level, whereas all manner of features that entail a deferred cost at higher levels (e.g., through overspecialization) are seen as consistent with the more traditional Darwinian perspective, and are perhaps too readily assumed to have arisen as organismal adaptations because of their prevalence at the organismal level. If a character is frequent among species, then blind reference to organismal adaptation represents a double fallacy. First, invoking organismal adaptation as the null hypothesis for explaining frequent occurrence of a trait at the individual level is a questionable research program; recognition of the potential influence of several levels of selection increases this difficulty. Second, as we have emphasized throughout, the frequent occurrence of a trait among species does not translate to frequent occurrence among individuals: substantial variation in the abundances of different species is a fact of nature.

Apparent nonorganismal exceptions to "normal" evolutionary processes are derived from an unarticulated major premise that holds the individual level to be the focus of natural selection: when this premise is abandoned, these "exceptions" fall into perspective as parts of an integrated theoretical framework. This is not to say that the individual level is empirically unimportant, but, rather, that it does not occupy any special or unique position in the structure of the evolutionary hierarchy.

Conclusions

Several important results derive from the recognition of hierarchically diverse mechanisms of branching and persistence. First, it requires that adaptation, selection, and fitness be approached from an explicitly hierarchical standpoint, thus allowing a limited autonomy for the study of each level. Second, this provides the basis for a consistent methodology at all levels, which we explore using various expansions of Price's (1970, 1972) covariance equations.

Hierarchical structure appears in two forms in our discussion.

(1) There are distinct measures of evolutionary change associated with biological entities such as alleles, individuals, and species. Each measure defines and is defined by particular mechanisms of branching and persistence; yet at all levels the operation of these mechanisms jointly determine the measure of focal level fitness, which is a generalized Malthusian parameter.

(2) Each focal measure of evolutionary change may exhibit the influence of selection operating at other levels. Selection acting at lower levels appears as a bias in the inheritance of characters, and it determines, along with stochastic processes operating at lower levels, the variation available for focal level selection. Higher-level selection may appear as a significant "treatment effect" in an analysis of covariance between focal level fitness and character values, though these higher-level effects will not necessarily reflect only the influence of higher-level branching and persistence.

We believe that this approach has additional benefits. Phenomena that were previously viewed as exceptions, peripheral to the "central" issue of natural selection at the organismal level, such as segregation distorters in *Drosophila,* are placed in perspective as the products of selection at lower levels, and analysis of these situations is guided by the same logic as at all levels. The hierarchical approach has value when individual selection is sufficient to predict the qualitative result as well, since it yields a more precise model of the rates of change in character frequency, and points out the "other level" implications of adaptation at the individual level. The result is a more complete and tractable picture of the evolutionary process and an explicit awareness of the limitations of the particular focal measure of evolutionary change as a window on these processes.

If we step back now and look at the hierarchy as a whole, a picture emerges of a highly interrelated system, in which selection at a given level can be opposed, reinforced, or unaffected by processes operating at other levels. If this concept emphasizes the complexity of interrelations in the evolutionary process, it also underscores the essential unity of its theoretical structure: no single level can be fully understood except in the context of its position in the evolutionary hierarchy. Moreover, the diverse mechanisms that operate at the various levels are manifestations of a common principle: heritable variation in branching and persistence. If we are to operate within the selection paradigm, then recursive and hierarchical application of the logic embodied in the theory of natural selection is not only possible but necessary to explain fully the processes of change at all levels within the domain of biology. Thus, paradoxically, by incorporating nonorganismal selection into our theoretical structure, we preserve the abstract conceptual content of Darwin's insight as the cornerstone of evolutionary theory.

Acknowledgments

The authors gratefully acknowledge P. Alberch, R. L. Dorit, W. Fink, S. Fink, R. Z. German, N. L. Gilinsky, S. J. Gould, J. Imbrie, P. S. Kitcher, R. S. Lewontin, C. E. Mitchell, E. Sober, J. T. Webb, E. E. Williams, P. G. Williamson, and W. C. Wimsatt, whose comments and insights contributed to the conceptual development of this paper.

References

Bernal, J. D., 1951. *The Physical Basis of Life*, London, Routledge and Kegan Paul.

Crow, J. F., and Kimura, M., 1970. *An Introduction to Population Genetics Theory*, Minneapolis, Burgess, 591 pp.

Crow, J. F., and Nagylaki, T., 1976. "The rate of change of a character correlated with fitness," *Am. Nat.,* 110:207–213.

Doolittle, W. Ford, and Sapienza, C., 1980. "Selfish genes, the phenotype paradigm and genome evolution," *Nature,* 284:601–603.

Eldredge, N., and Gould, S. J., 1972. "Punctuated equilibria: An alternative to phyletic gradualism," in *Models in Paleobiology,* ed. T. J. M. Schopf, San Francisco, Freeman, Cooper, pp. 82–115.

Fenner, F., 1965. "Myxoma virus and *Oryctolagus cuniculus,*" in *The Genetics of Colonizing Species,* ed. Baker, H. G., and Stebbins, G. L., New York, Academic Press, 588 pp. (pp. 485–501).

Fisher, R. A., 1930. *The Genetical Theory of Natural Selection,* Oxford, Clarendon.

Fisher, R. A., 1941. "Average excess and average effect of a gene substitution," *Ann. Eugen.,* 11:53–63.

Fisher, R. A., 1958. *The Genetical Theory of Natural Selection,* 2nd ed. New York, Dover Press.

Gould, S. J., and Eldredge, N., 1977. "Punctuated equilibria: The tempo and mode of evolution revisited," *Paleobiology,* 3:115–151.

Gould, S. J., and Lewontin, R. C., 1979. "The spandrels of San Marco and the Panglossian paradigm: A critique of the adaptationist programme," *Proc. R. Soc. Lond.,* B205:581–598.

Hamilton, W. D., 1977. "Innate social aptitudes of man: An approach from evolutionary genetics," pp. 133–187, in *Biosocial Anthropology,* ed. Robin Fox, London, Malaby Press, pp. 133–187. Reprinted in part in this volume.

Hamilton, W. D., 1978. "Evolution and diversity under bark," in *Diversity of Insect Communities,* ed. Mound, L. A., and Waloff, N., *Proc. R. Entomol. Soc.,* 9:154–175.

Hansen, T. A., 1980. "Influence of larval dispersal and geographic distribution on species longevity in neogastropods," *Paleobiology,* 6:193–207.

Hull, D. L., 1978. "A matter of individuality," *Philos. Sci.,* 45:335–360.

Hull, D. L., 1980. "Individuality and selection," *Annu. Rev. Ecol. Syst.,* 11:311–332.

Lewontin, R. C., 1965. "Selection for colonizing ability," in *The Genetics of Colonizing Species,* ed. Baker, H., and Stebbins, G. L., New York, Academic Press, pp. 77–94.

Lewontin, R. C., 1970. "The units of selection," *Annu. Rev. Ecol. Syst.,* 1:1–18.

Maynard Smith, J., 1964. "Kin selection and group selection," *Nature,* 201:1145–1147.

Mayr, E., 1963. *Animal Species and Evolution,* Cambridge (Mass.), Harvard University Press.

Orgel, L. E., and Crick, F. H. C., 1980. "Selfish DNA: The ultimate parasite," *Nature,* 284:604–607.

Price, G. R., 1970. "Selection and covariance," *Nature,* 227:520–521.

Price, G. R., 1972. "Extension of covariance selection mathematics," *Ann. Hum. Genet.,* 35:485–490.

Raup, D. M., 1978. "Cohort analysis of generic survivorship," *Paleobiology,* 4:1–15.

Robertson, A., 1966. "A mathematical model of the culling process in dairy cattle," *Anim. Production,* 8:95–108.

Robertson, A., 1968. "The spectrum of genetic variation," in *Population Biology and Evolution,* ed. Lewontin, R. C., Syracuse, Syracuse University Press, pp. 5–16.

Seilacher, A., 1970. "Arbeitskonzept zur Konstruktions–Morphologie," *Lethaia,* 3:393–396.

Simon, H. A., 1957. *Models of Man: Social and Rational Human Behaviour in a Social Setting,* New York, Wiley, 297 pp.

Simpson, G. G., 1963. *This View of Life,* New York, Harcourt Brace and World, 308 pp.

Sober, E., 1981. "Holism, individualism, and the units of selection," in *PSA 1980,* Vol. 2, ed. Giere, R. and Asquith, P., East Lansing, Michigan, Philosophy of Science Association, pp. 93–121.

Stanley, S. M., 1975. "A theory of evolution above the species level," *Proc. Natl. Acad. Sci. U.S.A.,* 72:646–650.

Stanley, S. M., 1980. *Macroevolution: Pattern and Process,* San Francisco, W. H. Freeman, 332 pp.

Van Valen, L., 1973. "A new evolutionary law," *Evol. Theory,* 1:1–30.

Wade, Michael J., 1976. "An experimental study of group selection," *Evolution,* 31:134–153.

Wade, Michael J., 1978. "A critical review of the models of group selection," *Q. Rev. Biol.,* 53:101–114. Reprinted in this volume.

Wade, Michael J., 1979. "The evolution of social interactions by family selection," *Am. Nat.,* 113:399–417.

Williams, G. C., 1966. *Adaptation and Natural Selection,* Princeton, Princeton University Press. Chapter four is reprinted in part in this volume.

Wimsatt, W. C., 1980. "Reductionistic research strategies and their biases in the units of selection controversy," in *Scientific Discovery: Case Studies,* ed. Nickles, T., Boston, Reidel, pp. 213–259. Reprinted in part in this volume.

Acknowledgments

1 "Charles Darwin and Group Selection," by Michael Ruse. Originally entitled "Reproduction and Selection in Evolution," reprinted by permission of *Annals of Science* and the author.

2 "The Roles of Mutation, Inbreeding, Crossbreeding, and Selection in Evolution," by Sewall Wright. Reprinted by permission of the author.

3 "Theories of Group Selection," by Sewall Wright. Extracts reprinted by permission of *Evolution* and the author.

4 "Intergroup Selection in the Evolution of Social Systems," by V.C. Wynne-Edwards. Reprinted by permission of Macmillan Journals, Ltd. and the author.

5 "Group Selection," by George C. Williams. Extracts copyright © 1966 by Princeton University Press, reprinted by permission of Princeton University Press and the author.

6 "The Unity of Genotype," by Ernst Mayr. Reprinted by permission of H. Bohme and R. Rieger, Editors, *Biologisches Zentralblatt,* and the author.

7 "Reductionistic Research Strategies and Their Biases in the Units of Selection Controversy," by William C. Wimsatt. Extracts copyright © 1980 by D. Reidel Publishing Company, Dordrecht, Holland, reprinted by permission. Figures 23 (p. 274) and 24 (p. 280) from R. C. Lewontin, *The Genetic Basis of Evolutionary Change* (New York: Columbia University Press, 1974), reprinted by permission of Columbia University Press.

8 "Artifact, Cause and Genic Selection," by Elliott Sober and Richard C. Lewontin. Reprinted by permission of the Philosophy of Science Association and the authors.

9 "The Levels of Selection," by Robert N. Brandon. Reprinted by permission of the Philosophy of Science Association and the author.

10 "Units of Evolution: A Metaphysical Essay," by David Hull. Reprinted by permission of Harvester Press and St. Martin's Press, New York.

11 "Replicators and Vehicles," by Richard Dawkins. Reprinted by permission of Cambridge University Press and the author.

12 "Innate Social Aptitudes of Man: An Approach from Evolutionary Genetics," by W. D. Hamilton. Extracts reprinted by permission.

13 "The Theory of Kin Selection," by Richard E. Michod. Copyright © 1982 by Annual Reviews, Inc., reproduced by permission from Annual Reviews, Inc. and the author.

14 "Group Selection," by J. Maynard Smith. Reprinted by permission of *The Quarterly Review of Biology* and the author.

15 "A Critical Review of the Models of Group Selection," by Michael J. Wade. Reprinted by permission of *The Quarterly Review of Biology* and the author.

16 "Individual Selection and the Concept of Structured Demes," by David Sloan Wilson. Extracts reprinted by permission of Benjamin/Cummings and the author.

17 "The Theory of Evolution by Natural Selection: A Hierarchical Expansion," by Anthony J. Arnold and Kurt Fristrup; this article first appeared in *Paleobiology* 8 (1982), reprinted by permission of *Paleobiology* and the authors.

Index